Hervé Ryssen

# JEWISH FANATICISM

# Hervé Ryssen

Hervé Ryssen (France) is a historian and an exhaustive researcher of the Jewish intellectual world. He is the author of twelve books and several video documentaries on the Jewish question. In 2005, he published *Planetary Hopes*, a book in which he demonstrates the religious origins of the globalist project. *Psychoanalysis of Judaism*, published in 2006, shows how intellectual Judaism displays all the symptoms of hysterical pathology. There is no "divine choice", but the manifestation of a disorder that has its origins in the practice of incest. Freud had patiently studied this question on the basis of what he observed in his own community.

France is home to one of the largest Jewish communities in the Diaspora, with a very intense cultural and intellectual life. Hervé Ryssen has been able to develop his extensive work on the basis of numerous historical and contemporary sources, both international and French.

## *JEWISH FANATICISM*

*Le Fanatisme juif: Égalité - Droits de l'homme - Tolérance*, Levallois-Perret, Baskerville, 2007.

Translated and published by
Omnia Veritas Limited

www.omnia-veritas.com

© Omnia Veritas Limited - Hervé Ryssen - 2023

All rights reserved. No part of this publication may be reproduced by any means without the prior permission of the publisher. The intellectual property code prohibits copies or reproductions for collective use. Any representation or reproduction in whole or in part by any means whatsoever, without the consent of the publisher, the author or their successors, is unlawful and constitutes an infringement punishable by articles of the Code of Intellectual Property.

# PART ONE ............................................................................................................ 13

## REVOLUTIONARY HOPES ..................................................................................... 13

### 1. The way out of the ghetto ................................................................. 14
- The "home zone .............................................................................. 14
- The mission of the Jews ................................................................. 23
- The revolutionary militant ............................................................. 30
- Judeo-Bolshevism .......................................................................... 35
- Stalin and the Jews ........................................................................ 40
- The Spanish Civil War .................................................................... 52
- The German invasion ..................................................................... 59
- Resistance to Nazism ..................................................................... 65
- USSR 1945 ....................................................................................... 76
- The Hungarian uprising ................................................................. 83
- Poland freed from its "ghosts". ..................................................... 94
- Liberated Romania ....................................................................... 101
- Lustration in Czechoslovakia ...................................................... 106
- East Germany ................................................................................ 109
- Refuge in Israel ............................................................................. 110

### 2. Planetary democracy ........................................................................ 119
- The cosmopolitan mutation ........................................................ 119
- The planetary project .................................................................. 124
- Bringing Islam to heel .................................................................. 132
- The liberal model ......................................................................... 136
- Wars and revolutions, "in the name of human rights". .......... 145
- A world war, if necessary ............................................................ 152

# PART TWO ......................................................................................................... 160

## THE TALMUDIC SPIRIT ........................................................................................ 160

### 1. The cosmopolitan mentality .............................................................. 160
- On our knees before Israel .......................................................... 160
- A great intolerance to frustration .............................................. 169
- The media dictatorship ............................................................... 175
- Criticising Israel ............................................................................ 180
- Lies and slander ............................................................................ 189
- Repression against historians ..................................................... 192
- Cruelty ........................................................................................... 198
- The theology of revenge ............................................................. 211
- The passion to destroy ................................................................ 218
- Insolence ....................................................................................... 225
- The pacification of the world ..................................................... 231

### 2. Anti-Semitism .................................................................................... 238
- The scapegoat .............................................................................. 240
- The folly of men ........................................................................... 245
- Innocence ..................................................................................... 250
- The accusatory inversion ............................................................ 261
- Anti-Zionism as accusatory projection ...................................... 267
- Lanterns and tall tales ................................................................. 270

  3. Jewish identity .................................................................... 278
    The hyper-patriots ............................................................ 278
    Dual ownership ................................................................ 284
    Duplicity .......................................................................... 292

## PART THREE .................................................................................. 298

### PSYCHOPATHOLOGY OF JUDAISM ............................................. 298
  Paradise Mombassa ............................................................. 298
  Sex maniacs ........................................................................ 303
  Violations in psychiatry ....................................................... 310
  Paedocriminality ................................................................. 317
  Sexual ambiguity ................................................................ 323
  Feminism ........................................................................... 334
  Incest ................................................................................. 342
  Jewish anguish ................................................................... 353
  Dementia ........................................................................... 368

## OTHER TITLES ............................................................................... 385

# THE JEWISH FANATICISM

The Jewish people are promoting a project for the whole of humanity; a grandiose project that they have been carrying out for centuries against all odds: the establishment of universal peace on the face of the earth. The notion of "Peace" is at the very core of Judaism, and it is no coincidence that this word (*shalom* in Hebrew) appears so frequently in all the speeches of the Jews of the world. It is not just a religious concept, or a belief in the advent of a better world, God's work in the distant future, but a guiding principle that determines the commitment and actions of Jews in their daily lives. Indeed, Jews, through their work, their actions and their involvement in politics, work every day to build "Peace".

In that perfect world they are building, all conflicts will have definitively disappeared from the face of the earth, and, first and foremost, conflicts between nations. It is for this reason that, wherever they are, Jews campaign tirelessly for the abolition of borders and the dissolution of national identities. Nations are supposedly generators of war and disorder, and must therefore be weakened and eventually abolished in favour of a world government, the only one capable of guaranteeing happiness and prosperity on earth.

This idea is found, more or less developed, both in the writings of Marxist intellectuals - from Karl Marx to Jacques Derrida - and in the discourses of liberal thinkers such as Karl Popper, Milton Friedman, Alain Minc or Guy Sorman. The aim is to unify the world by all means and to level out all cultural differences, supposedly sources of conflict. This is the goal for which Jewish intellectuals all over the world work tirelessly. Whether left or right, Marxist or liberal, believer or atheist, Zionist or "perfectly integrated", they are the most fervent supporters of the global empire.

They are also, of course, the best propagandists of plural society and planetary miscegenation. Thus, we see how Jews have always encouraged immigration in all the countries where they have settled, not only because the multicultural society corresponds to their politico-religious project, but also because the resulting dissolution of national identity protects them from a possible nationalist outburst against the power they have gained, especially in finance, politics and the media system. All Jewish intellectuals, without exception, focus on the question of the "plural" society and exercise a constant "anti-racist vigilance", regardless of their political divergences.

From this "planetary" perspective, the former communists of the 1970s had little difficulty in joining the neo-conservative liberal right. Lately, the danger, according to them, comes mainly from Islam and young Afro-Maghrebi immigrants, and no longer from the "extreme right". It is therefore a matter of consolidating this multicultural society that they have done so much to create and which is already at risk of disintegration. In France, intellectuals such as Alexandre Adler, André Glucksman and Pascal Bruckner, who currently support the liberal and pro-American hard right, are merely reacting in the exclusive interests of their community.

As we can see, Judaism is essentially a universal political project whose goal is the unification of the world, a prelude to global pacification. It is a long work, but the Jews are absolutely convinced that they can achieve it, for they are so imbued with the "mission" God has assigned them. As the prophet Isaiah stated: "The wolf shall dwell with the lamb, and the tiger shall lie down with the kid; the calf and the lion and the fatling together, and the fatling shall walk together, and a little child shall lead them..." (Isaiah, XI, 6–9).

The aim is not to convert the world to Judaism, but to incite other peoples to abandon their racial, national and religious identities in order to foster a spirit of "tolerance" among people. This is how the Jews continually campaign to convince the whole world to adopt their project. They are a people of propagandists and it is not without reason that they are so influential in the media systems of democratic societies. The incessant campaigns to blame Europeans for slavery, colonisation, the plundering of the third world or Auschwitz, have no other purpose than to eradicate their feelings of collective identity. When only the Jews are left on this earth to preserve their faith and traditions, they will finally be recognised by all as God's chosen people. The Messiah of Israel, whose arrival has been expected every day for more than two thousand years, will then re-establish the kingdom of David and give the Jews an empire over the entire universe. There are many very explicit texts on this subject, as we shall see below.

# PART ONE

## REVOLUTIONARY HOPES

The Jewish people played a key role in the 20th century. At the beginning, they devoted themselves completely to the cause of communism, providing this ideology with its main doctrinaires and activists. From the very beginning of the Soviet regime in 1917, a large number of its leaders were Jewish. The aim was not only to abolish private property and establish a collectivist system, but also to liberate the whole of humanity by abolishing borders, religions, nationalities and all traditions, in order to level out all the differences between people and thus bring about the emergence of a new man in a perfect world.

In reality, the Bolshevik regime turned out to be a ruthless tyranny for the "people of the past". Millions died of hunger, cold, famine or simply shot in the back of the head by the agents of the GPU (State Political Directorate). The early Bolsheviks were also victims of the great Stalinist purges of the 1930s, but despite this nothing could shake the faith of the countless revolutionary militants all over the world. Among them, many were Jews guided by a communist ideology that corresponded exactly to the hopes of Israel. Karl Marx was of Jewish descent, as were Lenin and Trotsky, and most of the Bolshevik leaders. It took many decades for the Jews to realise their mistake. It will probably take many more for them to acknowledge it publicly.

Most of them, even within the Western bourgeoisie, had supported the Bolshevik regime from its inception out of hatred for the tsarist autocracy. Adolf Hitler's rise to power in Germany in 1933 further reaffirmed the powerful Western Jewish communities in their unconditional support, whatever the cost, for the Soviet Union. Eventually, after the victory over National Socialism, this enthusiasm began to wane among some of them. The turning point came in 1948. It was from that date onwards that the Stalinist regime, which had already begun to remove the main "cosmopolitan" Jewish leaders, stepped up its purges at the highest levels of power.

In the West, socialist ideas continued to flourish in various forms and political alternatives, fuelling debates during the uprisings of 1968. But it soon became clear that liberal capitalist society had succeeded where communism had failed and proved incomparably more effective, both in breaking down national borders and identities and in creating material wealth. After the fall of the Berlin Wall in 1989, the collapse of the Soviet Union guaranteed the triumph of democracy. We then witnessed an unprecedented proliferation of global propaganda through the entire media system. The advent of a world without borders and universal peace was at hand. This time, the Messiah would finally arrive.

# 1. The way out of the ghetto

## The "zone of residence"

The kingdom of Poland has played a special role in the history of European Judaism. In the Middle Ages, while Jews were expelled from all the other kingdoms and principalities of Europe, this country was a haven for them. From 1264, a charter granted them freedoms and great privileges that were the basis of their religious, national and economic existence. In 1334, King Casimir III, under the influence of his mistress Esterka, confirmed the Kalisz charter and welcomed them extensively into his kingdom. This is why the Jewish population was very important there before the Second World War.

Poland was also the only old country in European history to have completely collapsed, to the extent that it was successively partitioned among its Prussian, Austrian and Russian neighbours at the end of the 18th century. After a brief revival under Napoleon, most of the country became part of the Russian Empire. By an *Ukase* (imperial decree) of 23 December 1791, Tsarina Catherine II had granted her subjects of Jewish origin the right to reside in the western provinces, to the exclusion of all others. This "zone of residence", which stretched from the Baltic to the Black Sea, encompassed most of the Jews of the East. The first census of the Jewish population of the Russian Empire dates back to 1897. Out of 126.5 million inhabitants, just over five million were Jews, 5% of the population of European Russia[1]. The census also showed the extreme urbanisation of the Jewish population. They accounted for more than 50% of the urban population of Belarus and Lithuania. In Minsk, 52% of the population was Jewish; it was 63% in Bialystok and 41% in Vilnius.[2]

In annexed Poland, the urbanisation of Jews was at odds with the almost total rurality of Poles. 91.5% of Poland's Jews lived in cities, while 83.6% of non-Jews resided in the countryside. Polish Jews thus made up 43% of the total urban population. In Warsaw, the proportion of Jews rose from 4.5% in 1781 to 33.9% in 1897[3]. In Lodz, it rose from 7% in 1793 to 40.7% in 1910. However, of the 3,250,000 Jews in the new Polish Republic in 1931, more than two million still lived in small villages, Jewish villages called "shtels".[4]

This is what the writer Marek Halter wrote about it: "Before the war, some towns, some regions of Poland were one hundred percent Jewish. Warsaw, my home town, had about one million inhabitants, three hundred and sixty-eight thousand of whom were Jewish, with its elementary schools and yeshivas[5], six theatre companies, newspapers, magazines, fifteen or so publishing houses and as many political parties. These women and men thought, spoke and wrote in Yiddish. From Alsace to the Ural, Yiddish was then the language of ten million people, a living language in which beings sang, cried, laughed and above all dreamed of the salvation of all mankind[6]."

In 1917, the area of residence counted seven million Jews, representing more than 10% of the population. Most of these Jews were engaged in

---

[1] Henri Minczeles, *Histoire générale du Bund*, 1995, Denoël, 1999, p.20.

[2] Alain Brossat, *Le Yiddishland révolutionnaire*, Balland, 1983, p.47.

[3] Mark Zborowski, *Olam*, Plon, 1992, p.447.

[4] Béatrice Philippe, *Les juifs dans le monde contemporain*, MA éd., 1986, p.199.

[5] A yeshiva: a Jewish university

[6] Marek Halter, *La force du bien*, Robert Laffont, 1995, p.11. Yiddish was the mother tongue of 96.6% of the Jewish population in the area of residence in 1898. It consists mainly of German and Hebrew words, with Polish, Russian, Slovenian and French words being added later. Yiddish uses the Hebrew alphabet and is written from right to left.

trade-related activities in the urban centres, although the crafts sector was also important (tailors, shoemakers, weavers, carpenters, locksmiths, etc.). There were also workers: "It is this miserable rabble of the workshops and small industry that will form the basis of the Jewish workers' movement at the end of the 19th century[7] ", wrote Alain Brossat and Sylvia Klingberg in their book entitled *The Revolutionary Yiddishland.*

The famous Russian writer Aleksandr Solzhenitsyn, for his part, painted a somewhat different picture of the situation of his fellow Jews in the Russian Empire before the 1917 revolution than the one usually presented by Jewish historians. In his well-documented book *Two Hundred Years Together (1795–1995),* published in 2002, Solzhenitsyn provided, for example, the valuable testimony of Senator Gabriel Romanovitch Derjavine, who was sent by the Tsar at the end of the 19th century to elucidate the causes of the famines that plagued Belarus. This statesman, who was later minister of justice under Alexander I, reported that in the Belarusian countryside the Jews were mainly engaged in the production of firewater, going through the villages, especially in autumn, at harvest time: "They water the peasants and their immediate people, collect their debts and deprive them of their last subsistence... They cheat the drunks and rob them from head to foot, leaving them in complete destitution". It is true that the peasants, "when the harvests are over, sin by their excessive spending; they drink, eat, feast, pay the Jews their old debts, and then, to pay their drunkenness, all that the latter demand of them; so that when winter comes they are in want." These excesses were favoured by the presence of numerous taverns: "In every village," wrote Derjavine, "there is one or sometimes several taverns built by the owners, in which vodka is sold day and night for the greater profit of the Jewish distillers... In this way, the Jews manage to extort from them not only their daily bread, but also their agricultural tools, their goods, their time, their health, their very life." They make use of "all sorts of tricks and subterfuges" which "reduce the poor and stupid villagers to hunger[8]".

This situation explained why the regulations of 1804 and 1835 forbade Belarusian Jews to reside in the countryside. In Ukraine they could live anywhere except Kiev and some villages; nowhere in Russia were

---

[7] Alain Brossat, Sylvia Klingberg, *Le yiddishland revolutionnaire,* op.cit, p.48.

[8] Alexandre Soljenitsyne, *Deux siècles ensemble,* tome I, Fayard, 2002, pp.51-54.

ghettos within cities mandatory. In the second half of the century, under Alexander II, the limitations imposed on Jews fell one after the other, so that they could distil and sell alcohol in their places of residence. In 1872 they "owned 89% of the distilleries[9]" in the Southwest.

Solzhenitsyn also recalled that the government had taken measures to encourage Jewish agriculture: the Russian authorities had allocated more than 30,000 hectares for this purpose, at a rate of 40 hectares of state land for each Jewish family, whereas in Russia the average peasant's plot was a few hectares, rarely more than ten hectares. These lands in southern Ukraine, among the most fertile in Europe, were given to them in hereditary ownership. They had been given cash loans and were even offered to build wooden *isbahs* for them. This programme was, however, suspended in 1810. In 1812, it turned out that of the 848 families who had settled there were only 538 left. The oxen had been slaughtered, stolen or sold, the fields were sown too late… Solzhenitsyn explained the mentality of some of these "shock" farmers: "They feared that if it was proved that the Jews were "capable of working the land", they would be forced to do so".[10]

The mass of Jews certainly lived miserably, but some were immensely wealthy. The famous Israel Brodski owned seventeen sugar factories. Many large Jewish fortunes had also been built on the exploitation of Russian natural resources, especially the export of timber abroad and the extraction of gold. They also played a leading role in the export of agricultural products: "from 1878, 60% of grain exports passed through Jewish hands; soon it would be 100%". The Guinzbourg family stood out notably. Others, such as Samuel Poliakov, invested in railways, becoming known in the 1880s as the "railway king", although the Russian state would later become the main builder. Banking was naturally their area of predilection: "More than half of the credit, savings and loan institutions were located in the Zone of residence", and "in 1911, 86% of their members were Jews[11] " By the beginning of

---

[9] Alexandre Soljenitsyne, *Deux siècles ensemble*, tome I, Fayard, 2002, pp.153,175.

[10] Alexandre Soljenitsyne, *Deux siècles ensemble*, tome I, Fayard, 2002, pp.79-86.

[11] Alexandre Soljenitsyne, *Deux Siècles ensemble*, tome I, Fayard, 2002, pp.175, 333-335. This was confirmed by the Sephardic sociologist Edgar Morin: "Seventeen Polish banks out of twenty were Jewish Gentiles in the mid-19th century" (*Le monde moderne et la queston juive*, Seuil, 2006, p.117).

the 20th century, Jews had gained strong positions in vital sectors of the Russian economy and had settled down to live in the capitals despite regulations forbidding them to do so: There were 16 000 in Moscow in 1880, 30 to 40 000 in St Petersburg in 1900, 81 000 in Kiev in 1913, and the number of Jews settled outside the area of residence was increasing year by year. Tsar Alexander II had authorised young Jewish university graduates to settle throughout Russia. The same measure was approved in 1879 for pharmacists, nurses and dentists.

With the arrival of Alexander II in 1855, the regime was effectively liberalised and a policy of assimilation was to prepare Jews for full citizenship. Jews were thus able to enrol in high schools and universities. From 1874, they flocked to general education establishments, which was a privilege, since until 1914, only 55% of Russians were enrolled in school. In 1881, Jews accounted for about 9% of students, in 1887 this figure grew to 14.5%, but in some universities this percentage was much higher: the medical faculty in Kharkov had 42% Jews, and 41% at the law faculty in Odessa[12]. In the last decades of the 19th century, this Russian-speaking Jewish *intelligentsia was to play* a key role in the intellectual and political movements that were to undermine traditional Russian society. Tsarist power had itself helped to train in its universities those who were to be the main promoters of its downfall.


Until 1844, the Jews of the East were organised in a separate state, administering their own affairs under the authority of the rabbinical Kahals. Thus, they had the right to elect their own rulers and had their own courts for minor matters. The rabbinical administration, the Kahal, was the legal authority under which they lived, as well as the organisation responsible to the central government. Permission from the local Kahal was required to live in the community or to own shtetl land. The Kahal collected funds for the social needs of the Jews, established rules governing trade and industry, and was the exclusive body for collecting taxes[13].

The leading figure in the community was the rabbi. "The authority of the rabbi is limited to three main functions, explained Shmuel Trigano: defining what is permitted and what is forbidden, presiding over the

---

[12] Alexandre Soljenitsyne, *Deux siècles ensemble*, pp.180,231.

[13] David Bakan, *Freud et la tradition mystique juive*, 1963, Payot, 2001, pp.117,118,155.

local rabbinical court and teaching the Torah in public[14]". Judicial rulings were therefore within his competence, as was the interpretation of a Talmudic question. He proclaimed rulings in civil matters and was consulted in all cases where it was a question of whether or not an act was permitted by law.

Aleksandr Solzhenitsyn quoted the testimony of a certain Pestel, a Russian officer and fervent republican, who in the first half of the 19th century had drafted a government programme in which one could find these remarks: "The spiritual leaders of the Jews, whom they call rabbis, keep the people in an incredible dependence, forbidding them, in the name of faith, any other reading than the Talmud… The dependence of the Jews on the rabbis is such that every order given by them is piously carried out without a murmur[15]".

The Kahal was officially abolished in 1844, but the Jewish communities remained highly structured. The emancipation of Jews from the tutelage of the rabbis had begun in the previous century under the influence of the "Enlightenment". In Judaism, this intellectual current, called Haskalah, had been developed by the German Jewish philosopher Moses Mendelssohn, who favoured secular education, the use of local languages and the integration of Jews into gentile societies. But the main danger for the rabbis at that time came from the powerful Hasidic religious movement, which undermined their authority. The rabbis put all their energy into containing the influence of both.

The Hasidic movement had represented a new form of Judaism. Founded in the 18th century by Israel Ben Eliezer, nicknamed Baal Shem Tov—the Teacher of the Good Name—this pietistic movement had an immense influence on the Jewish communities of Eastern Europe. Hasidism emphasised the pleasant aspects of life. It emphasised prayer, fervour, singing and dancing and was a counterbalance to the pure scholarship and severity of rabbinic teachings. It was no longer necessary to be a scholar to partake of divine grace.

The Hasidim were grouped around a charismatic leader called the tzadik (the Righteous), or rebbe. Unlike the rabbis, the tzaddik did not owe his high office to his education. The position and authority with which he was invested came not from a bookish knowledge, but from a mystical communion with God. The lack of scholarship of some

---

[14] Shmuel Trigano, *La Société juive à travers l'histoire*, t.I, Fayard, 1992, p.515.

[15] Alexandre Soljenitsyne, *Deux siècles ensemble*, tome I, Fayard, 2002, p.76.

tzaddikim was, indeed, the subject of popular ridicule by those who did not share their beliefs. "Rarely does the tzaddik possess the necessary diploma for the function of rabbi that is awarded by a jury of rabbis at the end of yeshiva studies," wrote Mark Zborowski. Therefore, the tzaddik did not intervene in matters of the Law. He did not encroach on the strictly ritual life of the shtetl, which was the province of the rov, the rabbi. "The tzaddik is one who, through his hard mystical work and through his genetic and spiritual affiliation with the great master Baal Shem Tov or his disciples, has attained the highest level conceivable for a mortal; that of being the intermediary between God and his unhappy sinful children, the people of Israel". Having attained the highest level, the tzaddik literally spoke with God and possessed miraculous endowments: "Thanks to his eminent position, his practice of esoteric kabbalah and his knowledge of the Name (God's, unrevealed), he is able to work miracles for his adepts."

The activity of the tzaddik was essentially to assist and help those who came to him for comfort or advice, and to expound his teachings to them. Here is what Mark Zborowski wrote in his great study of pre-war Jewish communities in Eastern Europe: 'A remedy, an amulet, a blessing or advice is expected… Sometimes, accompanied by their children, women also come to present their problems to the miracle-worker. The sick await a spectacular cure. The insane are brought to the court so that the rebbe can "drive away their dybbuk". Hundreds of people came to consult him. "This is how the most reputable tzaddikim, those most surrounded by adepts, especially if they are descended from Baal Shem Tov or his disciples, have often enjoyed remarkable fortunes." Certainly, there was in these Jews a "fanatical devotion to the tzaddik[16] ", and they came from all over the world to see and hear him.

The tzaddik had his court, which varied according to his popularity, and in which women were naturally excluded: "The great autumn festivals can attract to the residence of a famous Polish tzaddik several thousand khossidim[17] who come to spend the terrible days at their master's side… For his faithful, he is the "Holy Man", "the Master of miracles", "the Intercessor". For some, he is no more and no less than a Saint," wrote Zborowski. "Do you know what a tzaddik is? I will tell you. There are in the Jewish religion six hundred and thirteen mitzvot. The common

---

[16] Mark Zborowski, *Olam*, 1952, 1992, pp.157-164

[17] Pronounce the kh like the Spanish j. Chassidim

man cannot fulfil them all. Only the tzaddik is capable of doing them. They are usually part of the dynasty of the Righteous, whose origin can be traced back to the founder of Hasidism, the Baal Shem Tov, or one of his direct disciples. All Tzaddikim are grandchildren of a great patriarch of the dynasty[18]." Once acquired, the mystical powers of the tzaddik were passed down hereditarily from father to son, even to sons-in-law through daughters. Weaker or weaker or stronger depending on the generations, these powers were never completely lost.

The English writer Israel Zangwill seemed rather reserved about these manifestations of popular fervour. In *The Ghetto Dreamers*, in 1898, he wrote: Each community has its own tzaddik, "a unique source of blessing, a unique source of grace. Each houses him in a palace (transformed into a place of pilgrimage during festivals, as in the Temple of old), each pays him a tribute in gold and valuables". Everywhere, the tzaddik "monopolises the worship and devotion that should be rendered to God.[19]" Henceforth, as Shmuel Trigano wrote, "it would be the tzaddik, and not the rabbi, who would be perceived as the symbol of religious ideals[20]."

The Hasidic Jews, whose teachings clashed head-on with the strict rabbinical doctrine, had to face the hostility of the rabbis for a long time. In 1772, the "Gaon of Vilna" and the heads of the Lithuanian Jewish community declared them heretical. Years later, to retaliate, the Hasidim denounced the rabbis to the authorities who arrested the members of the Vilnius kahal "for improper withholding of taxes collected[21]." It took a long time for the Jewish tradition to finally assimilate Hasidism. But although this mass movement helped, as Israel Zangwill put it, to liberate "peoples under the tyranny of the rabbis[22]", the Jewish communities of Eastern Europe at the end of the 19th century were far removed from the Western intellectual universe.

---

[18] Mark Zborowski, *Olam*, 1952, Plon, 1992, pp.157,158. Of the 613 commandments, 365 are negative commandments ("thou shalt not") and 248 are positive commandments.

[19] Israel Zangwill, *Rêveurs du ghetto*, t II, 1898, Éd. Complexe, 2000, pp.70,71.

[20] Shmuel Trigano, *La société juive à travers l'histoire*, TI, Fayard, 1992, p.515.

[21] Alexandre Soljenitsyne, *Deux siècles ensemble*, tome I, Fayard, 2002, p.41.

[22] Israel Zangwill, *Rêveurs du ghetto*, t II, 1898, Éd. Complexe, 2000, p.79

Eastern Jews' feelings of communal belonging were also simply geographical. The community came together to confront another community. They never cease to criticise and mock the neighbouring shtelt," wrote Zborowski, "but all the towns and cities of one region can unite around a cause against another region. Across borders, Eastern European Jews are united in a common contempt for German Jews, branded as cold and accused of tending towards assimilation. But whatever their differences and antagonisms, the regional groups of Jews belong to Klal Israel, the Totality of Israel in the world." And this is where Mark Zborowski unveiled an important piece of information, which gave us an idea of the strength of Jewish communal feeling: "One who has only one Jewish parent is willingly admitted to Klal Israel. Religious observance is not a criterion. Even one who violates the commandments is still a Jew, as is one who eats forbidden food. One who abjures his faith is disowned by his family, even mourning his loss, but he may repent and return. Even though he has renounced, there is still something of the Jew in him? Whatever he does, "he always remains a Jew[23]".

The famous Elie Wiesel confirmed this idea that Jews are a nation apart: "Between a merchant from Morocco and a chemist from Chicago, a rag-picker from Lodz and an industrialist from Lyon, a kabbalist from Safed and an intellectual from Minsk, there is a deeper kinship, more substantial because more ancient, than between two citizens of the same country, the same city and the same profession. Even when alone, a Jew is never alone[24]." Elie Wiesel further wrote: "He feels closer to the prophet Elijah than to his neighbour on the landing... everything that struck his ancestors affects him. Their mourning weighs on him, their triumphs cheer him[25]."

---

[23] Mark Zborowski, *Olam*, 1952, Plon, 1992, pp. 408–410. "Even a renegade Jew is a Jew!" (*Israel Magazine*, April 2003); "He is a Jew and remains a Jew... come what may" writes France's Chief Rabbi Joseph Sitruk (*Tribune juive*, October 2004): it is a question of retaining Jews in their community, by all means. However, these declarations do not prevent thousands of Jews from forgetting and moving away from Judaism and their community of origin for good.

[24] Elie Wiesel, *Le Testament d'un poète juif assasiné*, 1980, Points Seuil, 1995, p.57.

[25] Elie Wiesel, *Memoires 2*, Editions du Seuil, 1996, p.46

In the shtelt, "the highest compliment that can be paid to a Gentile is: 'he has a Jew's face', or 'a Jew's heart'...". A true Jew, they incessantly repeat to the children, is moderate, reserved and intellectual; any departure from this ideal is open to severe reproaches: "a Jewish child does not ride a bicycle, a Jewish child does not laugh like an idiot!""And Mark Zborowski added: "Passing through the shtelt, visitors had noticed that the children had a serious look, that they made faces but did not smile". Compared to the Polish children whose main activity was playing games, "the contrast was striking"[26]

## *The mission of the Jews*

Visitors to the shtelts at that time probably did not penetrate all of Israel's secrets during their short walk through the muddy streets of these Polish villages. On the surface, the Jewish population of these "ghettos" could give the strange Western tourist a peaceful and picturesque image of communal life. But what happened later evidently strengthened the certainties of many Russians, Poles and Ukrainians about the uniqueness of the Jewish people.

Despite appearances, the Jewish people are not exactly a people like any other people. They are God's "chosen people". If this idea does not mean much to a goy, it certainly has much more significance for a Jew, convinced that he has a mission to fulfil on this earth. And this mission is to bring "Peace" to the world (shalom). It is incumbent upon every Jew to work towards this goal, as it is a precondition for what is even more important: the coming of the Messiah. This is why so many Jews threw themselves body and soul into the Bolshevik adventure, and why, after the collapse of communism, so many Jews are today the most ardent propagandists for globalism and the multicultural society. The disappearance of nations is part of the same egalitarian programme of world pacification as the earlier project of abolishing social classes and the differences between bourgeois and proletarians.

These hopes have been leading the Jews for centuries. A celebrated novelist of Jewish literature, the Englishman Israel Zangwill had expressed this idea at the time in *The Ghetto Dreamers,* a novel

---

[26] Mark Zborowski, *Olam*, 1952, Plon, 1992, pp.441,328

published in 1898: "Human brotherhood is what we strive for, he wrote... The Jew will be the world's messenger of peace[27]."

We have already dealt with this issue in our previous books, but there is no shortage of texts on this subject. One can cite, for example, Gershom Scholem, who was one of the most important Jewish intellectuals of the 20th century. He also confirmed that the religious faith of the Jews was based first and foremost on the hope for the establishment of a final peace and the coming of a messiah: "The Messiah will come and restore the kingdom of David to its original power, he wrote. He will rebuild the sanctuary and reunite the scattered Jews of Israel". Gershom Scholem here quoted Maimonides, who already wrote in the 12th century in his *Code of Laws*: "In those times, there will be no more famine and war, no more envy and discord, for the land will be possessed in abundance. The whole world will have no other concern but the knowledge of God. Then the children of Israel will be wise men of renown[28]."

These beliefs have traversed the centuries without becoming outdated. Naturally, contemporary Jewish thinkers think no differently. Let us listen to Théo Klein, former president of the Representative Council of Jewish Institutions in France (CRIF), talk about the "special mission" of the Jewish people. According to him, this people is "the bearer of an idea, of a project which it must strive to implement... In my opinion, this project is universal. Reread Genesis chapter 18, verse 18. Doesn't it say: "For Abraham will become a great and mighty nation, and through him all the nations of the earth will be blessed"[29]."

A second-rate writer like Jean-Michel Salanskis also expressed these messianic hopes when he wrote: "There is the hope that the nations will listen to and understand the greatness and the profound Jewish millenarian reflection", in order to "make possible the consummation of the universal, when the nations of the earth will be gathered around the last kingdom of the Messiah[30]."

---

[27] Israel Zangwill, *Rêveurs du ghetto*, t II, 1898, Éd. Complexe, 2000, pp.245,248.

[28] Gershom Scholem, *Le Messianisme juif*, 1971, Calmann-Levy, 1974, pp.57-59.

[29] Théo Klein, *Dieu n'était pas au rendez-vous*, Bayard, 2003, p.69.

[30] Jean-Michel Salanskis, *Extermination, loi, Israel*, Les Belles Lettres, 2003,

Indeed, this world of "peace" that the Jews want to build—this Empire of peace—is confused with the arrival of the messiah that they have been awaiting for two thousand years against all odds. A liberal media intellectual like Guy Sorman provided the testimony of a certain Leon Askenazi, born into a family of rabbis in Oran. He explained that the Jews were actually expecting two messiahs: the son of Joseph and the son of David: "The first gathers the exiles. Obviously, he is already at work. We see how humanity, scattered since Babel, is in search of a universal union; let's call it world order. It is the babbling of this search for the Messiah. The second messiah, the son of David, will establish universal peace and raise the dead. He is the object of faith: it is up to each Jew, in the secret of his heart, in his personal intimacy, to imagine this son of David. This experience is not shared. But since the first messianic phase is already underway, the second phase, that of the transformation of the human soul by the grace of God, should not take too long[31]."

This is what Maurice-Ruben Hayoun also wrote in 1996 in his *Intellectual History of Judaism*: "The coming of the true Messiah, son of David, was to be preceded by that of the Messiah, son of Joseph, who was to succumb in the war between Gog and Magog.[32]". This idea was confirmed by the American author David Bakan: "The warrior Messiah, (the Messiah-ben-Joseph or ben-Ephraïm, or ben-Manassé), will be killed, but he will come before the Messiah-ben-David who will reign after the Redemption[33]."

Gershom Scholem confirmed this once again: "The Messiah, son of Joseph, is the Messiah who dies, overwhelmed by the messianic catastrophe... He struggles and ends up failing—but he does not suffer for it... He is the redeemer who redeems nothing, on whom alone is concentrated the final combat against the powers of this world. His end coincides with the end of history. On the contrary, in this distribution of roles, it is in the Messiah, son of David, that all the utopian aspects are

---

pp.105,92

[31] Guy Sorman, *Le Bonheur français*, Fayard, 1995, p.68.

[32] Maurice-Ruben Hayoun, *Une Histoire intellectuelle du Judaïsme*, tome I, J-C Lattès, 1996, p.390.

[33] David Bakan, *Freud et la tradition mystique juive*, 1963, Payot, 2001, p.195.

concentrated. He is the one in whom the new world dawns... He represents the positive side of this complex process[34]."

Before the destruction of the second Temple by Titus' legions in 70 CE, Jewish eschatological writings evoked salvation without a messiah, explained Stephen Sharot. It was only after the failure of the second revolt against the Romans that apocalyptic authors began to mention a saviour messiah. "The messiah was to restore David's kingdom, rebuild the temple, restore the ancient laws and sacrifices, and reunite the scattered Jews... Rabbinic literature presented the messiah as a redeemer, as the instrument by which the kingdom of God would be established, and also as the future ruler of that kingdom." In addition, the Jews "expected the coming of certain personages before that of the messiah. The most important of these was the prophet Elijah, whose miracles and preaching would lead the people to repent and prepare for the coming of the messiah". The Talmudic literature "was, however, full of contradictions and the Middle Ages did not inherit a coherent and unified conception of the messiah... The Jewish messiah remained a diffuse and anonymous figure, allowing a wide range of personalities to claim this role".

The rabbinic mainstream did not encourage the imminent arrival of the messiah, but it was nevertheless an article of faith for medieval and modern Jews to constantly await his coming. "The twelfth principle of the best known formulation of Jewish religious doctrines, Maimonides' "The Thirteen Principles of the Jewish Faith" declared: "I believe by pure faith in the coming of the Messiah, and though I must tarry, I will wait for his coming every day". The affirmation of this belief, wrote Stephen Sharot, was a recurring theme of Jewish prayers: in some daily blessings, in thanksgivings after dinner, at weddings, and on feast and fast days. In private and business letters, holiday wishes and congratulatory formulas often ended with the wish that those concerned would witness the coming of the messiah and the reunion of all exiles[35]."

This was the secular messianic faith that structured the mental universe of hundreds of thousands of revolutionaries who militated in communism in the 19th and 20th centuries. All, in their respective parties,

---

[34] Gershom Scholem, *Le Messianisme juif*, 1971, Calmann-Levy, 1974, p.45.

[35] Shmuel Trigano, *La société juive à travers l'histoire*, TI, Fayard, 1992, pp. 263-267.

had faith in their historical mission. They nurtured an optimistic vision of the future and faith in the advent of a world where all injustice and discrimination would be outlawed. "This militancy is messianic, optimistic, oriented towards the Good" wrote Alain Brossat in *The Revolutionary Yiddishland*. "The great utopia of the new world, of the New Alliance that takes shape in the narratives of the socialist thinkers of the second half of the 19th century, consolidates with the growth of the workers' movement at the beginning of the century and launches its assault on the heavens with the Russian Revolution."

These were the hopes of these Ashkenazi Jews, as Alain Brossat acknowledged: "It is probably true that, since the mid-1880s, Jews have occupied a particularly important place in Russia's revolutionary movements[36]."

But the massive commitment of Yiddishland Jews to communism might seem paradoxical, in the sense that these highly religious, traditionalist and structured Jewish communities were not a priori conducive to being a breeding ground for militant revolutionaries. This issue is mentioned in a book by Elie Wiesel, *The Testament of a Murdered Jewish Poet*. Wiesel recounted the fate of a young man, Paltiel Kossover, a Jewish poet from Bessarabia, born in 1910, and converted to communism like so many of his peers. One of his friends had initiated him into the doctrine of Karl Marx:

Yes," he said, "I got my first lesson in communism from Ephraim that night in the Study House. Funny, isn't it? Ephraïm, the communist agitator! Ephraim, the future rabbinical judge, distributed clandestine leaflets. He hid them in the desks and—don't laugh—in the backpacks of holy books and ritual objects... —Have you lost your mind, Ephraïm? Are you abandoning the sacred texts for that?" And he would reply: "I have not lost my mind, Paltiel. Listen to me well. I still wish to save mankind, to rid society of its evils; I still wish to bring about the coming of the Messiah. Only I have discovered a new method, that is all. I tried meditation, fasting, asceticism, without success. There is only one way that leads to salvation." And that way is action: "I'm not talking to you about action on God, but on history, on the events that create history." Paltiel Kossover was puzzled: "If Ephraim had used the properly Marxist theses, I would have turned my back on him. But instead of

---

[36] Alain Brossat, Sylvia Klingberg, *Le yiddishland revolutionnaire*, Balland, 1983, pp.77, 78,227.

quoting Engels, Plekhanov and Lenin, he evoked our common messianic hope. And I could not but agree with him".

Indeed, this Ephraim saw in communism his hope in the coming of the Saviour: "Every morning, I pray that he will come, that he will hasten to come. Like you, I recite the prayer. But it is a long time to wait; and the burden of exile is heavy and hard to bear". And then he explained to Paltiel his conception of the world: "Only communism enables man to triumph quickly over oppression and inequality... Communism is a kind of messianism without God, a secular, social messianism, awaiting the other, the true one". And Ephraim exclaimed to himself, exalted: "We must make the revolution, because God commands it! God wants us to be communists[37]!"

But Paltiel Kossover had not completely detached himself from the ancestral faith of his people: "In appearance, I led the life of a communist; but only in appearance. Inge often reminded me: 'You are not a communist; I mean, not entirely. —That's true. I think too much of the Messiah. Some people are waiting for him; the communists, they run to him."

And so we see clearly that Judaism is by essence an activist religion: "My questions always revolved around the Messiah. I longed so much to hasten his coming. To abolish the gap between rich and poor, humiliated and happy, beggars and owners. To put an end to pogroms and wars. To unite justice and compassion... Rejoice, O Israel, the hour of your deliverance is at hand[38]!"

In his *memoirs,* Elie Wiesel also gave us an interesting account of the links between the Jewish world and socialism: "The phenomenon of the religious Jew who chooses communism continues to fascinate me... In the course of my research, I discovered to my astonishment that there were even some in my small town. Prestigious and less famous names were mentioned to me. Yes, these Talmudic students gathered at night in a dark Bet Midrash and analysed Lenin and Engels with the same

---

[37] Elie Wiesel, *Le Testament d'un poète juif assassiné*, 1980, Point Seuil, 1995, pp.63-68.

[38] Elie Wiesel, *Le Testament d'un poète juif assassiné*, 1980, Point Seuil, 1995, pp.128, 61, 62

religious fervour that they manifested during the day when they studied the teachings of Maimonides[39]."

However, commitment to revolutionary movements implied a certain break with ancestral traditions. Here is the eloquent testimony of a communist militant who recounted his first experience at the age of ten. A comrade invited him to go with him to the *Red Pioneers*. "He praised the many activities of this organisation so highly and so well that I decided to go with him. "There is a small problem, he tells me, you can't come with your peyos\*, your curls, they would make fun of you... "Never mind, I decide to go and have them cut. The hairdresser is astonished: "Did you ask your father's permission? —No—you know you're going to get a good beating? I insisted and he cut them. But he wasn't wrong: when I returned home, my father beat me to a pulp. I had committed one of the most serious crimes imaginable. Nevertheless, I continued to frequent the *Red Pioneers on* the sly[40]."

As Maurice Rajsfu wrote: "Lenin's Capital and the complete works of Lenin had replaced the Torah of his childhood[41]." The great historian of Judaism, Leon Poliakov, also wrote as much: a good part of those Jews "gradually abandoned the ancestral faith, at least in certain respects... moving towards a secularisation that in the 19th and 20th century would transform the descendants of the Talmudic Jews into passionate revolutionaries[42]."

Ashkenazi Jews in Central Europe and Russia accounted for about 90% of world Jewry at the end of the 19th century. For centuries, they had remained secluded in their villages, keeping as far away from the population as possible. Under the influence of the emancipatory ideas of the French Revolution, and then under the influence of Marxism, the rabbinical yoke had been loosened. Hundreds of thousands of individuals, filled with messianic hope, were to leave the walls of their community to preach and spread the good word throughout the world.

---

[39] Elie Wiesel, *Mémoires*, tome I, 1994, pp44,45.

\* It's those long locks of hair that orthodox Jews let fall from their temples.

[40] Alain Brossat, Sylvia Klingberg, *Le yiddishland revolutionnaire*, Balland, 1983, p.58.

[41] Maurice Rajsfus, *L'an prochain la révolution*, Editions Mazarinne, 1985, p.16.

[42] Leon Poliakov, *The Samaritans*, (Seuil, 1991, Anaya Group, 1992), p.85.

## *The revolutionary militant*

At the beginning of the 20th century, Russia and Romania were the only two European countries that did not recognise Jews as members of their national community, despite pressure from Western governments. In these two countries, Jews had no access to public office, and in Russia, moreover, the Zone of Residence had not yet been abolished, despite the liberalisation policy of Tsar Alexander II's regime. On 1 March 1881, he was assassinated by members of the People's Will, which had the effect of provoking repression, breaking the process of liberalisation and radicalising revolutionary groups. Solzhenitsyn noted in his book that "the Tsar was assassinated on the eve of Purim", the annual holiday on which Jews celebrate victory over their enemies. We also read that the assassination attempt had been prepared at the home of one Hessia Helfman [43]. Henri Minczeles wrote: "Among the revolutionaries arrested was Hessia Helfman, a young Jewish girl who had stored dynamite in her garret[44]."

The assassination of the tsar lit the fuse of the powder keg, and numerous pogroms broke out, mainly in Ukraine. The pogroms always broke out exclusively in the south-west of Russia, Solzhenitsyn pointed out. The destruction was impressive, but no one was killed. The laws of May 1882 did, however, restrict the economic influence of the Jews. In 1891, 20,000 Jews were expelled from Moscow and more than 2,000 from St Petersburg.

After 1881, the most important pogrom was the Kichinev pogrom in 1903, in which 42 people died, including 38 Jews[45]. In 1905, in Kiev, Odessa and other Ukrainian cities, clashes broke out between Ukrainians and Jews. The latter had formed paramilitary groups, gathering thousands of fighters.

From 1880 to 1910, more than 2.5 million Jews left Russia. Jewish historians argue that it was the pogroms that broke out after the assassination of the Tsar that prompted Jews to flee the country. Alain

---

[43] Frank L. Britton, *Behind communism*.

[44] Henri Minczeles, *Histoire genérale du Bund*, 1995, Denoël, 1999, p.31

[45] The historian Arkadi Vaksberg wrote: In April 1903, a pogrom "decimated the Jewish population of Kichinev". (*Staline et les juifs*, Robert Laffont, 2003, p.17). Jewish organisations and witnesses had claimed 500 dead; the number was later revised and lowered.

Brossat also stressed the importance of the anti-Semitism of the Russian and Ukrainian population in explaining this phenomenon, while neglecting to explain the causes, as most Jewish historians do. Aleksandr Solzhenitsyn provided another explanation: In reality, the emigration of Jews had been mainly motivated by the establishment, in 1896, of the state monopoly on spirits and the suppression of all private production. This measure, designed to protect the peasantry and force Jews out of the countryside, had "dealt a severe blow to the economic activity of the Jews of Russia". It was from then on that Jewish emigration out of Russia was seen to "amplify markedly[46]".

Among the main organisers of Russian populism, Solzhenitsyn cited Marc Natanson, the most important, and Leon Deutsch of Kiev. Also a certain Grigory Goldenberg: "He had shot down in cold blood the governor of Kharkov and asked his comrades for the supreme honour of killing the Tsar with his own hands (but his comrades, fearing popular anger, turned him away because he was a Jew; apparently, Solzhenitsyn added, this argument was often used by populists to designate Russians to carry out the attacks): after being arrested carrying a load of dynamite, he suffered an attack of anguish in his cell in the Trubetskoy bastion and his resistance broke down, finally betraying the whole movement[47]."

Between 1901 and 1906, the Social Revolutionary Party adopted the methods of the People's Will and carried out assassination attempts on Russian dignitaries. Assassinated were, among others, Education Minister Bogolepov (1901); Interior Minister Sipiaguine (1902); Governor Bogdanovitch (1903); Prime Minister Vyacheslav von Plehve (1904); Grand Duke Sergius, uncle of the Tsar (1905); and General Dubrassov (1906). The head of these terrorist operations was a Jew named Grigori Guerchouny. He was always at the scene of the attacks. In charge of the combat section was Yevno Azev, the son of a Jewish seamstress, and one of the founders of the party. He was executed in 1909.

"The execution of the attacks was always entrusted to Christians," wrote Solzhenitsyn, but "the bombs used for the assassination of Plehve, the Grand Duke Sergius and the Ministers of the Interior Boulyguine and Dournovo, were made by Maximilian Schweitzer, who, in 1905,

---

[46] Alexandre Soljenitsyne, *Deux siècles ensemble*, tome I, Fayard, 2002, p. 326.

[47] Alexandre Soljenitsyne, *Deux siècles ensemble*, tome I, Fayard, 2002, p. 249.

was himself the victim of the device he was making". Arrested by chance, Guerchouny was condemned to death, then pardoned by the Emperor without even having requested it. In 1907, he escaped from prison via Vladivostok to America and later to Europe. Among the most prominent terrorists were Abraham Gotz, who took an active part in the attacks on Dournovo (Minister of the Interior in 1905–1906), Akimov, Chouvalov (diplomat and politician) and Trepov (Deputy Minister of the Interior in 1905–1907)[48].

Pyotr Stolypin dominated Russian political life from 1906 to 1911. Thanks to his reformist policies, two million peasant families became landowners. In 1916, 6 million families benefited from the government's measures. The victim of an assassination attempt in 1906, Stolypin was finally assassinated in 1911 by a Jewish lawyer named Mordechai Bogrov: "Ironically, the first head of the Russian government who had honestly tried, despite the Emperor's resistance, to solve the question of equality for the Jews would fall under the blows of the Jews", wrote Solzhenitsyn. It is also true that Stolypin had vigorously suppressed the revolution of 1905–1906.

Although they represented only 5% of Russia's population, i.e. 6 million people, in 1903, Jews accounted for 50% of the revolutionaries, Solzhenitsyn reported. General Sukhotin, commander of the Siberian region, had established statistics by nationality on 1 January 1905 of the political convicts under his supervision throughout Siberia. The result was as follows: 1898 Russians (42%), 1678 Jews (37%), 624 Poles (14%) and 167 Caucasians[49].

The presence of Jewish militants was even stronger in the leadership of the revolutionary movements. Leon Poliakov confirmed this: "Jews quickly became the subversive ethnic group par excellence in the Russian empire... Their proportion among the politically condemned doubled from decade to decade, reaching 29 per cent in 1902–1904... This proportion was even higher in the central committees and other leading positions of anti-government organisations, in which young Jews played a decisive, even inciting role[50]."

---

[48] Alexandre Soljenitsyne, *Deux siècles ensemble*, tome I, Fayard, 2002, p.395.

[49] Alexandre Soljenitsyne, *Deux siècles ensemble*, tome I, Fayard, 2002, p.263.

[50] Leon Poliakov, *Histoire de l'antisemitisme, tome II*, Point Seuil, 1981, p.331.

The conditions of detention of revolutionaries were then incomparably more humane than the methods employed by the Bolsheviks after the revolution. The historian Simon Sebag Montefiore, author of a monumental biography of Stalin, wrote of the deportations in Siberia: "Those banishments were a far cry from Stalin's brutal concentration camps: the tsars were very inept as policemen. They were almost a reading holiday in remote Siberian villages, in the company of a part-time gendarme, during which the revolutionaries had time to get to know (and hate) each other, correspond with their comrades in St. Petersburg or Vienna... When the call of freedom or revolution became more imperative, they would escape, crossing the taiga until they found the nearest train[51]." Stalin thus escaped up to six times from these Siberian villages.

In 1897, the same year that Theodor Herzl founded the Zionist movement in Basel, the Bund, a specifically Jewish Marxist movement, was born. The aim of the Bund was neither the assimilation of Jews into European society nor their emigration to Palestine, but the achievement of cultural autonomy and the fulfilment of the socialist project.

At the beginning of the 20th century, the Bund was the main Jewish political organisation in the area of residence. It had thousands of militants, wrote Alain Brossat, between 25,000 and 30,000 between 1903 and 1905: "They had a very popular press, they led protests tirelessly: in one year, between 1903 and 1904, they held 429 political rallies, organised 45 demonstrations, 41 political strikes, and distributed 305 leaflets and pamphlets. In 1904, 4500 Bund activists were in prison. They set up a youth organisation and publish a newspaper. Their influence culminated in 1905 when they took part in the Revolution, their role being essential in their area of residence[52]."

All politicised Jews were not Bund militants. While the Bund claimed to represent the entire Jewish proletariat, others, who wanted to structure a socialist party for the entire working class of Russia, joined the various Russian socialist movements. But the Bund had at its disposal at that time material means and an organisation infinitely superior to those of the Russian and Polish socialists:

---

[51] Simon Sebag Montefiore, *La corte del Zar rojo*, 2004, Crítica-Barcelona, p. 6.

[52] Alain Brossat, Sylvia Klingberg, *Le yiddishland revolutionnaire*, Balland, 1983, p.35.

"It is he who, in the western part of the Empire, helps the Russian Social-Democrats to print their first publications and send them clandestinely to the industrial centres. It is he who, on May 1, 1899, organised the first great public demonstration of the Jewish proletariat in Russia. It was he who, after the Kishinev pogrom of 1903, organised the Jewish self-defence. When the 1905 revolution broke out, the Russian party had about 8500 members. The Bund already has about 30,000[53]."

When the Bolsheviks finally seized power thanks to the October 1917 coup d'état, all the militants, whatever their differences, let their joy burst forth, as Elie Wiesel expressed it through Paltiel Kossover, his "murdered Jewish poet":

"If Ephraim's words were true, the Messiah had left Jerusalem to come to Moscow. —You see, he said to me, overexcited, the prophecy of Isaiah, they have fulfilled it; the comfort of Jeremiah, they have proved it… There are no more rich and poor, no more bosses and workers, no more oppressors and oppressed. There is no more ignorance, no more terror, no more misery. Do you hear me, Paltiel? All men are brothers before the Law? And all this because the Revolution has triumphed. It has engendered a new man—the communist man—who has defeated capitalist power, the dictatorship of the rich, the fanaticism of superstitions".

In Berlin in 1928, Paltiel Kossover wrote to his parents who remained in Russia: "More than ever, I am convinced that we are destined to save the world". My father must have thought: we, the Jews. I thought: we, the idealists, the young people; we, the revolutionaries[54]."

These profound changes caused a complete restructuring of the political forces in Yiddishland. Numerous Bund militants and hundreds of thousands of Jewish youth from all over the world swelled the ranks of the communist movement. This is the testimony of Shlomo Szlein, who was in Poland in the 1920s: "The adherence of the Jewish youth to the communist movement was so important that one could almost say that it was a Jewish national movement". Bronia Zelmanovicz also stated, "For us Polish communists, five-year prison sentences were

---

[53] Alain Brossat, Sylvia Klingberg, *Le yiddishland revolutionnaire*, Balland, 1983, p.49

[54] Elie Wiesel, *Le Testament d'un poète juif assassiné*, 1980, Point Seuil, 1995, pp.79, 123.

commonplace, but nevertheless we were unshakably optimistic, convinced that our children would know true freedom, happiness and emancipation of the human race." Alain Brossat explained, "This is how tens of thousands of Yiddishland revolutionaries are going to follow, between the two wars, the many paths of their utopia in the four corners of Europe... It is the Jewish common people in their entirety, the proletariat of tailors, shoemakers, furriers, carpenters, tinsmiths, and other Yiddish weavers in the miserable workshops of Warsaw, Byalistock and Vilno, born in the spirit of revolt and struggle, for trade union and political organisation, and the internationalism of the exploited. " "[55]

Yiddishland was truly the breeding ground for the revolutionaries who were going to fight fascism and set fire to the whole of Europe. They were in all the revolutionary battles of that time: "We find Yiddishland fighters in all the incandescent places of the revolution, wrote Brossat, from the barricades of Lodz and the Petersburg Soviet in 1905, to Berlin in November 1918, Munich and Budapest in 1919, in Poland between the two wars, in Extremadura against the Spanish generals in 1937, in the French Resistance, in Belgium, in Yugoslavia and even fighting in Auschwitz and Vorkouta, in the very heart of the concentrationary universe." As the historian Pierre Vidal-Naquet formulated it: "Eastern European Judaism has truly been the blood bank of the proletarian revolutionary movements[56]."

## *Judeo-Bolshevism*

The new regime born of the February 1917 revolution had immediately abolished the zone of residence and declared equal rights. Suddenly, numerous Jews occupied the Russian administration. Arkadi Vaksberg recounted, for example, in his book *Stalin and the Jews*: "Sign of the times, the Jew Heinrich Schreider became the mayor of Petrograd, and another Jew, Oscar Minor, the mayor of Moscow". It is true, however, that there were no Jewish ministers in the successive provisional governments. "Abraham Gotz, leader of the revolutionary socialists and vice-chairman of the Russian central executive committee, and the

---

[55] Alain Brossat, Sylvia Klingberg, *Le yiddishland revolutionnaire*, Balland, 1983, pp. 84, 88, 80,128

[56] Pierre Vidal-Naquet, *Les Juifs, la mémoire et le présent*, Maspéro, 1981, p.160 in Alain Brossat, *Le Yiddishland révolutionnaire*, pp. 19, 15.

Menshevik Fedor Dan, a member of the Presidium of that committee, refused to enter the government precisely for fear of provoking a wave of anti-Semitism... However, several Jewish deputy ministers were appointed to exercise technical functions, outside any public representation[57]."

In October, the Bolshevik revolution brought them to the summit of power. They played a leading role in the insurrection: "The first "commander" of the Winter Palace, stormed by the Bolsheviks, was Grigory Tchoudnovsky, that of the Moscow Kremlin, Emelan Yaroslavsky (Minay Gubelman was his real name). It was Mikhail Lachevitch who took over the telegraph and the state bank. Zinoviev was elected head of the Petrograd Soviet, and Kamenev of the Moscow Soviet." Other Jews took charge of maintaining order in the capital and its environs. Moïssei Ouritzki, at the head of the Petrograd Tcheka, "reigned a merciless terror." Moïssei Volodarski (Goldstein) was the commissar in charge of the press in Petrograd. "From that position, he banned all opposition newspapers and fiercely repressed any attempt to circumvent this ban[58]."

We know that Lenin did not have a single drop of Russian blood. His origins had been carefully kept secret after his death. In 1938, Marietta Chaguinian's book, *The Examination of History*, had been immediately withdrawn from sale on Stalin's orders. "Lenin had German, Swedish (through his mother), Kalmykia and Chuvash blood, but not a drop of Russian blood[59]!" He was also partly of Jewish origin, on his mother's side. Arkadi Vaksberg recalled a letter from Lenin's elder sister, Anna Oulianova, who had written to Stalin on 19 December 1932, encouraging him to combat anti-Semitism: "The study of my grandfather's origins—and therefore of Vladimir Ilitch's—has revealed that he came from a poor Jewish family, and that he was, as his baptismal certificate indicates, the son of Moïchka Blank, a bourgeois

---

[57] Arkadi Vaksberg, *Stalin et les juifs*, Laffont, 2003, pp.23, 24.

[58] Arkadi Vaksberg, *Stalin et les juifs*, Laffont, 2003, pp. 31, 32.

[59] Simon Sebag Montefiore, *Staline, la cour du tsar rouge*, 2003, Éd. Des Syrtes, 2005, p. 101 "At the beginning of the 1920s, a common joke presented Lenin as the Shabbat Goy of the political bureau of the Russian Communist Party", wrote Maurice Rajsfus, explaining that: "The Shabbat Goy is the mercenary used by the religious to cook on the Sabbath or to perform some of the tasks forbidden on this day of complete rest". (Maurice Rajsfus, *L'an prochain, la révolution*, Editions Mazarine, 1985, p.36).

from Zhytómir[60]." But these revelations had not left the narrow circle of the party hierarchy. This letter, as Arkadi Vaksberg revealed, was "until recently classified: 'Strictly secret. Do not disclose to anyone'.

Trotsky, the head of the Red Army, was actually called Lev Davidovitch Bronstein. Kamenev, the head of the Moscow Soviet, was called Rosenfeld; Alexander Zinoviev, who headed Leningrad, had the real name of Apfelbaum; Karl Radek, Moscow's spokesman abroad, had the real name of Sobelsohn. The first head of the Bolshevik state was another Jew named Yakov Sverdlov, Lenin's close collaborator and adviser\*. The list of Bolshevik Jews at the head of the new regime is endless.

The Jews of Yiddishland also played a major role in the revolutions that shook Europe at the end of the First World War. First in Berlin, where the insurrection of November 1918 was led by Karl Liebknecht and Rosa Luxemburg. Then in Hungary, where a Soviet Republic was proclaimed in March 1919 by Bela Kun, who bloodied the country for 133 days. "Himself Jewish, twenty-five of his thirty-two commissars were also Jewish," recalled historian John Toland. Bela Kun's triumph emboldened the Bavarian left. In Munich, the revolution's spiritual leader was Kurt Eisner, who was later replaced by an anarchist, Ernst Toller. "Then the Red intelligentsia seized power, led by Eugen Leviné, originally from Petrograd and the son of a Jewish merchant. The Communist Party had sent them to Munich to organise the revolution. Having arrested Ernst Toller, they soon transformed the movement into a real soviet[61]...".

In his monumental *History of the German Army*, Jacques Benoist-Méchin had presented these facts to explain the reaction of many Germans after the defeat of 1918: "What did they see? Crowds raising red flags, storming power and seeking to eradicate, in the name of the class struggle, the last glimmerings of national instinct. But these crowds do not obey a spontaneous impulse. They are led by a legion of militants and agitators. And who are these agitators? In Berlin, Kurt

---

[60] Arkadi Vaksberg, *Stalin et les juifs*, Laffont, 2003, pp. 72, 73.

\* Yakov Sverdlov was also a close friend of Filipp Isayevich Goloshchokin, also a Jew and military commissar of the Ural Soviet. The two of them were the main masterminds behind the assassination of the Tsar and his family.

[61] John Toland, *Hitler*, New York, 1976, Éditions Robert Laffont, Paris, 1983, p. 76, 77.

Eisner, Lipp, Landauer, Toller, Léviné and Lewien; in Magdebourg, Brandés; in Dresden, Lipinsky, Geyer and Fleissner; in the Ruhr, Markus and Levinson; in Breerhaven and Kiel, Ulmanis. As many names as there are Jews. It may no doubt be objected that there are only two Israelis—Hirsch and Heine—out of the one hundred and forty deputies of the Prussian Landtag, but they are respectively President of the Council and Minister of the Interior. When the left-wing parties decide to set up a Commission of Inquiry for the purpose of bringing Hidenburg and Ludendorff to trial, who are the organisers? MM. Kohn, Gothein and Zinsheimer, and so on, the list could go on ad infinitum. How can we fail to see a real conspiracy? And should we now tolerate that a Jew [Rathenau] should take over the direction of the Reich's foreign policy? This is impossible[62]."

This is why the very rich electricity magnate Walter Rathenau was assassinated on 24 June 1922[63].

Indeed, it was this situation that partly explained the Hitlerite reaction in Germany, as the Jewish historian John Toland put it: "The hatred of Jews that was brewing within him had just been activated by what he was witnessing on the streets of Munich. Everywhere, Jews in power? The conspiracy that Hitler had suspected was becoming a reality[64]." John Toland further added: "Hitler is not alone in the world in having seen the Jews as the source of revolution and communism." Winston Churchill, who had enlisted the help of the white general Denikine to fight Lenin and Trostski, also spoke bluntly of this "sinister gang of anarchist Jews". It was also Winston Churchill who had made a speech to the House of Commons denouncing "a formidable sect, the most powerful in the world[65]." In an article in the *Sunday Herald* in February 1920, entitled *Zionism versus Bolshevism*, Winston Churchill mentioned a "world-wide conspiracy aimed at overthrowing civilisation": "At present, a gang of extraordinary characters, drawn

---

[62] Jacques Benoist-Méchin, *Histoire de l'armée allemande*, Robert Laffont, 1964, 1984 edition, pp.448, 449.

[63] On the German situation after the war, cf Stefan Zweig, *Yesterday's World, Memoirs of a European*, in *Planetary Hopes*, pp.314, 315.

[64] John Toland, *Hitler*, New York, 1976, Éditions Robert Laffont, Paris, 1983, p. 80.

[65] John Toland, *Hitler*, New York, 1976, Éditions Robert Laffont, Paris, 1983, p. 898.

from the underworld of the great European and American cities, have seized the Russian people by the throat and have become the undisputed masters of an immense empire[66]."

In any case, it seems that the presence of "so many Jews in the command posts of the new state apparatus[67] " was reassuring for many Jews in Russia. Here is the testimony of Esther Rosenthal-Schneidermann, a young Communist from Poland who came to Moscow to take part in the first congress of Jewish militants specialising in education: "She was thrilled to discover this aspect of the new reality: 'Until then, she says, I had not seen a Jew occupying the position of a high official, let alone an official speaking our dialect, Yiddish. And lo and behold, from atop the rostrum of the House of Congress of the People's Commission for Education, high-ranking officials speak Yiddish on behalf of the colossal Soviet power[68]."

Jewish historians always neglect to mention the role that their fellow Jews played in the atrocities that took place in Russia at that time. However, the truth is that Jewish doctrinaires, Jewish officials and torturers bore a heavy responsibility for the destruction of churches, the ruthless repression of the population and the countless massacres of Christians committed at that time by the men of the cheka. Aleksandr Solzhenitsyn has sufficiently demonstrated this in a book which we ourselves have summarised[69].

In 1927, the Austrian novelist Joseph Roth, author of *Radetsky's March*, wrote pungently: "Today, Soviet Russia is the only country in Europe where anti-Semitism is forbidden, though it has not ceased to exist... The history of the Jews knows no example of such sudden and complete liberation[70]."

---

[66] Ernst Nolte, *La guerre civile européenne*, 1917-1945, Munich, 1997, Editions de Syrtes, 2000, p. 139.

[67] Alain Brossat, Sylvia Klingberg, *Le yiddishland revolutionnaire*, Balland, 1983, p.229.

[68] Alain Brossat, Sylvia Klingberg, *Le yiddishland revolutionnaire*, Balland, 1983, p. 232.

[69] See *Planetary Hopes*, Part Two, pp. 209–270.

[70] Joseph Roth, *Judíos errantes (Wandering Jews)*, Acantilado 164, Barcelona, 2008

It is true that, at that time, Jews enjoyed special consideration from the regime. This is what Arkadi Vaksberg explained to us with this example:

"When it came to professional disputes between the administration and the Jewish employee, the latter always ended up winning, because no judge wanted to be seen as an anti-Semite". People were brought to justice for a mere hint of Jewish solidarity. Vaksberg summed it up: "The 1920s and the early 1930s will be remembered as the golden age of the Jews in Russia[71]."

## Stalin and the Jews

After Lenin's death in 1924, Stalin had to eliminate his main rivals, such as Leon Trotsky, Grigori Zinoviev and Lev Kamenev. However, these were Jews, as were their entourage: Grigori Sokolnikov, Mikhail Lachevitch, Ephraïm Sklianski and others. Zinoviev and Kamenev were also the closest friends of Lenin and his wife, Nadejda Kroupskaia[72].

Arkadi Vaksberg started from this observation in an attempt to show that Stalin was basically anti-Semitic, but that he had always played a double game, until the day when he was able, after the war, to dispense with Western aid. Meanwhile, the elimination of the old Bolsheviks only revealed the strong presence of Jews at the highest levels of power, and Stalin continued to be surrounded by close advisers of Jewish origin.

Stéphane Courtois, the author of the famous *Black Book of Communism*, wrote in the preface to Arkadi Vaksberg's book: "Numerous Jews gravitated in the spheres of power, to such an extent that in 1936 nearly 40% of the high command of the political police were Jews. Two of the men closest to the 'Father of the Peoples', Kaganovitch and Mejlis, were Jewish".

In the early 1930s, the Soviet Union was led by a triumvirate of Stalin, Molotov and Kaganovitch.

Molotov, the regime's number two after Stalin, had married a Jewish woman named Polina Karpovskaia, who was a full-fledged leader and a true Bolshevik. He was "cruel and spiteful". In January 1930, Stalin and Molotov planned the elimination of the kulaks, those small peasant landowners reluctant to collectivise. "The GPU and the one hundred

---

[71] Arkadi Vaksberg, *Stalin et les juifs*, Robert Laffont, 2003, p.67, 64

[72] Arkadi Vaksberg, *Stalin et les juifs*, Robert Laffont, 2003 p.51.

and eighty thousand Party collaborators sent from the cities resorted to guns, lynchings and the concentration camp or Gulag system to wipe out the villages. More than two million people were deported to Siberia or Kazakhstan; in 1930 there were 179,000 people working as slaves in the gulags; in 1935 there were almost a million. " "[73]

But above all, the regime planned the famine to wipe out the Ukrainian peasants. The death toll caused by the 1932 famine, wrote Sebag Montefiore, "would be between four and five million people to, at most, ten million, a tragedy without parallel in the history of mankind, except for the terror of the Nazis and the Maoists".

Fifteen million people had been deported, many of whom had died during the collectivisations. At that time, cases of cannibalism had been reported in the Ukraine and the Ural[74].

In 1930, Lazar Kaganovitch, who had just turned thirty-seven, became Stalin's deputy. He was the youngest of five brothers, three of whom were leading Bolsheviks. Kaganovitch, a shoemaker's apprentice, born in the border areas of Ukraine and Belarus, "had an explosive character," noted Sebag Montefiore. "He often hit his subordinates or grabbed them by the lapels. Politically, however, he was cautious, quick and clever." He was a good orator, "despite his strong Jewish accent". He was responsible for the militarisation of the party-state. "In 1918, at the age of twenty-four, he conquered Nizhny Novgorod and spread terror in the city. In 1919 he demanded the establishment of an iron dictatorship, calling for the imposition of the military discipline of 'centralism'."

It was he who designed and polished the gears and mechanisms of what was to become "Stalinism". "After heading the appointments section of the Central Committee, "Iron Lazar" was sent to administer Central Asia and later the Ukraine, until he returned in 1928 to join the Politburo as a full member at the 16th Congress in 1930". He had just come from crushing peasant revolts from the North Caucasus to Western Siberia. "Molotov's successor as Moscow's top leader and the hero of a cult like Stalin himself, Iron Lazar undertook the vandalistic creation of a Bolshevik metropolis, enthusiastically dynamiting numerous historic

---

[73] Simon Sebag Montefiore, *La corte del Zar rojo*, 2004, Crítica-Barcelona, p.46. The Soviet secret police was first called the cheka, before being renamed GPU in 1922, NKVD in 1934, and finally NKGB, KGB, in 1954.

[74] Simon Sebag Montefiore, *La corte del Zar rojo*, 2004, Crítica-Barcelona, p.68, 228.

buildings[75]." After Stalin's death, Lazar Kaganovitch never had to worry about his involvement in the extermination of the peasants, and passed away peacefully in his comfortable Moscow flat in 1991 at the respectable age of 97.

Genrikh (Enoch) Yagoda, the head of the secret police, was another emblematic figure of the Stalinist regime. He was half bald and small in stature, but motivated by ruthless ambition. This poison specialist was the son of a Jewish jeweller from Nizhny Novgorod. With his ferret face and "Hitler-like" moustache, he frequented the house of Gorky, the president of the Writers' Union. He loved French wines, German pornography and sex toys. "His great achievement, with Stalin's support, was the creation, thanks to slave labour, of the immense economic empire of the gulags. "[76]

Yagoda oversaw the first of the famous great Moscow trials in the summer of 1936. Eleven of the sixteen defendants were Jews, reflecting their significant presence among the older generation of Bolsheviks that Stalin had begun to liquidate. For six days, Zinoviev and Kamenev, accused of being anti-Soviet Trotskyist dissidents, confessed to their alleged crimes with a docility that astonished Western onlookers, acknowledging that they had planned to assassinate Stalin and other leaders.

Obviously, they were sentenced to death and shortly afterwards taken to the place of execution. Zinoviev shouted that Stalin had promised to spare his life. "Please, comrade, for God's sake, call Iosiv Vissarionovich! Iosiv Vissarionovich promised to spare our lives! — Kamenev remarked: "Serves us right for our unworthy attitude at the trial," and told Zimoniev to shut up and die manfully. Zinoviev made so much noise that an NKVD lieutenant took him to a cell nearby, where he was liquidated. They were all shot in the back of the head."

Stalin, who was fascinated by the behaviour of his enemies at the crucial moment of death, asked Pauker, the chief of his bodyguards, to tell him about the scene. Pauker was burly and bald, often perfumed, and occasionally plied his former trade as a barber, for which Stalin had given him a Cadillac as a thank-you for his services. "Pauker, who was

---

[75] Simon Sebag Montefiore, *The Court of the Red Tsar*, 2004, Crítica-Barcelona, p.44, 45, 46

[76] Simon Sebag Montefiore, *La corte del Zar rojo*, 2004, Crítica-Barcelona, p. 79, 215.

Jewish like Zinoviev, had specialised in telling Stalin Jewish jokes with a proper accent, forcing the R's and dragging himself on the floor," Sebag Montefiore recounted. "For God's sake, call Stalin! Some versions claim that he even grabbed the feet of the cheka agents and licked their boots." Paukner "played a Zimoniev who cried out and raised his hands to heaven in sobs:" Listen Israel, the Lord is our God, the Lord is the only one!" Stalin laughed so hard that Paukner had to repeat the routine. Stalin was almost sick with laughter and had to ask Paukner to stop".

Kamenev and Zinoviev were both shot in the back of the head and their bodies incinerated. "The bullets, their tips crushed, were removed from the skulls, cleaned of blood and brain fragments, and handed to Yagoda, probably still warm. The latter labelled them, proudly storing these macabre relics among his collection of erotic objects and women's stockings[77]. Paukner was quietly shot in 1937, like most of the former Chekists whom Stalin no longer trusted.

The death of two of Lenin's closest comrades constituted for Stalin a stage towards the regime of terror that was to be directed against the party. The NKVD was the bastion of old Bolsheviks, "the last stronghold of Bolshevik cronyism, full of Poles, Jews and Latvians of dubious credentials[78].", so the dictator needed someone to control it from the outside and subdue this over-confident elite.

At the end of September 1936, Yagoda was accused of diamond theft and corruption. He was removed from office and replaced by Nicolai Yezhov. As Yezhov had assured him that his close associates and protégés would be pardoned, Yagoda implicated many personalities. But "the rule in Stalin's world was that when one man fell, all those connected with him, whether friends, lovers or protégés, fell as well[79]."

Nicolai Yezhov, a protégé of Kaganovitch, had become the most powerful man in the USSR after Stalin. He was also one of history's great monsters. Between 1936 and 1938, he was the main organiser of

---

[77] Simon Sebag Montefiore, *La corte del Zar rojo*, 2004, Crítica-Barcelona, p. 192, 193.

[78] Simon Sebag Montefiore, *The Court of the Red Tsar*, 2004, Crítica-Barcelona, p.195, 196

[79] Simon Sebag Montefiore, *La corte del Zar rojo*, 2004, Crítica-Barcelona, p. 216.

the Great Terror directed against the Party and the people of the past, aristocrats, priests, bourgeois, peasants, who had hitherto survived the class terror. In fourteen months, more than seven hundred thousand people were shot and millions deported.

The son of a forest guard and a servant, he was a short, nervous man, skinny and small, measuring no more than 151 cm. He was also an enthusiastic bisexual, Sebag Montefiore reported, having "fornicated" with soldiers at the front "and even with high-ranking Bolsheviks like Filipp Goloshchokin, who led the assassination of the Romanovs". A friend of the poet Mandelstam, he had remarried Yevgenia Feigenberg, barely twenty-six, "a vivacious and seductive Jewess originally from Gome... as promiscuous as her new husband[80]."

Under his orders, in a year and a half, five Politburo members out of fifteen, 98 Central Committee members out of 139 and 1108 of the 1966 delegates to the XVIIth Congress were arrested. On some days, such as 12 November, Stalin and Molotov signed 3167 execution orders. Of the 28 commissars who were under Molotov's orders at the beginning of 1938, twenty were executed. Every morning, "the bloody dwarf", fresh from the torture chambers, went straight to the Politburo for meetings:

"One day Khrushchev noticed bloodstains on the hem and cuffs of Yezhov's peasant blouse. Khrushchev, who was certainly no angel, asked what the stains were. Yezchov replied with a glint in his blue eyes that anyone could be proud to wear those stains, for they were the blood of the enemies of the Revolution."

Each region was to contribute its quotas. Khrushchev, then First Party Secretary in Moscow, ordered the execution of 55,741 officials, more than the initial quota of 50,000 set by the Politburo. Zhdanov oversaw the detention of 68,000 people in Leningrad. Beria, a true cheka professional, scrupulously fulfilled his initial quota of 268,950 arrests and 75,950 executions. Apart from these, the other regional leaders were also crushed shortly afterwards. "All the hierarchs undertook bloody tours of the country. Zhdanov carried out purges in the Urals and the Middle Volga region. Ukraine had the misfortune to be visited by Kaganovitch, Molotov and Yezhov."

Sebag Montefiore presented another shocking image in his book: "So many railwaymen were executed that an agent telephoned Poskrebishev

---

[80] Simon Sebag Montefiore, *La corte del Zar rojo*, 2004, Crítica-Barcelona, p. 161, 162-163.

to warn him that a line had been completely stripped of its infrastructure[81]."

During the Great Terror, Voroshilov had been given the task of mass purging of the army. He later boasted that he had led to the arrest of forty thousand officers and the promotion of one hundred thousand new recruits. Tukhachevsky, the most able general of the revolution, had been arrested and tortured. He confessed that he was a German spy, colluding with Bukharin to seize power. In all, three of the five marshals, fifteen of the sixteen commanders and sixty of the sixty-seven corps commanders had been executed.

To perpetrate this massacre, Voroshilov benefited from the collaboration of Lev Mejlis, who was suddenly thrust into the limelight. "Even Stalin called him a fanatic," wrote Sebag Montefiore. "With a sort of crest of black hair encircling his head and an elongated bird-like face, Mejlis played in his own way as important a role as Molotov or Beria. Born in Odessa in 1889 into a Jewish family, he left school at fourteen, and did not join the Bolsheviks until 1918, after flirting with other parties, but during the civil war he served as a commissar in the Crimea, where he acted ruthlessly, executing thousands of people." He became one of Stalin's assistants and the confidant of all his secrets. He was "fervently devoted to his "dear comrade Stalin", for whom he worked with a neurotic frenzy[82]."

In 1930, Stalin appointed him editor-in-chief of Pravda, a post in which he behaved with "extreme brutality" towards writers. Mejlis, who had left the Tsar's army with the rank of artilleryman, was promoted deputy commissar of defence and head of the Red Army's political administration.

During the war, in 1942, Stalin's protégé directed operations in the Crimea: it was "a resounding failure, the result of the unhinged rise of terror applied to military science. He forbade trenches to be opened "so that the offensive spirit of the soldiers would not be undermined", and stressed that anyone who took "basic security measures" would be accused of "spreading panic". And so they all ended up in a "mass of flesh and blood". He bombarded Stalin with messages calling for more

---

[81] Simon Sebag Montefiore, *The Court of the Red Tsar*, 2004, Crítica-Barcelona, p.229, 238, 245, 250, 252

[82] Simon Sebag Montefiore, *The Court of the Red Tsar*, 2004, Crítica-Barcelona, p.223

terror measures... He raced along the front in his jeep at full speed, wielding a pistol to try to stop the retreat, he showed... the stupid tyranny and the utterly arbitrary ways of his military unculturedness. The events had disastrous consequences. On 7 May Manstein's counter-attack led to Mejlis's total retreat from the Crimea and enabled the capture of a tremendous booty: some 176,000 men, 400 aircraft and 347 armoured cars." Mejlis cursed against everything, begging Stalin to send him a great general, a Hindenburg, but Stalin scolded him, "If you had launched the aviation against the enemy armoured cars and soldiers instead of using it in diversionary operations, the Germans would not have managed to break through the front... You don't have to be a Hinderburg to understand something so simple... [83]"

Arkadi Vaksberg concluded: "This general had on his conscience the death of a hundred thousand fallen Soviet soldiers during the evacuation of Kertch, carried out in spite of common sense, and other equally dubious operations[84]."

In 1949, Lev Mejlis, Stalin's most faithful lieutenant, was the victim of an attack. As he was dying in his datcha, Stalin, remembering his old comrade, appointed him a member of the new Central Committee. "Mejlis died delighted and happy, and Stalin organised a magnificent funeral in his honour."


Alexander Poskrebishev was another leading figure, as he was Stalin's chief of staff for most of his reign. This former nurse had married "Bronka" Masenkis, a Lithuanian-born Jewess from a family of sugar magnates. Her best friend was Yevgenia Yezhova, editor and unrepentant follower of the literati and wife of Nikolai Yezhov. "These two funny, flirtatious kittens, both Jewish, one of Polish and the other Lithuanian origin, always charming, were very much alike," wrote Sebag Montefiore, "moreover, Yezhov and Poskrebishev maintained a close friendship; they used to go fishing together while their wives were busy gossiping." Yevgenia "maintained a close friendship with all the great names in the world of the arts and slept with most of them. The charming Isaac Babel was the headliner [of her parties]..., Solomon Mijoels, the Jewish actor who played *King Lear* for Stalin, Leonid

---

[83] Simon Sebag Montefiore, *La corte del Zar rojo*, 2004, Crítica-Barcelona, p.433-434.

[84] Arkadi Vaksberg, *Stalin et les juifs*, Robert Laffont, 2003, p. 162.

Utesov, the jazz bandleader, the film director Eisenstein, Mikhail Sholokhov, the famous novelist, or the journalist Mikhail Koltsov, came to the salon of this charming casquivana. At parties held in the Kremlin, Yezhova never stopped moving to the rhythm of the foxtrot and never missed a dance. Look at that!—remarked Babel on one occasion, "our girl from Odessa has become the first lady of the kingdom,[85] "!

"It was well known that Stalin was surrounded by Jewish women," Sebag Montefiore noted. In addition to the wives of dignitaries, there were the mistresses. Beria's son recounted in his *Memoirs* "that his father amused himself by keeping a list of the Jewish women with whom Satlin had relations. These Jewish girls hovered around Stalin, but they were all of 'dubious' origins".

Kato Svanidze had been Stalin's first wife. Nadejda (Nadia) Alliluyeva was the second. She was the daughter of Sergei Alliluyev, a Russian, and Olga Fedorenko, who had Georgian, German and Gypsy blood. With her he had a daughter, Svetlana. After Nadia's death, it was rumoured that Stalin had married Lazar Kaganovitch's sister Rosa:

"It was a rumour that was widely spread and believed by many: photographs of Rosa Kaganovitch were even published showing her as a beautiful brunette... The importance of the rumour lay in the fact that Stalin had married a Jewish woman, wrote Sebag Montefiore, a fact that could prove very useful to the Nazi propaganda apparatus... The Kaganovitches, both father and daughter, denied this fact so strongly that perhaps their protests were excessive, but it seems that the whole story was fabricated[86]."

Stalin had had a son from his first marriage, Yakov. He had a pleasant character, but Stalin was displeased when Yakov married, against his will, a Jewish woman from Odessa, divorced from a Chekist guard, Yulia Isaacovna Meltzer[87]. When his daughter Svetlana did the same with a Jew named Kapler, Stalin sent him to prison for five years. True, this Kapler was much older than she was, and he also had the reputation of being a Don Juan.

---

[85] Simon Sebag Montefiore, *La corte del Zar rojo*, 2004, Crítica-Barcelona, p. 268-269.

[86] Simon Sebag Montefiore, *La corte del Zar rojo*, 2004, Crítica-Barcelona, p. 269.

[87] Arkadi Vaksberg, *Stalin et les juifs*, Robert Laffont, 2003, p.127

The presence of so many Jewish women also attracted the attention of historian Arkadi Vaksberg: "In the 1920s and 1930s, many Russian members of the Central Committee and Politburo had married Jewish women: Molotov (Perle Karpovskaia, alias Paulina Khemtchukhina), Voroshilov (Golda Gorbman), Bukharin (Ester Gurvitch, later Anna Lourié), etc. Even Stalin's faithful secretary Alexander Poskrebishev had taken Bronislava Weintraub as his wife[88]."

Sebag Montefiore underlined the "incestuous" character of this Bolshevik world: "Kamenev's wife was Trotsky's sister; Yagoda was married to a woman of the Sverdlov family; Poskrebishev, Stalin's secretary, was married to the sister of Trotsky's daughter-in-law. Two prominent Stalinists, Shcherbakov and Zhdanov, were brothers-in-law. Later, the sons of Politburo members would intermarry[89]."

Jewish artists were being praised to the skies. This is what Vaksberg Arkadi wrote, also expressing the characteristic tendency of Jewish intellectuals to praise their fellows: Around the writer Mikhoels, "a company of excellent Jewish actors was formed, among whom the genius of Benjamin Zuskin shone. The Jewish Theatre, which had been given precious premises in the centre of the capital, was to be for many years one of the busiest in Moscow." Isaac Babel "quickly became one of the most popular authors of his time. Around him, other Jewish writers had taken pseudonyms, although they did not conceal their origins, which, moreover, were very present in their works.

The author went on to cite a list of complete unknowns, each one more "brilliant": "They were studied in class, the press talked about them, their books were sold, they were praised and decorated". Boris Pasternak and the poet Ossip Mandelstam were less praised by the regime than Ilia Ehrenburg and Vassili Grossman. Jews "were to constitute the hard core of Soviet cinema: Dziga Vertov (Kaufman), Abram Room, Grigori Kozintsev, Leonide Trauberg, Friedrich Ermler, Iossif Heifetz, Grigori Rochal, etc." The musicians who received the generous praise of the Soviet authorities "were all Jews, except in rare cases: David Oistrakh, Emil Guilels, Yakov Zak, Rosa Tamarkina, Arnold Kaplan, Grigori Guinzburg, Maria Grinberg, Mikhail

---

[88] Arkadi Vaksberg, *Stalin et les juifs*, Robert Laffont, 2003, p.75

[89] Simon Sebag Montefiore, *La corte del Zar rojo*, 2004, Crítica-Barcelona, p.31-32. Footnote.

Fihtengolz, and many more. Their names were everywhere, in the press, on the radio, Stalin was decorating them left and right and subsidising them generously with cash." Vaksberg added, tellingly, "Obviously, the Jewish community had always been fertile and talented, even though until then it had been impossible for it to express itself. But its 'disproportionate' fulfilment and fulfilment was interpreted by the sullen and ignorant crowd as a 'Jewish plot' against Slavic culture[90]."

Vaksberg sought to prove again and again in his book that Stalin was an anti-Semite. He wrote: "No reasonable person could have suspected the anti-Semitism of the country's leader". And he added, somewhat comically: "Stalin waited in silence. The Jews were enjoying the 'advantages of the revolution'. The time of persecutions had not yet come."

Meanwhile, the Russians were the victims of the regime. By the end of the 1920s, the former St. Petersburg Academy of Sciences, a "reactionary stronghold", had been purged. World-renowned scientists accused of anti-Semitism had been sentenced to death and executed. Arkadi Vaksberg noted that "these accusations had been notified to the academics only by investigating judges of Jewish origin (Lazar Kogan, Lazar Altman and Heinrich Luchkov)", but once again detected an underhand manoeuvre by Stalin: "For some authors, this specific choice of Jewish investigating judges was proof of a premeditated provocation ordered by the Kremlin guru[91]". But it remains true that those who were executed were Russians, and that, in this case, their executioners were Jews.

In the mid-1930s, Jews were still numerous at the top of the state. "They were members of the Council of People's Commissars: Maxim Litvinov (Wallach-Finkelstein) in Foreign Affairs, Genrij Yagoda (Yehuda-Ghenakh) in Interior (i.e. in the NKVD), Lazar Kaganovitch in Transport, Arkadi Rosengoltz in Foreign Trade, Moises Kalmanovitch in the Sovkhoz (Soviet State Farms), Moises Rukjimovitch in War Industry, Isidore Lubimov in Light Industry, Alexander Bruskin in Mechanical Constructions, Grigori Kaminski in Public Health. Dozens of other Jews were deputy commissars."

Arkadi Vaksberg went on to explain Stalin's ploy to remove Jews from important positions without arousing suspicion: "Stalin knew perfectly

---

[90] Arkadi Vaksberg, *Stalin et les juifs*, Robert Laffont, 2003, p.61, 62, 89, 90

[91] Arkadi Vaksberg, *Stalin et les juifs*, Robert Laffont, 2003, p. 65.

well that the "Jewish pre-eminence" would not last forever" and that "the large proportion of Jews among the victims of the hecatomb would not go unnoticed". In order to mislead, he stepped up repression against "anti-Semites":

"In the mid-1930s, wrote Vaksberg, we witnessed a spectacular increase in the number of anti-Semitic trials... One could be prosecuted as an anti-Semite without having committed anything criminally condemnable, simply for having shown little sympathy for the Jews. Complaints of anti-Semitic words, passed on by hand to police informers, were enough to set the judicial machine in motion. Remarks exchanged between friends along the lines of "the Jews make life miserable for us" were enough to justify an indictment for "incitement to ethnic hatred"... By repressing all these outward signs of anti-Semitism, Stalin was thus diverting attention from the truly Judeophobic motivations behind his actions[92]."

And it was probably also to "divert attention" that Stalin continued to reward deserving Jews: "For the completion of the work on the Baltic-White Sea canal, carried out by the gulag slaves, he awarded the order of Lenin to the heads of the Lubyanka, all of whom were Jews: Lazar Kogan, Matvei Berman, Semion Firine, Yakov Rappoport and many others". Vaksberg was again indignant: "From now on everyone knew who were the comrades of the convicts of socialism."

At the second major trial in Moscow in January 1937, there were six Jews out of seventeen in the dock. Of the four main convicts (Piatakov, Radek, Sokolnikov and Serebriakov), Stalin spared the lives of Karl Radek (Sobelson) and Grigori Sokolnikov (Brilliant), "both Jewish and known in the West". Vaksberg concluded: "Yet another argument to refute Stalin's anti-Semitism[93]."

In early February 1938, Yezhov led a great purge in Kiev where, aided by Khrushchev, he proceeded to arrest thirty thousand people. 106,119 people had fallen victim to the Terror in Ukraine that year, and almost the entire Ukrainian Politburo had fallen. Yezhov then returned to Moscow to launch the third and final major trial of the "anti-Soviet Trotskyist and right-wing organisations". This debuted on 2 March

---

[92] Arkadi Vaksberg, *Stalin et les juifs*, Robert Laffont, 2003, p. 90, 91.

[93] Arkadi Vaksberg, *Stalin et les juifs*, Robert Laffont, 2003, p.96, 97. Radek and Sokolnikov were murdered in prison in May 1939 by their cellmates, common law criminals.

1938, with Bukharin, Rykov and Yagoda next to go through the shredder. Of the 21 defendants, there were only four Jews, Vaksberg noted. "However, the last hearing ended with an overtly anti-Semitic coup on the part of prosecutor Vychinski, when he read in a Jewish accent a passage from the Torah from a fragment found on the accused Arkadi Rosengoltz." His wife had slipped it into his pocket as a protective talisman, but it did not prevent him from being shot.

After the Great Terror of 1936–1938, the proportion of Jews in the state apparatus had declined considerably. Jews, who constituted 39% of the NKVD leadership in 1936, became 21% in 1938 and only 4% in 1939, while the proportion of Russians rose from 31% in 1934 to 65% in 1941[94].

But Yezhov was beginning to be left over. "He led a vampire's night life, indulging in his drinking and torture sessions. Stalin kindly proposed that he hire someone to help him run the NKVD. Kaganovitch then suggested Lavrenti Beria, a Georgian. In 1938, Beria was sent to Moscow with his Georgian henchmen to break up the Yezhov gang. He was finally arrested in April 1939, "had to be dragged by the arms", and executed shortly afterwards. The writer Isaac Babel, who was related to Yezhov's wife, was also convicted and executed at the same time. After his death, Yezhov was regarded as a bloodthirsty renegade who had slaughtered innocents behind Stalin's back, and his name was erased from official history. The new master of the police, Beria, was hated by many of the dictator's close associates, for he was a born schemer, capable of the worst revenge and endowed with great energy. He was a "talented manager, the only Soviet leader one could imagine becoming president of General Motors", as his daughter-in-law[95] would say.

Although he was a good family man, he was still a "dangerous sexual predator" who abducted and raped women who came to plead with him on behalf of their families. On 17 January 2003, the Russian prosecutor's office confirmed the existence of a 47-volume dossier on Beria's crimes, including the testimonies of dozens of women who accused him of raping them. Beria was also a sadistic executioner. Like Yezhov, he personally tortured his victims. On the day he officially took office, Stalin and Molotov signed 3176 convictions. The executioners

---

[94] Arkadi Vaksberg, *Stalin et les juifs*, Robert Laffont, 2003, p. 104,105.

[95] Simon Sebag Montefiore, *The Court of the Red Tsar*, 2004, Crítica-Barcelona, p.280

had their work cut out for them. The Great Terror would not end until the 18th Party Congress on 10 March 1939.

## *The Spanish Civil War*

After Moscow, Berlin, Budapest and Munich, the revolutionary storm cloud was to gather over Spain, taking advantage of the terrible civil war that began in the summer of 1936. The unleashing of the nationalist insurrection in Spain had been the trigger which had convinced them of the imminence of the confrontation "between the forces of darkness and the forces of light". The historic test of strength began there. Thousands of Jews from all over Europe and the whole world threw themselves into the battle by enlisting in the International Brigades.

This is what we read in Alain Brossat's book: "Coming from Poland, Hungary, Romania, Yugoslavia, France, Belgium, Palestine, Germany, the United States, Argentina and even Australia and South Africa, they went from July 1936 to the Republican Spain they carried in their hearts, towards a combat in which all their energy and all their revolutionary optimism seemed to converge and concentrate". Indeed, among the brigadists, there was a large number of Eastern European Jews: "It is enough, today, to look at the endless lists of the "internationals" who fell in Spain to be convinced of the importance of the proportion of Jews, fighters from Yiddishland, who came to Barcelona and Albacete, from Melbourne, Buenos Aires, Chicago, Paris, Liège, and not only from Warsaw or Lodz".

In his book, Alain Brossat provided the testimony of former brigade member Pierre Scherf. He declared that, "three quarters, without exaggeration, of the 600 Romanian volunteers who took part in the Spanish war were Jews". One day he was called by his boss to help him with a delegation of militiamen from the apparently very angry American Lincoln Brigade, for whom a translator was urgently needed. Could Pierre Scherf take care of the translation? "But I don't know English! he replied. —Get to grips with it, the other replied, you know so many languages! Scherf scratched his head and suddenly had an idea: "Do any of you speak Yiddish?" Numerous hands went up and the display of complaints began: "We don't get our mail, the food is disgusting!

Pierre Scherf was very proud of his militant record: "Near Madrid, in Guadalajara, in Brunete or in Zaragoza, wherever our Brigade was fighting against the mortal enemy of humanity, fascism, the Jewish volunteers were in the front line, thus giving an example of heroism and anti-fascist consciousness[96]."

These facts were confirmed by the historian of communism Stéphane Courtois: "Those militants from all over Europe, but also from all over the world (Latin America, Canada, Australia, New Zealand, and even... Palestine), flocked en masse in 1936 to the international Brigades organised by the communist movement, to fight with arms in hand in Spain. Of the 32 000 volunteers in the Brigades, it is estimated that a quarter (7 to 8000) were Jewish, half of them were Polish, and they had a common language, Yiddish; the German, Czech, Polish and American battalions were composed mostly of Jews; an exclusively Jewish unit was even created, the Botwin company (named after a militant killed in Poland). "[97]

In his book entitled *Shalom Libertad, Jews in the Spanish Civil War*, Arno Lustiger—a close relative of the Cardinal*—wrote the following commentary which made clear the national character of the intervention: "From the first day of the outbreak of the civil war, the Jewish working-class press supported the Republic. The strong pro-Republican statements of the bourgeois circles of Jewish public opinion are also very noticeable. The editors of Jewish magazines outnumbered non-Jewish journalists in their advocacy of the Spanish Republic[98]."

Regarding the number of volunteers, Arno Lustiger considered that it was certainly underestimated, "since Jews used to change their surnames and therefore cannot be identified as such in the files and lists of the International Brigades... Many American Jews changed their surnames to Anglo-Saxon ones, following orders from the CP USA, in order not to attract attention in their agitation work among the non-Jewish workers[99]."

---

[96] Alain Brossat, Sylvia Klingberg, *Le yiddishland revolutionnaire*, Balland, 1983, p. 130, 124, 132

[97] Stéphane Courtois, in Béatrice Philippe, *Les juifs dans le mode contemporain*, MA éditions, 1986, p.53

* Aaron Jean-Marie Lustiger (1926–2007), Cardinal and Archbishop of Paris.

[98] Arno Lustiger, *Shalom Libertad, Judíos en la guerra civil española*, Flor del Viento Ediciones, Barcelona 2011, p.64

[99] Arno Lustiger, *Shalom Libertad, Judíos en la guerra civil española*, Flor del Viento Ediciones, Barcelona 2011. p. 70, 72.

Arno Lustiger added that there was a large factor of inaccuracy in these figures: "Many Jewish volunteers were wandering Jews of the world revolution, who had already been active in several countries before going to Spain. David Kamy, for example, left Russia, went through China and Japan and reached Palestine, from where he went to Belgium and then to Spain, hence his name appears on the Belgian list. Many Polish Jews reached Spain via France and Belgium, so they are most likely to be counted double or triple. Volunteers from Palestine of Polish origin are also counted as Poles… The Jews, with their 7,758 volunteers, ranked second among the national contingents, behind the 8,500 French who came from the neighbouring country. But if we subtract from the latter figure the 1043 Jews who were counted in the French contingent, the Jews who fought alongside the French were not strictly speaking French, but political refugees who had only recently arrived in France, for example from Poland[100]."

The international volunteers were trained at the new base in Albacete, halfway between Madrid and Valencia, under the command of André Marty. Of Catalan blood and born in Perpignan, this son of a worker had distinguished himself in 1919 by taking the lead in the mutiny of the French fleet in the Black Sea to protest against the order to support the White Russian armies. The leading historian of the Spanish Civil War, the Englishman Hugh Thomas, wrote of him: "The post he held at the Albacete base was given to him by virtue of his alleged military knowledge and thanks to the support of Stalin, who had not forgotten that, seventeen years earlier, Marty had refused to take up arms against the fledgling Soviet Union". In Spain, he was initially called the "mutineer of the Black Sea", and later "the butcher of Albacete".

Hugh Thomas recounted a scene in which André Marty was seen addressing the brigadistas in the barracks courtyard: "The Spanish people and their army have not yet defeated fascism. Why? For lack of enthusiasm? No, and a thousand times no. They have lacked three things that we must not lack: political unity, military leadership and discipline." Hugh Thomas added: "Referring to the military leaders he pointed to a small, grey-haired figure, his cape buttoned up to his neck. It was General Emilio Kleber. Kleber was forty-one years old and was apparently from Bukovina, which was then part of Romania and at the time of his birth was incorporated into the Austro-Hungarian Empire.

---

[100] Arno Lustiger, *Shalom Libertad, Judíos en la guerra civil española,* Flor del Viento Ediciones, Barcelona 2011, p73.

His real name was Lazar Manfred Stern and his nom de guerre was taken from one of the most able generals of the French Revolution. During the First World War he served as a captain in the Austrian army. Captured by the Russians, he was interned in Siberia. At the outbreak of the revolution he managed to escape and joined the Bolshevik Party... He eventually joined the military section of the Komintern." In 1933, he had been sent to Shanghai as a military adviser to the Chinese Communist Party. "Now he arrived in Spain, as the top leader of the first International Brigade... Just as Marty was introducing him, Kleber stepped forward to salute with a clenched fist, provoking a storm of applause[101]."

At the end of August 1936, this professional military expert of the world revolution arrived with the first Soviet ambassador, Manfred Rosenberg. Rosenberg was the former Deputy Secretary General of the League of Nations. He was accompanied by numerous specialists from the army, navy and aviation, as well as senior officers of the secret police and journalists. At the end of October, large quantities of war material arrived from the Soviet Union, paid for out of the gold reserves of the Republican government. The Spanish fighting forces were organised on the Red Army's major-state model. Each unit had a political commissar assigned to it alongside the military command. Arno Lustiger wrote: "Almost all the political commissars in Spain were Jews[102]."

Manfred Rosenberg also wanted to incite the head of the republican government, the socialist Largo Caballero, to remove General Asensio from office and to take some of the measures desired by the communists. "After two hours of animated conversation... Largo Caballero jumped up: 'Get out! Get out! You must know, Mr. Ambassador, that we Spaniards may be poor and in need of help from abroad, but we have enough pride not to accept that a foreign ambassador should try to impose his will on a Spanish head of government[103]." Rosenberg was replaced shortly afterwards by his chargé d'affaires, L. Y. Gaikins, also Jewish.

---

[101] Hugh Thomas, *La guerra civil española, Tomo I*, Grijalbo Mondadori, Barcelona 1976. p. 494-496.

[102] Arno Lustiger, *Shalom Libertad, Judíos en la guerra civil española*, Flor del Viento Ediciones, Barcelona 2011.p.53

[103] Hugh Thomas, *La guerra civil española, Tomo II*, Grijalbo Mondadori, Barcelona 1976, p.580.

The Komintern's man in Spain was Erno Gerö. He was in charge of leading the Communists in Catalonia. His real name was Ernst Singer. After the war he was to become deputy prime minister of Hungary and was also Khrushchev's creature during the bloody suppression of the Hungarian insurrection of 1956.

Ernst Toller is back in Spain. Born in 1893 near Poznan, Poland, into a family of Jewish merchants, he was deputy chairman of the Workers' Council and commander of the Bavarian army during the brief Munich revolution of 1918. He had been sentenced to five years in prison and expelled from Bavaria in 1924. He emigrated to the USA, where he tried unsuccessfully to settle in Hollywood, before moving to Mexico, where he founded the "League for German Culture". He returned to the USA and wrote plays before enlisting and leaving for Spain. He organised a collection for the "republicans" in England and the USA, but also in Finland, Sweden, Denmark and Norway, where the socialists were in power. He was constantly appealing for donations and met with numerous politicians, ministers and clergymen.

The journalist and writer Ilya Ehrenburg was born in 1891 in Kiev into a wealthy, religious Jewish family. He was the chief foreign correspondent of the Izvestia in Paris, from where he moved to Spain to "cover the war". There he met Hemingway. He was later called upon by Stalin to direct the USSR's war propaganda against Germany. The main reporter for the Soviet press at the front, he wrote, together with the other "great" Soviet writer, Vassili Grossman, the "Black Book" on Nazi crimes against the Jews. He always supported the Soviet regime, even after the purge of the Jewish Anti-Fascist Committee and the trial of Jewish writers in 1952.

Hugh Thomas also mentioned that the chief of staff at the Albacete base was "a comrade of Marty's, a councillor in the Paris town hall, named Vital Gayman, known in Spain by the common surname of Vidal". In 1938, he was "accused of embezzlement and left for Paris. He and his henchmen had apparently seized many of the volunteers' personal effects[104]." He was replaced by a German, Wilhelm Zaisser.

Jakob Smuschkewitsh, who was commander-in-chief of the Republican air force, can also be mentioned. He had taken the pseudonym "General Douglas". In 1936, one hundred and fifty Soviet aircraft were

---

[104] Hugh Thomas, *La guerra civil española, Tomo I y II*, Grijalbo Mondadori, Barcelona 1976, p.494, 840.

dispatched, along with their pilots and ground personnel. Colonel Selig Joffe, a Soviet Jew, was head of the technical service. "In June 1938, Jakob Smusschkewitsch was relieved... he arrived in Moscow on 18 June, was promoted to corps commander and received the post of deputy commander-in-chief of Soviet aviation. He was also awarded the Order of Lenin, and during a reception in the Kremlin, Stalin awarded him the decoration of Hero of the Soviet Union[105]." He too was to be a victim of the Stalinist purges.

With the advance of the Nationalist troops, the atmosphere among the international volunteers soon deteriorated. They were closely watched by the men from Moscow, and many volunteers were held against their will once their period of commitment was over. In early 1938, during the debacle on the Aragon front, "arbitrary executions followed one after another; there was no lack of cases of officers being shot in front of the troops", wrote Hugh Thomas (p.861). In volume 10 of *Tabou* magazine, Marty acknowledged having personally executed 500 volunteers, "a figure surely below the truth" (p.153). (p.153).

At the time, Spain held the fourth largest gold reserve in the world. Most of it was deposited in the Banco de España in Madrid. In September 1936, the Republicans had deemed it preferable to transfer the treasury to a safe place. It seemed risky to rely on Britain and France given their unwavering policies of non-intervention. On 25 October 1936, the gold was finally shipped to the Soviet Union. That gold reserve became a kind of current account with which the Republic could pay for its arms and oil.

The loading operation was carried out with the utmost secrecy. Sixty sailors worked three nights in a row, sleeping during the day on top of the crates full of gold, not knowing what they contained. Alexander Orlov, the head of the Soviet secret police, had been appointed to supervise the transport to the USSR. He was also responsible for organising the repression of the Trotskyists and for having their leader, Andreu Nin, assassinated.

When the shipment was completed, Undersecretary of State Méndez Aspe compared his figures with Orlov's. He said there should have been 7,900 boxes, but Méndez Aspe counted only 7,800. According to him, there should have been 7900 boxes, but Méndez Aspe counted only

---

[105] Arno Lustiger, *Shalom Libertad, Judíos en la guerra civil española*, Flor del Viento Ediciones, Barcelona, 2011, p.135.

7800. Each truck that had secured transport to the port of Cartagena was loaded with fifty boxes. The cargo of two trucks was therefore missing. "Orlov did not mention the discrepancy to Méndez Aspe, since, if the latter's accounts were correct, he would have had to account for the missing boxes". The gold then left for Odessa. "According to Orlov, Stalin celebrated the arrival of the gold with a banquet at which he declared that "the Spaniards will no more see the gold than anyone can see his own ears"."

This gold, however, was used to finance the purchase of weapons for the Reds. An NKVD agent named Zimin then set up an organisation capable of buying arms throughout Europe. He worked on this matter with Ignace Poretsky (Ignace Reiss), the head of the NKVD in Switzerland. In the notes on page 478, Hugh Thomas stated that Ignace Poretsky had been a member of a group of Jewish communists from Poland. He added that they found paid agents who "often had the characteristics of characters in espionage novels":

"There was, for example, a certain Dr. Mylanos, a Greek based in Gdynia. Another was Fuat Baban, also Greek, a representative in Turkey of the Skoda, Schneider and Hotchkiss companies, who would later be arrested in Paris for drug trafficking. And then there was Ventoura. Here Hugh Thomas used a note from the German Ministry of Foreign Affairs identifying him and sent to the national side: "Of Jewish origin, born in Constantinople, who was convicted of swindling in Austria, with a false passport, and lived with a woman in Greece, although he was domiciled in Paris, in a hotel on Avenue Friedland." It added finally that "numerous characters of this kind... supplied expensive and often antiquated armaments to the commission for the purchase of arms of the republican government[106]."

The Spanish gold affair seems even clearer in the light of other information. When Orlov was summoned to return to Moscow, "instead of presenting himself to the Soviet embassy in Paris, he managed to flee to Canada". He lived in Cleveland, Ohio, until his death in 1973, wrote a very discreet Arno Lustiger[107]. In a book published in 2006, Edgar Morin informed us that the real identity of Orlov, the NKVD chief in

---

[106] Hugh Thomas, *La guerra civil española, Tomo I*, Grijalbo Mondadori, Barcelona 1976, p.485-487.

[107] Arno Lustiger, *Shalom Libertad, Jews in the Spanish Civil War*, Flor del Viento Ediciones, Barcelona 2011, p.164-165.

Spain, was "Leiba Lazarevitch Feldin". A refugee in the United States, "he was kept alive by the fact that he informed Stalin that his death would trigger the publication of capital revelations[108]."

Republican Spain was defeated, but the "forces of light" were still alive and at work throughout the world. As Roger Bramy wrote in the United States at the time, in an article in the *Jewish Journal*: "Nazism and fascism recognise no territorial boundaries, they are microbes that will attack the whole world, including the Jews in America, and we must be prepared for them[109]."

## The German invasion

Before the outbreak of the Second World War, Jews in the USSR were still numerous and influential in the regime's leadership. However, they had lost ground since the great purges that had decimated the former Bolsheviks. Arkadi Vaksberg recalled that in the 1920s and 1930s, 'Moscow was represented by Jews in the main Western capitals: Maksim Litvinov (Wallach), Grigori Sokolnikov (Brilliant), then Ivan Maiski (Israel Lakhevetzi) in London, Adolf Iofe in Paris, Boris Stein in Helsinki and then in Rome, Marcel Rosenberg and then Leon Gaykis in Madrid, Konstantin Umanski in Washington, and Lev Khintchuk and then Yakov Souritz in Berlin, when the new Nazi regime was already showing its hatred of Jews." It was almost a provocation, wrote Vaksberg, who concluded, paradoxically, "Numerous facts attest that Stalin willingly manifested a particular sympathy for Jews[110]."

In 1939, Stalin, while offering his neutrality to the highest bidder, decided to go for Hitler's offer. On 4 May, he dismissed his foreign minister, Maksim Litvinov, as well as most of his Jewish collaborators, thus sending a very clear signal in the direction of Nazi Germany.

Litvinov was replaced by Molotov. Years later, Molotov would reveal the following: 'In 1939, when Litvinov was recalled and I came to the

---

[108] Edgar Morin, *Le monde moderne et la question juive*, Seuil 2006, p.85, note 1.

[109] Arno Lustiger, *Shalom Libertad, Judíos en la guerra civil española*, Flor del Viento Ediciones, Barcelona 2011, p.62

[110] Arkadi Vaksberg, *Stalin et les juifs*, Robert Laffont, 2003, p.71, 72. Stalin realised that Litvinov was an obstacle to rapprochement with Hitler. He ordered Mejlis, the editor of Pravda, to use pseudonyms in the paper.

Foreign Ministry, Stalin said to me: "Clean out the Jews in the Commission". It is fortunate that he asked me to do so, because Jews formed an absolute majority in the leadership and among the ambassadors... Of course, Stalin distrusted the Jews".

Sebag Montefiore agreed in his biography: "The application of terror to Stalin's diplomats was intended to attract Hitler: 'Purge the Jews from the ministry,' he said, 'clean out the synagogue. Thank God he uttered those words, Molotov (who was married to a Jewess) would comment. The Jews formed an absolute majority and many ambassadors... "So that, "Molotov and Beria were engaged in terrorising the cosmopolitan diplomatic establishment, many of them Jewish Bolsheviks who knew the great capitals of Europe perfectly well".

On the long list of those dismissed was Ievgueni Gnedine (Parvus). He was the son of Alexander Gelfand (Israel Parvus), a native of Belarus who emigrated to Switzerland, where he distinguished himself as a philosopher, businessman, publisher and revolutionary. Close to Trotsky and Lenin, he was the one who financed the transfer of Lenin and his clique from Switzerland to Russia in March 1917 before his death in 1924. Stalin nevertheless declined to organise a grand trial of the diplomats, considering that the dispersal of the "synagogue" was a sufficient gift to Hitler. Litvinov remained a member of the Central Committee.

Arkadi Vaksberg wanted to prove the anti-Semitic intentions of the master of the Kremlin, which is why he again insisted on his double-dealing. According to him, this explains why Stalin, anxious to preserve his public image as a communist, also appointed Rosalia Zemliatchka (Zalkind) as Deputy Prime Minister (i.e. deputy to the Chairman of the Council of Commissars, hence to Molotov), "the same one who distinguished herself in a cruel and barbaric manner in 1920 in the repression of the White army and the civilian population of the Crimea...". She had the reputation, wrote Vaksberg, of being a mediocre civil servant, and the Crimean massacres were the only noteworthy part of her biography... It was a reassuring gesture for the Jews but of no real significance. But when the charade was no longer necessary, Zemliatchka was dismissed in August 1943. No one had noticed his presence in the post of Deputy Prime Minister."

Similarly, Salomon Lozovski (Dridzo), hitherto relegated to the background at the head of the Trade Union International (Profintern), was given the enviable post of deputy people's commissioner for foreign affairs. "Who would dare, therefore, to say that the diplomats dismissed had been dismissed because of their ethnic origin? Lozovsky was of average intelligence and a docile executor of the dictator's wishes. He was a perfect mirage[111]."

After the signing of the Ribbentrop-Molotov Pact in Moscow on 23 August 1939, the anti-Nazi discourse and the denunciation of anti-Semitism and persecution of Jews in Germany and Nazi-occupied countries suddenly disappeared from communist propaganda until the German invasion of 1941.

In *Testament of a Murdered Poet*, Elie Wiesel's hero, Paltiel Kossover, a religious Jew turned communist militant who had joined the international brigades in Spain, was returning to Moscow at the time. He was astonished: "In Paris, we fought and denounced Nazism day and night in our newspapers, magazines and speeches, all in the name of the communist revolution. And here, you keep quiet! I don't understand."

The German invasion on 22 June 1941 and the Soviet Union's subsequent entry into the war were to be celebrated in style: "I greeted the outbreak of hostilities with a sense of relief. I was not alone. Listening to Molotov's speech, I felt a powerful, inordinate urge to shout out my joy: Hurrah, we are finally going to do battle against Hitler and the Hitlerites! Hurrah, we are going to be able to give free rein to our anger! I left the printing press and ran to the Club. Panting and over-excited, I joined my comrades surrounding Mendelevitch. At this hour, I wanted to be together with my own, among them, to congratulate them, to embrace them, to weep with joy like them, to weep with pride, to laugh with them, to sing like them, having a few drinks." And Wiesel continued, "No war in history has ever been embraced with such passion and fervour. Ready to offer everything, to do everything to defeat the worst enemies of our people and of humanity, we finally had the feeling of belonging to this country[112]."

---

[111] Simon Sebag Montefiore, *La corte del Zar rojo*, 2004, Crítica-Barcelona, p. 309, 310 and Arkadi Vaksberg, *Stalin et les juifs*, Robert Laffont, 2003, p. 110-113.

[112] Elie Wiesel, *Le testament d'un poète juif assasiné*, pp. 240, 247, 249. This scene reminds us of the scene in Roman Polanski's film *The Pianist* (2001), where we see a Polish Jewish family bursting with joy when they hear on the radio the entry into war of the United Kingdom and France: "It is wonderful! In Ariel Zeitoun's film, *The Navel of the World* (1993), we also see Tunisian Jews euphoric with joy at the announcement of France's declaration of war on

However, events quickly turned to disaster. When, in 1939, German armies crossed the Polish border, "hundreds of thousands of Jewish and Polish refugees" took refuge in the east of the country, part of which was to be, a few weeks later, annexed by the Soviet Union. Alain Brossat's book presented the testimony of Isaac Safrin:

"When the Wehrmacht invaded Poland, Isaac Safrin, a radical student, was on holiday working in a children's shelter in Warsaw. "Go away at once! his father urged him, 'go to Russia! He knew that his son had attracted attention at the university with virulent anti-Nazi articles published in the capital's political and cultural magazines… As night falls, Safrin and the children arrive in a small town on the Bug: it is the demarcation line. The place is swarming with smugglers and traffickers of all kinds. But the Soviet border guards block the crossing. Thousands of refugees are there, stranded, Jews for the most part. Safrin sees the first Red Army soldier of his life: "He wore that funny pointed cap… The next morning, they opened the border and we were able to reach Bialistok"… It seems that during this exodus, some 300,000 Jews were able to evacuate the German-occupied territories and flee eastwards[113]."

The cities of Bialistok and Brest-Litovsk were often the first stop for these refugees. Another Jewish activist, Yakov Greenstein, gave this testimony: "The situation in Bialistok was astonishing: there were tens of thousands of Jewish refugees from Poland who, on the one hand, danced and partied with the Red army in the streets, but who, on the other hand, by their very presence created total anarchy, sleeping in the streets and living in deplorable hygienic conditions[114]."

In this new partition of Poland, the Soviets had taken 26,000 Polish officers prisoner. On 5 March 1940, the Politburo decided their fate: 14,700 Polish officers and policemen, as well as 11,000 "counter-revolutionary" landowners were declared "spies and saboteurs" and were to be executed. Blojín, "a tough forty-one-year-old cheka agent with a stocky face and backcombed black hair", had been in charge of the Lubianka prison and the executions since 1921. He was the man of the situation, wrote Sebag Montefiore. "Blokhin went to the Ostashkov

---

Germany.

[113] Alain Brossat, Sylvia Klingberg, *Le yiddishland revolutionnaire*, Balland, 1983, pp. 197, 198.

[114] Alain Brossat, Sylvia Klingberg, *Le yiddishland revolutionnaire*, Balland, 1983, pp. 270, 271.

concentration camp, where, together with two other cheka agents, he set up a barrack with padded and soundproofed walls and decided to impose a truly stakhanovist quota of 250 executions every night. He took with him a leather apron and a butcher's cap which he used to carry out one of the most prolific acts of mass murder ever executed by a single individual, killing exactly seven thousand men in twenty-eight nights, with a German-made Walther pistol, to prevent future identification. The corpses were buried in various places, but the four and a half thousand officers imprisoned in the Kozelsk camp were buried in the forests of Katin."

"He was one of the most prolific executioners of the century, personally killing thousands of individuals, often donning a butcher's leather apron to avoid staining his uniform. Nevertheless, the name of this monster has slipped through the fingers of history [115] ", the historian was surprised. Blokhin retired after Stalin's death with Beria's thanks.

"Jews were still numerous in the upper echelons of the Lubianka, wrote Arkadi Vaksberg, not to mention in scientific research, in economic life and in the war industry... When he was confronted with the thorny Finnish problem in 1939, he turned to Ambassador Boris Stein... and Lubyanka Colonel Boruch Rybkin... in order to be able to present and argue his ultimatum to the leaders of that country[116]."

The Israeli historian Sever Plocker mentioned a certain Leonid Reichman, head of the NKVD department, an interrogation specialist, who was "a particularly cruel sadist".

The Poles were not the only ones to suffer from the occupation of their country. The Balts were also able to experience the harshness of communist methods: "As fate would have it, the first People's Commissar of the Interior in Soviet Latvia was, for a few weeks, the Jew Semion Schuster," wrote Arkadi Vaksberg. He was the one who started the purge and deportation of Latvians who did not seem to be to the occupiers' liking. Naturally, the Latvians' detestation of the tyrant Schuster extended to all "Moscow" Jews[117]."

---

[115] Simon Sebag Montefiore, *La corte del Zar rojo*, 2004, Crítica-Barcelona, p. 343, 191.

[116] Arkadi Vaksberg, *Stalin et les juifs*, Robert Laffont, 2003, p.117

[117] Arkadi Vaksberg, *Stalin et les juifs*, Robert Laffont, 2003, p. 121.

The fate of the Jews in the regions annexed by the USSR in 1940—the Baltic countries, eastern Poland, Moldavia and northern Bukovina—was quite different. The Soviet regime immediately took immediate steps to protect them, sending hundreds of thousands of Jews eastwards, thus sheltering them from advancing German troops. Haim Babic, who had also taken refuge in Brest-Litovsk, confirmed the testimonies of Marek Halter and Samuel Pisar[118]: "The authorities had decided to deport the Jews from Poland who had taken refuge in that region. We were transported to the east of the Ural, to the Tavda region, a camp in the middle of the forest... I arrived with my wife and children in Astrakhan, on the edge of the Caspian Sea. Astrakhan was a dead end where millions of refugees converged. I found a job in a factory, we were housed in a collective flat". But the German armies soon approached Astrakhan, along the Volga: "We had to flee again. The trains were overcrowded... We set off thousands of kilometres from there, to the centre of Russia. I had friends in a kolkhoz who took us in and helped us[119]."

Obviously, rumours spread that the Jews remained in the rear, far from the combat zones. The Jews were supposed to be hiding in Tashkent, the capital of Uzbekistan. "Ivan fights in the trenches, Abram deals in the market", was a popular saying. In the collective consciousness of the Soviets, Tashkent had always been the city of plenty, where life was good. Arkadi Vaksberg, who declared himself against the myth of the "crouching Jew", seemed, once again, to be throwing stones on his own back: "Of the Jews transferred to the East, only 5% had arrived in Tashkent or its environs. But these were mainly well-known people—scholars, intellectuals, artists... In reality, most of the Jews had taken refuge in the cities of the Urals and Siberia where they shared the harsh hardships of the war with the local population. But they were indeed an important part of the "evacuated" masses, as they were called[120]."

The French daily *Actualité juive* of 5 May 2005 recalled that 500 000 Jews fought in the Red Army during the Second World War. 167,000 were officers, including 276 generals or admirals and 89 division

---

[118] Hervé Ryssen, *Les Espérances planetariennes*, Baskerville 2005, pp. 279-282.

[119] Alain Brossat, Sylvia Klingberg, *Le yiddishland revolutionnaire*, Balland, 1983, pp. 273, 279.

[120] Arkadi Vaksberg, *Stalin et les juifs*, Robert Laffont, 2003, pp. 130, 131.

commanders. Five fronts were commanded by Jewish generals. There were also 30,000 Jewish guerrillas in Belarus and 25,000 in the Ukraine. In total, 198,000 Jewish soldiers died in combat. "This death rate is higher than that of any other ethnic group of Soviet soldiers," we were assured.

Vaksberg also mentioned that 160,000 were decorated and that the title of "Hero of the Soviet Union", the supreme distinction rewarding military valour, was awarded to 120 of them[121]. However, Stalin played down this commitment. Certainly, in view of the Jewish population of the USSR at the time, the proportion of the dead is three or four times lower than it should have been.

## *Resistance to Nazism*

In 1939, when the defeat of the Spanish Republicans was certain, thousands of them found refuge in France, making their contribution to the subsequent resistance. Naturally, here too, the Jews of Yiddishland played a considerable role.

Since the end of the 19th century, Jews from the East had arrived in successive waves and began to populate certain neighbourhoods of Paris, from the most popular, such as Belleville, to the more bourgeois ones in the west of the city. Between the two wars, the capital saw another major wave of emigration from Germany and Eastern Europe. Republican France was a land of welcome that nourished all the hopes of these persecuted Jews.

Most of the Jews arriving from Germany and Poland were highly politicised. Here is the testimony of a certain Grynberg, presented in Alain Brossat's book:

"It was by attending political rallies and listening to the great orators of the Popular Front that I learned French. However, working conditions could be quite difficult, he commented: "As in Poland, our bosses were Jewish. Only they accepted to make us work clandestinely in such conditions[122]."

---

[121] This reminds us of the legions of honour distributed in France each year in handfuls to members of the community.

[122] Alain Brossat, Sylvia Klingberg, *Le yiddishland revolutionnaire*, Balland, 1983, p. 110.

The MOI (Immigrant Manpower) was an organisation created in 1924 by order of the Komintern (Communist International), in order to provide a reception structure and to frame and train for the struggle the numerous émigrés and political refugees arriving in France. Unlike the French Communist Party, the MOI remained very active in the anti-fascist struggle even after the Hitler-Stalin pact in August 1939. The party leadership applied the political line defined by the Kremlin within the framework of the German-Soviet pact, and condemned all resistance activity against the Germans. During this period, the French police persecuted communists for collaborating with the enemy. About 6000 of them were arrested and charged with treason.

In October 1940, the clandestine leadership of the party then decided to create the OS, Special Organisation. It was made up of armed groups intended, not to fight the Germans, but to protect the leadership against the French police. It was also responsible for executing party traitors, i.e. those who rebelled against orders or who had left the party to join Jacques Doriot's PPF. For these rather special tasks, the most fanatical militants were recruited, those without scruples capable of killing former comrades or other Frenchmen: "From the beginning of the war, the Jewish group of the MOI was the best structured and the most active. From it would come the commanders of the "OS", the special organisation in charge of terrorist and sabotage actions, wrote Alain Brossat; it would also provide almost all the militants of the "TA", the German Work, i.e. the work of propaganda and demoralisation of the German troops-an infinitely risky job, internationalist par excellence and carried out essentially by women: in bars and public places frequented by Wehrmacht soldiers, young women who spoke German tried to make contact... [123]"

In his *Critical History of the Resistance*, the historian Dominique Venner confirmed the essential role of the Jewish militants of Yiddishland in the organisation: 'Thanks to them, a new leadership of the MOI was put in place. They made up the central troika: Son Lerman (Bruno), Kaminski (Hervé) and Athur London (Gérard). Czarny was appointed head of the southern zone in 1943, seconded by Albert Youdine, Jacques Ravine and Mina Puterflam. In the northern zone, Therese Tenenbaum and Herman Grymbert coordinated the two regions... One of the main agents of the Komintern within the MOI is

---

[123] Alain Brossat, Sylvia Klingberg, *Le yiddishland revolutionnaire*, Balland, 1983, p. 183.

Michel Feintuch (Jean Jerôme), a Polish Jew, former quartermaster of the International Brigades and a future eminence grise within the PCF leadership[124]."

The MOI was thus waging a kind of private war against the Germans, against the orders of the PCF and against the opinion of General de Gaulle's National Council of Resistance (CNR). Individual attacks and terrorism were, at that time, condemned by the communist party. However, while the Communist Party did not give such an order, the Komintern probably had sufficient authority to give it. Pierre Georges, the future "Colonel Fabien", was to commit the first attack on a German officer in Paris: "On 23 August 1941, the future Colonel Fabien executed a German officer at the Barbès metro stop. "I have avenged Titi," he says in retreat—"Titi", that's Tyszelman. In this action, considered the first armed initiative against the Germans in France, Fabien was accompanied by another militant with a foreign name: Brustlein[125]."

A cycle of attack-repression then began, provoking, as expected, a German reaction against the French population. But instead of executing civilian hostages at random, the Germans, knowing where the blows were coming from, executed communist Jews from Eastern Europe. Let us remember here that the usages of war, tacitly accepted by all belligerents, permit the execution of civilian hostages who have assaulted men in uniform.

In February 1942, the underground leadership of the communist party decided to expand the combat groups. The MOI fighters joined the OS to form the FTPs (Franco riflemen and guerrillas). The party gave the go-ahead to form the FTP-MOI units. A first FTP-MOI battalion was created in Paris in March 1942 under the command of Lisner, a former member of the international brigades. In Paris, the man at the head of the FTP was Colonel Gilles (Joseph Epstein), a Yiddishland revolutionary, a former Spanish Civil War veteran and an escapee from a stalag.

The FTP-MOI groups were generally made up of very young men, largely recruited from the Union of Jewish Youth (UJJ), a communist

---

[124] Dominique Venner, Histoire critique de la Résistance, Éditions Pygmalion 1995, p. 231.

[125] Alain Brossat, Sylvia Klingberg, *Le yiddishland revolutionnaire*, Balland, 1983, p. 179.

transmission belt and a veritable breeding ground for armed action. These fighters were to be at the centre of most of the attacks organised in the Paris region, wrote Dominique Venner. "A chronology of a few weeks in the summer of 1942 is very eloquent:

- 4 August, assassination in Seine-et-Oise of the former communist Gachelin, Jacques Doriot's secretary.

- 6 August, grenade attack on Luftwaffe soldiers training at the Jean-Bouin stadium: two dead, several wounded.

- 7 August, derailment of a German transport near Melun.

- 9 August, an Italian detachment sets fire to a German depot at Sartrouville.

- 11 August, Lisner, Simon and Geduldik detonate a bomb in a German hotel on Avenue Iéna.

- 28 August, in Villepinte, the two sentries of the Tirpitz-Kazerne are shot dead. On the same day, a time bomb explodes in the Clichy cinema where Marceal Déat is holding a meeting: one dead, 27 wounded.

- 1 September, Group 3 of the Valmy detachment of Jewish partisans led by Rayman attacks a German section in Rue Crimée with grenades. On the same day, Yone Geduldik and two others throw an incendiary bomb at a German office near Lyon station.

- 3 September, arson attack on the premises of the francist party in the 13th district.

- 10 September, Anka Rychtyger and two other resistance fighters set fire to four German vehicles, Rue de Charonne, etc.".

The most important exploit of these groups is the attack on 28 September which cost the life of Dr. Von Ritter, head of the STO (Compulsory Labour Service) in France. "The action is carried out by Fontano and Rayman. Wounded by Fontano's pistol as he left his house unprotected, Von Ritter was shot a few metres further on by Rayman's parabellum... In the southern zone, the FTP's actions do not begin until the German troops enter it. As in Paris," wrote Jacques Ravine, "the Jewish groups of the FTP in the southern zone were the first to be formed. They are an integral part of the FTP-MOI military organisation and are divided into four units: the *Carmagnole*, later renamed *Carmagnole-Fried*, in Lyon; *Liberté* in Grenoble and its region; the Marcel Korzec Company in Marseille; the 35th Brigade, later named after its creator, Mendl Langer, operates in Toulouse and the south-west region; it later grew to a more significant size with immigrants of various origins. *Carmagnole* de Lyon recruits young people from the Union of Jewish Youth and functions as a veritable school of commanders. These commandos are then sent to the other towns in the south. It provided mobile commandos who were active in Lyon as well as in Marseille, Toulouse and Nice. The first organisers of these groups were almost always former volunteers of the International Brigades. This was the case in Lyon with Krakus and Tcharnecki, in Marseille with Boris Stcherbak, and in Toulouse with Mendl Langer. The latter was arrested and guillotined in 1943[126]".

In his book entitled, *Next Year's Revolution,* Maurice Rajsfus quoted the same source: "Of the dozens of daring operations carried out by the militants of the 35th brigade after Langer's death, Jacques Ravine cites the following specifically French "targets" attacked by Jewish guerrillas:

- 13 July 1943: In broad daylight, bomb attack on the private home of Dr. Berthet, leader of the "Collaboration" group in Toulouse. On the same day, attack with two bombs on the home of the notary Bachala (future Gauleiter of Toulouse). Bachala was seriously wounded, his flat destroyed.

-20 August 1943: In broad daylight, the partisans of the 35th brigade attack Felicien Costes, secretary general of the Fascist militia's Free Guard, Gestapo agent and informer, at gunpoint. He was killed. During the intense firefight, two policemen were killed.

- 24 August 1943: At nine o'clock in the morning, execution of Mas, head of the second office of the Militia.

- 20 September 1943: To celebrate the victory at Valmy, the partisans plant two bombs in the arsenal. Two militiamen were killed and four wounded.

- 10 October 1943: Advocate General Pierre Lespinasse, who had demanded the death penalty against Langer, was shot dead.

- 2 November 1943: Militia leader Lionel Berger is executed in his home with Major Bru, cantonal commander of the French Legion of combatants.

---

[126] Dominique Venner, *Histoire critique de la Résistance*, Éditions Pygmalion 1995, p. 238.

- 15 November 1943: General Philippon, a militia leader, is shot dead in the streets of Toulouse. "[127]

This was the testimony of Jean Lemberger, a Polish Jew, quoted by Maurice Rajsfus: "When press releases reported the actions of French patriots, we reacted with humour. I remember that with Marcel Rayman we could not stop laughing: 'As French patriots, the little Jews of Paris are particularly representative'[128]."

The Jewish militants are indeed the most fierce. They did not fight for France or against Germany, but against international fascism, and especially against European National Socialism. Alain Brossat confirmed this:

"Trains derailed, Nazi collaborators and officers executed, fuel depots set on fire, grenades thrown into restaurants and theatres frequented by Germans, sabotage in industry or in workshops working for the occupiers, posts and pillars collapsed... There was no action of this kind that Jewish fighters did not take part in, that they did not organise, by the dozens, on all fronts and at all levels. There was no difference between big and small actions[129]."

Alain Brossat also informed us that Jewish anti-fascist militants were specialists in the production of false documents and banknotes. In Paris, Pierre Scherf was in charge of the MOI's "Romanian-speaking group". He was in charge of the small daily tasks of the Resistance: "selling bank notes, food vouchers expropriated by the combatants, making false documents of all kinds, organising solidarity with the families of deportees...". Later he was given the task of organising liaison with MOI groups in northern and eastern France, where Polish and Italian miners were particularly active: railway tracks sabotaged, electricity lines shot down, German soldiers disarmed and executed, organised strikes in the mines and sabotage, etc.".

During the Paris insurrection, Pierre Scherf was commander of the patriotic militias. "Later, he took part in the liberation of northern

---

[127] Maurice Rajsfus, *L'an prochain la révolution*, Éditions Mazarine, 1985, p.221

[128] Maurice Rajsfus, *L'an prochain la révolution*, Éditions Mazarine, 1985, p.231

[129] Alain Brossat, Sylvia Klingberg, *Le yiddishland revolutionnaire*, Balland, 1983, p. 190.

France, following in the footsteps of the American army. But as early as December 1945, he was called up for more pressing tasks: Romania is falling to the side of Stalin's 'socialism', so the Communist Party needs all its commanders[130]."

However, not all Jews played a heroic role during the war. Some of them preferred to continue to prosper with their businesses. Here is a testimony from the book by Alain Brossat and Sylvia Klinberg: "In Paris, during the war, Jewish partisan commandos organised raids against Jewish workshops in the faubourg Poissonnière, whose owners prospered by making equipment for the Wehrmacht; some of these fighters were arrested during these actions, denounced by those "good" Jews, then shot or deported. In the ghettos, the shadow fighters liquidated the most diligent members of the Jewish police and the collaborationists of some Judenrat[131]."

We know that some Jews built fortunes by collaborating with Germany. Among them, two men particularly stood out: Mandel Szkolnikoff, also known as "Monsieur Michel", and Joseph Joanovici, also known as "Monsieur Joseph".

Monsieur Michel was of Russian origin. He specialised in textiles and foodstuffs. Thanks to his German wife—an Aryan—he did not hesitate to warn his SS friends in order to have other Jewish competitors arrested and thus take over their warehouses and business premises. Monsieur Michel was the one who led the German police to the warehouses in the Sentier*. The occupied zone was his hunting ground. His profits were so large that he was able to buy the biggest hotels on the Côte d'Azur, to take over hotel, real estate and commercial companies in Paris, as well as restaurants and cafés. In 1945, his real estate fortune was estimated at two billion francs, about 900 million euros today.

At the same time, Monsieur Joseph, a Romanian Jew who had started out as a rag-picker, was raiding all the non-ferrous metals useful to the German war machine. Joanovici also took over the leather market, a commodity highly coveted by the Nazis, who had just invaded the

---

[130] Alain Brossat, Sylvia Klingberg, *Le yiddishland revolutionnaire*, Balland, 1983, pp. 195, 196.

[131] Alain Brossat, Sylvia Klingberg, *Le yiddishland revolutionnaire*, Balland, 1983, p. 206.

* Jewish shopping district of Paris.

Soviet Union. In those years, Monsieur Joseph's monthly turnover was around 5 million euros today. More skilful than Szkolnikoff, he managed to get in touch with the head of the French Gestapo in rue Lauriston, the famous Henri Lafont.

By the end of 1943, the tables had turned. Monsieur Michel fled to Spain with his German muse, accompanied by some of his French and Jewish agents. But in his wife's suitcases, the French police found jewels and precious stones worth 300 million euros. Monsieur Joseph, on the other hand, played the opposite card; he bought back from Lafont the weapons parachuted by the Allies and seized by the French Gestapo, to supply a resistance network within the Paris police headquarters. But at the same time, he equipped and clothed the Guardia Franca de la Militia and the North African Brigade fighting against the Maquis. The prefecture's policemen held him up as a real role model. Monsieur Joseph was the god, the saviour who would bring about the liberation of Paris. Thanks to his influential friends, he would manage to escape the worst punishment: five years in prison, a ridiculous fine and a declaration of his national unworthiness, which mattered little to this stateless man. As for Monsieur Michel, a refugee in Spain, he was extorted by former Gestapo agents who fled from the execution squads. His body was found on 17 June 1945 in a field outside Madrid.

It remained true, however, that the role of Jews in the Resistance had been important, even if it had been overlooked for a long time. "Poliakov himself quotes the figure of between 15 and 30% of Jews in the French Resistance[132]," wrote Alain Brossat. For a community that represented 1% of the French population, this is a considerable proportion.

In *The Testament of God*, the philosopher Bernard-Henri Levy makes the same observation: "Where does the legend come from, according to which the Jews did not resist Hitlerism, and that they allowed themselves to be led to the slaughter like lambs to the slaughter? Being 1% of the French population before the war, they constitute 15–20% of the various resistance movements[133]."

---

[132] Alain Brossat, Sylvia Klingberg, *Le yiddishland revolutionnaire*, Balland, 1983, p. 180.

[133] Bernard-Henri Levy, *Le Testament de Dieu*, Grasset, 1979, p. 275.

"Why, in proportion, were there so few Frenchmen in the patriotic Resistance in France, why was the percentage of foreigners so large, especially Eastern European Jews?" asked Alain Brossat. It was enough to "scratch lightly the veneer of the "Patriotic Resistance" in Paris, from the summer of 1941 onwards, and analyse more closely its numerous armed actions, to find the indelible mark of the Jewish immigrant worker, of the militant of the communist MOI (Immigrant Worker's Labour)[134]."

And in the same way, it was enough to "analyse carefully what was the 'Great Patriotic War' declared by Stalin, behind the German lines in Belarus and the Baltic countries, the partisan fighting in those regions, to find, there too, the mark of the Jewish fighters who fled from the ghetto, the 'Vilna Avengers' and other members of the maquis in the Minsk region". For example, of the 130 fighters in a detachment of "Russian" partisans fighting in the Ivenitz forest, "70 are Jews who fled from the Minsk ghetto. The leadership of the detachment is also largely made up of Jews,[135]," wrote Alain Brossat.

The Polish "patriots" presented an even more caricatured image than that of the French "patriots". Questioned by Aain Brossat and Sylvia Klingberg in Israel, where he finally settled after the war, David Grynberg gave his testimony: "In 1945, I was in Moscow. I was an active member of the Committee of Polish Patriots, which dealt, among other things, with the repatriation of Polish refugees in the USSR. Shortly before the committee ceased to function, before our departure for Poland, we organised a small party. I proposed inviting Peretz Markish; to which another committee member, Kinderman, a man of the apparatus, objected: "And why invite a Jewish author? we are a Polish patriotic committee, not a Jewish committee! True, I replied, but look around you: there are fifty of us here, and there are only three who are not Jewish."[136]."

For thirty years, the role of Jews in the Resistance has been largely downplayed, even outright silenced by the Communist parties. Alain

---

[134] Alain Brossat, Sylvia Klingberg, *Le yiddishland revolutionnaire*, Balland, 1983, pp. 180, 185, 186.

[135] Alain Brossat, Sylvia Klingberg, *Le yiddishland revolutionnaire*, Balland, 1983, pp. 168, 213.

[136] Alain Brossat, Sylvia Klingberg, *Le yiddishland revolutionnaire*, Balland, 1983, pp. 288, 289.

Brossat and Sylvia Klingberg asked: "Does it harm the patriotic image of the Resistance to admit that, throughout 1943, the main actions of the partisans in Paris were carried out by foreigners, MOI activists, until the great autumn raid came upon them? Is it a sin against internationalism to recognise that behind the "Polish", "Hungarian", "Romanian", "Czech" partisan, there is the revolutionary of Yiddishland, his traditions of struggle, his culture, his language and the particular consonance of his name[137]?"

In his *Critical History of the Resistance*, historian Dominique Venner posed the same question: "Did the Communists fear to arouse a latent xenophobia against them by mentioning the essential role within their ranks of Jewish fighters from Central Europe[138]?"

It is true that after the arrests of twenty-four members of the Manouchian group at the end of 1943, the Germans had revealed their identities by widely displaying their photos on the walls of France's major cities. The famous Red Poster painted an unflattering picture of the "French" resistance and had become a symbol. The Germans pilloried the "Hungarian Jew" Elek, the "Polish Jew" Rayman, making their Jewishness an argument against the Resistance and designating the whole Resistance as an "army of crime", a "fifth column of metecos".

For the Communist Party, the Jewish resistance had always been an integral part of the French resistance, and there was no need to mention it. Maurice Rajsfus wrote: "It was not until the 1970s that Jewish militants published books on the Jewish resistance. Despite the strong patriotic accent of these works, they had to wait twenty-five years to come to light[139]."

The essayist Guy Konopnicki also rightly wrote: "Gaullists and communists joined hands to write history, they fabricated together, a posteriori, a national resistance when in reality the dividing line was not

---

[137] Alain Brossat, Sylvia Klingberg, *Le yiddishland revolutionnaire*, Balland, 1983, pp. 185, 186.

[138] Dominique Venner, *Histoire critique de la Résistance*, Éditions Pygmalion 1995, p. 230.

[139] Maurice Rajsfus, L'an prochain la révolution, Éditions Mazarine, 1985, p. 333.

between French and Germans, but between fascists and anti-fascists of all countries[140]."

In fact, the Jews' motivations were certainly very different from those of the patriots in the countries where they fought.

Even so, Dominique Venner's analysis invited us to put into perspective the importance of the militants' combat: "There were almost never any losses on the part of the perpetrators of the attacks during the action. Depositing a disguised time bomb in an ordinary package is not as difficult or dangerous as throwing a grenade in a shop window. Clearly, this did not mean that such acts could be executed without courage or daring, and "the perpetrators had no illusions about their fate if caught[141]."

The testimony of Colonel Passy, head of the BCRA, gives an even better understanding of the reality of the FTP's actions: "The account he left of his meeting with Ginsberg (Villon), the main leader of the Front nationale, shows that he was not gullible," wrote Dominique Venner. This is what Colonel Passy wrote: "Villon told us for twenty minutes about the exploits of the Snipers and Partisans (FTP), how they had killed a sixty-year-old Landsturm at Armentières, how they blew up a newspaper kiosk at Epernay, how they recovered two dozen grenades and six crossbeams at Mézières or Sedan, etc, etc... We were a little astonished to hear this long monologue, recited like a litany, which had no more interest than the chronicle of ordinary events in a pre-war newspaper. But when he had finished, Villon announced to us, by way of conclusion, that, in the face of such warlike exploits, fighting France had only to bow down, and that it was clear that the National Front had the vocation of federating behind it the whole of the French Resistance[142]."

General de Gaulle had a similar reaction to the "great resistance fighter" Colonel Ravanel, who was responsible for the resistance in Toulouse.

---

[140]Guy Konopnicki, *La Place de la nation*, Olivie Orban, 1983, p.41

[141] Dominique Venner, *Histoire critique de la Résistance*, Éditions Pygmalion 1995, p. 238.

[142]*Missions secrètes en France*, Plon, Paris, 1951, p. 162.

\* The expression Deuxième Bureau commonly refers to the information service of the French Army, with reference to the 'Second Bureau' of the General Staff.

In fact, Ravanel controlled it with other partisans, many of whom were Spanish communists. Toulouse resembled, according to an English historian, "Barcelona in July 1936": with "thirty-seven private "Deuxièmes Bureaux*" where each office had its own prison, usually an underground cellar, where victim and executioner were the only witnesses to abominable scenes[143]".

When General de Gaulle came to inspect the region to try to restore some order after the departure of the German troops, Ravanel presented himself to him, squaring his shoulders: "Colonel Ravanel, at your service!" His only reply was a dismissive: "Second Lieutenant Asher, at ease!"

## USSR 1945

In 1942, Stalin had finally agreed to the creation of a 'Jewish Anti-Fascist Committee' (JAC) bringing together the most famous Jewish personalities of the Soviet intelligentsia. For six years, until 1948, the Jewish Anti-Fascist Committee, under the patronage of Lavrenti Beria, was at the centre of an intense revival of Jewish life in the USSR. In 1942, its main objective was the international mobilisation of the Jewish people and fundraising in Jewish communities abroad, and especially the rich and highly influential Jewish community in the USA. The celebrated actor Solomon Mijoels, director of the Moscow Yiddish theatre, was the chairman of the committee, while the writer Ilya Ehrenbourg was the most active spokesman.

In 1943, representatives of the Jewish Anti-Fascist Committee set out on a long tour of the United States to make contact with Jewish organisations. The official aim was to raise funds for the purchase of weapons, food and medicine. But the secret aim of the trip was actually to build bridges between the physicists of the two countries in order to accelerate the implementation of the Soviet atomic programme.

All Soviet atomic fission researchers were Jews, wrote Arkadi Vaksberg. "Stalin was therefore counting on the reputation of the members of the Committee and their relations with the international community to extort information that would speed up the development of the nuclear weapon. This should be facilitated by the fact that most of the American scientists, including Einstein, were also Jewish".

---

[143] *Rivarol* Weekly of 11 April 1997

Stalin entrusted Beria with the task of extracting these secrets and securing effective collaboration. Solomon Mijoels and other members were to be supported on the spot by Soviet agents. Months later, the results of Mijoels' tour had exceeded all expectations. "The emissaries of the CJA brought bundles of enthusiastic articles about their stay in the United States... They also brought cheques for several million dollars donated by wealthy American Jews to continue the war against Nazism in the name of the universal Jewish cause[144]."

"With very rare exceptions," wrote Vaksberg, the Soviet espionage networks were made up of Jews. "In Belgium, the highly effective Red Orchestra coordinated the espionage activities of Leopold Trepper and his wife Lioubov Broido, both Polish Jews, and the famous "Kent", the Russian Jew Anatoli Gourevitch... The title of best spy of all time was unanimously attributed to "Sonia", the German Jew Ruth Werner, who worked together with her brother Jurgen Koutchinski (later an academic in communist Germany). In the United States, Grigori Heifetz, Lisa Gorskaya-Zarubina (Rosenzweig) and others were major suppliers of atomic secrets to the Kremlin", and added: "Stalin undoubtedly suffered from being dependent on Jewish secret agents, especially since most of them had been recruited at a time when the secret services were run by the Jews Meyer Trillisser, Abram Sloutski and Sergei Spiegelglass, who have since been shot. He could afford to order mutations and promotions within the state and party apparatus, but he could not dismiss an agent who already possessed contacts or who was infiltrated into some structure of the adversary[145]."

Arkadi Vaksberg considered that Stalinist anti-Semitism really manifested itself from 1942 onwards, when several reports were written about the influence of Jews in the cultural sphere. For reasons of age or health, "people of Jewish origin" began to lose their positions of responsibility. "The struggle against the Jewish presence began in the

---

[144] Arkadi Vaksberg, *Stalin et les juifs*, Robert Laffont, 2003, pp. 147, 151. In her biography of Beria, Amy Knight wrote that the Soviets had an effective source of information: "The spy network set up in New York by an American Communist couple, Morris and Lona Cohen. Morris Cohen had been recruited by the Soviets during the Spanish Civil War. He managed to pass on to Vasili Zarubin, head of Soviet intelligence in New York from 1941 to 1944, information provided by an American physicist". (Amy Knight, *Beria*, 1993, Aubier, 1994, p. 203).

[145] Arkadi Vaksberg, *Stalin et les juifs*, Robert Laffont, 2003, pp. 128, 129.

cultural sphere, Vaksberg wrote. The archives have also preserved numerous similar documents denouncing the "Jewish invasion" of the social sciences. They did not yet dare to do the same for physicists, chemists and mathematicians. In wartime, Stalin could not attack science and industry... By 1942, the evolution towards state anti-Semitism had become visible, almost self-evident[146]."

Stalin, however, continued his ostentatious distribution of awards and decorations to Jewish personalities. In no way could he renounce the financial support, necessary for the purchase of armaments, equipment, food and medicine, which had to be extorted from the American "bourgeoisie", continually reminding them that only the Soviet Union was capable of protecting the Jews from total extermination.

Vaksberg nevertheless recalled the "massive presence" of Jews in key positions in the state apparatus, in the scientific and industrial sectors, especially in the war industry, during the war. "Stalin had no other solution but to turn to them. Even as state anti-Semitism began to spread, Stalin thus created the illusion, not only that the Kremlin was not responsible for it, but, on the contrary, encouraged a certain Judeophilia.

Numerous Jews were at that time at the top of the executive power, holding the titles of people's commissars or generals: "In addition to Lazar Kaganovitch, Deputy Chairman of the Government and Commissar of Ways of Communication, Boris Vannikov (released from prison at the beginning of the war and quickly appointed Commissar of Armaments), Isaac Zaltzman (first Jew to be honoured with the title of Hero of Socialist Labour, Commissar of the Armoured Car Industry), Semion Guinzbourg, Vladimir Grossman, Samuel Shapiro were appointed People's Commissars." Not counting the dozens of deputy commissars of the people. "Almost every day, Stalin received Jews, generals of industry, and talked with them for hours (General Aron Karponossov, deputy chief of staff, responsible for equipping the armies, was a fixture at Stalin's headquarters)." Vaksberg added, somewhat paradoxically, "Thus took shape the myth of Stalin's special benevolence towards the Jews[147]."

Khrushchev, who was now in the Politburo, probably harboured anti-Semitic sentiments. Historian Simon Sebag Montefiore recounted how, in the immediate post-war period, when he administered Ukraine,

---

[146] Arkadi Vaksberg, *Stalin et les juifs*, Robert Laffont, 2003, pp. 139, 140.

[147] Arkadi Vaksberg, *Stalin et les juifs*, Robert Laffont, 2003, pp. 132, 133.

Khrushchev had refused to give back his houses to Jews when they found them occupied: "An unrepentant anti-Semite, he complained that the 'Abramovichs' were raiding his fiefdom like crows". The affair provoked a real debate in Stalin's entourage, wrote Sebag Montefiore. Miloels complained to Molotov, who passed the complaint on to Beria. The latter demanded that Khrushchev help the Jews. Stalin "would later suspect that Beria was too close to the Jews, and that may have been the origin of the rumour that Beria himself was a "secret" Jew[148]."

He seems to have had real sympathy for Jews, wrote Amy Knight in her biography of Beria: "The descriptions we have of him often emphasise that he could physically pass for a Jew, and the rumour that he was a Jew spread. Although these rumours seem unfounded, they may have made Beria associated with Jews in public opinion." In fact, after the war, Beria, while in charge of the Party in Georgia, had launched a programme of rehabilitation of Georgian Jews, including the creation of a Jewish pious works society and a Jewish ethnological museum in Tbilisi. "We may add, wrote Amy Knight, that his sister had married a Jew, and that he had several Jewish friends among his faithful followers: Milstein, Raïkhman, Mamulov, Sumbatov-Topuridze and Eitingon, to name but a few[149]."

From 1946 onwards, the reports denounced, page after page, the influence exerted by American Zionist organisations on the Committee. Any manifestation of Jewish particularism was suspect. This did not prevent Stalin from initially supporting the creation of the state of Israel. But in September 1948, the visit of Golda Meir, the Israeli foreign minister on an official visit to Moscow, provoked great enthusiasm among Soviet Jews, which in turn provoked Stalin's anger. A month later, on 20 November 1948, Stalin ordered the dissolution of the Jewish Anti-Fascist Committee, decreed a "bourgeois Jewish nationalist organisation".

---

[148] Simon Sebag Montefiore, *The Court of the Red Tsar*, 2004, Crítica-Barcelona, p.586

[149] Amy Knight, *Beria*, 1993, Aubier, 1994, p.223. Eitingon was commissioned to assassinate Trotsky. Stalin "entrusted the task of eliminating his old enemy Trotsky to the Jews Naoum Eitingon, Grigori Rabinovitch and Lev Vassilevski, as well as to Pavel Sudoplatov, married to a Jewess". (Arkadi Vaksberg, *Stalin and the Jews*, Robert Laffont, 2003, p. 117)

Shortly afterwards, almost the entire CJA leadership was behind bars. In January, Mikhoels's body was found in Minsk, sticking out of the snow. The corpse was taken to Moscow, "to the laboratory of Professor Boris Zbarski, the (Jewish) biochemist in charge of the preservation of Lenin's mummy; despite seeing the contusion of the head and the bullet wound, he was ordered to prepare the victim of the "traffic accident"[150]".

On 19 January 1949, Pravda published an editorial "about an unpatriotic group of cosmopolitan critics". The official anti-Semitic campaign had begun. The aim was to expose a large American espionage network linked to the Zionists. A few days later, Polina Molotova, Molotov's wife and the most influential Jewish personality at court after Kaganovith, was quietly relieved of her duties.

The operation to liquidate the CJA was not completed until the summer of 1952, after six years of investigation. Victor Abakumov, a close associate of Beria's who had been appointed Security Minister after the war to replace Beria himself, was dismissed and arrested in July 1951 for dragging his feet. He was replaced by Semion Ignatiev, and Riumine was appointed deputy security minister. As in 1937, terror descended on the leadership itself.

"Since the pre-war period, when Beria headed the Lubyanka, the Lubyanka's management included a good number of Jews, wrote Vaksberg. Riumin then ordered the arrest of Léonid Raïhman, Naum Etigon, Norman Borodin (Gruzenbrg), Lev Schwartzman, Mikhail Makliarski, Salomon Milstaein, Aron Belkine, Efimm Libensn, Andrei Sverdlov (son of the first Soviet 'president'), and many other generals and senior officers of the Lubyanka[151]."

Sebag Montefiore also presented the case of one Naun Shvartsman: "Colonel Naum Shvartsman, one of the most vicious torturers since the late 1930s and a journalist skilled in publishing confessions, claimed to have had sexual relations not only with his own son and daughter, but also with Abakumov himself[152].". All were accused of being involved in a Zionist conspiracy.

---

[150] Simon Sebag Montefiore, *La corte del Zar rojo*, 2004, Crítica-Barcelona, p. 620.

[151] Arkadi Vaksberg, *Stalin et les juifs*, Robert Laffont, 2003, p. 233.

[152] Simon Sebag Montefiore, *La corte del Zar rojo*, 2004, Crítica-Barcelona, p. 662, footnote

One hundred and ten members of the CJA had been imprisoned and tortured. "More than one hundred and ten prisoners, mostly Jews, suffered the "French struggle" at the hands of the bloodthirsty Komarov in the Lubyanka, wrote Sebag Montefiore. I was merciless with them," Komarov later boasted, "I broke their souls... Even the minister did not frighten them as much as I did... I was particularly violent with the Jewish nationalists (whom I hated the most)[153]." Five died.

In the summer of 1952, the trial of the "Zionists" finally took place. It lasted three months, behind closed doors without prosecutor or lawyers, in the Lubyanka building. In the end, thirteen people appeared in the dock. Salomon Lozovski, deputy foreign minister, opened the list. He was accused of having promoted the idea of creating a Jewish republic in Crimea. Then came the writers and poets Itzik Fefer, Perec Markish, Lev Kvitko, David Bergelson. They were all shot on 12 August 1952.

The Soviet dictionary itself changed the meaning of the word "cosmopolitan", reported Alain Brossat; "the "cosmopolitan" is no longer an "individual who considers the whole world as his homeland" (1931 definition), but an "individual devoid of patriotic feelings, detached from the interests of his homeland, alien to his people and with disdainful behaviour towards his culture" (1949 definition).

On 13 January 1953, the fifth anniversary of Mikhail's assassination, the Soviet press published the official communiqué denouncing the "White Coat" conspiracy, the starting point for a new campaign directed against "Zionists" throughout the country. Of the nine doctors accused of attempting to kill Zhdanov and Stalin, six were Jews. It was at this time that Stalin planned the forced transfer of all Jews to Central Asia, which, according to Arkadi Vaksberg, was to begin on 15 March. This plan did not prevent him from continuing his double dealing with the Jews, for example by awarding the Stalin Prize to Ilia Ehrenbourg on 27 January. But after the official announcement of the doctors' plot, Stalin lived only 51 days. His death on 5 March 1953 is still shrouded in mystery.

At 10 p.m. on 1 March 1953, Stalin was found unconscious in his dacha in Kutsevo, 80 kilometres from Moscow. Four hours after the dignitaries had been informed, a delegation turned up at 3 a.m. on Monday morning. "No one knows who stopped the anti-Semitic media

---

[153] Simon Sebag Montefiore, *La corte del Zar rojo*, 2004, Crítica-Barcelona, p. 634.

campaign that night. Suslov was the secretary of the Central Committee in charge of ideological questions, but... who ordered him to stop the campaign? but who ordered him to stop the campaign? The answer remains an unknown[154]."

Beria and Malenkov, Stalin's trembling and punctilious secretary, had arrived first. As Stalin lay dying, with a callus of blood on his brain, they did not call the doctors until the day after the drama. Beria was generally accused of not having helped Stalin, but Khrushchev and Ignatiev did not do much either. Sebag Montefiore wrote: 'Recent research indicates that he may have spiked Stalin's wine with an anticoagulant drug based on crystalline sodium, which, after several days, was the trigger for the stroke. Perhaps Khrushchev and the other hierarchs were complicit, so it was in everyone's interest to cover up the affair. The four then decided to return to their respective homes and not to tell their families about it[155]."

As the doctors were not called in until the day after the drama, it will never be known whether a quicker intervention would have saved Stalin. In any case, Beria made no secret of his joy: "I did it myself!—he would later say in a boastful tone to Molotov and Kaganovich, "I saved all of you! Stalin opened his eyes when Kaganovich arrived and glanced at his lieutenants one by one, then closed them again. Unlike the despotic Beria, Molotov and Kaganovich were deeply dismayed. Tears streamed down their cheeks... It is possible that twenty million individuals had been murdered; that another twenty-eight million had been deported, eighteen million of whom had been forced to do hard labour in the gulags. Yet, despite so much blood and so much pain, they remained true to their creed". Sebag Montefiore hinted here at a facet of Beria's personality: "When Stalin's incapacity was demonstrated, Beria "spewed out all the hatred he felt for Stalin", but whenever the dictator's eyelids began to tremble or he opened his eyes, Lavrenti, terrified that he might recover, "knelt down and began to kiss his hand" like an oriental vizier at the foot of a sultan's bed. When the dictator slipped back into a deep sleep, Beria would practically spit in his face, revealing

---

[154] Simon Sebag Montefiore, *La corte del Zar rojo*, 2004, Crítica-Barcelona, p. 692. Footnote.

[155] Simon Sebag Montefiore, *La corte del Zar rojo*, 2004, Crítica-Barcelona, p. 694.

his overweening ambition..." That scoundrel! That filth! Thank God we got rid of him[156]!"

In 1948, Beria's political status was less important than it had been at the end of the war. He was already only number four in the leadership, behind Molotov, Zhdanov and Vorochilov (Chief of the Armies) and his loyalists had been removed from the Central Committee. Because of his dubious relations with the Jewish Anti-Fascist Committee, Stalin distrusted him and even insinuated that he was a crypto-Jew. "After Stalin's death, Beria was not content merely to denounce the doctors' plot as a farce, wrote Amy Knight in her biography, but also tried to promote the revival of Jewish culture[157]."

He was the new strongman of the collegial leadership, having regained control of the secret services and retained the post of deputy prime minister. Molotov and Mikoyan sat again in a reduced presidium and resumed their respective portfolios of Foreign Affairs and Trade. Khrushchev remained a pillar of the Party, but was excluded from the government. Malenkov succeeded Stalin as party general secretary and head of government. Beria was triumphant, and everyone thought he was the man with the best future. At no time did he doubt himself. But on 26 June, during the extraordinary meeting of the Presidium, Khrushchev rose to speak and attacked Beria. Bulganin joined him, as did Malenkov. He panicked and gave the signal to enter to the generals waiting outside. Marshal Zhukov entered the room and arrested Beria.

On 22 December, he was sentenced to death by a secret tribunal. Undressed, in his underwear, handcuffed and tied to a hook on the wall, he screamed and begged for his life. He was so loud and noisy that a napkin had to be stuffed into his mouth before he was shot in the head with a rifle. His body was cremated. Beria was retrospectively accused of most of the crimes committed during the Stalin era. Khrushchev was now emerging as the new master of the Soviet Union.

## *The Hungarian uprising*

In the immediate post-war period, communist leaders of Jewish origin also played a notable role in the countries of Eastern Europe. Refugees

---

[156] Simon Sebag Montefiore, *La corte del Zar rojo*, 2004, Crítica-Barcelona, p. 694, 695, 697, 702.

[157] Amy Knight, *Beria*, 1993, Aubier, p. 223

in Moscow during the war, they were packed into Red Army boxcars to go and administer the invaded countries. The example of Hungary is the most emblematic. The Soviet troops that had entered Hungary in 1945 were partly composed of Asian soldiers. Years later, the English historian David Irving recounted some rather evocative testimonies: "When we saw the Russian soldiers arrive, we wondered whether they really belonged to the human race... Their dress was indescribably filthy. They burst into the flats throwing grenades. Instead of talking, they would grunt. They aimed at people, and if they did not get what they wanted, they killed them... They did not know toothpaste and smeared it on bread. They drank Cologne. Telephones frightened them and shot at them. They washed themselves in the toilets. They didn't know showers, when they saw water gushing from the wall they got scared and shot at them".

David Irving described in his book the torments the Hungarian population had to endure: gang rape, murder and pillage. "But, above all, the rapes hung over the country like a calamity, accompanied by syphilis". The Hungarians therefore have a rather painful memory of that "liberation", as can be perceived in this somewhat sarcastic expression: "Our country has known three disasters in the course of its history: the defeat by the Mongols, the Turkish conquest, and the liberation by the Red Army[158]."

The Red Army brought to power a group of communist leaders of Jewish origin. Most of them were leaders of the communist Republic of Bela Kun who had fled to Moscow after the fall of that regime in 1919. There they had attended Soviet party schools and had been chosen by Stalin to lead the Hungarian communist party.

Matthew Rakosi, the country's leader until 1953, was actually called Matthew Roth. The son of a Jewish grocer, he was "one of the most ruthless despots of the 20th century", wrote David Irving. He had been taken prisoner by the Russians during the 1914 war and interned in Siberia, where he became a communist. He met Lenin in Petrograd in 1918 and returned to Hungary during Bela Kun's brief Republic of Soviets. After the defeat, he took refuge in Austria, and in Moscow in 1920. Four years later, the Komintern sent him back to Hungary to rebuild an underground communist party. He was captured and

---

[158] David Irving, *Insurrection, L'enfer d'une nation: Budapest 1956*, Albin Michel, 1981, p. 28, 26.

sentenced to death, but his sentence was commuted to eight years in prison thanks to an international protest campaign. Tried again in 1935 for the execution of 40 political opponents under Bela Kun's government, he transformed the dock into a political tribune from which he made his trial world famous. Finally, on 30 October 1940, Horthy released him in exchange for the Hungarian flags taken by the Tsar in 1848. He remained the head of the Hungarian communist party in exile in Moscow during the war years[159]. He was not well liked by his comrades, who accused him of having betrayed militants during the 1935 trial. Beria called him "the first Jewish king of Hungary".

"The four men who held real power in Hungary were Jews," explained David Irving. In addition to Rasoki, the "Jewish quartet" included Ernst Gero, who ran the country's economy. Born Ernt Singer, it was he who recruited Ramon Mercader to assassinate Trotsky in 1940. M.Farkas was in command of the army and defence. Born Wolf, he was an NKVD officer in Moscow and a former member of the International Brigades in Spain, as was Gero. The third was Joseph Revai, to whom the regime's Ministry of Culture and Propaganda was handed over.

It seems that the Hungarian population was well aware of the situation: "According to Jay Schulman, an American sociologist who studied the phenomenon, "the communist leaders were seen first and foremost as Jews by nearly 100% of the people surveyed". For example, a well-educated and well-trained engineer stresses that the Jews who introduced communism in Hungary were the ones who suffered the least and who shared the most interesting positions. Almost all permanent members of the Party and senior officers of the secret police are Jews[160]."

A book written by two Jewish journalists from Milan, *The Jews and Communism after the Holocaust*, published in 1995, confirmed this:

"In no other country in Eastern Europe did the Communist General Staff have such a large number of Jews[161]." In May 1945, they wrote,

---

[159] David Irving, *Insurrection, L'enfer d'une nation: Budapest 1956*, Albin Michel, 1981, p. 31.

[160] David Irving, *Insurrection, L'enfer d'une nation: Budapest 1956*, Albin Michel, 1981, p. 37.

[161] Gabriele Eschenazi, Gabriele Nissim, *Les juifs et le communisme après la Shoah*, 1995, Éd. De Paris, 2000, p 84

"of the 25 members of the central committee, 9 were Jews; the party secretariat consisted of eight people, half of whom were Jews: at the head of the security forces was Gabor Peter and his deputy Itstvan Timar, and a host of collaborators who were in their service. The chief of police was André Szebenyi, while Geza Revesz headed the army's purge control committee. The percentage of Jews in the propaganda sector was very high: they were present everywhere, from the editorialists of *Szabad Nep* (Free People), the party newspaper headed by Oszkar Betlen, to the state radio and the official press agencies." However, "the totalitarian steamroller made no ethnic distinctions. Both Hungarians of Jewish origin and non-Jewish Hungarians were crushed in the same way[162] ", the two authors asserted.

In his 2006 book *Budapest 56,* Victor Sebestyen described how Gabor Peter "was the most hated character in Hungary after Rasoki". "He had worked as a tailor's assistant before embracing a career devoted entirely to violence." He was "married to the beautiful and terrifying Jolan Simon, a KGB agent, Rakosi's personal secretary... They lived surrounded by servants in a luxurious villa on Rozsadomb (Rose Hill) which enjoyed a unique view over the Danube below." On the walls of his office, "a picture of him toasting with Stalin occupied a prominent place[163]."

David Irving revealed that his real name was Benjamin Auschpitz. He was responsible for the creation of the regime's all-powerful political police, the AVH (State Protection Authority), and its installation in the famous building 60 Andrassy Avenue in Budapest.

"Peter demands that the command of the AVH, from officer ranks upwards, be made up solely of Jews. Many were born in Hungary; most were trained by the MVD, Stalin's secret police... Almost every Hungarian family suffered from the actions of the hated AVH members, Irving wrote. The AVH knew no laws but its own. Everyone had heard of their methods. For example, rumours, probably well-founded, and also numerous prisoner accounts mention some cases in which a probe was inserted into the penis of the detainee and then punched out...

---

[162] Gabriele Eschenazi, Gabriele Nissim, *Les juifs et le communisme après la Shoah*, 1995, Éd. De Paris, 2000, p.92,93

[163] Victor Sebestyen, *Budapest 56, les douze jours qui ébranlèrent l'empire soviétique*, Calmann-Levy, 2006, p.62

Thousands of prisoners definitely went mad in the dungeons of the AVH".

A certain Janos Szabo, one of the leaders of the Hungarian insurrection "speaks unequivocally of "those damned Jews who run the whole organisation", i.e. the political police... The man was tortured: his fingernails pulled out, his upper and lower molars replaced by rudimentary prostheses".

The methods of this militia were undoubtedly worthy of those of the Bolshevik commissars of the USSR: "That torture was a common practice in the AVH premises is unfortunately a certainty,..." "What a marvellous place 60 Andrassy Avenue. What a wonderful place, 60 Andrassy Avenue: the Danube is not far away, it is very convenient when you want to make someone disappear". Indeed, the disappearance of the victims seems to have been carefully planned: "'The corpse crusher' of the AVH is mentioned in a number of interviews after the uprising[164] ", wrote David Irving.

The two Italian Jewish authors, Gabriele Eschenazi and Gabriele Nissim, were also forced to recognise this: "The presence of a Jewish leadership in power accentuated the misunderstanding that reigned between Jews and Hungarians after the Holocaust". The population "saw the presence of Jews at the top of power as the sign of a foreign will". They pointed out that in 1945, the Jewish bourgeoisie had preferred to support the communists rather than see the Hungarian "small landowners" party in power, which had won the first elections after the war and desperately defended private property:

"The Jewish bourgeoisie... felt more protected by a party which seemed to be the standard-bearer of the struggle against anti-Semitism than by that of the small proprietors. Those Jews, even if they were far removed from socialism, considered more trustworthy those who promised exemplary punishment for fascist criminals, than those who showed no enthusiasm in condemning Hungarians co-responsible for Nazi crimes[165]." In short, if we understand it correctly, the Jewish bourgeoisie

---

[164] David Irving, *Insurrection, L'enfer d'une nation: Budapest 1956*, Albin Michel, 1981, p. 40, 47, 48, 41.

[165] Gabriele Eschenazi, Gabriele Nissim, *Les juifs et le communisme après la Shoah*, 1995, Éd. De Paris, 2000, p.85,86

felt some "selective affinity" with the Jewish communists, beyond political divergences.

Jewish power in Hungary would eventually be overthrown, not by Stalin, but by the 1956 revolution. The two authors, Eschenazi and Nissim, immediately tried to explain that the Hungarian revolt had no anti-Semitic character. Ferenc Fetjó, a Jewish historian who prefaced their book, "the most eminent historian of the people's democracies", was surprised to note the "absence of any notable manifestations of anti-Semitism" during the 1956 Hungarian uprising. "The truth be told, the two authors acknowledged, there were some small incidents (anti-Semitic slogans written on the façades of some Jewish houses during the great popular demonstration of 23 October), but they were always isolated events[166]."

According to Eschenazi and Nissim, it turned out that, after Stalin's death in 1953, Khrushchev's de-Stalinisation policy had generated "an ideological crisis that led many leaders of Jewish origin to support the reform attempt". It remains true, however, that some Jews seem to have had a bad memory of the 1956 revolution.

The testimony of journalist Erno Lazarovitz, who became vice-president of the Jewish community after 1989, contradicted the above statements: "I will never forget the night of the 23rd. I was returning from the station and heard demonstrators chanting anti-Semitic slogans. I was moved. I had two children. From then on, I was terrified to go out on the streets. I wanted to leave the country. If I didn't, it was only because in the end the Russians arrived... How could I have explained to people that the Jews had nothing to do with "the gang of four[167] "?

It seems that the anti-Semitic incidents were not just isolated events. In fact, the Jews rightly feared Hungarian reprisals, but the Jews' great fear disappeared with the arrival of the Soviet soldiers. On 4 November Janos Kadar set up his new government. He ordered thousands of arrests, hundreds of death sentences and stifled anti-Semitism. "Anti-

---

[166] Gabriele Eschenazi, Gabriele Nissim, *Les juifs et le communisme après la Shoah*, 1995, Éd. De Paris, 2000, p. 111, 112

[167] This was the name given to the four communist leaders of Jewish origin: Rakosi, Gerö, Farkas and Revai.

Semitism was strictly forbidden [168] ", and order reigned again in Budapest.

David Irving is even more explicit about the anti-Semitism that erupted during the revolt. During the 1956 insurrection, he wrote, "the mostly Jewish heads of the AVH are evicted from their holes." AVH commander F. Toth "is rounded up in his house near Lenin Boulevard... The mob pounces on Toth and hangs his corpse from a tree on the boulevard. Another AVH officer is lynched nearby on Aradi Avenue; the ten thousand guilders in banknotes found in his pockets are stuffed into his mouth... An AVH colonel is lynched on Kalman-Mikszath Square and the thirty thousand guilders he was carrying are stuck in his chest[169]."

The *Paris-Match* correspondent Paul Mathias, who had managed to leave Budapest when Russian troops were about to invade Hungary, was invited by the President of the French Republic, René Coty, to be questioned about the situation in the country. The journalist reportedly explained: "The two million inhabitants of Budapest have simply lost their fear... They have become enraged. A whole city, a whole country has gone mad with exasperation". The common people were finally freeing themselves: "A huge bonfire was burning, burning literature and propaganda in a thick smoke[170]."

Let us note, however, that David Irving did not focus solely on this question: of the 521 pages of the French edition, the passages we have presented here are the only ones that are explicit enough to understand the anti-Semitism of the Hungarians at the time. However, if we look at the edition of the original text, we realise that the French version by the French publisher Albin Michel has been singularly watered down. The English version of 751 pages was indeed a little more abrasive. At the beginning of the book, when the Hungarian personalities were introduced, the English version systematically reported the Jewish identity of the main protagonists. Matias Rakosi, for example, was introduced in the English version as follows: "64 years old, Jew, head of the Hungarian émigrés in Moscow from 1940 to 1944, general

---

[168] Gabriele Eschenazi, Gabriele Nissim, *Les juifs et le communisme après la Shoah*, 1995, Éd. De Paris, 2000, p. 120, 128

[169] David Irving, *Insurrection, L'enfer d'une nation: Budapest 1956*, Albin Michel, 1981, p. 325, 326.

[170] David Irving, *Insurrection, L'enfer d'une nation: Budapest 1956*, Albin Michel, 1981, p. 22, 352.

secretary of the Hungarian Communist Party from 1944 to 1956; prime minister from 1947 to 1953". Of the 56 individuals presented, the Jewish identity, mentioned in the English version, has been deleted 28 times in the French version.

The description of the group of four managers was also more accurate in the English version (page 52): Ernest Gero was described as a man "black-haired, genial organiser, cool and aloof, a ball of energy". Michael Wolf, Rakosi's "sinister" defence minister after 1948, "had spent ten years structuring a youth movement in Czechoslovakia, later becoming an NKVD officer in Moscow, but he never lost his Slovak Jewish accent". The fourth man in the gang, journalist Joseph Revai, "became the dictator Rakosi's 'Dr Goebbels', his Minister of Propaganda". David Irving added: "The dominant position of Jews in the regime was the cause of the deep unease of the Hungarian people."

The Red terror was taking its toll on everyone, irrespective of the rank of the victims. Janos Kadar, for example, an irreproachable communist, was arrested in April 1951. He had taken the reins of the underground CP in 1942 and had been Minister of the Interior in 1948. The French edition said of him (p.65): "In prison, he was subjected to the cruelest tortures, no humiliation was spared him. He was not released until three years later." The English version (p.98) gave more details:

"He was tortured until he collapsed, and when he came to, Colonel Vladimir Farkas—the son of Rasoki's Jewish minister—was pissing on his face. When Kadar was released three years later, a CIA agent wrote in his report: 'the fingernails of his left hand have been pulled out. He was interrogated with unimaginable cruelty on the personal orders of M. Farkas".

In the original text, we find the testimonies of American researchers who questioned peasants in the Hungarian provinces, whose statements undoubtedly reflected the mood of a large part of the population. In Nyiracsad, for example, a small town of 6000 inhabitants ten kilometres from the Romanian border, we see how the communists never succeeded in extirpating Christianity. At the May Day demonstrations, "they stand on the sidelines, while the regime's officials and employees of the agricultural cooperative parade".

The Orthodox population never spoke openly about political issues, but after making sure that no one could overhear their conversation, the peasants revealed to the researchers: "When they returned to Hungary in 1945, they didn't have a penny," one peasant blurted out. Now, all the local officials are Jewish... The peasants in this village know perfectly well that they are the bosses of the communist regime[171]." The American journalists noted: "Here, the hatred of Jews is really terrible". Another peasant recounted how in 1948 the regime paid the Gypsies to repress the local population, seizing crops, livestock and anything else of value. It is enlightening how ethnic minorities can sometimes be useful in silencing the majorities. Obviously, these considerations do not seem to be to the liking of M. André Berelovitch, the French translator, who did a good job here for the sake of "concord".

On the fiftieth anniversary of the insurrection, several books published in French were available in bookshops. Victor Sebestyen's, quoted above, was translated from English by Johan-Frederik Hel Guedj. Although he informed us very briefly of the nationality of the four leaders, "who were all Jews", he implied above all that these Jews were communists: "Never short of ideas and witticisms, Rakosi, without fear of ridicule, became one of the most fervent anti-Semites in Hungary" (p.55). (p.55). Victor Sebastyen, as we see, is not afraid of ridicule either. The quoted sentences were the only ones that touched on the subject in the 406 pages of his book.

André Farkas' book *Budapest 1956, The Tragedy as I Saw and Lived It* (Tallander, 2006, 288 pages) did not contain a single mention of the role of the Jews in post-war Hungary. François Fetjö's *1956, Budapest, the Insurrection* (Complexe Publishing House, 2005) did not contain a single line about this painful subject either.

Henri-Christian Giraud's book, *A History of the Hungarian Revolution* (Le Rocher, 2006), demonstrated perfectly how the Goy learn to respect the perimeter of freedom of expression, without this preventing them from occasionally criticising "intellectual terrorism".

After the bloody crushing of the Hungarian insurrection, the number of Jewish leaders was limited. "The strict limitation of the number of Jews at the top did not have the effect of "Aryanising" the party, as was the case in Poland in 1968 with Gomulka, wrote Gabriele Eschenazi. Kadar continued to employ managers of Jewish origin in the press, television and the various economic sectors, and to place them in key positions within the state administration", so that it could be said that "under communism, the best time for the Jews was the one during which Kadar exercised power".

---

[171] David Irving, page 156 of the English version

Anti-Semitism was forbidden, and "the fact that there were no longer any managers of Jewish origin at the top of the Party prevented the population from identifying them with power...". By occupying leading positions in the mass media, scientific institutions and the economic world, a large number of Hungarians of Jewish origin acquired important professional prestige. Most of the time, according to Gabriele Eschenazi, they were the first to become involved in the reform movements and to take an interest in the modernisation projects authorised by the Kadar regime. This is why they were considered the most open, the most modern and the most 'Western' technical and economic leaders".

In 1967, when the Six-Day War broke out in the Middle East, the Hungarian government aligned itself with the other communist countries, breaking off diplomatic relations with Israel. But any anti-Semitic campaign was banned, and 'Kadar, under the guise of official "anti-Zionism", allowed the few Jews who wished to travel freely to Israel[172].'"

A survey conducted between 1983 and 1988 showed that Hungarian Jews had "never fully integrated": "Of the 109 people questioned, only 43 fully accepted their origin; 20 concealed it completely, while 46 preferred to evaluate the situation before deciding whether or not to disclose it. However, among their parents, who were Holocaust survivors, 63% categorically denied their Jewish identity and tried hard to convince their children to do the same[173]."

Thus, although the number of Jews at the top of power had been voluntarily limited, there could still be hidden Jews, as Gabriele Eschenazi recounted: "The story of Aczel, the Minister of Culture, whose views were highly respected by Kadar, is the most extreme but also the most emblematic example of the existential concerns that Hungarians of Jewish origin had". He had been in his youth a "courageous militant Zionist of the Hashomer Hatzair... When, under Kadar's reign, he was suddenly propelled to the pinnacle of power, he did everything he could to conceal his identity and, above all, his

---

[172] Gabriele Eschenazi, Gabriele Nissim, *Les juifs et le communisme après la Shoah*, 1995, Éd. De Paris, 2000, p. 127-131

[173] Andras Kovacs, *Identity and Ethnicity*, p. 4 (manuscript). Gabriele Eschenazi, Gabriele Nissim, *Les juifs et le communisme après la Shoah*, 1995, Éd. De Paris, 2000, p. 131-133.

Zionist past. Vasarhelyi recalls: "In his life as a high communist dignitary, his past was a terrible burden. He wanted at all costs to present himself with 'the moustaches of a real Hungarian'. In his youth he had been an actor, but he still acted, pretending not to have Jewish origins[174]."

With the collapse of communism in 1989, Jews were once again gripped by fears. The "spectre of anti-Semitism" returned. Listen for example to Istvan Csurka, playwright and vice-president of the Democratic Forum: "Why don't the Jews admit that they have been in power in the times of Bela Kun and that they were also in power when they returned with the Russians? Why don't they recognise their responsibilities?"

Once again, as we see, the Jews were to serve as scapegoats. "In this way, Eschenazi and Nissim wrote without laughing, they could lay the collective guilt on the Jews and whitewash the rest of society. The Jews are called upon to take over the process of moral reconversion that the country itself is unable to carry out".

Istvan Csurka seemed rather to designate a scapegoat: "The capitalist he publicly points to as a symbol of the new Jewish careerism is George Soros, the Hungarian-born American financier who, during the last years of Kadar's reign, helped and financed the birth of an independent culture".

It is true that in Budapest, the Soros Foundation had awarded scholarships worth several million dollars to Hungarian intellectuals "in order to enable them to study and undertake research without being hindered by the totalitarian power". In such a case, how could one reproach this generous and patriotic Hungarian millionaire? Csurka, "who started a political campaign against Soros, actually accuses him of helping the former Jewish nomenklatura to convert to capitalism[175]." To this Istvan Csurka, who saw Jews behind both communism and liberalism, the two Italian writers replied, feigning incomprehension: "How is it possible to make Jews the symbol of two antithetical ideologies, of two opposing political systems?"

---

[174] Gabriele Eschenazi, Gabriele Nissim, *Les juifs et le communisme après la Shoah*, 1995, Éd. De Paris, 2000, p. 136

[175] Gabriele Eschenazi, Gabriele Nissim, *Les juifs et le communisme après la Shoah*, 1995, Éd. De Paris, 2000, p. 145, 147, 150

The answer is however very simple: it is a question of finding a new formula for building this world without borders, this new "kingdom of David", in which the people of Israel will finally be recognised by all as the people of God.

## *Poland, freed from its "ghosts"*

There, too, Jews had returned in the wake of the Red Army. "Never in the history of Poland had Jews held such important political positions, Eschenazi acknowledged. The new regime employed leaders of Jewish origin in strategic sectors, such as the army, security and the party apparatus, because the Russians trusted them more than the Poles[176]."

The Polish Communist Party was nevertheless trying to present itself to the public as a truly national party. The task was not easy. As Berman, the regime's "number two", explained: "Like Bierut, I had opposed the fact that there were too many Jews at the top of power. I saw this as a necessary evil to which we had been driven at the time of the seizure of power[177]." It was therefore necessary to "ask the communist Jews to become Poles". To this end, the Party issued a decree allowing Jews to change their surname "with extreme ease". "If they were "proper", they could come into contact with the population, otherwise they were given tasks for which contacts were limited; if they had a very marked physique, they were relegated to the background in the section of political work, among Jews." To enter the administration, "not only were they required to change their Jewish surname to a typical Polish one and to speak with a perfect Polish accent, but they also had to redo the identity papers of their whole family. For everyone, this was a cover-up operation designed to conceal the foreign and Jewish character of the new power. Thus, Eschenazi lamented, the Jews, even if they had Polish surnames and were perfectly integrated, became the most suspicious individuals for the rest of the population[178]."

---

[176] Gabriele Eschenazi, Gabriele Nissim, *Les juifs et le communisme après la Shoah*, 1995, Éd. De Paris, 2000, p. 199

[177] Gabriele Eschenazi, Gabriele Nissim, *Les juifs et le communisme après la Shoah*, 1995, Éd. De Paris, 2000, p.222-227

[178] Gabriele Eschenazi, Gabriele Nissim, *Les juifs et le communisme après la Shoah*, 1995, Éd. De Paris, 2000, p. 218, 219, 199

Nevertheless, they were very well integrated, especially in the ministries. We can also read this in Alain Brossat's book, through the testimony of a certain Adam Paszt: "We knew that the population was anti-Semitic, so we tried to conceal the fact that there were Jews in the higher positions... We advised the Jews who had responsibilities to change their surname. We would "promote" those who were blond, who had a "good face"—that's how we put it—those who spoke the language well. The others were not allowed to occupy positions of responsibility or representative functions[179]."

Hilary Minc, one of the leaders of the new regime, was easily identifiable: "Several Jewish communists who were in Russia waiting to return home with the Polish army were locked up for several days in a hovel. As they began to lose patience, they asked to speak to Minc to find out what was to become of them. He openly told them that if they wanted to return to Poland, they would have to change their surnames and hide their origins, otherwise they would generate anti-communism disguised as anti-Semitism. One of them, who had been enraged by this explanation, took out a mirror and told him to look in it, for with the face he had, it would be impossible for him to fool anyone".

The charade did not really seem to fool anyone, neither the Jews nor the Poles. Szapiro recalled how he and other Jews felt during that period: "I was reassured to see that the Zionist Sommerstein was in the Ministry of Education. For most Jews, the presence of Jews at the top of the state was a kind of guarantee against anti-Semitism, or at least proof that there would be no official anti-Semitism[180]."

Alain Brossat also quoted the testimony of Bronia Zelmanovicz: "One day, when my daughter Ilana was still small, I left her in her cot to go shopping—to queue to buy meat. Some people came and cut in line. I protested and they replied: "You wanted it, this regime, didn't you?" They had seen in my face that I was Jewish. For them, the familiar "Judeo-communism" equation worked perfectly[181]."

---

[179] Alain Brossat, Sylvia Klingberg, *Le yiddishland revolutionnaire*, Balland, 1983, p. 329.

[180] Gabriele Eschenazi, Gabriele Nissim, *Les juifs et le communisme après la Shoah*, 1995, Éd. De Paris, 2000, p.231

[181] Alain Brossat, Sylvia Klingberg, *Le yiddishland revolutionnaire*, Balland, 1983, p.337.

Eschenazi and Nassim's book is full of contradictions and paradoxes, but at least it has the merit of highlighting a certain Talmudic spirit. By putting the facts back in order, the authors' analysis takes a surprising turn. Eschenazi and Nissim explain that this situation actually concealed an identity drama: "Between the two wars, many had embraced communism in order to get out of the ghetto, to free themselves from the burden of orthodox tradition... For them, modernity was to be found outside the shtetl. After the war, however, communism became, beyond any ideological motivation, an obligation. Most of those who joined the Party... did so not out of a desire for a career, but rather out of a kind of desperation... Faced with the necessity of living, they committed themselves reluctantly to the path of communism... They signed a moral contract with communism for the simple reason that they wanted to live. And in order to live in Poland, one had to be a member of the Party[182]." We have to understand, then, that it was a great pain for them to end up working in the ministries.

It was therefore also with great desperation that the Jews became massively involved in the terrible security apparatus of the Polish state: "The section in which the Jews were most confused with the communist power was very special, because it was the security apparatus," acknowledged Gabriele Eschenazi. The *Służba Bezpieczeństwa, the* Security Service (SB), "controlled practically the whole of civil society. Its officials read private mail, conducted searches and raids, and censored newspapers".

The presence of many Jews in the repressive system certainly helped to fuel anti-Semitism: "The Party's mistake was to employ Jews in such a sensitive section, with the risk of further arousing the hostility of the people towards the government. What is certain is that "the Poles believed that the Security Service was entirely run by Jews."

During the Stalinist years, "a relatively large number of Jews" held high positions in the secret police: "Some did so out of idealism, others because they fervently desired revenge". For example, "Colonel Iosef Swiatlo, who had fled to Berlin in September 1953 under obscure circumstances: "He was a Polish Jewish petty criminal who thought only of enriching himself and taking revenge for everything, for his

---

[182] Gabriele Eschenazi, Gabriele Nissim, *Les juifs et le communisme après la Shoah*, 1995, Éd. De Paris, 2000, p.217, 219

origins and even for his poverty. He was the master of the fate of thousands of people. It was a horrible thing"[183]."

Khrushchev, who was leading the de-Stalinisation of the USSR, was in favour of the purge of the Jewish leadership. In 1955, during the sessions of the 20th congress, the sudden death in Moscow of Beirut, the secretary of the Polish Communist Party, came as a bombshell. Rumours circulated that he had died in dubious circumstances. Berman and Radkiewicz found themselves out of the government and out of the Party's Political Bureau. A popular uprising took place in Poznan in June 1956, which saw an angry mob storm the various Party headquarters and take over the city for two days. The repression claimed 75 victims. Right after this, in July, Deputy Prime Minister Zenon Nowak, during the Central Committee meeting, put forward a proposal, "after having carefully clarified that he was not an anti-Semite: 'The Jews alienate the people from the Party and the Soviet Union... It is therefore the duty of the Party to ensure that Poles, and not Jews, occupy the most important posts".

Under pressure from the people, Gomuka was elected party secretary, and the Stalinist Jews were eliminated: "The year 1956 was marked by the disappearance of the Stalinist Jews from the political scene. The powerful Berman was excluded from the political bureau, as was the Minister of Economics, Minc, and soon after, the army chief, Zambrowski. At the time, however, the purge was not particularly anti-Semitic in character: it targeted both Jews and non-Jews. Kersten noted that: "Berman, Minc, and other personalities working in the Security ministries were removed from their functions not so much because they were Jews, but because they were considered Stalinists, conservatives and dogmatists[184]."

All in all, "1956 was a truly traumatic year" for this generation of Jewish communists. "They had opted for the USSR full of messianic hopes, and suddenly Khrushchev's revelations at the 20th Congress called everything into question". It was thus a new drama in Jewish history: "As soon as the new Gomulka regime reopened the borders to appear liberal, fifty thousand Jews had already packed their bags" and

---

[183] Gabriele Eschenazi, Gabriele Nissim, *Les juifs et le communisme après la Shoah*, 1995, Éd. De Paris, 2000, p. 222-227

[184] Gabriele Eschenazi, Gabriele Nissim, *Les juifs et le communisme après la Shoah*, 1995, Éd. De Paris, 2000, p. 251, 253

left the country. One wonders what they were afraid of to flee like that: had they not, after all, become true Poles, "perfectly integrated", as Eschenazi and Nissim repeated in their book?

"Now that communism seemed to be collapsing, they harboured a feeling of emptiness. They no longer had an identity and they felt threatened... The news from the Soviet Union added to the prospect of being once again, as Jews, the scapegoats of a tottering regime, which further increased their unease... They had entered the Party and the police full of hope, but suddenly everything collapsed. They felt defeated[185]."

After the war, many had already preferred to leave the country because of tensions with the Poles. Of the 350,000 Jews living in Poland after the war, the vast majority were returning from the Soviet Union; 250,000 had left for Israel or Western Europe. In February 1947, Poland closed its borders, although it was still possible to obtain visas to travel to Israel[186].

After the 1956 exodus, the Polish Jewish community numbered no more than thirty thousand people. "Those who had remained constituted the hard core of assimilated Jews. Despite everything, they still felt completely Polish, wrote Gabriele Eschenazi without a hint of irony. Many were Gomulka's supporters" and "would participate in the new attempt at communist reform with the same enthusiasm as in the past[187]." They could therefore start afresh on a new basis, on new "hopes".

Unfortunately, another drama unfolded. The Six-Day War between Israel and the Arab countries inaugurated the anti-Semitic campaign in a big way. For the Polish press, from the day the fighting began on 5 June 1967, every assimilated Jew was considered a potential Zionist:

"Purges were carried out in all institutions that harboured Jews and in which there could be any nesting of opposition to the regime. Naturally, cultural circles, newspapers, cinema and universities that had shown signs of intellectual anti-conformism were targeted first. In addition, it

---

[185] Gabriele Eschenazi, Gabriele Nissim, *Les juifs et le communisme après la Shoah*, 1995, Éd. De Paris, 2000, p.254-258

[186] Gabriele Eschenazi, Gabriele Nissim, *Les juifs et le communisme après la Shoah*, 1995, Éd. De Paris, 2000, p. 205, 212

[187] Gabriele Eschenazi, Gabriele Nissim, *Les juifs et le communisme après la Shoah*, 1995, Éd. De Paris, 2000, p. 258

was made clear that, within the police and the army, power belonged to the "real" Poles. The Jews, who had been fully integrated the day before, were "evicted" one by one as if they were "moles" of a criminal organisation operating in the shadows. A special "security" commission drew up a list of Jews to be investigated. However, the top positions were particularly targeted. From the second half of 1967 until the end of 1969, 341 officers of Jewish origin were dismissed from the army and expelled from the party. In Warsaw alone, between March and May 1968, more than 500 managers were dismissed; of these, 365 worked in ministries, 49 in academic institutions, 21 in press agencies and 39 in various services. There were also four ministers, fourteen under-secretaries, seven directors-general and fifty-one department directors. In October, 2100 people were expelled from the Party. The hunt for the "Zionist" was particularly fierce in the schools and universities, where Gomulka wanted to deal a mortal blow to the rebellion of the youth. Dozens of academics and university professors lost their posts. To replace these "enemies of Poland", 576 new professors were quickly promoted. The 1600 or so students who were expelled from the universities were banned forever and could not resume their studies in Poland. Accused of being Zionists, hundreds of Jews were immediately dismissed and found themselves overnight without a home, without medical care, without friends… The 'enemies of the people' were publicly reproached and pilloried[188]."

The despair of the Jews was further deepened by the fact that, lest we forget, "most of them felt fully assimilated: they spoke Polish, had completely forgotten Yiddish, did not go to synagogue, did not practise Jewish religious rites and had brought up their children according to Polish educational principles, wrote Eschenazi… And yet these former Jews were suddenly accused of being Zionists and of being part of a fifth column of the 'enemies of Poland'[189]."

It was thus a "cold shower" for all those assimilated Jews who "had believed that the party would allow them to feel totally Polish and forget about the hostility around them. But suddenly, the Party around which they had built their lives was turning against them. Everything collapsed.

---

[188] Gabriele Eschenazi, Gabriele Nissim, *Les juifs et le communisme après la Shoah*, 1995, Éd. De Paris, 2000, p.276

[189] Gabriele Eschenazi, Gabriele Nissim, *Les juifs et le communisme après la Shoah*, 1995, Éd. De Paris, 2000, p.260

We have, for example, the case of a certain Szchter Michnick, one of those "perfectly assimilated" Jews: "For fifty years he had been a communist intellectual, as well as the editor of Karl Marx's works. He carried out research on Lenin's "mistake" that had opened the door to the degeneration of socialism. In 1968, after having concealed his origins all his life, he suddenly remembered that he came from a Jewish family and had been educated to be a rabbi. From one day to the next, he became a fervent Zionist. He wanted his son to settle in Israel to contribute to the defence of the Jewish state[190]."

The Jews, once again, had been "designated as the enemies", the "scapegoat", on whom the party had "laid the responsibility for its own shortcomings". Their helplessness was so great that approximately twenty thousand Jews left the country for Switzerland, Denmark or the United States. Few, at the time, left for Israel. Worst of all, Eschenazi explained, was that "the great majority of the population was indifferent to the fate of the Jews... The moral loneliness in which the Poles left the Jews was very hard to bear... In 1968, the intellectuals as well as the Polish Church were content to observe the events without taking sides against the anti-Semitic campaign. The undisputed head of the Polish Church, Cardinal Wszynski, who was internationally recognised as the representative of the bastion of anti-communist resistance, did not bother to intervene[191]."

On the other hand, why would the Church have intervened on behalf of people who had not stopped persecuting it? The reality—and it is a terrible thing to say—was that the Poles were most likely happy about the situation. The result was that "after 1968, the Jews who remained in Poland were very few, no more than three or four thousand". How were the Poles to cope now?

After the collapse of the communist bloc, the 1991 presidential campaign was conducted in a confused atmosphere. Lech Walesa, the former trade union leader, was running against the liberal Catholic Prime Minister Tadeusz Mazowiecki: "Soon strange rumours began to circulate about the latter. Important personalities did not state it explicitly, but everyone thought it: Mazowiecki was a Jew in disguise.

---

[190] Gabriele Eschenazi, Gabriele Nissim, *Les juifs et le communisme après la Shoah*, 1995, Éd. De Paris, 2000, p.282

[191] Gabriele Eschenazi, Gabriele Nissim, *Les juifs et le communisme après la Shoah*, 1995, Éd. De Paris, 2000, p.260, 278-280

At first, his collaborators of Jewish origin had sowed doubts, but then he too was accused of being a 'Jew disguised as a Catholic'".

Anti-Semitism was thus unfortunately still very virulent in Poland. There is only one solution to this kind of issue, Gabriele Eschenazi recommended: "It is likely that such episodes will be repeated in the years to come, and this will happen as long as anti-Semitism is not declared illegitimate. If this must be done, it is not to satisfy the Jews, or to show solidarity with them, but because of the Poles' own need to get rid of their ghosts[192]."

## *Liberated Romania*

In Romania, too, Jewish leaders played an important role in the establishment of communism after the Second World War[193]. Eschenazi and Nissim's book presented the eloquent testimony of a certain Lya Benjamin, a Jew who was also a fervent communist:

"During the war, in the years of the underground, most of the Communist leaders were Jews; after 23 August 1944, the Jews rejoiced at the arrival of the Soviet Communists and many wished to become part of the new regime. Because of their ardent anti-fascism, the *Securitate* secret services regarded them as trustworthy elements, so they took in large numbers of them. Idealism led these Jews to communism. They believed so much in that ideal that they turned out to be more fanatical than their Romanian comrades, who had often joined the Party only out of opportunism. Surely many Jews were motivated by the desire to take revenge, not only on fascism, but also on the Romanians. After so long having been cut off from society, they felt that the time had come for them to play a new role... The Jews harboured great hopes for a possible new life in their country... "And it will come as no surprise to learn that this witness was a "perfectly

---

[192] Gabriele Eschenazi, Gabriele Nissim, *Les juifs et le communisme après la Shoah*, 1995, Éd. De Paris, 2000, p.289, 287

[193] The inter-war period has been studied by Lucien Rebatet. One can read his articles in the weekly *Je Suis Partout* of 15 April 1938, and those published between 23 September and 28 October 1938, devoted to Romania and the Iron Guard. These articles were reprinted in a book entitled *Les Juifs et l'antisemitisme*, published in 2002.

integrated" person: "I didn't feel very Jewish: I had been brought up in such a way that I felt Romanian[194]."

Incidentally, it is precisely for that reason that she married a Zionist Jew, which, on reflection, is very consistent.

Many Jews changed their names to prevent anti-Semitism in the population from growing. Alain Brossat's book presented us with the testimony of Pierre Sherf: The Party, he said, "feared that the resentment of the population would grow because of the large number of Jews within the Party leadership; like many others, I had to "Romanise" my surname; I was no longer called Pierre Sherf, but Petre Sutchu[195]."

Just as in Hungary, where the great Marxist ideologist was George Lukacs, and whose renown went far beyond the borders of the country, the great official Romanian thinker was another Jew: "Salomon Catz who, under the name of Constantine Dobrogeanu-Gherea, became the greatest Romanian Marxist ideologist".

The new leaders of Romania were the so-called "Muscovites", i.e. the Romanians who left the Russian capital and entered in September 1944 in the vans of the Red Army. Their leader was the daughter of an Orthodox Jew, Ana Pauker. She belonged to the leading "troika" together with Georghiu Dej, the head of the Party, and Vasile Luca. In Moscow, Ana Pauker worked for Soviet propaganda and was a teacher at the Komintern. Marcel Pauker, her husband, whom she had met in Switzerland, came from a secular Jewish family. He had been one of the founders of the communist movement and a high official in the Komintern. He was a victim of the purges and liquidated in Moscow in August 1938. She had been imprisoned in Romania since 1936 for being a member of an outlawed party. In 1941, she was released from prison thanks to a prisoner exchange agreement and returned to Moscow, where she remained for the duration of the war. During her stay in the USSR, she searched in vain for information about the whereabouts of her husband, whose fate she did not know. But nothing

---

[194] Gabriele Eschenazi, Gabriele Nissim, *Les juifs et le communisme après la Shoah*, 1995, Éd. De Paris, 2000, p.419

[195] Alain Brossat, Sylvia Klingberg, *Le yiddishland revolutionnaire*, Balland, 1983, p. 340.

could shake Ana Paulker's blind faith in communism. She returned to Romania in September 1944 to take part in the communist takeover.

Gabriele Nissim provided the testimony of Tatiana Pauker, Ana Pauker's daughter, whom he questioned in 1991 in Bucharest: "Ana's father was an orthodox Jew with a very rigid religious culture. His name was Rabinson... She was very close to her family. She had excellent relations with her brother Enea (or Zalman, his Hebrew name) who was an observant Jew. She had a sincere affection and great respect for him... He never concealed his identity. When asked if she was Jewish, she never denied it. She had kept her husband's surname, but at the same time she wanted to be considered a Romanian. Unlike many Jews who, after becoming communists, preferred to avoid contact with other Jews so as not to be accused of favouritism towards the community, she surrounded herself with Jews in her foreign ministry... This shows that my mother had no complexes about being Jewish and that she felt free to surround herself with Jewish friends and collaborators. In public, she never refused to perform symbolic acts that might betray her origins. At her mother's funeral, she followed Jewish tradition, and at the cemetery, she tore her clothes to stop the cycle of death. I also remember the day when, after his dismissal in 1952, we went to the Jewish theatre in Bucharest. The shows were performed in Yiddish, and we had to wear headphones for instant translation, but she, who understood Yiddish, refused them. It was an almost symbolic gesture[196]."

Anne Pauker was a convinced atheist: "Communism had enabled her to overcome Judaism". This is probably also what motivated her to try to stifle Christianity and persecute the Orthodox clergy. "She was the Party's ideological commissar on Stalin's behalf, and it was she who sponsored the first political trials from 1947 to 1949. In 1950–1952, she supported Stalin's "death canal" project, the construction of which forced thousands of prisoners to work in inhumane conditions to build a canal connecting the Danube to the Black Sea. It was a veritable gulag in which 120,000 people perished in two years[197]."

---

[196] Gabriele Eschenazi, Gabriele Nissim, *Les juifs et le communisme après la Shoah*, 1995, Éd. De Paris, 2000, p.444

[197] Gabriele Eschenazi, Gabriele Nissim, *Les juifs et le communisme après la Shoah*, 1995, Paris, 2000, p. 442. De Paris, 2000, p.442. The exact phrase is: "120 000 people, including many Jews, perished". This statement would certainly merit careful study.

To enhance Gabriele Nassim's rather bland analysis, let us recall here this passage from Stéphane Courtois' book, *"History and Memory of Communism in Europe"*, which mentions the case of Colonel Nicolski, famous for his cruelty: "whose real name was Boris Grünberg, KGB agent in Romania, deputy director of the sinister *Securitate* since 1948—the political police—personally responsible for thousands of murders and inventor of the terrifying "re-education" experiment of the Pitesti prison. Nicolski died peacefully in his splendid villa in Bucharest on 16 April 1992[198]."

In Romania, as in Czechoslovakia, the first political purges began in 1949. Dozens of Jewish leaders were arrested. Faced with the offensive by Georghiu Dej, the party secretary, Ana Pauker had the same reaction as Slansky and the other Jewish communists on trial in Prague: she believed that Stalin would not betray her. She went to Moscow to defend herself and to accuse Dej, but the Kremlin's doors remained closed. During a meeting with Dej in 1951, Stalin allegedly asked her for an "iron hand" against the agents of Titoism and Zionism. Vasile Luca, the Minister of Finance, and Teohari Georgescu, the Minister of the Interior, were dismissed in May 1952. This repression also affected many Jewish managers in the lower echelons.

Anna Pauker, Minister of Foreign Affairs, was dismissed in July 1952, excluded from the Party in September, arrested in February 1953, and finally released a few weeks later after Stalin's death. She had been accused of numerous misdeeds, notably "having had contacts with foreign secret services through Israel, where her father lived, and having deposited money in Switzerland". However, she was never explicitly branded a Zionist and, unlike in Czechoslovakia, there was no immediate purge of the Jews at the top of the Party. Proof of this was that in Pauker's place in the foreign ministry, Dej appointed another Jew: Simon Bughici.

After Anne Pauker had been eliminated, Dej undertook a silent purge of Jews from public life, first excluding them from the press and the university professoriate. The army, security and judiciary were barred from access to Jews, although the exclusion was gradual. No anti-Jewish campaign was launched from Bucharest, let alone with the scope and international resonance of the Prague campaign. In 1957, the last

---

[198] *Du Passé faisons table rase, Histoire et mémoire du communisme en Europe*, collective work, edited by Stéphane Courtois, Ed. Robert Laffont, 2002, p.49.

Jew still present in the Politburo, Chishinevsky, was dismissed. "The accusations against the Jews were not of an anti-Semitic character, there was no talk of Zionism but rather of ideological deviationism and petty-bourgeois and anarchist tendencies."[199]." Only a few Jews continued to occupy any key posts, but they were neither in the Politburo nor in the Party Secretariat. Dej had almost completely eliminated them from the Party.

Ceausescu, his successor, also facilitated the departure of Jews from Romania, to such good effect that between 1961 and 1975, 150,000 Romanian Jews emigrated to the State of Israel. "Among them were many former ministers and important party officials. Ceausescu let them leave in return for Israel's payment of between $2,000 and $8,000 per individual". By 1975, there were only 60,000 Jews left in the country, the equivalent of 15% of the post-war population[200]."

The "selling" of Jews to the Hebrew state was a common arrangement to which the community had been accustomed since ancient times: "In the Middle Ages, Eschenazi explained, Jews had always bargained for their lives. The great rabbis always offered money to the powerful... In feudal Germany, when Jews were expelled from a duchy, they would turn to another nobleman and offer him money so that he would agree to take them in. They would stay until the duke became anti-Semitic and then emigrate again[201]." It was thus that Rabbi Moses Rosen, Ceausescu's emissary, was able to negotiate the departure of tens of thousands of his people.

But unlike the other communist countries, Romania did not have a hostile foreign policy towards Israel. It did not break off relations with Israel after the Six-Day War, as the USSR and its satellites did, and established economic and military relations with the Jewish state. These privileged relations between Romania and Israel were celebrated with Golda Meir's visit to Bucharest in May 1972. Similarly, in August 1987,

---

[199] Gabriele Eschenazi, Gabriele Nissim, *Les juifs et le communisme après la Shoah*, 1995, Éd. De Paris, 2000, pp.436-438.

[200] Gabriele Eschenazi, Gabriele Nissim, *Les juifs et le communisme après la Shoah*, 1995, Éd. De Paris, 2000, p. 460

[201] Gabriele Eschenazi, Gabriele Nissim, *Les juifs et le communisme après la Shoah*, 1995, Éd. De Paris, 2000, p. 471

Prime Minister Yitzhak Shamir and Rabbi Rosen stood side by side in the Bucharest synagogue to applaud Ceausescu.

The fall of the dictator in December 1989 was for the Western media the opportunity for large-scale manipulation. The Timisoara massacre had claimed the lives of 90,000 victims. Ceausescu was summarily executed, and a pro-Western regime was installed. Investigators eventually discovered that the number of victims in Timisoara was 96, almost a thousand times less than originally claimed.

In 2000, there were only 9,000 Jews out of Romania's 23 million inhabitants. But as in Poland, Gabriele Nissim explained that there was "anti-Semitism without Jews". Despite the fall of the communist regime, some members of the chosen people returned to leadership positions: "Petre Roman, whose Jewish origins were distant (on his grandfather's side), had been a leader of the 1989 revolution and of the National Salvation Front, as well as Prime Minister between 1990 and 1991[202]". Brucan, "a communist Jew from the beginning" and who had been part of the opposition in the last years of the Ceausescu regime, became the target of numerous attacks from May 1990 onwards. The kind of slogans that could be heard at protest demonstrations were: "Roman and Brucan in Palestine!" Apparently, the Jews had not left good memories in the population...

## Lustration in Czechoslovakia

From the creation of the Czechoslovak Republic in 1918, Tomas Mazaryk, its founding father, ensured that any hint of anti-Semitism was immediately quashed. At the time, there were 360,000 Jews on the census, or 2.5% of the population, two-thirds of whom lived in Slovakia and in Rutena subcarpathia in the east of the country. The war had encouraged some rapprochement: In London, Czech resistance leaders had been in permanent contact with the Jewish Agency, so that when the Jewish state was proclaimed, Czechoslovakia was the first country to immediately request the establishment of official diplomatic relations. The weapons used by Israeli soldiers to conquer Palestine were of Czechoslovakian manufacture, and the Israeli air force had been

---

[202] Gabriele Eschenazi, Gabriele Nissim, *Les juifs et le communisme après la Shoah*, 1995, Éd. De Paris, 2000, p.487

founded on Czech territory. The communist coup d'état in February 1948 did not alter the friendly relations between the two states.

1948 also saw the withdrawal of Tito's Yugoslavia and the first anti-Semitic purges in the USSR. In September 1949, the first show trial took place in the Hungarian capital, at the direct request of Moscow: Laszlo Rajk, the former Interior Minister, had been accused of being a Tito spy acting in the service of the USA. In Czechoslovakia, the main communist leaders were arrested, as well as hundreds of senior state and Party officials and army and security service officers. Thousands of second-rank communists were sentenced to long terms of detention following expeditious prosecutions. They were accused of espionage, sabotage, bourgeois nationalism and Zionist crimes. "Almost all the Slovak communist leaders... were found guilty of" bourgeois nationalism", wrote Nissim. It was another way of saying that they were Jews, behind their Slovak surnames. Such was the fate, for example, of the powerful head of the secret police: Karel Svab [203]." Numerous journalists, administrators and officials were revoked and removed from society.

The trial of Party General Secretary Rudolf Slansky in 1952 had international repercussions. Of the fourteen defendants, eleven were Jewish, and all were accused of having participated in a worldwide Jewish conspiracy. Slansky had also been accused of allowing "capitalists" to leave the country with large amounts of gold, silver and jewellery[204].

Unlike Janos Kadar in Hungary, Klement Gottwald decided to give the Czechoslovak communist party an anti-Semitic twist that was to continue after Stalin's death. During the trial, the Jewishness of the defendants was continually alluded to. The prosecutor, journalists and even the defendants themselves took pleasure during their "confessions" in recalling their origins, citing their former surnames if they had changed them.

However, Gabriele Nissim tried to explain that they were good Czechoslovaks, "perfectly integrated", because as loyal communists they had opposed Zionism, Jewish nationalism and the Jewish religion:

---

[203] Gabriele Eschenazi, Gabriele Nissim, *Les juifs et le communisme après la Shoah*, 1995, Éd. De Paris, 2000, p.534, 548

[204] Gabriele Eschenazi, Gabriele Nissim, *Les juifs et le communisme après la Shoah*, 1995, Éd. De Paris, 2000, p.550, 551

"Communist Jews put aside their Jewish identity in order to show that communism was an overcoming of Judaism".

Here is the testimony of Eduard Goldstücker, the chairman of the Writers' Union: "The Jewish Communists were convinced that they were part of a great movement, of a great human community, not Jewish, not other than Human. They had the feeling of participating in the attempt to build a state, a society founded on brotherhood and equality among all men. It was a kind of religion that replaced the Jewish religion, a religion that was, shall we say, humanist[205]."

Comrade Slansky defended himself by arguing that his pro-Israeli policies were directed against British colonialism. "He married a woman who was not Jewish, and did not pass on any Jewish consciousness to his children, explained one witness. Today, his son does not deny his Jewish ancestry, but he does not feel Jewish... "However, on the following page, Gabriele Nissim presented the testimony of Pavel Bergman: "His daughter Marta Slanska told me that she had always thought that her father had encouraged emigration to Israel because he wanted to help his people". These contradictions and paradoxes are very frequent in the books of Jewish intellectuals, who almost always put forward the same arguments to explain their disappointments: "Stalin and his allies were looking for scapegoats for the sole purpose of foisting the failures of the regime on them".

After the outbreak of the Six-Day War in June 1967, the Novotny regime launched the most intense and violent anti-Israeli and anti-Zionist campaign of any country in Eastern Europe. Czechoslovakia was the first communist state after the Soviet Union to break diplomatic relations with Israel, and the first to send a large political and military delegation to Egypt and Syria.

1968 was the year of the Prague Spring. The revolt was crushed by Warsaw Pact troops. Of the 18,000 Jews who remained, some 6,000 left the country between 1968 and 1970. After the fall of the Berlin Wall, Vaclav Havel, leader of the Prague Spring, became prime minister of the new Czech Republic, giving full democratic guarantees to the Western world. Gabriele Nissim wrote naively: "As had already happened in many other Eastern European countries, the international

---

[205] Gabriele Eschenazi, Gabriele Nissim, *Les juifs et le communisme après la Shoah*, 1995, Éd. De Paris, 2000, p. 542, 543

credibility of the new democratic regime depended on its attitude towards the Jewish question[206]."

## East Germany

In East Germany, created in the autumn of 1949, the same script unfolded as in the other satellite countries of the USSR. Jews "immediately occupied important positions within the Party... In fact, they had the feeling of returning to Germany as victors[207]." The new constitution explicitly condemned anti-Semitism, but the idyll between Jews and Communists did not last long. "One of the first to be investigated was the first Jewish Minister of Propaganda and Information, Gerhart Eisler. In July 1950, he was excluded from the Central Committee and accused the following year of having been disloyal to Stalin because he had criticised his policies in 1927 and 1928. Despite much criticism, Eisler managed to keep his position in the ministry until 1953[208]."

Relations with "the international Jewish community" were largely determined by the question of war reparations. "The Jewish state, where 500,000 concentration camp survivors had taken refuge[209], had hardly decided to normalise its relations with the Germans[210]," Gabriele Nissim pointed out. While the Federal Republic of Germany had obeyed the orders of the Allies, Israel and the World Jewish Congress, paying large reparations, the GDR (German Democratic Republic), which already paid war reparations to Poland and the USSR, did not consider itself the successor of the Hitler regime, refusing to assume any moral and material responsibility towards the Jews and the Jewish state[211]. This position irritated 'the international Jewish community', all

---

[206] Gabriele Eschenazi, Gabriele Nissim, *Les juifs et le communisme après la Shoah*, 1995, Éd. De Paris, 2000, p. 565, 566, 546, 599

[207] Gabriele Eschenazi, Gabriele Nissim, *Les juifs et le communisme après la Shoah*, 1995, Éd. De Paris, 2000, p. 614, 615

[208] Gabriele Eschenazi, Gabriele Nissim, *Les juifs et le communisme après la Shoah*, 1995, Éd. De Paris, 2000, p.628

[209] They are the "miraculous survivors" of the "death camps".

[210] Gabriele Eschenazi, Gabriele Nissim, *Les juifs et le communisme après la Shoah*, 1995, Éd. De Paris, 2000, p. 630

[211] "By 1990, the Bonn governments had paid $37 billion (current exchange

the more so as the German communist regime was the most pro-Arab of all. It had been supplying arms to the Palestinians since the late 1960s, and in 1971 it was to receive an official visit from Yasser Arafat, the head of the PLO.

After the fall of the communist regime, the World Jewish Congress, led by billionaire Edgar Bronfman, stepped up the pressure. On 13 April 1990, the newly elected parliament "adopted a declaration in which the GDR confirmed that it took moral responsibility for the Holocaust, and apologised for the anti-Israeli policy of previous governments and the country's treatment of Jews[212]." East Germans were also going to have to pay.

## *Refuge in Israel*

The truth is that the communist system had decidedly turned against the Jews, even though they had been the first to inspire and even establish it. "In this field of ideological ruins, wrote Alain Brossat, Israel appeared, for lack of anything else, as a safe haven, as a refuge... Since the other peoples continue to live in the narrowness of their national egoisms, our interlocutors often repeat, what else can be done but to affirm ourselves as a nation, as a state[213]?"

Many communist militants left for Palestine after the war to build the Jewish state. It was in Israel, in the early 1980s, that Alain Brossat and Sylvia Klinberg collected these testimonies: "Back from so many illusions", they wrote, these activists seemed to have settled down after so many years of revolutionary wandering: "It is not a spectacular ideological shift that leads them to come to live a 'normal', peaceful life, retired from politics, in a modest housing estate on the outskirts of Tel Aviv, it is above all a conversion to 'realism'".

Since the first Zionist congress in Bale in August 1897, the Zionist idea had come a long way to penetrate people's minds. Theodor Herzl, who had realised that the Jews were unassimilable in Europe, had become

---

rate) to the Israeli government and to the surviving Jews, including those in East Germany", p. 631.

[212] Gabriele Eschenazi, Gabriele Nissim, *Les juifs et le communisme après la Shoah*, 1995, Éd. De Paris, 2000, p. 677

[213] Alain Brossat, *Le Yiddishland révolutionnaire*, Balland, 1983, p.341, 342.

their tireless prophet. At the time there were only 25,000 Jews in Palestine out of a total population of 450,000, but that Jewish population was to grow steadily after the Balfour Declaration of 1917, and the creation of a "Jewish home" in Palestine.

The coming of the messiah of the Jews does not only coincide with the establishment of a world of "Peace", a perfect world in which all conflicts will have disappeared. The messianic expectation also nourishes the hope of the "return of the exiles" to Palestine, the return to Zion, and the rebuilding of the Temple. This hope of return has never disappeared. Jews have always prayed towards the East, towards Jerusalem. For 2000 years, their nostalgic psalms have repeated ad infinitum: "Next year in Jerusalem". We find this spell in the prayers, liturgy, feasts and celebrations of the Jewish people.


In 1945, there was still a war to be fought against the British power occupying the region under international mandate, which was also opposed by the Arab populations who did not intend to let their land be plundered without reacting. The Haganah was this Jewish army that would fight victoriously. It was supported by activist groups such as the Irgoun and the Stern group. After the assassination of Abraham Stern in February 1942 in Tel-Aviv, the leadership of the group passed to Nathan Yalin-Mor. In the introduction to his book published in 1978, one could read the following: "The Stern group (at that time they called it the Stern gang) dynamites, shoots at will and kills without mercy. That is true. But in the three or four years preceding the creation of the State, it is they, with Yalin-Mor at their head, who make life impossible for the British in Palestine. They killed Wilkin and Martin, the two "secret" inspectors from Tel-Aviv who were rounding them up. They attack convoys, blow up railways and dynamite barracks with the stubborn perseverance of real terrorists[214]."

The representative of British imperialism, Lord Moyne, a friend of Churchill's, was shot on 6 November 1944 in Cairo: "Benny's first shot instantly killed the resident general. The driver, who was trying to crawl out, was shot by Zebulon[215] ", wrote Yalin-Mor. The Jews were no

---

[214] Nathan Yalin-Mor, *Israel, Israel, Histoire du groupe Stern*, Presses de la Renaissance, 1978, p. 18.

[215] Nathan Yalin-Mor, *Israel, Israel, Histoire du groupe Stern*, Presses de la Renaissance, 1978, p. 178.

longer just taking it out on the local authorities, they were daring to attack the Empire. But the most symbolic action of this Jewish war in Palestine was the bombing of the King David Hotel. On 2 July 1946, the men of the Irgoun blew up the seven floors of the British-occupied wing. The toll was 200 dead and wounded.

Irgoun had also specialised in terrorist actions against Arab civilians: market bombings, raids on buses and companies employing Arab personnel. According to a widely spread version in Israel, the Haganah, the regular army, did not take part in any of these acts of which members of the Irgoun were guilty. But some testimonies are at odds with the official version. Alain Brossat's book presented the testimony of Yankel Taut, which contradicted the official version. After an attack on the large refinery in Haifa, which had claimed the lives of seven Arab workers at the end of 1947, the Arabs took revenge by killing seven Jewish workers. Yankel Taut, left for dead, was the only survivor. He recounted: "After this whole affair, the Haganah made a raid on the two Arab villages between Haifa and the refinery, killing part of the population and expelling the other part, systematically killing all the Arab refinery workers they found in the area. What happened in Deir Yassin was far from being an isolated case[216]."

The creation of the State of Israel was proclaimed in May 1948. Two years later, on 5 July 1950, commemorating the 45th anniversary of the death of Theodore Herzl, the Israeli parliament adopted a law—"the law of return"—granting any Jew who so wished the right to come and settle in Israel and automatically acquire Israeli nationality on arrival. Solidarity among Jews around the world once again found an opportunity to manifest itself. The billionaire Baron Guy de Rothschild, of the famous banking family, left an interesting testimony in his memoirs published in 1983. He recounted how in 1945 he had helped a woman involved in the "construction" of the State of Israel: "André Blumel, the former head of Léon Blum's cabinet with whom I was close friends, asked me to help him save Léa Knout, a young woman wanted for terrorism. I did so willingly and have since kept in touch with this woman, who today leads a peaceful life as a mother". This unfailing solidarity, as we can see, works even with terrorists. And Guy de Rothschild added: "On the day Israel declared its independence in May 1948, Alix and I joyfully demonstrated by parading arm in arm on

---

[216] Alain Brossat, *Le Yiddishland révolutionnaire*, Balland, 1983, p.319.

the Champs Elysées with Madame Mendès France, whom we had met there in the crowd[217]."

After the victory over the Arabs in 1967, the exactions continued during the occupation of the West Bank and Gaza. Professor Israel Shahak listed in 1975 the 385 Arab villages destroyed, bulldozed, out of 475 in 1958. From June 1967 to November 1969, more than 20,000 Arab houses were dynamited in Israel and the West Bank. Houses, fences and enclosures, even cemeteries were razed to the ground.

We will not recapitulate here the long litany of violence committed by Jews in Palestine; firstly because there are already many studies on the subject, and secondly because resorting to extreme violence to conquer a land is by no means a Jewish specificity. The French armies of Louis XIV, led by Louvois, also committed a number of atrocities during the sack of the Palatinate, and we know that the conquest of Languedoc by Philip Augustus was not only cultural. We will also remember, for example, that what the Palestinians suffered is small compared to what the Arabs suffered at the time of Genghis Khan's conquests. Unfortunately, states, like great civilisations, are not built on philosophy alone. In the preface to Nathan Yalin-Mor's book, one could read this common sense reflection: Yalin-Mor "is rightly one of the founders of the State of Israel... It is no coincidence that, to this day, his surname has been systematically concealed. Indeed, very few nations confess, after gaining their independence, that they owe their existence to the political sense of their men of action[218]."

The idealistic and revolutionary vision of the Zionist movement of the 1950s, and of that ideal of the Kibbutz, those collective farms that made so many young militant socialists dream, has completely expired. For many Jews, today's Hebrew state is part of the process of redemption, which must lead to the liberation of the Jews of the whole world.

After the victorious war of 1967, the charismatic Rabbi Zvi Yehudah Hacohen Cook explained to his students "that the State of Israel was God's chosen instrument for the Redemption of His people... that the land of Israel is holy, holy the trees that grow in it and the stones that

---

[217] Guy de Rothschild, *Contre bonne fortune...*, Belfond, 1983, p.353.

[218] Nathan Yalin-Mor, *Israel, Israel, Histoire du groupe Stern*, Presses de la Renaissance, 1978, p. 12.

carpet it and the houses that stand there; that it is God's inalienable gift to His People, and that no one can arrogate to himself the right to cede to the gentiles the smallest plot of land; and that their sacred right was to populate it[219]."

The Yom Kippur war in October 1973, though an Israeli victory, cost 2,500 dead and its political repercussions dealt a lethal blow to the triumphalism of 1967. These difficulties shook Israelis' feelings of security, strength and self-sufficiency. It was then, in 1974, that the Gush Emunim (The Faith Bloc) movement was created, whose leaders had been students of Rabbi Hacohen Cook.

This movement incorporated the nationalist and pioneering themes of Israelis within a messianic religious framework: "The land of Israel, for the people of Israel, according to the Torah of Israel" was its slogan. "The leaders of the Gush Emunim claimed that the messianic process of redemption of the Jewish people had begun and that the Jews had an essential role to play. The most important mitzvah at the time was the settlement of the Land of Israel, wrote Shmuel Trigano... The turmoil that reigned in Israel after the 1973 war was perceived as one of the pains of the birth of the Messiah". For the Gush Emunim, "the Jewish people have a sacred right to the Land of Israel and it is their sacred duty to take back possession of the country and populate it in every part[220]." Within this group, the mosques on the Temple Mount were seen as the main stumbling block to the Redemption process, and their destruction is now the order of the day.

This vision of Israel's destiny is also the one expounded by the former resistance fighter Victor Tibika in 1970, in a Zionist propaganda book entitled *Awakening and Unity of the Jewish People*. For him, "the hour of return has come". Israel's destiny "has been announced by the prophets, who unanimously foretold: the Destructions of the Temple, the Exodus, the Exile, the Persecutions, the Banishment, the Restoration

---

[219] Eli Barnavi, *Las Religiones asesinas*, Turner publicaciones, 2007, Madrid, p.67

[220] Shmuel Trigano, *La société juive à travers l'histoire*, tome I, Fayard, 1992, p.303. Some members of the Gush Emunim have merged into ultra-orthodox Judaism by adopting its way of life and outward appearance (the Jaredis), but most continue to dress according to contemporary standards and pursue careers within the modern economy.

of Israel, the Return, the Liberation of Jerusalem and the coming of the Messiah[221]."

This is no ordinary nationalism, equivalent to that of the Goyim, but a grandiose vision of history, embracing all nations: "It must not be forgotten," Tibika continued, "that Israel is a blessing both for the Jews and for humanity. This state has not been re-established to divide the world, but to bring blessing upon all nations, for it is through Israel that the world will be blessed[222]." From the same perspective, Theo Klein, the former president of the Representative Council of Jewish Institutions in France (CRIF), recalling his first visit to the Wailing Wall in 1967, wrote in turn: "I was not in front of the Wailing Wall: I was in front of the wall of hope[223]."

This eschatological conception of Judaism that integrates the state of Israel at its core can also be seen as dangerous for world Judaism. Elmer Berger, a Reform rabbi and former president of the American Council for Judaism, has spoken out on this issue: "The prophetic tradition clearly shows that the holiness of the land does not depend on its soil, nor on that of the people or their presence on the land. Only the divine covenant, which is expressed in the behaviour of its people, is sacred and worthy of Zion. Now, the current State of Israel has no right to identify itself with the culmination of the divine project of a messianic era? That is the pure demagogy of land and blood... Zionist totalitarianism... makes the Jewish people a people like any other[224]." And precisely, Jews do not want to be "like other people".

Jean-Christophe Attias expressed the religious antagonism on this question very well: "Zionism proposes a break with the passive attitude of the Jews, who have been waiting too long for the Messiah. It advocates that the Jews themselves take the reins of Jewish destiny, a

---

[221] Victor Tibika, 1967, *Réveil et unité du peuple juif*, 1970, p. 88.

[222] Victor Tibika, 1967, *Réveil et unité du peuple juif*, 1970, p. 39.

[223] Theo Klein, *Dieu n'etait pas au rendez-vous*, Bayard, 2003, p. 103.

[224] Elmer Berger, *La foi des prophètes et le Sionisme*, conférence à l'Université de Leiden (Pays-Bas), 20 mars 1968, in *Le XXIe siècle, Suicide planétaire ou résurrection?*, L'Harmattan, Paris 2000, p. 106.

will to achieve here and now on earth, and by human means, something that until then was only a diffuse horizon in the hands of God."

This secularised messianism thus constitutes a break with Jewish tradition. Zionism is thus perceived by some orthodox groups "as a veritable desecration of the religious ideal[225]." These groups condemn Zionism and the State of Israel because they believe that the Jews have been exiled by divine decree, and that the return and regrouping of the exiles, as well as national independence, can only legitimately occur by divine decree. In this sense, "Zionists seriously compromise Israel's mission in exile. Indeed, Israel is not only in exile for the punishment of its sins, but to assume, in the midst of that exile, an ethical, mystical and redemptive function alongside the Nations... Such is the mission of Israel in exile: scattered and even humiliated, it is there, everywhere, to redeem this world[226]."

The State of Israel is therefore just another element in the process of redemption in which Jews all over the world are working. The destruction of this state would not change their mission. For them, Israel has no vocation to host all the Jews of the world. It is primarily a refuge, where those Jews who wish to do so can go from time to time to replenish their strength. It is a refuge for "neurotic" Jews—as the American novelist Philip Roth wrote—who can no longer bear the contradiction between their apparent loyalty to their host country and their Judaism. It is also a refuge for former communist militants, for pensioners, for the "persecuted" and for crooks and criminals of all kinds, who know they will never be extradited. We have seen in *The Planetary Hopes* numerous examples of this. This is why, in spite of everything, most Jews still support Israel. The most virulent anti-Zionist leaders of the extreme left are no exception. "All left-wing organisations in Europe are led by anti-Zionist Jews[227] ", wrote the famous press director Jean Daniel Bensaïd. But more often than not, the

---

[225] Esther Benbassa, Jean-Christophe Attias, *Les juifs ont-ils un avenir?* J. C. Lattès, 2001, p.82, 83

[226] Esther Benbassa, Jean-Christophe Attias, *Les juifs ont-ils un avenir?* J. C. Lattès, 2001, p. 95

\* *Les Espérances planétariennes*, Hervé Ryssen, Ed. Baskerville 2005

[227] Jean Daniel Bensaïd, *L'Ère des ruptures*, Grasset, 1979, p.117

anti-Zionist discourse they spout in the mainstream press is nothing more than a façade[228].

Before the war, many Jews believed that the creation of a state would be a new ghetto. Here is what Elie Wiesel thought, in the words of his *murdered Jewish poet,* who wrote in 1936 in a newspaper opposed to the Zionist project: "I explained my principled opposition to Zionism. Either you are religious, and therefore forbidden to rebuild the kingdom of David before the coming of the son of David; or you are not, and in that case Jewish nationalism would endanger the Jews it claims to protect. He went on to say: a Jewish state in Palestine would be a ghetto, and we are against ghettos... We are in favour of a humanity without borders... Instead of barricading the Jews from humanity, we try to integrate them into it, to weld them together; it is not enough to liberate the Jew, we must liberate man, and then the problem will be solved[229]."

This idea of "humanity without borders" that structures the background of the mental universe of Jews all over the world is recurrent and we have heard it many times.

Journalist Guy Konopnicki had the same apparent misgivings about the State of Israel: "I cannot therefore share this new Jewish yearning, which would also turn them into a banal nation-state with defined borders. The Judaism I am calling for remains wandering and cosmopolitan, without land or roots. It is from everywhere and nowhere, just like my cultural heritage[230]."

The former leader of May 1968, Daniel Cohn-Bendit, also expressed himself along the same lines in a dialogue book with the former socialist minister Bernard Kouchner, who later switched to the "hard" right: "For me, the Jew is still the Jew of the Diaspora who lives everywhere and not in a country where Jews are in the majority. As soon as they have a state and a nationality, they are no longer Jews as we have known them for twenty centuries, but Israelis".

But for intellectuals and politicians such as Guy Konopnicki, Bernard Kouchner and Daniel Cohn-Bendit, feelings towards Israel are

---

[228] See, for example, the testimonies of Marek Halter and Guy Konopnicki, in *Les Espérances planétariennes,* Baskerville, 2005, p. 172, 173.

[229] Elie Wiesel, *Le Testament d'un poète juif assassiné,* 1980, Point Seuil, 1995, p. 164, 165.

[230] Guy Konopnicki, *La Place de la nation,* Olivier Orban, 1983, p. 24.

sometimes ambivalent, as is often the case in Judaism. Bernard Kouchner added in the following pages: "I know many Jews who would not go to live in Israel, but who want the State of Israel to exist[231]."

The Jews of the USSR, for example, did not all go to live in Israel—far from it. After the collapse of communism, hundreds of thousands of "perfectly integrated" Jews left the country without regret or remorse. Some left for Israel, but most decided to settle in the United States and East Germany, where immigration from Russia had been declared completely free for Jews of German ancestry. This decision, which had been taken by the parliament of the declining GDR as a gesture of contrition, was subsequently retained by reunified Germany. As a result, within fifteen years Germany's Jewish community grew tenfold, reaching 220,000 members in 2005.

Admittedly, the German state was generous. A Russian Jew who decided to settle in Israel received only 28,000 euros, while a Russian Jew who decided to settle in Germany was welcomed with open arms and a donation of 140,000 euros. A Jewish family of four thus received 560,000 euros from the German taxpayer in a single hosting bonus.

*Le Figaro* of 20 January 2005 stated: "Tens of thousands of Jews from the former USSR who immigrated to Israel are said to have taken advantage of their trips to the countries of the former Soviet bloc to destroy their Israeli passports and apply for admission to Germany[232]."

The process of "Redemption", as we see, continues mainly in "exile", among the nations.

---

[231] Daniel Cohn-Bendit, Bernard Kouchner, *Quand tu seras président*, Robert Laffont, 2004, p. 344, 346

[232] On 1 January 2006, Germany finally abolished immigration rights for Jews from Russia and former Soviet bloc countries. This measure was not taken by the Germans because they were frightened in advance of disturbing the international Jewish community, but at the request of the Israeli government itself, which was concerned about the flight of its citizens. (*Faits et documents* du 15 janvier 2006)

## 2. Planetary democracy

*The cosmopolitan mutation*

Jewish hopes are today much better represented by the ideal of the democratic society than by the old, largely discredited communist project. The two Marxist and liberal systems, far from being antagonistic, are effectively two complementary ideological machines working in the same direction for the construction of the universalist New World Order so desired by Israel, in which peoples, nations and borders will have disappeared.

Jacques Attali, one of President Mitterrand's closest advisers, makes an apology for unbridled cosmopolitanism in all his books. This socialist intellectual is currently quite close to the liberal right, but he retains an understandable esteem for Marx.

In the introduction to his biography of Karl Marx, published in 2005, he wrote:"… long before everyone else, he saw how capitalism constituted a liberation from previous alienations… he made the case for free trade and globalisation, and foresaw that revolution, if it came, would only come as the overcoming of a universal capitalism. He is the first "world" thinker. He is the spirit of the world."

Guy Ponopcki in turn recalled that Karl Marx had in *Capital* "praised the commodity and the capitalist revolution" in order to sweep away the traditional European society he hated. Konopcki also quoted these words: "To bring our country out of its backwardness, it must be infused with American practicality", adding: "This expression is Lenin's, who dreamed of putting an end to the dreadful national character of Russia[233]*".

It is no coincidence if Marxism came from the brain of a son of Israel. Morchedai Marx Levy, Karl Marx's grandfather, was a rabbi from Trier. His second son Herschel, born in 1777, "is not inclined to the rabbinate;

---

[233] Guy Konopnicki, *La Place de la nation*, Olivier Orban, 1983, p. 159.

* Lenin "had little regard for the Russians, whom he considered lazy, soft and not too clever. When you meet a clever Russian," he told Gorki, "he is almost always a Jew or has Jewish blood in his veins", in Richard Pipes, *The Russian Revolution*, 1990, Debols!llo, Penguin Random House Editorial, 2018, Barcelona, p. 380–381.

he is even far removed from religion". In 1817, after the death of his mother, "he decides to take the leap: he renounces Judaism and changes his name from Herschel Marx Levy to Heinrich Marx. However, he does not break with his community, in particular with his brother. In order to make it clear that his conversion was only political, and certainly temporary, he opted not for the dominant religion of the city, Catholicism, but for Lutheranism, the religion of the Berlin chiefs… Herschel Marx Levy may have hoped to become the lawyer he had dreamed of, but the King of Prussia, Frederick William III, made it compulsory for the Jews of his country to convert in order to exercise a liberal profession or public office… In 1814, in the synagogue of Trier, he married a Dutch Jewess, Henrietta Pressburg, (who) came from a Jewish family of Hungarian origin, long settled in the United Provinces… Their first son is born in Trier on 5 May 1818. He was neither circumcised nor baptised according to the Lutheran rite. As if by provocation, according to Jewish tradition, he was named after his father and his grandfather, the former rabbi of the city: Karl Heinrich Mordechai… In 1824—the year the first electric motor was manufactured in London—Heinrich made up his mind and, despite his wife's opposition, had his four children baptised in a Lutheran church in the city. The break with Judaism was henceforth complete, both for him and for his children[234]."

This last assertion was, however, denied three pages later, but we know that contradictions and paradoxes are frequent with Jewish intellectuals: "Karl is twelve years old, the age at which young Jews, his cousins, prepare their *bar-mitzvah*. He knows the Jewish community in the city, but has hardly been there since the death of his uncle. He even knows that his father had to convert in order not to give up his profession and that his mother, who has always considered herself Jewish, still attends the services; he intends to assimilate. Although he reads Hebrew, which his mother instilled in him, he rejects the image of the usurious Jew denounced by his father, whose heir he acknowledges[235]."

In March 1843, Karl Marx wrote his views on the emancipation of the Jews, and while he informed us that he "hates the Jewish faith", it was also clear that his motivations were fully in line with the secular

---

[234] Jacques Attali, *Karl Marx o el espíritu del mundo*, Fondo de cultura económica de Argentina, 2007, p. 13-15, 19- 25.

[235] Jacques Attali, *Karl Marx o el espíritu del mundo*, Fondo de cultura económica de Argentina, 2007, p. 28.

struggle of the Jews against Christian society: "The aim is to make as many breaches as possible in the Christian state and insidiously introduce the rational into it".

In this emancipatory perspective, stateless capitalism and globalised materialistic society, which uproot all ancestral traditions, represent the most effective weapons to dissolve nations and extirpate religions.

Marx "wrote the most beautiful pages ever published in praise of the bourgeoisie, and it is worth rereading them today," said Attali:"The bourgeoisie cannot exist except by incessantly revolutionising the instruments of production, which is as much to say the whole system of production, and with it the whole social regime(…) The epoch of the bourgeoisie is characterised and distinguished from all others by the constant and agitated displacement of production, by the uninterrupted upheaval of all social relations, by an incessant restlessness and a ceaseless dynamic. The unshakable and mouldy relations of the past, with all their retinue of old and venerable ideas and beliefs, collapse, and the new ones grow old before they take root. Everything that was believed to be permanent and perennial vanishes (…) The need to find markets spurs the bourgeoisie from one end of the planet to the other (…). The bourgeoisie, by exploiting the world market, gives to the production and consumption of all countries a cosmopolitan stamp (…) The low price of its goods is the heavy artillery with which it demolishes all the walls of China, with which it forces the most barbarous tribes to capitulate in their hatred of the foreigner (…) The bourgeoisie subjugates the countryside to the empire of the city. It creates huge cities, intensifies the urban population in a high proportion to the peasantry, and wrenches a considerable part of the rural people into the cretinism of rural life[236]"."

With such "cosmopolitan" convictions, it is not surprising that Karl Marx was in the crosshairs of anti-Semites: "at that time, he himself suffers countless anti-Semitic attacks, since he is regarded as Jewish and brown by all those—among them his daughters—who designate him, kindly or not, as "the Moor"[237]."

---

[236] Karl Marx, Frederick Engels, *Manifesto of the Communist Party*, Ed. Fundación de Investigaciones Marxistas, Madrid, 2013, p. 54, 55, 56.

[237] Jacques Attali, *Karl Marx o el espíritu del mundo*, Fondo de cultura económica de Argentina, 2007, p. 204.

In England, where he began writing *Capital*, the police kept an eye on "this stateless man with planetary relations". In his new residence, "not a single republican or socialist comes from the Continent or North America without dropping in to see him, either to receive his instructions or to listen to his oracle. He talks to them indifferently in English, French, German, Spanish, and even Russian, which he now learns to distract himself, particularly when he suffers from his boils[238]."

By sweeping away traditional cultures, capitalism thus opens the way to the establishment of the global empire, which is supposed to prefigure the advent of universal brotherhood. Indeed, Marx and Engels were convinced that they were witnessing the emergence of a world market, of a system of production and consumption on a planetary scale that would abolish national and cultural borders. It was a development they saw with good reason, for in such a planetary market, nationalisms and religions were destined to become extinct:

"When it has so exhausted the commodification of social relations and used up all its resources, capitalism, if it has not destroyed humanity, could also give way to a global socialism. To put it another way, the market could make room for fraternity… Every man would become a citizen of the world, and finally the world would be made for man. Then we will have to reread Karl Marx", wrote the very liberal Jacques Attali in the conclusion of his book; "from there we will draw the reasons for not repeating the mistakes of the last century[239]."

We can therefore sum it up as follows: communism appeared too early, and perhaps too brutally. It should be no more than a natural consequence of liberal globalisation and the planetary uniformisation engendered by materialistic society and democracy. Due to the failure of communism's project of "universal brotherhood", planetary intellectuals have temporarily shifted their hopes to the liberal project, whose aim is identical: to create the Empire of Peace.

Liberal economists, such as Thomas Friedman, for example, were also convinced that globalisation was only compatible with one economic

---

[238] Jacques Attali, *Karl Marx o el espíritu del mundo*, Fondo de cultura económica de Argentina, 2007, p. 239.

[239] Jacques Attali, *Karl Marx o el espíritu del mundo*, Fondo de cultura económica de Argentina, 2007, p. 413.

system: the liberal democratic one, capable of ending war, tyranny and poverty.

In this perspective, the student revolt of May '68 represented the swan song of communist hopes. It is known that the main leaders of the protest movement were Jews. Indeed, it was Jewish militants who led the revolutionary, Trotkyist, Maoist or anarchist movements, inspired by a specifically Jewish messianism, even if it was apparently secularised. An Israeli academic, Yaïr Auron, noted this in a book entitled *The Jews of the Far Left in May '68*, published for the thirtieth anniversary of those "events": "Of the four main leaders of May '68, Daniel Cohn-Bendit, Alain Krivine, Alain Geismar and Jacques Sauvageot, the first three are Jews[240]."

The Jewish community magazine *Passages* devoted its eighth issue to these events. Benoît Rayski wrote: "There was, in May '68, a compact crowd of Jewish volunteers, both at the top and at the bottom of the parties, movements and groups that were at the forefront of that insurrectionary event… They occupied a pre-eminent place, totally disproportionate to the number of Jews in France… They all, or almost all, came from a well-defined geographical location: Central or Eastern Europe. Almost all came from families who had sacrificed their lives in the name of the revolutionary ideologies of the 20th century: Bolshevism, communism, Trotskyism, Bundism, anarchism… There were, in a rush of people, the martyrs of l'*Affiche rouge (Red Poster)*, the Jews of the Komintern, tireless representatives of the world revolution, the Jewish and communist leaders of the international brigades, the young insurrectionists of the Warsaw ghetto, etc.". So, rather than a dress rehearsal for a hypothetical great revolutionary evening, May '68 was more like a great farewell party. It was, according to Benoît Rayski, "a kind of revolutionary pavane of an extinct world".

But Jewish intellectuals tend to forget all too quickly the atrocities caused by Marxist doctrine throughout the world, and especially the irrefutable responsibilities of Jewish doctrinaires, officials and executioners during the Soviet period. The Israeli historian Sever Plocker recalled, however, in an article entitled *Stalin's Jew's*, published in 2007, that the number of victims of the cheka amounted to at least 20 million. According to him, Ghenrij Yagoda was definitely "the

---

[240] Read the chapter: *Les Espérances planétariennes*, Hervé Ryssen, pp. 265-270

greatest criminal of the 20th century", as he was "responsible for at least 10 million deaths". "We must not forget," wrote Sever Plocker, "that some of the greatest criminals of modern times are Jews... Many Jews sold their souls to the demon of the communist revolution and have blood on their hands for all eternity." Let us stress, however, that this Sever Plocker is an exception, and that Jewish intellectuals, as a whole, have always refused to acknowledge to the general public their enormous responsibility for the communist tragedy.

## *The planetary project*

Planetary intellectuals are the most unbridled propagandists for immigration, miscegenation and open borders. Whether left or right, Marxist or liberal, atheist or believer, Zionist or "perfectly integrated", they tirelessly campaign for the construction of a multicultural society and the advent of a world without borders.

Among them, Jacques Attali is one of the most influential. *In A Brief History of the Future,* published in 2006, he once again believed himself to be inspired like the prophet Elijah himself, announcing the coming of the Messiah: "The situation is simple: market forces have taken over the planet. This triumphal march of money, the ultimate expression of the triumph of individualism, explains most of the recent upheavals in history... If this evolution comes to an end, money will destroy everything that can harm it and, little by little, it will destroy all states, including the United States. Once it has become the sole law of the world, the market will create what I am going to call the *hyper-empire, an* ungraspable and planetary network, a creator of mercantile riches and new alienations, of fortunes and extreme miseries; nature will be totally subjugated; everything will be private, including the army, the police and the justice system".

Attali continued prophetically:"... a new infinite horizon of freedom, responsibility, dignity, self-improvement and respect for others will open up. This is what I will call *hyperdemocracy*. It would lead to the establishment of a democratic world government, as well as a set of local and regional institutions". In this new configuration of the world, the domination of the American empire will have given way to a planetary democratic system: "I am convinced that, by the year 2060, we will see the victory of hyperdemocracy, the highest form of human organisation, the ultimate expression of the engine of history: freedom[241]."

This hyper-empire will be "an empire without a land, without a centre, that is to say open... Individuals will be loyal only to themselves; companies will no longer have a nationality; the poor will be one market among others; laws will be replaced by contracts, justice by arbitration, and the police by mercenaries".

States will disappear in the face of the new power of corporations and cities. "Altruistic and universalist forces, which are already active today, will take power on a global scale, under the rule of ecological, ethical, economic, cultural and political necessity". A "Planetary Criminal Court will ensure the compatibility of jurisprudence developed on each continent... A World Water Agency will protect the availability of water; a universal market authority will control monopolies and the respect of the right to work. The quality control of consumer products, in particular foodstuffs, will be in the hands of another body. And yet another will control the major insurance companies, the other organs of government and the large enterprises essential to life[242]."

Of course, we can ask ourselves what are these "altruistic forces" of which Jacques Attali speaks. To this question the author gave an honest answer, and those who know Judaism will rejoice in his sincerity:

"The masters of the hyper-empire will be the stars of "circuses" and "theatre companies": holders of the capital of "circus companies" and nomadic assets, financial or business strategists, owners of insurance and leisure companies, software architects, creators, jurists, financiers, authors, designers, artists, designers of nomadic objects; I will call them *hypernomads* here. They will number in the tens of millions, both women and men, many of them self-employed... they will constitute a new creative class, a *hyperclass*, which will lead the hyper-empire". (p.176). But Jacques Attali's visions contain gaps, obviously voluntary ones.

Pending those happy days when the hyper-Jews will be able to run the planet, the hyper-Goyim should be encouraged to meekly accept the

---

[241] Jacques Attali, *Breve historia del futuro*, Ediciones Paidós Ibérica, 2007 Barcelona, p.13, 14.

[242] Jacques Attali, *Breve historia del futuro*, Ediciones Paidós Ibérica, 2007 Barcelona, p. 20, 233.

options proposed to them. So that, from now on, the Europeans, in this case the French, will have to put aside their whims. Let us recall how, in the referendum of 25 May 2005, the French voted massively "no" to the draft European constitution, despite all the warnings of their hypercommunicators (the Netherlands and Ireland also voted against it). The whims of spoiled children must cease, as Attali prescribed:

"France will have an interest in helping to create the *hyper-democracy* that will protect its values and its own existence. It should therefore propose the creation of world government bodies with their own resources... At the European level, it will have to encourage the establishment of a true continental government".

The French will also have to accept even more immigrants, for their salvation depends on it. They must understand, Attali wrote, "that the influx of population, well controlled and integrated, is the condition of their own survival" (p.129). (p.129). All this, of course, "for the greater benefit of humanity[243]."

At the beginning of his book, however, he warned us that this globalisation would not be without upheavals: "Long before the American Empire disappears, long before living conditions become almost unbearable, populations will fight over territories, and countless wars will take place; nations, pirates, mercenaries, mafias and religious movements will equip themselves with new weapons" (p.20). (p.20). Indeed, everything seems to indicate that the weakening of states, wars and general chaos are favourable to the coming of the Messiah.

Finally, the Spanish edition included a short epilogue on Spain, in which the author gave his views on the historical and future role of the Spanish. His analysis could not have been more typical and synthetic: "Spain had several occasions to become the dominant power in Europe... It never became one", because "it has never managed to form, raise, or welcome a *creative class*" (p.241). (p.241). Attali thus sentenced: "Spain has never become a "heart" because at no time did it know how to adhere to the laws of the history of the future that I have just described in these pages" (p.241).

The solution is therefore simple: "Spain's future will henceforth depend on its ability to comply with these laws and follow the rules of success", such as "an immigration policy that is accepted and accompanied by an

---

[243] Jacques Attali, *Une brève Histoire de l'avenir*, Fayard, 2006, p, 421, 423

appropriate integration policy, a path that Spain seems ready to take" (p.242). (p.242)

## *Multicultural society*

For the sociologist Edgar Morin, the planetary project should first be tested in European countries. Europe, Morin wrote, should "become a place of experimentation for the new and original concepts that will then be proposed to the whole world". It must "integrate into itself that which is different from itself, but at the same time not reduce it to this integration: it must become a microcosm such as the planetary civilisation is[244]."

In a book entitled *A Wish for Politics,* Daniel Cohn-Bendit insisted on the need for Europeans to open their borders wide. The model now proposed by the former anarchist Cohn-Bendit was that of the liberal United States, where a multiracial society had been set up under the leadership of a powerful lobby: "Europe must think of itself as a region of immigration, just like the United States[245]". It is indeed the only way to enter modernity.

Cohn-Bendit defended an argument often adduced by cosmopolitan discourses: "First of all, we must convince ourselves that there will always be a flow of immigration because of the strong inequality between the industrialised countries and the developing countries of the Maghreb and Africa… This is valid for the whole of Europe[246]."

Alain Minc, the very rich and influential liberal essayist, supported the same discourse in *The Egalitarian Machine,* published in 1987, but with the emphasis of a biblical revelation. In the chapter entitled *The Ten Commandments, he* left no room for doubt, stating: "Between a Europe in full demographic decline and the overpopulated countries of the southern Mediterranean, the effect of communicating vessels is inevitable".[247]

---

[244] Edgar Morin, *Un nouveau commencement*, Seuil, 1991, p.94, 106.

[245] Daniel Cohn-Bendit, *Une Envie de politique*, La Découverte, 1998, p.92.

[246] Daniel Cohn-Bendit, *Une Envie de politique*, La Découverte, 1998, p. 90-92.

[247] Alain Minc, *La Machine égalitaire*, Grasset 1987, p.264

This was also what Jean Daniel—a man of the left—wanted to tell us in the magazine *Le Nouvel Observateur* of 13 October 2005: "Nothing will stop the movements of miserable populations towards an old and rich West... That is why, from now on, wisdom and reason consist in preparing to receive and welcome more and more migrants... We must realise that nations will no longer be what they are today".

The great migrations of the peoples of the South towards the North are inevitable; it is therefore pointless to try to oppose them. Let us remember, however, that in the old Marxist discourse, it was the "classless society" that was to be "inevitable". This analogy may leave us a little circumspect, considering the tragedies that this kind of prophecy seems to bring with it... But as you will have understood, these are not sociological analyses, but covert propagandist discourses intended to take away the idea of defending ourselves.

This tendency is in fact the reflection of a discourse that is very characteristic of the cosmopolitan mentality: they project us into the future on the back of "prophecies", declaring that all that was written must inevitably come to pass; fight no more, let go and all will be well! The efforts of Jewish intellectuals to make us accept immigration are nothing more than the concrete application of their messianism.

Obviously, if Europeans were content to accept the third-worldisation of their culture and territory with resignation and in spite of themselves, they would be demonstrating a certain meanness. They must therefore be convinced that welcoming immigrants will make them better off. Not only regular but also illegal immigrants should be the object of their attention. The doctrine of "human rights" is a terribly effective weapon to dissolve the old civilisation.

For the philosopher Etienne Balibar, freedom of movement on a planetary scale is an "imprescriptible right", as he put it in the prestigious daily *Le Monde* of 9 July 1998: illegal immigrants "have the right to demand equal treatment, to challenge the legality of the administrative procedures to which they are subjected... What is valid for some must be valid for all, even for the most wretched undocumented. They too have the right to present their situation and to discuss their fate... We, who support them and fear for them, tell you once again: Don't play with people's lives, really open the way to dialogue, mediation and help! Europeans, open your doors, open your hearts, open... everything! Of course, it would be nice if Etienne Balibar had the same words for his fellow Israelis, but it seems that for the Jews these words are a product exclusively reserved for export.

The next stages of the planetary argument are of a more prosaic nature. Journalist Philippe Bernard sought to answer a question often asked by those opposed to immigration: "Are immigrants profitable or a cost for France? In a book published in 2002 and entitled, *Immigration, the global challenge*, Philppe Bernard, a regular columnist for the daily *Le Monde*, endeavoured to answer this question conscientiously.

"With regard to the question of the cost of immigrants, it makes little sense, given that the French social security system is a pay-as-you-go system based precisely on solidarity between all categories: the healthy pay for the sick, the active for the retired, the single for large families, etc. Who is interested in knowing the cost of children or diabetics? In any case, he added, "there is no general social balance sheet in France on the subject[248]... "

However, any observer who visits a hospital in any town in France can see for himself the origin of the famous "hole" in the social security system. But on this point, Mr. Philippe Bernard showed above all the typical *"Chutzpah"* of his peers, that unmitigated impudence so characteristic of cosmopolitan thinking.

It would be good for Europeans to understand that this third-worldisation of their countries, far from being a catastrophe, is in fact an extraordinary benefit, an incredible good fortune, a real gift from heaven, the rejection of which would be a tremendous mistake. All these immigrants are truly indispensable to replace Europe's ageing population. At the end of the day, we must recognise that Jewish intellectuals are very concerned about the fate of Europeans.

Likewise, one of the key figures behind the US war in Iraq in 2003, Paul Wolfowitz, then deputy to US Defence Secretary Ronald Rumsfeld and later to become president of the World Bank, encouraged Russia to open its borders to mass immigration from the Third World. In a 2005 report on the Russian economy, he wrote:

"Russia would benefit from a substantial change in its immigration policy. Immigration is one of the main conditions for a stable economy in Russia. The country's population is ageing and declining... To compensate for this depopulation, an annual influx of one million immigrants would be necessary."

---

[248] Philippe Bernard, *Immigration le défi mondial*, Gallimard, 2002, Folio, p.161

Once again, you will understand that Paul Wolfowitz does not support this same immigration policy in the slightest when it comes to the Hebrew state.

In short, if one understands correctly, immigrants from the third world are coming to save us. An article in the daily *Libération* of 25 July 2005 confirmed this: "According to Eurostat projections presented by Serge Feld of the University of Louvain, the European Union will lose 14 million inhabitants by 2030". This is "a risk that can only be mitigated by maintaining immigration". By 2030, "immigration will make the EU gain 25 million inhabitants". This article, entitled "Immigration to Europe's rescue", was signed by a certain Eric Aeschlimann.

Obviously, it does not occur to all these intellectuals, who are so kindly concerned about our pensions, that Europeans can resort to natalist policies. This was clearly expressed by Daniel Cohn-Bendit: "A pro-natalist policy seems to me to be absolutely useless... The family is not a value in itself...". The family is not a value in itself", and then went on to promote homosexual couples: "What I value most are the relationships within the couple. Whatever the sex of the couple: a homosexual couple should have the same rights as a heterosexual couple". And Cohn-Bendit continued: "Why this sick desire to have your own child, when it is not possible, for whatever reason...? I don't see the point of artificial procreation. Why not make adoption easier?"[249]

Cohn-Bendit also declared himself in favour of a major immigration and integration policy controlled and financed by the taxpayer. We must "implement a policy of integration, schooling and housing. I am in favour of setting quotas to achieve this objective". Finally, he unveiled his grandiose plan for Europe: "As a whole, the European Union could allow 500,000 immigrants to enter... Periodically, every eight to ten years, a regularisation operation will have to be carried out by applying, as was done in France with undocumented immigrants, the "presumption of integration"[250] "

---

[249] Daniel Cohn-Bendit, *Une Envie de politique*, La Découverte, 1998, p.104, 105, 113.

[250] Daniel Cohn-Bendit, *Une Envie de politique*, La Découverte, 1998, p. 90-92.

This obsession with the miscegenation of European peoples is not new. As early as 1963, Charles De Gaulle's minister, Michel Debré, repopulated certain departments of the French metropolis with hundreds of children from Reunion Island. Forty years later, in September 2005, taking advantage of the general state of repentance of white Europeans, the Association des Réunionnaires de Creuse denounced the State before the administrative court of Limoges for the "deportation" of 1630 children from Réunion between 1963 and 1980[251]. So we see that liberals, socialists and former revolutionaries are in complete agreement: their opinions are determined not so much by their political commitment as by their messianic faith.

Muslim countries are also targeted by the "benefactors of humanity". In the name of "modernity", Daniel Cohn-Bendit called on Europeans to show common sense and agree to let Turkey join the European Union: "With regard to Turkey, I think the argument that Europe would be a Christian club is completely aberrant... To integrate Turkey into Europe would be to build a bridge of modernity to the whole of Central Asia and the Middle East and to deny the division between Islamic and Christian countries". And he added without laughing: "A large part of Turkey is already European "[252]

In the weekly *Le Point* of September 29, 2005, the billionaire philosopher Bernard-Henri Levy elaborated on this point and seemed to be in complete agreement with the former leftist Cohn-Bendit[253]. For him, Europe is essentially an idea, a concept, for, according to him, "it has no limit, no really prescribed or imposed frontiers... From this point of view, there is no longer any objection that a country of ancient Muslim culture like Turkey, insofar as it embraces the heroism of reason, cannot join the European constitution... I am one of those who believe that Europe has a function rather than a geographical location".

---

[251] Read in Emmanuel Ratier's indispensable letter, *Faits et Documents* (1 September 2005). Michel Debré, a former minister under General de Gaulle, was the grandson of a rabbi from Alsace.

[252] Daniel Cohn-Bendit, *Une Envie de politique*, La Découverte, 1998, p.224.

[253] BHL (Bernard-Henri Levy) sold its building materials company for CHF 2.6 billion.

One of Jacques Chirac's main advisors, Pierre Lelllouche, a deputy of the liberal right and president of the NATO assembly, stated it bluntly in *Actualités juives* of 23 December 2004[254]: "I want Turkey to join the European Union because it is a Muslim country". Moreover, Turkey was at the time an ally of Israel, which could secretly motivate Pierre Lellouche's political positions.

In the same issue of the weekly, Nicolas Sarkozy declared on 21 December 2004 after returning from Israel: "The problem is not Turkey, but Europe's identity. If we really want to expand in this part of the world, we must first integrate Israel, whose population, mostly of European origin, shares our values".

The phenomenon of the dissolution of peoples and states is in any case "ineluctable", as Philippe Bernard also wrote. To motivate us in such an undertaking, Bernard tried to stimulate us by prodding our national pride: "This progressive globalisation of the population is putting France's universalist pretensions to the test, for it faces considerable obstacles. Is the Republic so weak that it cannot meet these challenges? The French must mobilise and "cry out loud and strong" for the values of their country: "equality between men and women, the rejection of discrimination, education for all, the separation of religions and the state—while at the same time attenuating their Jacobinism to allow new mixed-race identities to enter and assert themselves, like the planet and, why not, to inspire future European Union legislation[255]."

Philippe Bernard's book ended with this beautiful optimism. I remember calling him one day, ten years ago. Despite being a very busy man, I managed to get him on the phone: "I have just one question, Mr Bernard, just one... Are you Jewish? Are you Jewish?" He got an awkward little laugh in reply... It was at the time when I was discovering that behind the most fanatically pro-immigration press articles, there was almost always a Jewish intellectual.

## Bringing Islam to heel

---

[254] Quoted in *Faits et Documents* of 15 January 2005, letter by Emmanuel Ratier. Jacques Chirac was President of the Republic at the beginning of the 21st century.

[255] Philippe Bernard, *Immigration le défi mondial*, Gallimard, 2002, Folio, p.279

The new multi-ethnic and multicultural society they have recently put in place already holds great dangers for the future. During the race riots of November 2005, 14,000 vehicles were set on fire and four native Frenchmen lost their lives. Jewish intellectuals obviously bore an overwhelming responsibility for this situation, just as Jewish doctrinaires had done for the thirty million victims of Bolshevism in the USSR.

Moreover, Jews themselves were beginning to reap the fruits of this new multiracial society. Since September 2000, the second Intifada in Palestine had given rise in the French suburbs to a solidarity movement among young Maghreb and sub-Saharan Muslims, who were beginning to display virulent anti-Semitism. We then witnessed a multiplication of anti-Semitic incidents. This prompted a section of the cosmopolitan intelligentsia to support a strong security policy. Alain Finkielkraut, Pascal Bruckner, André Glucksmann, Alexandre Adler, and others shed their progressive ideas to support the "hard" right and Nicolas Sarkozy's candidacy for the presidency in May 2007. It was now a matter of consolidating the multiracial society in danger of disintegration.

The weekly *Le Point* of 27 April 2006 published a dossier on anti-Semitism and the worrying emigration of French Jews to Israel. In it, Alain Finkielkraut denounced the aggressiveness of these immigrants who also declared themselves to be victims of the West, thus dangerously competing with Jewish victimhood propaganda:

"Today, the Jew is once again attacked in the flesh, and I have no intention of deserting the battlefield... There are in France imaginary slaves, imaginary natives who want to liquidate the Jews. No doubt they believe that the Holocaust is a choice and they are envious. I don't know if the Jews have changed, but the situation is new. I suffer it not only as a Jew, but also as a Frenchman, when two of the most common insults are precisely "damned Jew" and "damned Frenchman"". Double suffering, then, for Alain Finkielkraut.

In the same issue of *Le Point*, Julien Dray, one of the emblematic figures of the socialist party and a former Trotskyist, who was one of the founders of SOS Racisme, acknowledged some mistakes: "The truth is that the community has gone astray in this direction. It has become a lobby, a pressure group on France's foreign policy. It is a suicidal attitude, because, lobby against lobby, it cannot compete". It is clear that, compared to the formidable lobby of the Maghrebi shopkeepers, the Jewish lobby does not measure up.

Researcher Pierre-André Taguieff, as usual, lurked in the conspiracy influence: "The suspicion that Jews are not good citizens is not new and has become the main subject of accusations of modern anti-Semitism. Today, some even revive the spectre of the 'world Jewish conspiracy', renamed the 'American-Zionist' plot. This means that all Jews, including the French, are suspected of being part of the gigantic plot". And he declared unequivocally: "the Islamists are our sworn enemies".

Philosopher Bernard-Henri Levy urged that henceforth the Goyim should mobilise against the great danger threatening the Jewish community: militant Islam. "I am at war against contemporary Muslim fundamentalism[256]."

In *Le Point* of 2 November 2006, Elie Bernavi, former Israeli ambassador to France, interviewed by Elisabeth Levy after the publication of his book *Killer Religions*, also urged us to take tough measures against Islamists: "Faced with fundamentalist and revolutionary Islam, the West has let its guard down".

The influence of Islam in the French suburbs was of particular concern to him. According to him, the wearing of the Islamic veil was a worrying sign: "I want to be at home in our cities... Like it or not, the threshold of tolerance is being challenged... I don't want to have to choose between Islamic fascists and straight fascists... It is not a question of chasing the veil on the streets, but of conveying a club discourse. We belong to a club that is open to everyone, but it has its rules". Apparently, Jews don't feel as patriotic as when they feel threatened.

Of course, it was not at all a question of encouraging Europeans to expel the millions of Muslims who had recently landed in Europe, but rather of making Muslims abandon their religion, just as many European Christians had already done with theirs. Daniel Cohn-Bendit was quick to dot the i's and cross the t's: "It is clear that the Muslim religion must embark on a process of secularisation, following the path taken by the Catholic Church. It took many reforms and conflicts, sometimes bloody ones, for the European religions to accept their separation from the state... We will only achieve this by putting all religions on an equal footing". And Daniel Cohn-Bendit, so that no one could blame his ideas

---

[256] Bernard-Henri Levy, *Récidives*, Grasset, 2004, p.415-421

on his Jewishness, added: "I am an atheist, I am indifferent to all religions. But I want democracy. For everyone[257]."

But even so, the secular hatred of Christianity occasionally reared its head in Cohn-Bendit's egalitarian discourse: "The ringing of the Sunday bells bothers me too. If you can regulate the number of bells and their timing—for example, night-time—you can also regulate the muezzin's singing[258]."

It would indeed be more "modern". "Europeans should remember that their democracies could only develop against the background of the Reformation and the retreat of Christianity," wrote Cohn-Bendit. Bernard Kouchner replied: "I completely agree. In 1905, the law on the separation of church and state brought the country to the brink of civil war... We persecuted the congregations, forcing the orders into exile. There were clashes with the troops. Daniel Cohn-Bendit summed up the problem in a few words: "Like 19th and early 20th century Europe, Islam has a great secular reformation ahead of it. It will be done through struggle and with pain[259]." It is clear that it will be rather with pain.

The Grand Rabbi of France, Joseph Sitruk, undoubtedly agreed with these statements. But he tried to have his back covered and declared in the *Tribune juive* of October 2004: "I was undoubtedly the one who promoted the acceptance of Muslims in France the most". Jewish intellectuals cannot therefore be accused of racism.

The liberal economist Guy Sorman also presented to the public his slogans for governing Islam: "The Muslim world is not the hostage of the Koran, he wrote, it is not alienated by its religion, but is the victim of the dictatorship of its clerics: ulemas, ayatollahs and other imams. When they get rid of this clericalism, Muslims will recover their roots, with a religion that is in no way hostile to individual freedom. That social and religious revolution will be comparable to our Lutheran-Calvinist reformation [260]." And Guy Sorman dared to say: "The fundamentalists, who confuse the veil and Islam, are lousy Muslims;

---

[257] Daniel Cohn-Bendit, *Une Envie de politique*, La Découverte, 1998, p.86, 87.

[258] Daniel Cohn-Bendit, *Une Envie de politique*, La Découverte, 1998, p.122.

[259] Daniel Cohn-Bendit, Bernard Kouchner, *Quand tu seras président*, p. 183

[260] Guy Sorman, *Le Bonheur français*, Fayard, 1995, p.123, 124

they have misread the Koran²⁶¹." What is very clear, is that Daniel Cohn-Bendit, Bernard-Henri Levy and Guy Sorman know the Torah and the Talmud very well.

We see, in fact, how their critique of radical Islam was only aimed at favouring the integration of Muslim immigrants into European societies. After the uprisings in November 2005, Jewish intellectuals continued to promote their project of a multicultural society.

And yet we know that a policy of firmness is possible. On 7 January 2003, for example, India announced the expulsion of 20 million undocumented Bangladeshis. In a statement, the ministry justified this decision on the grounds of the serious threat posed by "the presence of a large number of undocumented migrants". While it is true that the mainstream Western media do not report such information, immigration is not an inevitable phenomenon, but rather a deliberate policy for the destruction of European civilisation. The multicultural and multiracial society seems to the Jews to be a guarantee that protects them from a national reaction of the European peoples against their political project. Elie Wiesel also recounted this very well in his memoirs during a trip to India: "I spend a Shabbat with a Jewish family in Bombay. I go to the synagogue. There the Jews tell me with satisfaction how fortunate they are. The Sassoons and the Kaduris are very rich families, dynasties, but no one would think of hating them because of their origins or their Jewish ties: there are so many ethnic groups, so many languages, so many cultures and traditions in this immense country, that the Jews do not attract attention²⁶²."

Indeed, the ideal is not to draw too much attention to oneself. Unfortunately, however, the entire history of the Jewish people shows that it is almost always difficult for them to submit to this imperative.

## *The liberal model*

---

²⁶¹ Guy Sorman, *Le Bonheur français*, Fayard, 1995, p. 132.

²⁶² Elie Wiesel, *Mémoires, Tome I*, Le Seuil, 1994, p.287. Anne Kling, author of the book *La France licratisée* [adjectival LICRA], (2006), pointed out that the Institute for Jewish People's Policy Planning, chaired by former US Ambassador Dennis Ross, had published a report in 2006 which contained a paragraph entitled: 'Support multicultural policies': '1.

Jewish economists are the champions of liberal deregulation and globalised market economics. Guy Sorman (Berl Zormann) is a liberal economist and prolific international essayist. In *French Happiness*, published in 1995, he explained that he is above all a disciple of Raymond Aron: "How can one claim to be French liberalism without having been, in one way or another, a student of Raymond Aron", he wrote. They met in the early 1980s when he collaborated with the magazine *L'Express,* of which Raymond Aron was the editorial director and Jimmy Goldsmith the owner[263].

Guy Sorman also has that very characteristic tendency in the Jewish community to extol the virtues of his co-religionists: "*Du Pouvoir* is the book that made me join liberal thought. It is one of the most beautiful texts ever written in French". He went on to specify that its author, Bertrand de Jouvenel, was, like him, of "Jewish origin". The men who helped shape his economic thinking are all great geniuses:

"Friedrich von Hayek, Karl Popper and Milton Friedman: these men have contributed to improving the human condition," Sorman wrote, adding mischievously: "And, by the way, the nationality of my main interlocutors is irrelevant.

"In the 1980s, any liberal thinker had to know Hayek. It was like an obligatory pilgrimage to listen to the most creative theoretician of our century. His conversation was worth the trip, for it dazzled the interlocutor even more than his austere books… His genius was almost as ignored in France as it was praised in Britain and the United States. Hayek came to us through Margaret Thatcher and Ronald Reagan… Of Czech origin, he studied in Austria and then went into voluntary exile in Britain in the 1920s; because of a love affair, he went to teach at the University of Chicago in the United States; from there, having reached retirement age, he was invited to the University of Freiburg in Germany, where he spent his last years. What was Friedrich von Hayek's nationality, if that question makes sense? He proudly replied that he was a British citizen because his children were British. Karl Popper also claimed to be British, even though he was born in Vienna, taught in New Zealand and came to Britain after the Second World War at an advanced age. Although his parents were not British, Milton Friedman, on the other hand, can only be American, for his thinking is very much

---

[263] Guy Sorman, *Made in USA*, Fayard, 2004, Livre de Poche, 2006, p.25, 26

imbued with the places where he lived. But this was not the case with Hayek and Popper, true cosmopolitans[264]."

Anglo-Saxon" thinking is a determining factor for liberal economists, and the United States today represents the model of society that the rest of humanity should imitate. In another book, *Made in the USA*, Guy Sorman gave us an idea of the place of Jews in that country: "Never in its history have Jews been so prosperous, numerous and secure as in the United States. Is it the Promised Land? For the Jews, it looks very much like it... Most are wealthy and influential, and have their own public schools and cultural centres... The influence of Jews, especially in the cultural industries, is so disproportionate-one percent of the population-that the rest of the world perceives it as a lobby that determines the country's foreign policy."

Of course, Guy Sorman hastened to add: "The suspicion is excessive, but the Jewish lobbyists do not deny it". Of course there is a Jewish lobby in the United States," acknowledges the leaders of the Zionist foundations in New York and Los Angeles, whose mission is to influence the US government. But a lobby in America, far from being an infamy, contributes to the democratic vitality of the nation[265]."

Bernard Henri Levy, another media philosopher, also praised the American model. In his book *American Vertigo*, published in 2006, he played the role of a journalist touring the "States", questioning certain characters who seemed to him to be emblematic of that country. For example, in the local Arab community, he tried to pick out the most "goy" of them all, in this case a naïve journalist from the Arab community in Michigan:

"Do you know what my model is? The Jews, obviously; this incredible American '*success story*' that is the constitution and triumph of the Jewish lobby; what the Jews managed to create, this power that they managed to obtain, to earn by the sweat of their brow, this path that they traced and that led them to the heart of all influences, how can you not be inspired by it? We are fifty years behind, it is true; they are ten times

---

[264] Guy Sorman, *Le Bonheur français*, Fayard, 1995, p.26-29

[265] Guy Sorman, *Made in USA*, Fayard, 2004, Livre de Poche, 2006, p. 137.

\* Snobbish Anglicism sometimes used in France.

stronger than we are, all right; but you will see how we will make it; one day we will be their equals[266]."

Bernard Henri seemed slightly circumspect here: "I do not say that this discourse is free of confusing elements". But, after all, he was glad that, for once, his community did not pass for an enemy, but a model—"an obscure object of desire", he wrote. It is true that, in this competition allowed by the liberal model, Jews have little to fear from the goyim overtaking them. The day when the latter know how to handle money like the Jews will have passed millennia ago.

Naturally, Bernard-Henri Levy could not fail to visit a Lubavitch rabbi in Brooklyn. The four-page interview is completely inconsistent, as it has no other aim than to show readers that Jews are a community like any other[267].

Nor did his interview with George Soros shed much light on the extent of the Jewish lobby mentioned by Guy Sorman. We learnt, quite simply, that some billionaires are capable of rapidly amassing immense fortunes: "On the one hand, the hyper-magnate who, when I ask him if he does not sometimes have a guilty conscience for these fortunes earned in such a curious way, is not far from answering me that attacking a currency, alarming the banking establishment, forcing them to react and invent, is not a crime, but a favour to society, a revolutionary gesture, a duty". But Bernard-Henri Levy, himself a hundred times a millionaire, seems to have a certain affection for this financial shark. For this George Soros is, in a way, also a philosopher, as well as a philanthropist. His admiration for Karl Popper was never exhausted[268]. He had admired him since his youth, and even wished he could be like the famous European philosopher. Finally, Bernard-Henri gave his opinion on what remains one of the worst financial predators on the planet: "All too human. Another incarnation of a system that, for half the planet, is a

---

[266] Bernard-Henri Levy, *American vertigo*, Editorial Ariel, 2007, Barcelona, p.46.

[267] Bernard-Henri Levy, *American vertigo*, Editorial Ariel, 2007, Barcelona, p. 137.

[268] On Karl Popper, see *Les Espérances planétariennes*, Hervé Ryssen, Baskerville, 2005, p.23, 140, 196, 322.

representation of the inhuman and that emotional and pathetic part of humanity[269]."

Certainly, after all, between a Jewish millionaire with a passion for philosophy and humanism and a Jewish humanist philosopher and millionaire, it is only natural that there should be some mutual respect, regardless of political differences.

Jewish financiers are indeed the kings of Wall Street. This undisputed financial supremacy was exemplified in an article in *Le Point* magazine of 9 February 2006, entitled "Steven Cohen, the Manitou of Wall Street".

Steven Cohen was the "star of the stock market". He liked to maintain secrecy around him: "The real boss of Wall Street does not live in Manhattan, but secluded in a house in Greenwich (Connecticut) enclosed by a four-metre high wall. Steven Cohen, 49, hardly ever shows himself… In 2005, he pocketed 500 million dollars. What is his secret? He knows everything before anyone else. With his eyes glued to the control screens, he analyses thousands of data and gets furious when Wall Street analysts don't give him the scoop on a piece of information. The investors who entrust him with their money (4 billion dollars) pay him dearly for his services: Cohen receives 3% of the sums as management fees (against an average of 1.44%) and 35% of the profits (against an average of 19.2%)". Cohen "professes total capitalism: 'You eat what you kill'," he tells his brokers, who are remunerated on the basis of their competence and performance."

George Soros is still, of course, the star of the show. He is one of the richest men on the planet and the symbol of international speculation. When he buys gold mines, the price of the yellow metal rises and falls if it is reported that he is selling. It was in 1992 that he reached the height of his glory when he pulled off one of the most resounding financial coups of the century. In a few days, sensing the weakness of the British currency, it mobilised nearly 10 billion dollars against sterling. The Bank of England faltered under the onslaught of speculation and finally had to devalue and withdraw its currency from the European Monetary System. Soros became "the man who broke the Bank of England". In the process, he pocketed more than a billion dollars in one week. His personal fortune was estimated (in 1998) at

---

[269] Bernard-Henri Levy, *American vertigo*, Editorial Ariel, 2007, Barcelona, p. 263, 264.

70 billion dollars. "Since the fall of communism in 1989, he has devoted most of his time to his *Open Society Foundation*. He defends the principles of freedom and human rights, "to preserve peace, order and law on a planetary level[270]". In this way, Soros funds cultural and scientific projects, supports writers, artists and "the independent and democratic press" (sic). In 1995, the Soros foundations had fifty offices around the world and employed a thousand people. These foundations teach and profess tolerance and the democratic values of the "open society", especially in the countries of Central Europe, where his family originated.

Before George Soros, the guru of Wall Street was another Jewish financier. Samuel Pisar, a successful businessman who knew the world's major stock exchanges, told us: "There is a guru on Wall Street. He is dedicated to the dollar and the dollar lovers. He is the chief economist of the mighty Salomon Brothers, which places the bond issues of most of the governments and multinationals of the world in the public eye. His name is Henry Kaufman. When he speaks, and he doesn't need many words, the world's stock markets begin to hope or tremble. His forecasts are followed in a second, recorded by banks, interpreted by chancelleries. Fortunes are made and unmade[271]."

Samuel Pisar had amassed his colossal fortune through fruitful collaboration with the Soviet Union. He had spent several stays there, especially with his friend, the famous Armand Hammer, president of the Western company Petroleum and a multimillionaire in his twenties:

"Hammer, at the age of twenty-three, went to the Soviet Union. The young American capitalist was to meet personally most of the Soviet leaders, befriend them, and eventually develop with them the first American-Soviet economic collaboration... Back in the United States, Hammer was to become the "king" of many things: whiskey, cattle, art, oil, etc., amassing one of the largest fortunes in the world and a power capable, if he so wished, of overthrowing the economies of many countries. His luxurious office in Los Angeles is full of photos with heads of state signed with praise". And Pisar specified: "It was with this

---

[270] George Soros, *La Crise du capitalisme mondial*, Plon, 1998, p.151.

[271] Samuel Pisar, *La Ressource humaine*, Jean-Claude Lattès, 1983, p. 24, 313.

fabulous and unfathomable Hammer that he arrived in Moscow in 1972[272]."

In his book on the Jews in Russia, *Two Hundred Years Together*, the Russian dissident Aleksandr Solzhenitsyn pointed out that Armand Hammer, as Lenin's favourite, had been granted the concession for the asbestos deposits at Alapayevsk as early as 1921. "Later, he shamelessly exported the treasures of the imperial collections to the United States. He returned frequently to Moscow, under Stalin and Khrushchev, to continue importing freighters full of Fabergé icons, paintings, porcelain and goldsmiths' wares."

These statements were confirmed by Jacques Attali: "Armand Hammer (...) became one of the leaders of East-West trade, reconciling his friendship with Lenin and his full adherence to the capitalist system. He exploited asbestos mines in the USSR, imported cars and tractors, and bought Russian works of art from the state in exchange for industrial products[273]."

We will not deal here with all those more or less mafia-like financiers who plundered all the wealth of Russia after the collapse of communism[274]. At the time, the Western media spoke of the "Russian mafia".

So we see that the Yiddish writer Cholem-Aleikhem was right when he wrote in 1913: "The biggest beasts and sharks on the stock exchange are mostly Jews. Their names can even be counted on the fingers of one hand: Rothschild, Mendelssohn, Bleichroeder, Yankl Schiff[275]." Manifestly, nothing has changed in that respect.


Jewish intellectuals may have some sympathy for the Protestantism of the Anglo-Saxons. The historian of Judaism Leon Poliakov had noted the affinities between the Anglo-Saxon world and Judaism. They were

---

[272] Samuel Pisar, *La Ressource humaine*, Jean-Claude Lattès, 1983, p. 170, 171.

[273] Jacques Attali, *Los Judíos, el mundo y el dinero*, Fondo de cultura económica de Argentina, Buenos Aires, 2005, p.403.

[274] Read *Les Espérances planétariennes*, Baskerville 2005, p.410-412 [and *La Mafia juive*, Baskerville, 2008].

[275] Cholem-Aleikhem, *La Peste soit de l'Amérique*, 1913, Liana Levi, 1992, p.295.

"due above all to the knowledge of the Old Testament, which was almost completely ignored, at least until the middle of the 20th century, by Catholics, including practising Catholics".

These affinities manifested themselves in England from the 17th century onwards. The country had just emerged from a civil war which had ended with the execution of King Charles I, and was in turmoil, subject to apocalyptic hopes. Cromwell had seized power and installed a dictatorship. One of his companions, Johm Sadler, proclaimed that the English were descended from the ten lost tribes of Israel. "As Cromwell himself announced, the English were the new chosen people; moreover, Poliakov added, medieval genealogists related the Britons to the ancestor Shem and, as a final proof, "Brit-Ish" meant in Hebrew "Man of the Covenant". In detail, their Danish ancestors descended from the tribe of Dana, their Gothic ancestors from Gad, and so on... Thus the sect of the "British Israelites" was formed.

The Puritans and other visionaries of the time referred to the Pope as the Antichrist. It was in this chaotic context that the Jews, who had been expelled in 1290, were reintroduced to the island: the Jews, Poliakov explained, "were still waiting for the Messiah who, according to belief, would not appear until they were scattered over the face of the earth. It was then, in those years, that Menasseh Ben Israel published his famous book *The Hope of Israel, a treatise on the admirable dispersion of the ten tribes and their inevitable return*".

The book was aimed primarily at a Christian audience, wrote Poliakov, for Menasseh Ben Israel's real ambition was to obtain the readmission of Jews to England. Having convinced his many English contacts of the relevance of his thesis, he presented himself to Cromwell in 1655, himself a supporter of readmission. "Finally, a group of wealthy Marranos was secretly admitted, awaiting a legalisation that did not take place until the end of the 17th century[276]."

The British Israelite sect developed and later Queen Victoria and King Edward VII became its honorary patrons. It ended up with hundreds of thousands of members and even published a weekly magazine, *The National Message*, which defended traditional British values. "As for Hebraic ancestry, the sect published in 1877 a work entitled *The Lost Ten Tribes of Israel*, which provided five hundred proofs drawn from

---

[276] Léon Poliakov, *The Samaritans*, Anaya & Mario Muchnik, 1992, Madrid, p.82

Scripture specially designed to demonstrate the biblical purity of their race, as opposed to the infidel Jews, those "bastards"[277]."

In the 1980s, British Israelites vehemently supported Margaret Thatcher's liberal policies. Today, they are but a small sect compared to their American offspring, the Mormons (The Church of the Latter Day Saint Movement).

This alliance of Anglo-Saxon Puritans and Jews, which was nourished by the sap of the Old Testament, was the true matrix of the capitalist, liberal and cosmopolitan society which today tends to expand over the whole planet. The triumph of the cosmopolitan spirit is due to this symbiosis, at once religious and vilely materialistic, which represents contemporary cosmopolitanism, "i.e. the Jewish and Protestant realism of capitalism which holds that profit is the motor of Creation[278] ", as Guy Konopnicki wrote.

During the second half of the 19th century, the United Kingdom had been the first European country to be led by a Jew. Benjamin Disraeli had become Prime Minister during the reign of Queen Victoria, of whom he was a friend. A champion of a strong British state, Disraeli secured Britain's control of the Indian routes by buying shares in the Suez Canal—earning him the nickname 'Sphinx'.

Israel Zangwill, a famous figure in Jewish literature, wrote of Disraeli in 1898 that "he regarded himself as coming from a race of aristocrats whose mission it was to civilise the world". And he added: "Like Heine, he senses that Puritan England, heir of ancient Palestine and whose State Church guards the generalised Semitic principle, is destined, by virtue of its physical and moral energy, to realise the ideals of Zion."

Disraeli's concern for the greatness of the British Empire should not be misleading: "His heart is always with his people, with their past glory, with their persistent power of ubiquity, in spite of the ubiquity of persecution. He considers himself a descendant of a chosen race, the only race to whom God has ever spoken[279]."

---

[277] Léon Poliakov, *The Samaritans*, Anaya & Mario Muchnik, 1992, Madrid, p.66, 67

[278] Guy Konopnicki, *La Place de la nation*, Olivier Orban, 1983, p. 193.

[279] Israel Zangwill, *Rêveurs de ghetto*, Tome II, 1998, Éditions Complexe, 2000, p. 213, 214.

## Wars and revolutions, "in the name of human rights".

It is common knowledge that the American evangelical movements were the most faithful supporters of Presidents George Bush Sr. and Jr. in the wars they waged against the "axis of evil". After a first war in Iraq in 1991, the US had invaded Afghanistan after the spectacular attacks of 11 September 2001, and finally Iraq again the following year.

It cannot be ignored, however, that numerous Jews were at that time very influential within the US administration: Paul Wolfowitz was Assistant Secretary of State for Defence; he was later appointed to head the World Bank. Richard Perle was head of the Advisory Committee to the Defense Policy Board; Douglas Feith was Deputy Secretary of State for Defense; Mickael Rubin was staff advisor to the Office of the Secretary of Defense on Iran and Iraq, etc. [280]...

The weekly *Rivarol\** of 12 May 2006 reported that some Israeli newspapers openly rejoiced at the decisive influence of numerous Jews in the US administration. "The key posts in the White House are filled by Jews". That was the cry of triumph in the *Jerusalem Post* of 25 April 2006: "After appointing Joshua Bolten as White House chief of staff, President George W. Bush chose another Jew, Joel Kaplan, as Bolten's deputy," the paper rejoiced. Other presidential aides, such as Homeland Security Secretary Michael Chertoff, Deputy National Security Advisor Elliott Abrams and White House pillar Jay Lefkowitz, etc., were also there. So much so, the Israeli daily stressed, that since Bush took office, it was approved to start every cabinet meeting with a short Jewish prayer. Bolton therefore asked the rabbis for help in "finding an appropriate Jewish prayer for the safety and well-being of the cabinet members". We would thus learn that Joshua Bolten read a prayer "aloud, in Hebrew and English, at every meeting." In addition, on the feast day of Purim, which commemorates the liberation of the Jews from Persia thanks to Esther, a religious service was held and the White House kitchens were duly "kashered" for the occasion.

It is true that there were even more Jews in the White House under President Clinton, recalled the *Jerusalem Post,* which cited the names of Robert Reich, Robert Rubin, Sandy Berger, Lawrence Summers,

---

[280] See: *Les Espérances planétariennes*, Hervé Ryssen, Baskerville, 2005, p. 134, 135.

\* Historical weekly of the French national right-wing founded in 1951.

Madeleine Albright, Aaron Miller, Dennis Ross and Martin Indyk. The newspaper did not mention that the latter two had been implicated in high-profile political and financial scandals.

The Jewish lobby was indeed extremely powerful within US governments in recent decades. Its influence on US politics, especially foreign policy, was first revealed almost officially by a report by two academics, Stephen Walt and John Mearsheimer. The report, entitled "The Israel Lobby and US Foreign Policy", masterfully demonstrated how the lobby, through the American Israel Public Affair Committee (AIPAC), had taken control of the US Congress and executive, and placed the military, finance and media at the service of the Hebrew state. The document was published by Harvard University, where Walt was a professor, and was recognised by the prestigious *London Review of Books*. In it one could read very eloquent passages about the unleashing of the Iraq war in March 2003:

"The war has been motivated, in large part, by a desire to increase Israel's security... In fact, the Israelis were so warmongering that their allies in the United States asked them to tone it down to keep everyone from learning that the war, if there was to be one, was going to be on behalf of Israel... "

"Neoconservative pundits wasted no time in implanting the idea in public opinion that the invasion of Iraq was essential to winning the war on terror. In the 1 October issue of the *Weekly Standard*, Robert Kagan and William Kristol called for an offensive to wipe out the Iraqi regime after the Taliban were defeated. On the same day, Charles Krauthammer argued in the *Washington Post* that when the US ended the war in Afghanistan, Syria had to be next on the list, followed by Iran and Iraq: *"The war on terror will end in Baghdad when we finish off the world's most dangerous terrorist regime"*. A relentless media campaign then began to persuade the public to invade Iraq. The crucial part of this was the manipulation of information in such a way that Saddam Hussein was believed to pose an imminent threat. For example, Libby pressured CIA analysts to find evidence in favour of war, and helped prepare the *briefing* given by Colin Powell to the UN Security Council.

"At the Pentagon, the *Policy Counter Terrorism Evaluation Group was* tasked with finding *al-Qaida*'s links to Iraq that the intelligence services were supposed to have missed. Its two main members were David Wurmser, a neo-conservative hardliner, and Michael Maloof, a Lebanese-American with close ties to Richard Perle. Another Pentagon group, the Office of Special Plans (OSP), was tasked with uncovering evidence that could be used to "sell the war". This office was headed by Adam Shulsky, a neo-conservative close to Wolfowitz, and included in its ranks recruits from pro-Israeli *think tanks*. These two organisations had been created in the aftermath of 9/11 and reported directly to Douglas Feith. Like almost all neo-conservatives, Feith is deeply loyal to Israel; he also has long-standing relations with Likoud".

The two authors concluded: "Given the neo-conservatives' devotion to Israel, their obsession with Iraq and their influence in the Bush administration, it is not surprising that many Americans suspected that the war was designed to further Israel's interests. There is little doubt that Israel and the *lobby* were the main influences that precipitated the decision to go to war. A decision the US would probably not have made without their efforts."

The British government was also strongly influenced by this lobby, which lobbied hard for the Israeli government. British Labour Prime Minister Tony Blair was evidently under its influence, as journalist and writer Israel Shamir noted and described:

"Michael Levy, also known as Viscount Reading, a friend of Ariel Sharon, is the grey eminence behind the Labour leader". This fervent Zionist had organised his election campaign. Israel Shamir quoted this testimony: "An honest Jew, Philip Weiss, acknowledges, in the *New York Observer* newspaper: "The Jews and the right wing have made an alliance... and together, they will push for war[281]."

As soon as the Iraqi question was resolved, Iranian President Ahmadinejad took on the role of spokesman for the Muslim resistance. The exaggerated warmongering of many Jewish intellectuals was once again verified, for example, in the weekly *Le Point* of 22 December

---

[281] Israel Shamir, *L'autre Visage d'Israel*, Éditions Al Qalam, 2004, p. 379, 394. The weekly *Le Point* of 20 July 2006 confirmed that this Michael Levy was a friend of British Prime Minister Tony Blair, whom he had met at a dinner organised by an Israeli diplomat. Levy had started fundraising for the Labour Party, which until then had been financed mainly by the trade unions. This had helped him to receive the title of Lord Lord after Tony Blair's victory in 1997. In the summer of 2006, the 60-year-old Lord was accused of having raised millions of pounds in loans from wealthy industrialists in exchange for honorary titles and seats in the House of Lords. The English have since nicknamed him "Lord Cashpoint".

2005. Bernard-Henri Levy entitled his article: "Is it still possible to stop the fascislamists in Teheran?" Compared to the current Iranian regime that threatened to get its hands on the atomic bomb, Saddam Hussein's "warlike veleities" were in reality "a gentle joke", wrote Levy. It was therefore a matter of overcoming the "pusillanimity of the free world": "We have to move fast," wrote the philosopher, "because we have very little time left".

In November 2004, Richard Perle, the "prince of darkness", took part in the 20th European Conferences at the Hebrew University of Jerusalem. Far from acknowledging his mistakes about the phantom "weapons of mass destruction" that had justified the invasion of Iraq, Perle took the opportunity to threaten Iran with US intervention, presenting it as a new crusade of democracies: "We must help the Iranians who live under the yoke of the mullahs and who are asking for our help. If all indications are that they may have nuclear weapons, we must intervene[282]."

Jewish intellectuals have a habit of portraying their enemies as the new Adolf Hitler. It was already the case in 1999 when they tried to paint Serbian president Milosevic as a bloodthirsty tyrant, and to push for war against Serbia; as it was also the case in 1991 to push the West to intervene against Saddam Hussein and his "fourth army of the world[283]". In the daily *Le Figaro* of 12 January 2006, MP Pierre Lellouche, a close adviser to Jacques Chirac, claimed that the new Iranian president, Mahmoud Ahmadinejad, was a new incarnation of Hitler: "At the dawn of the sixth year of the new millennium, Adolf Hitler was reincarnated in the guise of an obscure Iranian terrorist".

This is what the president of the European Jewish Congress, Pierre Besnainou, declared when he was elected president of the unified Jewish Social Fund[284] in June 2006: "Without any possible discussion, the priority must be the neutralisation of this new Hitler". The aim was to eliminate "the risk of seeing an undemocratic and dangerous dictator equip himself with a nuclear weapon to use against the countries of the region, including Israel. For me, the danger is focused on the Iranian

---

[282] Letter from Emmanuel Ratier, *Faits-et-Documents* of November 15, 2004.

[283] "It was the State of Israel, which had the fourth largest army in the world, and not Iraq." (JMB)

[284] http://www.guysen.com/articles.php?sid=4688

president". The journalist then asked: "Are you working to make European leaders aware of this danger?

—Yes, in my opinion this is important work. When Israel was exposed to the danger of terrorism and forced to defend itself, the world, which did not know the extent of this scourge, did not understand the reaction of the Hebrew state. With the attack on the World Trade Center, the United States and other European countries suddenly took the necessary measures. Today, the Iranian president is threatening to wipe Israel off the map, and while nations protest verbally, they still do not really realise how much this threat concerns them indirectly. The Iranian threat is not yet sufficiently perceptible in Europe, and we must act to awaken consciences."

You will have understood by now: if Israel is threatened, and if New York, the world's leading Jewish city and the heart of international finance, could have been the target of these attacks, then the West must strike back and declare war on the Muslim world and the "enemies of civilisation". Israel, indeed, seems to wage its wars only on the blood of others. But, after all, isn't it all about building the Empire of "Peace"?

In his 2006 book *The Great Global Disorder*, international speculator George Soros revealed some information about his role in the spread of democracy in the former Soviet bloc countries:

"I have set up capacity-building funds in several countries, including Georgia, following the 2003 Rose Revolution and the fall of President Eduard Shevardnadze's regime. These funds disbursed $1,200 a month to government ministers, plus a grant to police officers." But George Soros complained bitterly, "I have been the victim of a campaign of slander created and directed from Russia. I was accused of paying the Georgian government[285]."

Naturally, Soros was very concerned about the interests of Europeans and presented himself as the apostle of immigration and Turkey's entry into the European Union: "Given its ageing population, immigration is an economic necessity. The European Union, as the prototype of the

---

[285] George Soros, *Le grand Désordre mondial*, Éditions Saint-Simon, 2006, p. 137.

world's open societies, must welcome immigration and accept the entry of new members[286]."

His humanitarian commitment had also led him to support intervention against Serbia: "I took a position in favour of a more interventionist policy in the Yugoslav civil war, to curb human rights violations," he wrote. "At Christmas 1992, I announced a donation of fifty million dollars for humanitarian aid to the besieged city of Sarajevo... I joined a bipartisan group, the *Action Council for Peace in the Balkans*, which encouraged the Clinton administration to take a more aggressive position on Bosnia. Paul Wolfowitz belonged to the same group as I did, and together, we lobbied Secretary of State Madeleine Albright. I also supported NATO's intervention in Kosovo[287]."

Soros had also spoken out in favour of military intervention in Afghanistan in 2001, against those wretched Taliban, guilty of professing an "obscurantist" religion: "I supported the invasion of Afghanistan, home of Bin Laden and the Al-Qaeda training camps[288]". In 2003, however, he opposed George Bush and the neo-conservatives' war in Iraq, guilty, according to him, of being "supporters of American supremacy". He then denounced, without laughing, the most reactionary elements of this Christian and "nationalist" "right wing", the only ones responsible for the war: "In the United States today, the right-wing propaganda machine... has succeeded, remarkably, in imposing its interpretation of reality". He further insisted: "Bush's policy contains a strong nationalist theme". And it was here that he accused the two domesticated goyim, Vice President Dick Cheney and Defence Secretary Donald Rumsfeld, of having been the main protagonists of this bellicose adventure. These two are the ones who

---

[286] George Soros, *Le grand Désordre mondial*, Éditions Saint-Simon, 2006, p. 164, 167.

[287] George Soros, *Le grand Désordre mondial*, Éditions Saint-Simon, 2006, p. 83. In December 1996, US President Bill Clinton had revamped his foreign policy team. At the State Department, Madeleine K. Albright replaced Warren Christopher. Albright is the surname of her divorced husband, while the "K" stands for Korbel, a Jewish family from Czechoslovakia. At the Ministry of Defence, William Perry gave way to William S. Cohen. Lake's former deputy, Samuel R. Berger, now occupied the strategic post of national security officer, etc. Read *Les Espérances planétariennes*, p. 119

[288] George Soros, *Le grand Désordre mondial*, Éditions Saint-Simon, 2006, p. 109.

"have largely succeeded in imposing their views on the Bush administration[289]."

Let us simply recall, for formal reasons, the objectives pursued by George Soros: "My objective, he said, is the establishment of an open world society" in order to contribute to "peace" in the world.

The occupation of Iraq by US troops in 2003, and the ongoing civil war that devastated the country, proved catastrophic. After the Republicans' electoral defeat in 2006, the "neo-conservatives" projected their guilt onto a "scapegoat" in a very biblical manner. In the political weekly *Marianne* of 27 January 2007, one article read: "Several of them, including Richard Perle, Kenneth Adelman, David Frum and Michael Rubin, have just written jointly in *Vanity Fair,* an unprecedentedly virulent criticism of President Bush and his administration… The four "hawks" have no remorse: the idea of the war, they reiterate, was "good", but it was "its execution that turned out badly", due to the "incompetence" of the White House."

Once again, we must understand that the responsibility for these wars lies solely with Christians. Guy Sorman did, however, acknowledge the responsibilities of some Jewish leaders: "Is the Iraq war, therefore, a machination of Jewish intellectuals more concerned with Israel's security than with that of the United States? Certainly, the most fervent advocates of exporting democracy to the Middle East belong to an intelliguentsia of New York Jews, often on the far left, who describe themselves as neo-conservatives". But Guy Sorman was quick to add: "This Zionist conspiracy theory does not stand up to any analysis[290]."

According to him, the real culprits of the Iraq war were the 40 million American evangelists, Baptists and Pentecostals, irredeemable "imperialists", as he defined them.

Another well-known essayist, Pascal Bruckner, declared in *Le Figaro* of 5 November 2003: "Christianity and Islam have in common that they are two imperialist religions, convinced that they possess the truth and always ready to bring salvation to men, be it by the sword, the auto de fe or the burning of books… In the name of a merciful God, they have killed and liquidated, directly or indirectly, millions of individuals". On

---

[289] George Soros, *Le grand Désordre mondial*, Éditions Saint-Simon, 2006, p. 90-93.

[290] Guy Sorman, *Made in USA*, Fayard, 2004, Livre de Poche, 2006, p.304

the contrary, Judaism, as you will well understand, is a religion of Peace and Love.

This policy, which is both immigrationist in Europe and warmongering in the East, can only provoke resistance here and there. Indeed, Jacques Attali had perfectly perceived the dangers it represented: "We could be heading, in the worst of nightmares, towards an agreement between the two daughter religions against the mother, Islam and Christianity against Judaism[291]". Certainly, we know that the Jews have had a virtue for centuries: that of making the whole world angry and against them.

## *A world war, if necessary*

Even before the Second World War, nationalists in all European countries were alarmed by the unbridled warmongering of the representatives of the respective Jewish communities in their countries.

In a book aimed at combating the idea of Jewish "conspiracy", Norman Cohn reported that in the 1930s, French nationalists strongly denounced Jewish warmongering: "Throughout August and September 1938, *La France enchaînée* published articles with headlines such as "Danger of War: Jewish-Russian conspiracy in Czechoslovakia"; "The war is coming, the war of the Jews"; "Will the Jews dare to unleash the world war? The publication of the new edition of the Protocols was accompanied by the following announcement: "It is Judaism that has created the democratic front. It is Judaism that has brought the United States out of its splendid isolation. It is Judaism that wants war". Norman Cohn further added that, under pressure, "the French Government had to take the measure, which at the time was extraordinary, of limiting the freedom of the press. On 25 April 1939, a decree was issued prohibiting, on pain of a fine or imprisonment, all anti-Semitic propaganda[292]."

---

[291] Jacques Attali, *Los Judíos, el mundo y el dinero*, Fondo de cultura económica de Argentina, Buenos Aires, 2005, p. 499.

[292] Norman Cohn, *The Myth of the World Jewish Conspiracy. The Protocols of the Elders of Zion*, Digital Editor pdf: Titivilius, 2016, p.159. Robert Brasillach recounted this in *Notre avant-guerre*: "Anti-Semitism, despite the fact that M. Blum was removed from the government, was growing stronger. A strange decree law provided for sanctions against those who incited racial or religious hatred against the citizens of France, including its "inhabitants". Brasillach

Lord Beaverbrook, the head of the *Daily Express*, who was also the British Minister of Aircraft Production and Minister of State during the Second World War, had also noticed this tendency in the Jewish community. In his letters dated 9 March and 9 December 1939, preserved in the "Beaverbrook papers", he wrote:

"The Jews have a strong presence in the press... The *Daily Mirror* is perhaps owned by Jews. The *Daily Herald belongs* to Jews. The *New Chronicle* should be called the *Jews Chronicle*. I'm not sure about the *Daily Mail*... For years, I was convinced we would avoid war, now I am shaken. The Jews may drag us into war; I don't mean deliberately, but all things considered, their political influence is likely to drag us into it[293]."

A former socialist resister, Paul Rassinier, wrote a book on the subject in 1967, entitled *Those Responsible for the Second World War*. In it, he accused US President Roosevelt, a man of the left and a 32nd degree Scottish Rite Freemason: "His entourage is Jewish, at least most of his most important collaborators. Morgenthau, his Secretary of State for the Treasury is Jewish; his most influential advisers, Baruch and Weiman also; Cordell Hull, of the State Department, is married to a Jewess... "

Paul Rassinier recalled that when Hitler rose to power, the US *Daily Express* of 24 March 1933 headlined on its front page: "Jewish Peoples All Over the World Declare Financial and Economic War on Germany[294]." The *Jewish Chronicle* of 8 May 1942 recalled: "We have been at war with Germany from the first day of Hitler's seizure of power[295]." British Prime Minister Chamberlain, too, wrote in a letter to his sister on 10 September 1939: "It is the United States and the international Jewish world that have thrown us into the war."

In his 1942 pamphlet entitled *Jewish America*, Pierre Antoine Cousteau—the brother of the famous ocean commander, explorer and

---

ironically added: "From then on the Jews were called the 'inhabitants'".

[293] Quoted in Serge de Beketch's radio programme *Le libre Journal*, 17 March 2005.

[294] In Roman Polanski's film *The Pianist*, we see this father of a family exclaim: "Jewish bankers should convince the United States to declare war on Germany!"

[295] Paul Rassinier, *Les Responsables de la Seconde Guerre mondiale*, Nouvelles éditions latines, 1967, p. 74, 78.

documentarian—also recounted how Jewish publicists were poisoning the international situation. During one of his trips to the United States in 1935, he saw the extent to which the Americans were being incited by the press: "I had in my hands a magazine showing a "torture room" in a German concentration camp. Admittedly, the picture had been taken in such a way that it was quite confusing, but terrifying. It was difficult to tell that the torture room was actually a shower room[296]."

Pierre-Antoine Cousteau destroyed in a few lines the arguments put forward by the Jews, which were almost always the same: "People who deny Roosevelt's subjection to Judaism insist a lot on the fact that only one of his ministers (Morgenthau) is Jewish and that the congress does not count more than a dozen Jews, which can be considered a reasonable percentage. But once again, we must distinguish appearances from reality. The ministers are mere executors and the real power is exercised by the "brain trust", the one that made rivers of ink flow and is hardly spoken of anymore, although its power is still intact. However, this "brain trust" is a strictly Jewish affair".

Among Roosevelt's personal advisers, "the most senior was Bernard Baruch, whom the *Jewish Examiner* of 20 October 1933 tenderly calls 'the unofficial President'...". Before 1914, he had already amassed a colossal fortune by speculating on Wall Street in tobacco, sugar, copper and rubber. When the war broke out, he joined the "War Industries Committee"; he became a sort of dictator of the economy. No arms dealer can get credit without his approval. He also decides how much material the Allies will receive and how it will be distributed. The profits he pockets from the blood of others are beyond imagining. Indeed, he has admitted to a parliamentary committee of enquiry that questioned him—timidly, as always—about his chicanery: "He probably had more power than anyone else during the last war". When the peace conference opened in Paris, Bernard Baruch followed in Wilson's footsteps. He brought with him 117 collaborators, all Jews, who helped him to consolidate his prodigious profits in the corridors of the conference. This war profiteer, a man who amassed his extravagant fortune on the massacres of Europe, is also a cynic. He is often quoted as saying in the *Chicago Tribune*: "Patriotism is nothing but a lot of nonsense". Patriotism is perhaps a "load of nonsense", Cousteau replied, but when it comes to Jewish patriotism, guys like Baruch don't hesitate. They are ready to sacrifice everything for the salvation of their race.

---

[296] Pierre-Antoine Cousteau, *L'Amérique juive*, Éditions de France, 1942, p. 45.

Such is the "unofficial president", the man Roosevelt sees almost every day and without whom no important decision can be taken."

Another figure in the "brain trust" was Felix Frankfuter. This Marxist, born in Vienna in 1882, "was in charge of setting up the legal structure of the New Deal," wrote Cousteau. He immediately took advantage of the situation to place several of his race brothers: Herbert Feiss in the State Secretariat, Benjamin Cohen and Nathan Margold as financial advisers to the Ministry of the Interior, David-T Lilienthal at the head of the T.V.A. and Charles Wyzanski as technical adviser to the Ministry of Labour." In January 1939, he was appointed by Roosevelt as an immovable justice of the Supreme Court of the United States.

Felix Frankfurter had a key collaborator in the Supreme Court, another judge named Louis Dembitz Brandeis. He was undoubtedly the real father of the New-Deal. "He is said to have instigated the election of the Jew Lehmann to the post of Governor of the State of New York to replace Roosevelt. He is also said to have influenced the appointment to the Supreme Court of the Jew Samuel Rosenmann, whom Roosevelt called his 'right-hand man'. His requests also extended to the lawyer Samuel Untermeyer, Roosevelt's personal adviser, head of the organisation of the boycott of "racist" goods, whose communist sympathies were publicly known… Cousteau wrote that we could go on naming names. From the moment Roosevelt came to power, the Jews went after all the administrations and ministries, to such an extent that it looked like a gigantic manhunt. Even when the minister responsible is not Jewish, his immediate subordinates are". Cousteau cited a litany of names now forgotten, recalling in passing that France in 1937, under Léon Blum, suffered the same situation: "The stampede of the Jews, their rush to the squares (all posts and immediately!)[297]". The only difference was that in the United States, an Aryan was nominally the head of the government. But "the ideal is to rule through an intermediary, to manage a figurehead of proven subservience, a synthetic Jew. Mr. Roosevelt is that man[298]."

---

[297] Pierre-Antoine Cousteau, *L'Amérique juive*, Éditions de France, 1942, p. 71-77.

[298] "Perhaps it is the same fear, the same desire not to be in the limelight that explains the curious approach of the Chief Rabbi of Paris who, according to Blumel, went to meet Léon Blum to tell him: "If you refuse the presidency of the Council, "we" undertake to pay him a life pension equivalent to the salary of the head of the government" (Jean Lacouture, Sociologie de l'antisémitisme,

During the economic crisis of 1929, Roosevelt, a man of the left, lashed out strongly against the power of the financiers. His election in 1932 was not, however, a victory against capitalism. Pierre-Antoine Cousteau's analysis was very concise: "It was immediately clear that the conquest of money by the Jewish plutocrats was not without the conquest of the masses by the Jewish agitators. This same dualism, whose most perfect representation is the current alliance of Wall Street and the Kremlin[299]."

Pierre-Antoine Cousteau also told a particularly eloquent anecdote: "Already, on the eve of the other war, i.e. only twenty-five years before the start of the conquest, the Jews held such important positions in the United States that nothing could be undertaken without their consent. André Tardieu, who was France's High Commissioner in the United States from April 1917 to November 1918, recounted, with a certain naivety, in *L'Année de Munich*, how he had that revelation. His delegation had been received correctly, but nothing more, and he was met with a kind of smiling indifference which made his task particularly difficult. To be honest, the "Americans" did not care much for France, La Fayette, or the great historical memories that only served to enliven the speeches at the end of banquets. By contrast, the British mission operating in parallel got everything it asked for, and Monsieur André Tardieu suddenly realised that his boss, Viscount Reading, had been born Rufus Isaac. That Hebrew aristocrat wasted no time courting Aryans. He went straight to the point, besieging Judge Brandeis who was the confidant of the paralysed Wilson, and his officers who accompanied him, Jews for the most part, were only prospecting in Jewish circles. André Tardieu understood that this was the key to the problem, and that, if he wanted to avoid failure, he had to stop the cantankerous talk about La Fayette and seduce the real masters of the country. So he attached to the chaplains of his intelligence service two photogenic rabbis whom he displayed at all times and surrounded himself, he too, with highly decorated Jewish officers who told anyone who would listen about their warlike "exploits" and flattered their New York brethren as best they could. After that, Mr. André Tardieu received

---

Paris, 1977, p. 301-303, in François de Fontette, Sociologie de l'antisémitisme, PUF, 1984, p. 309). (Jean Lacouture, *Léon Blum*, Paris, 1977, p. 301-302, in François de Fontette, *Sociologie de l'antisémitisme*, PUF, 1984, p.38).

[299] Pierre-Antoine Cousteau, *L'Amérique juive*, Éditions de France, 1942, p. 58, 68.

from Pichon, our Minister of Foreign Affairs, a telegram written by himself and containing France's adhesion to the Balfour project for the creation of an Israeli home in Palestine. As soon as he had the telegram, Mr Tardieu brought it to Judge Brandeis, who, he says, "wept with joy". From then on, the case was won. Mr Tardieu concluded: "Our relations with the American government, American finance and the American press, which we badly needed, were greatly facilitated". It could not be more clearly explained that, as late as 1917, the Aryans had no place in the United States[300].

It is known that the philosopher Henri Bergson was also sent to the United States by Aristide Briand in early 1917 to convince the Americans to go to war with the Entente countries[301]. It was thanks to the American armies that the catastrophic situation in which the Allies found themselves in 1917, following the collapse of Russia and the mutinies of French troops, could be saved.

World War I had brought about the destruction of the great European monarchies, the German Empire, the Austro-Hungarian Empire, and the Russian Empire, as well as the Ottoman Empire. It is almost certain that many Jews thought at the time that the prophecies were being fulfilled. Maimonides, one of the greatest Jewish thinkers of the Middle Ages, still considered today as one of the main references in Judaism, explained in his *Epistle to Yemen*, in 1172, the changes that the Messiah would bring: "When he appears, God will make the kings of the earth tremble, and they will be horrified at the announcement of his coming. Their kingdoms will fall; they will be unable to rise up against him, either by war or revolt[302]."

However, some Americans had opened their eyes to the consequences of the conflict and to who would be the main beneficiaries. On 20 May 1920, the great industrialist Henry Ford launched his crusade against Judaism by creating a weekly newspaper, the *Dearborn Independant*, and writing a book soberly entitled *The International Jew*. His enemies organised a conspiracy of silence around the paper, until it got too far-reaching. A boycott of its automobile production finally caused it to

---

[300] Pierre-Antoine Cousteau, *L'Amérique juive*, Éditions de France, 1942, p. 32, 33

[301] Michel Winock, *Edouard Drumont et Cie*, Seuil, Paris, 1982, p. 173-174.

[302] Gershom Scholem, *Le Messianisme juif*, 1971, Calman-Levy, 1974, p. 57-59.

capitulate. In January 1922, the *Dearborn Independant* published "an embarrassed note in which he explained that he had to renounce his attacks, but invited all Goyim not to lose sight of the Jewish question. The Jews, Cousteau wrote, had silenced the richest businessman in America".

Among the American resisters, mention must be made of Father Coughlin, who harangued millions of listeners every week. He "censured capitalism and Marxism with a fierceness worthy of a fascist". He had supported Roosevelt with all his eloquence, but soon realised that the president was "betraying the cause of the humble, that he was handing the country over to the Jews, that he was leading the country into war." In 1935, he denounced for the first time at the microphone the role of the "international bankers". "The word Jew had not been uttered," Cousteau wrote, "but there was no doubt about it, and the rabbis of New York immediately rose up to accuse Coughlin of fomenting 'racial hatred'." Father Coughlin became increasingly clear and precise in his accusations, and ended up openly denouncing the" Jewish crusade". "But as soon as he began to denounce Israel's influence and the Jews' desire for war, the radio stations, one after another, as if by magic, took away his microphones. Excluded from radio, Father Coughlin was disarmed. They gave him the coup de grâce at the outbreak of hostilities by charging him with high treason, accusing him of being a sell-out to Germany."

That left Charles Lindbergh. National hero, the famous aviator who had flown across the Atlantic for the first time in 1927. He led the anti-war movement. "His courage, his intelligence and his probity are called into question. The victor of the Atlantic is now nothing but a sell-out, the leader of the "fifth column". Eager Jewish publicists, just as vile as the gangsters who murdered his son, are bent on dishonouring him[303]."

In his novel *The Plot Against America*, published in 2004, the famous American writer Philip Roth imagined a terrible storyline, mixing fact and fiction and inverting the situations, as Jewish intellectuals usually do: In 1940, Charles Lindberg defeated Roosevelt and won the election. Here is what you could read on the cover of the book: "fear invaded every Jewish home in America. Not only had Lindbergh publicly

---

[303] Pierre-Antoine Cousteau, *L'Amérique juive*, Éditions de France, 1942, p. 87-95.

## THE JEWISH FANATICISM

blamed the Jews for pushing the country into a senseless war with Nazi Germany in a speech broadcast over the nation's radio, but after taking office as the 33rd President of the United States he negotiated a cordial 'agreement' with Adolf Hitler". The Jews were, once again, the great victims, always persecuted, and always innocent.

In 1942, President Lindbergh's son was kidnapped: "At church services across the country, prayers are offered for the Lindbergh family. The three major radio stations cancel their regular programming to rebroadcast the mass at Washington National Cathedral, which is attended by the First Lady and her children. German radio rages against the organisers of the "plot": "The plot has been planned and organised by the warmongering Roosevelt (in collusion with his Jewish Secretary of the Treasury, Morgenthau, his Jewish Supreme Court Justice, Frankfurter, and the Jewish business banker Baruch) and is being financed by the international Jewish usurers Warburg and Rothschild and executed under the command of Roosevelt's half-breed hit man, the Jewish gangster La Guardia, mayor of Jewish New York City along with the powerful Jewish governor of New York State, financier Lehman, in order to get Roosevelt back into the White House and launch a total Jewish war against the non-Jewish world[304]."

Philip Roth expressed himself at the end of the novel through his character: "Mayor La Guardia says: 'There is a conspiracy afoot, of course, and I will gladly mention the forces driving it: hysteria, ignorance, wickedness, stupidity, hatred and fear. What a revolting spectacle our country has become! Falsehood, cruelty and evil everywhere, and brute force behind the scenes waiting to do us in. Now we read in the *Chicago Tribune* that for all these years Jewish master bakers in Poland have been using the blood of Lindbergh's kidnapped son to make Passover *matzohs*, a story as insane today as it was when first devised by anti-Semitic maniacs five hundred years ago. Their lies, and their trickery, are relentless[305]."

---

[304] Philip Roth, *La Conjura contra América*, Círculo de lectores de Barcelona, on loan from Grupo Editorial Mondadori, 2005, cover and p. 339, 341.

[305] Philip Roth, *La Conjura contra América*, Círculo de lectores de Barcelona, on loan from Grupo Editorial Mondadori, 2005, p.346.

# PART TWO

## THE TALMUDIC SPIRIT

## 1. The cosmopolitan mentality

### On our knees before Israel

Few Jewish intellectuals have a natural tendency to blame the rest of humanity. Of all the specificities of the chosen people, this character trait is undoubtedly one of the most obvious. In the first volume of his memoirs, Elie Wiesel recounted the following: "In 1979, during an official visit to Moscow, I met the Soviet General Vassily Petrenko who had, at the head of his troops, liberated the Auschwitz camp. We shared our memories. He describes to me how the units under his command had prepared for the assault, while I tell him how we were waiting for him and his soldiers". We were waiting for you as a religious Jew waits for the Messiah," Wiesel wrote, then reproached, "Why didn't you arrive a few hours earlier, why were you delayed? An advance party of one patrol would have been enough to save thousands of human lives!" Wiesel continued his guilt-ridden speech: "He gave me vague explanations, technical ones: strategy, meteorology, logistics. I was not convinced. The fact is that the Soviet army could have made an effort; it did not. And neither did the American army... Of the objectives set by the Allied General Staff, none envisaged the death camps; their liberation did not come about as a result of a priority directive but simply by chance." He added: "Cowardly, the men refused to listen[306]."

Men are cowards, and even, let's say it frankly, bastards, as we can read it under the pen of other authors: "When our children cried under the scaffold, the world was silent, the poet Nathan Alterman would say[307]."

---

[306] Elie Wiesel, *Mémoires, Tome I*, Le Seuil, 1994, p. 120, 133, 134.

[307] Victor Malka, *In Israel*, Guide Bleu, Hachette 1977, p. 27.

The final solution, we must believe, has been "imagined by the Hitlerites, with the at least passive complicity of a good part of humanity[308]."

Europeans were extremely indifferent to the poor Jews, always persecuted and always innocent. Manes Sperber, a committed intellectual who was a friend of André Malraux and Albert Camus, wrote in 1952: "We know the facts, the guilty parties. The complicity is not sufficiently emphasised. Certain circumstances are concealed: for example, neighbouring Russia, a friend of the Hitler regime until June 1941, could have saved the Jews of Poland; the powerful United States, neutral until December 1941, could have helped. When the countless days and nights of methodical murder came, the victims, a whole people in the middle of the world, were alone, alone like a child in its first nightmare". And this criminal policy, Sperber claimed, continued under Stalin: "Jews disappeared from the USSR without trial, without gas chambers, without attracting attention, without making a sound[309]."

In 1978 Manes Sperber was still lamenting: "The catastrophe organised by the Germans had been actively encouraged by other peoples and watched with indifference by the rest of the world… Memory cannot be dispelled, it recalls those ships full of escaped Jews wandering the oceans and eventually sinking miserably because no port, no country, from the most powerful to the most humble, would agree to grant them even temporary asylum; it reminds me of the Warsaw ghetto insurgents, who in the middle of an empty and depopulated moonscape, provoked an all-powerful enemy; they no longer expected anything, for even despair was vetoed for those young beings: they died in nothingness. But we live on, guilty of their disappearance without having committed any fault, guilty of everything[310]."

However, it would be a mistake to think that the Jewish people are completely alone in this world of hatred and hypocrisy. There are people, among the Goyim, who did not lose face in the eyes of Judaism. There are not many of them, of course, so it is important to give them a deserved place here. In *The Power of Good*, the writer Marek Halter showed us the way to wisdom, beginning with the comfort that "the Good exists", he wrote with a capital letter. He thus undertook a

---

[308] CinémaAction, Cinéma et judéité, Annie Goldmann (dir.), Cerf, 1986, p. 29.

[309] Manès Sperber, *Être Juif*, Odile Jacob, 1994, p. 124, 125.

[310] Manès Sperber, *Être Juif*, Odile Jacob, 1994, p. 28, 29.

"journey to the land of the Righteous" to pay homage to them: "By restoring their testimonies, silenced for so long, I wanted to create a "memory of the Good". For Good is hope. And without hope, one cannot live". "The world is based on thirty-six Righteous Ones", said Rabbi Rabbah? According to the Talmud, in every generation, they are present to sustain the world." They show that "there were individuals who enabled us not to lose faith in humanity[311]."

Marek Halter's journey naturally began in his native Poland, where so many Jews lived before the Second World War. "It has always been said that in Poland the Jews had no one to reach out to them, and here is a woman who, with the help of a few friends, managed to save so many children! Irena Sendler senses my surprise, my disbelief". We understand Marek Halter's surprise better when we hear the saying: "It took a thousand Poles to save one Jew. But one Pole was enough to denounce a thousand Jews".

Halter then recounted the unspeakable suffering of the Jewish people during that dark period, and asked the old woman: "Why did so many Poles, so many Catholics, do nothing to help the Jewish children? Sister Ludovica remained silent for a few seconds, then, with a clear look and voice, she began to laugh. "Ask them!"

—Why did you save the Jewish children?" He smiles. Behind his thick glasses, a warm simplicity shines in his eyes." For God of course. Because God said to help your neighbour. And besides… "He interrupts himself and in a limpid voice says: "We could not stop saving Jewish children, because when we saved a Jewish child, it was as if we were saving the child Jesus[312]."

At last, a healthy reflection from a good Catholic. It has to be said that all too often, the bad instincts and "death drives" of Catholics have manifested themselves to the detriment of other communities: "Why? Why against Muslims, Protestants, gypsies, homosexuals and so many others? Why the murder of these or those, sometimes? Why the murder of Jews, always[313]?" This is where we understand that Marek Halter wanted to reassure himself: since the Jews are not the only victims, it is

---

[311] Marek Halter, *La force du Bien*, Robert Laffont, 1995, p, 7, 8

[312] Marek Halter, *La force du Bien*, Robert Laffont, 1995, p. 14, 34

[313] Marek Halter, *La force du Bien*, Robert Laffont, 1995, p. 36.

that the Evil necessarily comes from the oppressors and not from themselves.

After Poland, Marek Halter continued his "initiatory journey to the land of the Righteous" until he reached the Netherlands: "This country has the largest number of Righteous in Europe: one third of the 9295—but paradoxically, it also has the largest proportion of deported Jews in Western Europe. Indeed, "in Anne Frank's country, eighty percent of the Jews of Holland were deported with the active collaboration of the population... How could there be so much apathy and complacency towards crime in a country that had demonstrated since ancient times its tolerance and its humanism, a country where the French Huguenots could take refuge, a country that welcomed the Encyclopaedists and the Enlightenment...? This question is a painful one, wrote Halter, and no one is able to provide an enlightening explanation or produce a definitive analysis".

There is indeed no valid explanation for anti-Semitism. For Marek Halter, anti-Semitism is a mystery. He added: "And suddenly we are faced with this paradox: the shame of the Righteous! They were ashamed of the behaviour of the majority of their fellow citizens, who were so willing to collaborate with the Nazis and denounce the Jews during the war, and who, now in peacetime, looked askance, with a guilty conscience and even with a certain veiled hostility, at those rescuers who had, unlike them, risked their lives to help persecuted people. Many of these rescuers left. Many went to South Africa to join the Boers... They preferred to be with the distant descendants of their Dutch ancestors, rather than to go on living, as if nothing had happened, in the midst of their contemporaries whose behaviour they had found odious during the war and hypocritical after the war. Others also emigrated far away: Canada, Australia, as if they wished to distance themselves as far away as possible from the Dutch[314]." This is how we like the Dutch: full of bad conscience and contempt for their own countrymen.

Marek Halter's pilgrimage led him to Lithuania, where he met Nathan Gutwirth: "What were you doing in Lithuania, Mr Gutwirth? —The Talmud," he replied. In 1936, I went to study Talmud at the yeshiva in Vilnius. I had left behind Holland, where I had completed my education and where my family lived. Vilnius then had one hundred and fifty-four

---

[314] Marek Halter, *La force du Bien*, Robert Laffont, 1995, p. 99-104.

thousand inhabitants, one third of whom were Jewish. Don't forget that, at that time, Vilnius was called the "Jerusalem of the North" because it had the largest yeshiva in the world: a sort of international university, with students from all over the world, from the United States and even Australia... In September 1939, we saw tens of thousands of Polish Jews arriving from invaded Poland, and Lithuanian Jews welcomed them with open arms.

Faced with the advance of the German armies, Lithuanian Jews thought only of trying to flee to the Far East: "The news has spread in the Jewish community, especially among the Polish refugees. Thousands of people crowded in front of the Japanese consulate: they all wanted a visa!" Tempo Sugihara, the Japanese consul then decided to bypass his government's ban and issue as many visas as he could: "Some six thousand visas would thus be hastily issued... These Jews, with papers in order, were to take whole trains to go eastwards through the Soviet Union. They would cross the whole of Russia, via Vladivostok, to land in Japan: a collective escape on the Trans-Siberian! Nathan Gutwirth recalls this journey: "Imagine arriving in Japan after a three-week journey on the Trans-Siberian, just after Pearl Harbor, on 7 December 1941: there were Wehrmacht military missions preparing projects with their Japanese army allies. And suddenly they saw thousands of Jews disembarking from Vladivostok, coming from the confines of Lithuania. They must have thought it was a nightmare... "The Japanese were surprised and totally unprepared. Evidently, they would dismiss the Lithuanian consul, Tempo Sugihara, and send all the Jews to Shanghai, the city they controlled. Thus the Jewish quarter of Shanghai was created[315]."

Tempo Sugihara, the Japanese consul in Vilnius, was therefore a Righteous Man, for he risked his life to save Jews. A few pages further on we learn that this Righteous man had a son called Nobuki: "Nobuki Sugihara, aged forty-four, is a diamond cutter in the gemstone capital of the world, Antwerp". Gemstone cutting in Antwerp is a "Japanese" speciality, as is well known.

In Denmark, Marek Halter was able to congratulate himself on the rescue of almost all of the country's 7,500 Jews whom the fishermen helped to flee to Sweden: "My research on the Righteous could not do without the country of the Righteous, wrote Halter". But let us not be

---

[315] Marek Halter, *La force du Bien*, Robert Laffont, 1995, p. 121-123.

too hasty with too much celebration, for if the Danes were blameless, they would not be goyim: "Curiously, far from what I might have believed, the fact that I learned that some Danish fishermen had not risked their lives entirely gratuitously for the Jews cheered me up. After all, these Danes are normal people. They too have their faults, their lowliness, their pettiness[316]."

However, we can ask ourselves in the face of so much selflessness and sacrifice on the part of these small Danish people: "A miracle? No, you had to have the will", replied Henry Sundoe... The Jews were our friends, they were Danes. We never had the slightest problem with them. Marek Halter confirms: "Arriving at the invitation of King Christian IV in 1662, the Jews had been in Denmark for two hundred and seventy-eight years when the Second World War broke out. Originally, they were Sephardim from Amsterdam and Ashkenazi from Hamburg... They quickly became Danes. This was constantly underlined by their rescuers".

Here is the testimony of a Dane to Marek Halter's liking: "The Jews? Danes like us, with their Sunday falling on the Sabbath, which never bothered anyone". One can perceive in these pages the writer's delight in referring to these words and how he secretly laughed at the goy's credulity. But this Danish goy went beyond his hopes: "If the Jews are indebted to the Danes (and they keep repeating it ever since), we Danes are also grateful to them for the opportunity and possibility they offered us to help them: they enabled us, by saving them, to safeguard our dignity[317]."

Marek Halter continued his search in France, together with his friend, the Cardinal-Archbishop of Paris: "You know, Cardinal Lustiger told me one day... those who we call "Righteous" and who saved many Jews... understood this fact: Israel is our source. You cannot pollute your own source, let it dry up. If we do so, if we accept that our source is damaged, we condemn ourselves to die of thirst. We cannot not love our source... I have noticed that true believers, true believers, profess an indescribable love: a true love for the Jews, the people of God, a

---

[316] Marek Halter, *La force du Bien*, Robert Laffont, 1995, p. 137-138.

[317] Marek Halter, *La force du Bien*, Robert Laffont, 1995, p. 141-150.

religious love[318]." This is how we like bishops and cardinals: full of admiration for Israel.

But it seems necessary here to specify Monsignor Lustiger's origins, which may have influenced his profound reflections: "Even today my civil status name is Aron. The fact that I am Jewish is no secret to anyone in Orleans, where I was during the war". His false identity papers had then been given to him by a mayor of the Orléans region, and established his surname Lustiger, as well as an invented name, Jean-Marie. "Despite those papers being in order, my father was discovered, and so was I. We fled to Toulouse. That's when we fled to Toulouse[319]."

But Catholics are not the only ones to recognise the ancient wisdom of the Jews. Marie Brottes, a Protestant from the Cévennes region, also spoke to Marek Halter: "What does a Jew mean to you? —Well, the Jews, they're... the people of God. So we respect that[320]." That's well said.

The financier Samuel Pisar, who left a painful testimony of his experience in the death camps in his book *The Blood of Hope*, also knew how to recognise the Righteous among the nations. He recalled in particular the gesture of Willy Brandt, the former German Chancellor, who "knelt before the memorial in the Warsaw ghetto, silently asking for forgiveness on behalf of the German people, he who had worn a foreign uniform to fight his country in madness[321]." This is how we like German chancellors: on their knees before Israel.

In 1992, four hundred years after the expulsion of the Jews, the time had come for the King of Spain to apologise as well. Journalist Serge Moati recalled this episode: "In 1992, Juan Carlos I, King of Spain, distant successor of Isabella the Catholic, solemnly abrogated the

---

[318] Marek Halter, *La force du Bien*, Robert Laffont, 1995, p. 172, 210-213

[319] Lustig is the name of a Jewish swindler of Czech origin who, in 1925, posed as the deputy minister in charge of the demolition of the Eiffel Tower. He had brought together the most important ferrous metal salvage companies at the Crillon Hotel on the Place de la Concorde to put them out to tender, and then fled to New York with the money he had pocketed.

[320] Marek Halter, *La force du Bien*, Robert Laffont, 1995, op.cit., p. 248.

[321] Samuel Pisar, *Le Sang de l'espoir*, Robert Laffont, 1979, p. 244.

expulsion decree of March 1492 and officially apologised to the Jewish people[322]."

Cosmopolitan intellectuals seem to be particularly fond of repentant goyim. On the other hand, the heads of the Jewish community do not tolerate being confronted and denied their demands. It is well known how the former French president, François Mitterrand, was severely harassed at the end of his career for refusing to acknowledge France's culpability for events during the German occupation. His successor, Jacques Chirac, immediately prostrated himself, as demanded, upon his arrival at the Elysée Palace in 1995. He officially acknowledged the state's responsibility, which automatically triggered claims and financial compensation procedures. This compensation was indeed an important and even indispensable point in the process of repentance.

But Europeans are not only guilty of having locked up the Jews in concentration camps. Indeed, their entire history testifies to the fact that they are to blame for almost all the evils of the earth, as the last two centuries suffice to prove. In the weekly magazine *Le Point* of 8 December 2005, the philosopher Bernard-Henri Levy repeated his repudiation of colonialism. Colonial ideology is "undeniably" a "criminal ideology", he said. He added: "The colonial idea was, in itself, a perverse idea; the colonial adventure has been, from the beginning, a dark page in our history; there is in the gesture and countenance of those who want to revise this evidence, in their aplomb, in their passion and satiated enthusiasm of old fogies who are finally giving free rein to their ideas, a smell of outdated backwardness that has not been felt for a long time. Levy had, however, elsewhere expressed his disgust at the "celebrated and fetid" song of the Africans. But apparently, these considerations of colonialism did not prevent the charming BHL (Bernard-Henri Levy) from taking advantage of the immense fortune amassed by his father in the exploitation and export of African timber.

The well-known sociologist Edgar Morin also expressed his disgust with European civilisation: "We must become aware of the complexity of this colossal tragedy. This recognition must include all victims, he wrote: Jews, blacks, gypsies, homosexuals, Armenians, colonised people from Algeria or Madagascar. It is necessary if we are to overcome European barbarism[323]."

---

[322] Serge Moati, *La Haine antisemite*, Flammarion, 1991, p. 96, 97.

[323] Edgar Morin, Culture et barbarie européennes, Bayard, 2005, p. 91, 92. On

This "European barbarism" still manifests itself today in the third world. For everyone agrees that when a child starves to death in Africa, it can only be the fault of the whites. And since the white man is finally lowering his head, this is the best time to take advantage of the situation. This is how charities and NGOs that help the third world thrive. The very liberal Guy Sorman explained to us how they work, revealing in passing some aspects that fit in quite well with our present study of Judaism.

In December 1979, he wrote, when Soviet troops invaded Afghanistan, "Françoise Giraud, the most famous and undisputed of us, launched an appeal for help in *Europe 1* in the form of a basic and forceful slogan: with a hundred francs, it would be possible to buy and send a tent to protect Afghans fleeing to the mountains of Pakistan from the cold. The next day the cheques piled up in big bags. Thus was formed the AICT (*Action Internationale Contre la Faim*), which was to become one of the largest and most effective French humanitarian organisations". Bernard-Henri Levy, "without whom the AICF would never have come into being", was of course also a member of the association. Levy "wanted above all to take revenge on Bernard Kouchner, who had kicked him out of his own association, 'a ship for Vietnam'" and who would later create *Médecins sans frontières (Doctors Without Borders)*.

Guy Sorman revealed an important piece of information here: "The average donor, a widow from Montargis, is unaware that when she donates a hundred francs to a good cause, only a few francs will go to the begging child she saw on the leaflet in the letterbox or on the poster designed to give her a bad conscience". At least half of his money will have gone to pay for the advertising campaign to blame the goyim, and the other half to pay for the association's expenses and staff salaries, which are "on the whole, comparable to those of private companies". It is also known that the directors of these associations enjoy untaxed CEO salaries, luxury housing, travel allowances, etc.... "The importance of the awareness campaign, fundraising and media hype is only a demonstration of strength and notoriety, acknowledged Guy Sorman. Once their notoriety is established, they can then canvass the real

---

blaming, see *Les Espérances planétariennes* and *Psychanalyse du judaïsme*, as well as the two chapters on cinema.

financial donors, which are local, national, European or global administrations[324]."

This relentless predisposition to blame others is, of course, a fearsome weapon of war to bring one's adversary to his knees (and in the process empty his pockets). In 1985, the novelist Geneviève Dormann expressed her thoughts loud and clear: "The Jews piss me off, I say it clearly. When, at the slightest opportunity, they throw in my face what we did to them, when I was still a little girl, trying to make me feel guilty or have a bad conscience, and rejoicing in it in a sadistic way, I get angry with them as I would with Vandeans who accuse me of having destroyed their villages and savagely murdered their ancestors... I claim the right to love the good Jews and to send the others for a walk[325]." Most French intellectuals do not have that courage, especially those who most cry out against "intellectual terrorism", "single thought" and "political correctness".

## *A high intolerance to frustration*

Cosmopolitan intellectuals can also be quick to lash out at their opponents, insulting them without qualms. One of the most emblematic cases occurred in the spring of 2000, when the writer Renaud Camus published a book that set the journalistic and publishing world abuzz. A man of the left and a homosexual, his prose had never troubled the media until the publication, in a book entitled *Campaign for France,* of some perfectly anodyne words that were judged to be anti-Semitic. Camus wrote on page 48 about the *Panorama* programme on public radio France Culture: "The Jewish contributors to *France Culture*'s *Panorama* exaggerate a little: there are about four out of five on each programme, or four out of six, or five out of seven, which, on a national and quasi-official radio station, constitutes a clear over-representation of an ethnic or religious group". In another passage of his book, on page 408, he insisted: "Five participants and what proportion of non-Jews? Minimal, if not non-existent. Well, this seems to me, not exactly scandalous perhaps, but exaggerated, and misplaced, incorrect. And no, I am not anti-Semitic, and yes, I consider the Jewish race to have made one of the highest spiritual, intellectual and artistic contributions to humanity. And I consider the anti-Semitic crimes of the Nazis to be

---

[324] Guy Sorman, *Le Bonheur français*, Fayard, 1995, p. 88, 91-94.

[325] *Le Crapouillot*, February 1985

probably the pinnacle of the abomination that humanity has reached. But no, no, I do not think it is appropriate that a talk show, prepared and announced in advance, i.e. official, about integration in our country, on a public service broadcaster, should take place exclusively among Jewish journalists and intellectuals or those of Jewish origin... Leave us alone with this terrorism that does not allow us to open our mouths on such matters! This programme and many others are deeply biased by the exaggeratedly biased composition of their participants." He added: "It bothers and saddens me to see how, in many cases, this [French] culture and civilisation has as its main spokespersons and organs of expression a majority of Jews."

The reactions to these words were very revealing of the climate of terror that had long reigned in France, especially in the cultural world. It was the journalist Marc Weitzmann who first sounded the charge, in *Les inrockuptibles* of 18 April 2000—the magazine of young people who think they are rebels. *Le Monde* of 20 April published an indignant article. Laure Adler, director of *France-Culture*, and Jean-Marie Cavada, president of *Radio-France*, announced their intention to sue him for racial hatred [326]. Catherine Tasca, Minister of Culture and Communication, publicly expressed her disapproval. Jean Daniel, the editor of the weekly *Le Nouvel Observateur*, was also indignant in the publication of 3 May 2000 in a rather particular way: "Mr. Renaud Camus does not even have the astute perversity to point out that since the Jews have renounced to present themselves as Jews, they have in fact denied themselves the exclusive possibility of speaking in the name of France". You have understood: the Jews do not exist; it is a mirage, an anti-Semitic hallucination. Mr. Renaud Camus is strongly urged to try to cure his "illness [327]".

In *Le Monde* of 4 May 2000, Patrick Kéchichian dismantled before our eyes the "rhetoric of anti-Semitic discourse", starting by denouncing the paranoia of the writer who declared himself the victim of a "witch-hunt" and a media "lynching". Patrick Kechichian correctly pointed out that Renaud Camus had previously shown signs of an "almost militant Judeophilia": "The scruple he expresses is revealing of his mentality...

---

[326] Jean-Marie Le Pen had been convicted of "incitement to racial discrimination" in 1986, mentioning the media influence of the media popes "Jean-François Kahn, Jean Daniel, Ivan Levaï, and Jean-Pierre Elkabbach".

[327] *Les Espérances planétariennes*, p.365, 366. *Psychanalyse du Judaïsme*, p. 219, 220

this protest of sympathy is a procedure as old as anti-Semitism itself… What a great culture! What a great culture! What an admirable people! What sufferings… But also: What an invasion! What an art of being everywhere! It is the stale and hackneyed refrain, reminiscent of the famous spectre of the Jewish "lobby", as seen recently in the words of François Mitterrand referred to by Jean d'Ormesson, which has not yet fallen into disuse and which, disguised behind false objectivity, spreads the same contempt. Over-emphasised admiration is only the symmetrical counterpart of an exasperation, of an unconfessed hatred[328]."

Everyone will have understood that it is completely useless to go into previous statements of admiration, in the vain hope of avoiding the infamous spittle, if one wants to express the slightest criticism of the media representatives of the Jewish community. Kechichian concluded his speech: "This way—very "old France", even in style—of pushing Jews outside the borders of French culture is absolutely unacceptable". For him, Renaud Camus' statements "are clearly tainted by this perversion of the spirit". It seems to be a leitmotif of Jewish intellectuals to accuse their opponents of mental disorder.

Faced with the extent of the protests, the director of Fayard editions, Claude Durand, decided to withdraw the book from sale and republish it without the incriminating passages. The cuts and corrections to the text of the *Campaign of France accounted* for about ten pages out of five hundred. Jean-Etienne Cohen-Seat, managing director of Hachette-Livres, a group owned by Fayard, tersely justified his decision: "Renaud Camus' book stinks".

But three weeks after the book disappeared from bookshops, *Campagne de France* continued to fuel the controversy. Michel Polac, former star presenter of a cultural television programme, wrote in the *Charlie-Hebdo newspaper* on 17 May 2000, denouncing "the anti-Semitic 'bullshit' of this little writer". The pages of Renaud Camus were, according to him, "vomitous". And he went on: "For this fool, a Jew without roots cannot understand French literature. Does one have to testify to a crusader ancestor to have the right to speak? And for the others, to establish a numerus clausus? And on top of that, this poor man has quoted names: he must have in his château library the *Dictionnaire*

---

[328] On François Mitterrand, cf. *Les Espérances planétariennes*, p. 332.

*des Juifs* and *Comment reconnaître un Juif*, books published during the German occupation in the same collection as *Bagatelles pour un massacre* and *Les Beaux Draps\**".

On 25 May, the very media-savvy Bernard-Henri Levy kindly headlined his article in the weekly *L'Événement du jeudi:* "You have to look shit in the face". As usual, Bernard-Henri went on at length, hurling invectives: "I hate the anti-Semitism that is heard in the *French campaign*. And I am very angry that some people try to deny or minimise the odious character of these pages... pages, words, absolutely pestilent" that can only provoke "horror" and "revulsion". "Renaud Camus practises a very old French anti-Semitism, influenced by Charles Maurras, which considers that a Jew—a foreigner, a Meteco—is incapable of understanding the subtleties of French culture. It's stupid, it's abject, there can be no debate about it." And Levy added: "All these lines, they are not only dubious, they are hateful... One cannot, in the face of so much reasoned perversity, contain a constant and diffuse nausea[329]."

As we can see, it was not about discussing the basic issue, namely the "overrepresentation of Jews in the media". However, "BHL" declared itself against censorship: "This book should not be withdrawn or censored. I don't think you can fight hatred with censorship or with the law. I don't believe that you can effectively 'ban' evil... You can't pretend that Celine didn't write *Bagatelles pour un massacre\**. A good civic education, from the earliest age, should be enough to contain the danger, provided that the media bombardment is permanent.

On 25 May 2000, a petition signed by Jacques Derrida, Serge Klarsfeld, Claude Lanzman, Philippe Solers, Jean-Pierre Vernant, etc., appeared in the daily *Le Monde.* "We believe that the campaign that tries to pass off the author of the *Campaign for France as* a victim is disturbing. It is urgent to state clearly that the words of Renaud Camus are criminal opinions, which as such have no right to be expressed... This has nothing to do with freedom of expression. He who thinks that, writes that and publishes that... thinks, writes and publishes criminal, racist and anti-Semitic opinions. This has nothing to do with freedom of expression... We declare that the words of Renaud Camus are criminal opinions, and that, therefore, to defend or republish his book in the

---

[329] *Le Point* of 26 June 2002

\* Louis-Ferdinand Celine's famous virulent pre-war anti-Semitic pamphlet.

name of freedom of expression or on any other grounds is, whether one wishes to or not, to defend and publish criminal and reprehensible opinions. The public must know this. This is not expunged... We declare that no obfuscation, no illusion is permitted. And to allow such opinions to be insinuated, from weakness or any other motive, is to consent to the insidious installation of the worst."

In the *Art Press* of June 2000, Jacques Henric issued his analysis, also pointing to the mental illness of Renaud Camus: "We are in the presence of an endemic illness, which periodically manifests itself again", he wrote, criticising "this nationalist withdrawal with xenophobic overtones" and "his plainly delirious words", "chauvinistic and reactionary".

On 18 June, set writer Philippe Solers had the opportunity to express himself in the daily *Le Monde:* "Claude Durand's mistake is above all literary, wrote Sollers: he believes that Renaud Camus is an important writer, when in reality it is mouldy prose... It is a decorous anti-Semitism, the most dangerous of all. It's also a symptom that hasn't gone away and is due to the Mitterrand era: in the morning I see Bousquet and in the afternoon I go to SOS Racisme. This old French anti-Semitism, a bit gloomy, is a tradition that must disappear".

The *Campaign in France* reappeared on 4 July in a new edition, in which the scandalous passages had been left blank. The director of the Fayard publishing house announced that the book had been purged of the controversial passages by the author himself, "with white strikethroughs, like scars inflicted on our freedom of expression, and, first and foremost, on the freedom to criticise".

The president of the League of Human Rights, Michel Tubiana, gave his point of view in the July 2000 issue of *Hommes et Libertés*, the association's magazine. His article, very pedagogical, was entitled: "Racism explained to a writer and his editor". It denounced the "unacceptable passages": "Whether we like it or not, this kind of account takes us back to precedents that we know are unbearable. More seriously, some of his words are utterly nauseating".

On the problem of "over-representation", Michel Tubiana also had a response of instinctive self-defence: "I refuse to answer to refute the words of Renaud Camus. The racist approach is obvious, and coming from a man of culture, it is even more unbearable". You can't argue: you attack.

For the League of Human Rights, the question should not be posed and debated in this way: "Let's put the debate on a real basis... Is it possible to judge individuals on the basis of their origins and not on the basis of their actions and thoughts? Instead of accusing us of censorship, these are the questions that Renaud Camus' friends and publisher should be answering". Precisely, the problem is that "acts" and "thoughts" are strongly related to "origins".

Michel Tubiana observed that, in republishing the book, the author and the publisher "had shown a strange and inexplicable obstinacy: we might have expected that the publisher would admit his mistake and that Renaud Camus would understand the nature of the debate he had provoked. To no avail. The editor wrapped himself in the folds of freedom of thought and expression, which were not in question, and the author adopted the posture of a misunderstood victim. They didn't understand anything or pretended not to understand". Definitely, these French are hopeless.

The reply from Claude Durand, the director of the Fayard publishing house, concluded thus: "Even the most hardened censors of the totalitarian regimes of the 20th century had not invented this new formula of today: the prohibition of white strikethroughs in any text."

The only two slightly discordant voices among the intellectuals of the "community" were those of Alain Finkielkraut and Elisabeth Levy. In *Le Monde* of 6 June 2000, Alain Finkielkraut wrote timidly of his peers: "In this case, it took less courage than opportunism to join in the fray. For her part, Elisabeth Levy, presenter of a cultural programme, quoted Renaud Camus's polemical words in her book *Les Maîtres censors*, published in 2002, but taking care to refer to them in a footnote: "The passages quoted have been reproduced numerous times in the press" This precaution, which allowed her to protect herself against possible legal action, said a lot about freedom of expression in France at the beginning of the 21st century. Regarding Bernard-Henri Levy, he wrote: "We could reply to the writer that it is always more urgent to refute than to denounce, to convince than to demonise. But this would probably be judged to be typical of a Munich spirit[330]." Elisabeth Levy was a courageous exception, which is why one should not say or point the finger at "the Jews" in general, even if the exception proves the rule.

---

[330] Elisabeth Levy, *Les Maîtres censeurs*, Lattès, Poche, 2002, p.346. The spirit of the Munich agreements (1938)

One of the greatest French thinkers of the 19th century, Ernest Renan, had already noted these very specific character traits. In his *Life of Jesus*, in 1863, he said: "One of the principal defects of the Jewish race is its harshness in controversy and the injurious tone in which it almost always involves itself... The lack of nuance is one of the most constant features of the Semitic spirit[331]."

## *The media dictatorship*

Of course, the writer Renaud Camus was not the first to notice the "overrepresentation" of Jews in the media. Far-right" journalists had already referred to the militant predisposition of the Jewish community. François Brigneau, one of the leading figures of national right-wing journalism in the second half of the 20th century, wrote in 1975: "In France, there are six hundred thousand out of fifty million French people, but they are preponderant in the press. I myself have spent more than half of my twenty-five years of career working on the newspapers of M. Lazareff and M. Lazurick: they are predominant in the cinema, radio, television, show business... We see them in banking, in all businesses; they play a very important role in the intellectual elite". François de Fontette, who reported these words, added, indignant and complaining that "the "Auschwitz moratorium" had expired": "Like the emigrants of yesteryear, the author of these lines has neither learned nor forgotten anything[332]."

These ideas are still strongly condemned in France today. The president of the National Front (FN), Jean-Marie Le Pen also had to face the outburst of the media tribe after some of his statements. Journalist Serge Moati referred to one such statement: 'On 26 October 1985, during the FN's "Bleu-Blanc-Rouge" party, he shouted to an ecstatic crowd: "I dedicate your welcome to Jean-François Kahn, Jean Daniel, Ivan Levaï, Elkabach, to all the liars in this country's press. These people are the shame of the profession". LICRA (International League Against Racism and Anti-Semitism) immediately denounced him. Jean-Marie Le Pen was convicted, and Serge Moati noted: "The recital of the sentencing court stipulates: "Anti-Semitism is not a Jewish problem but the problem of all. An anti-Semitic attack on one is in reality a threat to all". We can see how the jurisprudence had not yet integrated the

---

[331] François de Fontette, *Sociologie de l'antisémitisme*, PUF, 1984, p.9.

[332] François de Fontette, *Sociologie de l'antisémitisme*, PUF, 1984, p. 121, 122.

phraseology of the Jewish community, which, no doubt, would have preferred the expression: "a threat to all mankind".

In August 1989, Jean-Marie Le Pen's rhetoric rose to a higher level. In an interview with the daily *Présent, he* denounced "the big internationals such as the Jewish international which plays a notable role in the construction of the anti-national spirit[333]." But at the beginning of 1990, the European parliamentary immunity of the president of the National Front was waived to allow the judiciary to deal with the "Jewish international" affair. Here, too, he was harshly condemned. The publicist Alain Minc, outraged, even more so when these words were reproduced in the press, wrote: "Le Pen lashes out against the weight of the Jews in the media. It is the new collective mythology equivalent to the banking phantasmagoria of fifty years ago: the symbol of power in the shadows. And meanwhile, *Le Monde* allows pollsters to ask the question: 'Do Jews have too much power in the media? "Strange question. Strange publication, wrote Alain Minc: apparently, the taboos have disappeared for good, because according to the poll a third of the French answer in the affirmative[334]."

It is indeed scandalous that the French can complain about the "over-representation" of Jews in the media, since Jews are French like everyone else, "perfectly integrated". Worse still, *Le Monde*, despite being the "newspaper of reference", echoed these "nauseating stenches", thus making it clear that France was a hopelessly anti-Semitic country. Indeed, Alain Minc forgot to tell us that he was the president of the Société des lectors du *Monde* and that the paper was owned by people related to the powerful Bronfman family, which also ran the World Jewish Congress[335].

The weight of conformism also made it impossible to speak out on other issues, such as the migratory invasion and the third worldisation of France, or the inequality of races, for example. In September 1996, Jean-Marie Le Pen declared on LCI: "I believe in equality of opportunity, but I also believe in the inequality of races. I believe that there are inequalities between men in all fields, and also that there is a hierarchy within civilisations. History proves it. (*Rivarol*, 13 September

---

[333] Serge Moati, *La Haine antisémite*, Flammarion, 1991, p. 191.

[334] Alain Minc, *La Vengeance des nations*, Grasset, 1990, p. 128.

[335] Read the indispensable *Encyclopédie politique française* by Emmanuel Ratier.

1996). In this case too, the MRAP (Movement against Racism and for Friendship among Peoples), which is close to the Communist Party, was quick to denounce. Jean Kahn, the president of the Consultative Commission on Human Rights, declared himself "deeply shocked" and even "shattered".

We will not recapitulate here the countless complaints brought by ethnic minorities against French patriots who have denounced the Islamisation and Third Worldisation of their country in recent decades. Let us just mention the trial of the writer Jean Raspail for his article of 17 June 2005 published in *Le Figaro*. The author predicted that the indigenous French would be a minority in France by the 2050s. The massive migratory invasion, during the last twenty-five years of the 20th century, had indeed changed the French population.

In November 2005, serious riots broke out in the suburbs of the big cities, in which four French people lost their lives and more than fourteen thousand vehicles were set on fire. Unlike the other European media, especially the Russian media, French television never mentioned that the riots were clearly racial in character. *Le Monde* of 17 November 2005 quoted Hélène Carrère d'Encausse, a historian specialising in Russia and perpetual secretary of the Académie française, as saying in an interview with the weekly *Les Nouvelles de Moscou*: "French television is so politically correct that it has become a nightmare. We have laws that Stalin could have imagined. You go to jail if you say there are five Jews or ten blacks on TV. People are not allowed to express their opinion about ethnic groups, the Second World War and many other things".

Since 2001, numerous anti-Semitic incidents had occurred in France in parallel to the Middle East conflict. In 2004, the reaction against the influence of the "lobby" was strengthened by the very popular French-Cameroonian comedian Dieudonné. When he worked in duo with Elie Semoun, Dieudonné, together with many other cosmopolitan artists, had thrown himself into the fight against "the extreme right". But after becoming angry with his artistic partner and his denunciation of the "American-Zionist axis", Dieudonné had to face not only a media boycott, but also pressures to cancel his shows and even physical attacks on him and his audience, causing him to radicalise his discourse even more. He was vilified by all the media and ordered to apologise. His new show, a few months later, was ironically titled *"My Apology"*. In reality, it was a blistering indictment of the Jewish lobby and the State of Israel. Dieudonné, after winning his seventeen trials, embodied, as he himself amusingly put it, the "axis of evil alone".

In March 2005, in a radio programme on Meditérranée FM in which Dieudonné participated, the presenter declared: "The Jews of the Middle East have largely participated in the slave trade since many traders were Jewish". To which the black comedian replied:"... The truth is, indeed, that the Jewish people, who claim to have always been persecuted, have also participated in infamous persecutions. They must also face up to this. On 10 April 2005, another presenter had stated the following: "Judaism, I have already said it, remains a religion that is like a private club, you almost have to have a gold visa to be a member... it is a club of the privileged, a club of the rich, extremely closed to others... "

These "unbearable" words could not go unpunished. The CRIF therefore called for all measures to be taken "to contain the flood of audiovisual and radio anti-Semitism", and in October 2005, the High Audiovisual Council sent a cease and desist notice to the radio station.

Regarding Dieudonné, the "French" singer Shirel, a "new star" of reality TV, gave her opinion in the *Tribune juive* magazine in October 2004: "Why aren't Dieudonné and so many others, who utter anti-Semitic insults, behind bars? I don't understand. I wonder if this unbearable climate is not, perhaps, an appeal or a sign that the time has come for all the Jews of France to return home to Israel". This young woman who had gone to live in Israel for a while had followed the teachings of illustrious rabbis and understood the causes of anti-Semitism: "Rabbi Aviner, with whom I studied in Israel, analyses the causes of anti-Semitism as the rejection by other peoples of the word of Abraham, who gave the world the notion of conscience. It is uncomfortable to have to tell those around us that what they are doing is not just, good and right. It is true that explaining justice to men bothers them, but that is also the mission of the Jewish people".

Repression also hit representatives of ethnic minorities. Kemi Seba, the leader of a black youth movement, also strongly denounced the involvement of Jewish traders in the slave trade. His raw and unabashed denunciation of the "Zionist lobby" in his lectures, much more explicit than that of the French nationalists, earned him two months in jail in 2007. But his determination remained intact.

The links between the anti-Zionist left and the national right were clear. In October 2005, a press release by Jean-Marie Le Pen called for the resignation of the presenter Marc-Olivier Fogiel, against whom Dieudonné's supporters had also mobilised. Gathered in the association *République sociale*, they denounced Fogiel as "the mouthpiece of the dictatorship of political correctness in the public service". *République sociale* was waging a "republican battle against the media dictatorship" and for "the citizens' reconquest of the audiovisual public service".

After a visit by Dieudonné to the National Front's annual party in November 2006, Bruno Gollnish and a few other party leaders returned the visit, going to the Salle Zénith the following month to applaud his show; 5,000 people turned up, despite the media establishment's widespread boycott. French nationalists mingled surprisingly with suburban "youths" of Afro-Maghrebi origin.

On 28 September 2004, the anti-communist republican writer Alain Soral, who was signing dedications of his books in a Parisian bookshop, was also the victim of young Jewish activists who broke into the bookshop, smashed the shop window and assaulted the customers. A year after the events, the police had not made any arrests. Interviewed informally and colloquially during a televised street report a few days earlier, Alain Soral "seemed to have crossed the red line" when he declared: "For 2500 years now, every time they set foot somewhere, they get harassed after fifty years—because that's more or less their history…". When "with a Frenchman, a Zionist Jew, you say that maybe there are problems that come from them, that maybe they made some mistakes, that it's not systematically the fault of others if nobody can swallow them, you realise that the guy starts barking, screaming, he goes crazy. Everybody is wrong but them. You can't have a dialogue". Finally, Alain Soral drew this conclusion: "There is a psychopathology of Judaism-Zionism that borders on mental illness." Alain Soral was brought to justice for these words. Two years after his attack, he officially joined the National Front.

In *Operation Shylock,* the American novelist Philip Roth, however, confirmed these words through one of his anti-Semitic characters, who he pulled out his tongue: "The most anti-Semitic people in the world are those who have been married to a Jew or a Jewess. They all tell you the same thing: they're a bunch of fools". He continued: "They spend billions of dollars fighting anti-Semitism. And anti-Semitism has had no choice but to go underground… They are aware that nobody likes them. Why? Why is that? Because of the things they do… If you even think of saying anything, you immediately become [*whispering*] *an anti-Semite.* How can you be surprised that anti-Semitism has gone underground. What can you do about it. Because, come on, how can you *not be* anti-Semitic? Hell, they are born with the public relations gene implanted in them. They are born with that gene, as aggressive as it is[336]."

In the United States, the famous Australian actor and director, Mel Gibson, has also been in trouble for some of his statements. Arrested while intoxicated on a Malibu highway in late July 2006, Gibson had spoken words deemed anti-Semitic, claiming that Jews were "responsible for all the wars in the world". It is true that, at the time, the state of Israel had just launched a destructive offensive on Lebanon. The president of the highly influential American Anti-Defamation League, Abraham Foxman, had immediately called on Hollywood to distance itself from "this anti-Semite". Despite being very rich, after the worldwide success of his film on *The Passion of the Christ,* Mel Gibson had to get down on his knees. *Le Figaro* of 2 August 2006 transcribed his words: "There is no excuse, and there should be no tolerance for anyone who thinks or expresses anything anti-Semitic. I want to apologise to all members of the Jewish community for the violent and hurtful words I said to a policeman the night I was arrested. Please know that I am not anti-Semitic. I am not bigoted. Hatred, whatever it is, is against my faith." His contrition went even further: "I don't just ask for forgiveness. I would like to do more, and to meet with leaders of the Jewish community, with whom I could talk and find a way to repair the damage done. This mea culpa from Gibson seemed to satisfy Abraham Foxman: "We are happy that Mel Gibson finally accepts responsibility for his anti-Semitic remarks, and his apology seems sincere. When he has finished his rehabilitation [in his fight against alcohol], we stand ready to help him in his other rehabilitation to combat the disease of prejudice."

We see how Edouard Drumont was right, in 1886, when he wrote in *La France juive:* "The Jew will always lack, compared with the Christian, that which constitutes the attraction of social relations: equality. The Jew—bear this observation in mind—will never be equal to a man of the Christian race. He either throws himself at your feet or else crushes you under his heel; he is always above or below, never beside."

## Criticising Israel

---

[336] Philip Roth, *Operación Shylock*, Debolsillo, Editorial Mondadori, 2005 Barcelona, p. 296, 297, 299

Even the most cosmopolitan and conformist intellectuals can be victims of repression. To be prosecuted, it is enough to criticise the repressive policy of the Israeli state. In May 2002, Daniel Mermet, presenter and producer of a programme on the state radio *France Inter*, was summoned to appear before the Paris courts for incitement to racial hatred. The reason was a series of statements made during a series of programmes devoted to the situation in Israel. Daniel Mermet was accused of having complacently allowed listeners to express themselves on voicemail, in accordance with the programme's "intangible rule" of broadcasting messages in their entirety. Of the 35 messages broadcast that week, seven were considered hatefully racist, totally unbearable for the leaders of the French Jewish community. For example, this reaction from a listener about the State of Israel: "What kind of deadly power is it that indulges in the murder of children and mutilations, that justifies the unacceptable day after day with criminal impudence, and that has the infamous arrogance to treat us as racists when we dare, timidly, to protest against such unworthy behaviour?"

This was too much, and the aforementioned Mermer was denounced by the Union of Jewish Students of France (UEJF), the association of Lawyers Without Borders, and LICRA. Among the witnesses for the plaintiffs in this trial was the media personality Alain Finkielkraut. The philosopher wrote in *Le Monde* on 1 June 2002: "95% of French Jews are Zionists, in the sense that they have a solidarity of destiny with Israel. To banish this state as fascist or Nazi is to exclude, under the guise of anti-racism, all those who, as Jews, support it". However, this was not the view of Rony Brauman, former president of Médecins Sans Frontières, quoted by the defence, for whom Zionism "is both a national liberation movement and a colonial movement. In that sense, he added, it contains a part of racism."

Daniel Mermet was finally released. In an interview with the communist daily *l'Humanité* on 10 September 2002 (published on its website), he explained his version: "The damage suffered goes far beyond a favourable legal opinion. When you slander, there is always something left. My professional honour has been undermined. I have been called an anti-Semite, and not for nothing. For me, this accusation is tantamount to an attempt at moral assassination". Daniel Mermet assured that he would be at the Fête de *l'Humanité* to speak about this injustice: "The confusion between the State of Israel, the Jewish people and Zionism must be denounced. It has become a weapon of intimidation against the profession as a whole".

The planetary sociologist Edgar Morin was also brought to justice for an article published in *Le Monde* on 4 June 2002 entitled "Israel-Palestine: the cancer". In that article, Edgar Morin wrote: "it is hard to imagine that a nation of fugitives, coming from the most persecuted people in the history of humanity, which has suffered the worst humiliations and the worst contempt, is capable of transforming itself in two generations into a 'dominant and self-confident people' and, except for an admirable minority, into a contemptuous people, satisfied with humiliating others". Edgar Morin continued: "The Jews of Israel, descendants of the victims of the apartheid ghetto, in turn ghettoise the Palestinians. The Jews who were humiliated, despised, persecuted, humiliate, despise and persecute the Palestinians. The Jews who were victims of a ruthless order impose their ruthless order on the Palestinians. The Jewish victims of inhumanity show a terrible inhumanity. The Jews, scapegoats for all evils, now make scapegoats of Arafat and the Palestinian Authority, holding them responsible for attacks that they are prevented from stopping."

For Edgar Morin, Jews living in Israel appear to be of a very different nature from Jews in the diaspora. But the regular complainants judged that he was guilty of "generalisation": "by alluding "to an entire nation or almost an entire religious group" he had committed the offence of racial defamation. *Le Monde* of 30 March 2004 reported that, in this case, the sociologist had the support of a hundred intellectual figures, French and foreign, also critical of Ariel Sharon's Israeli policy. Their statement of support for Edgar Morin read: "Morin's accusers believe they are defending the State of Israel. In reality, they run the risk of reviving anti-Semitism if they completely identify the current policy of the Israeli government with the State of Israel and the Jewish people".

The Jewish associations' complaint was finally dismissed, but it was clear that Jewish intellectuals were not spared from legal proceedings either. Edgar Morin, a Jew of Sephardic origin, surnamed Nahoum, a supporter of a world without borders, gave his opinion in *Le Monde* of 23 July 2005: "Judaism is not a uniform bloc, and to reduce it to a religious or nationalist party is not only to mutilate it, but also to deny its universal contribution. After all, Spinoza himself was excluded from the synagogue, and his light still shines on us after his persecutors have been forgotten".

Ultimately, it is about quarrels between Jewish intellectuals who fight over their interpretation of Jewish universalism and messianism. Some think the State of Israel is criminal, others do not. Some think it is necessary, others think it is not.

The geopolitician Pascal Boniface, director of the authoritative Institute for International and Strategic Relations (IRIS), had also had a few run-ins with the Zionist lobby in France after publishing a book in 2003 entitled *Is it allowed to criticise Israel? in which he* studied the agents and political-media correspondents of the pro-Israeli lobby. In an interview for *Le Quotidien d'Oran* on 1 October 2003, he revealed that seven publishers had refused to publish his book: "I think that everyone who read the book could see that I could not be accused of racism. In France, there are laws that protect against racist expressions. The conclusion I draw from this is that the subject is so sensitive that publishers are afraid to commit themselves, which says a lot about the scale of the pressures. I can only imagine, because I have no explanation. And yet I have published about twenty books individually and as many collectively: I have never had that kind of difficulty... When one criticises the Israeli government, not as a state and its existence, but the political action of the Israeli government, one is quickly labelled anti-Semitic by the pro-Israeli ultras. This accusation of anti-Semitism is obviously a heavy one to bear... In addition to this accusation, there are other threats. As a result of my writings on the Middle East, there was pressure on IRIS board members to resign or to remove me from my position of responsibility. In turn, pressure was exerted on our partners to stop working with us". Pascal Boniface concluded: "As a reader, I note that it is much easier to criticise Arabs and Muslims in France. An example: when an Arab religious dignitary has problems or is attacked, hardly anyone reacts. Conversely, when Rabbi Farhi was stabbed in circumstances that were not perfectly elucidated, four former Prime Ministers rush to his bedside[337]. It is normal for the political class to show solidarity when an anti-Semitic aggression occurs, but the same should be done when an anti-Arab aggression occurs... "And Pascal Boniface could have added:"...and it would be even more normal to defend the native French when they are attacked by one or the other in their own country". But that would have been asking too much of him.

In April 2001, two years before leaving the socialist party, Pascal Boniface had sent the party's top officials, M. François Hollande and M. Henri Nallet, an internal report on the events in the Middle East, in which he drew attention to the Israeli policy of Ariel Sharon and the importance of the pro-Palestinian electorate in France: "Imagine: after

---

[337] The investigation showed that Rabbi Farhi had stabbed himself. Cf, *Les Espérances planétariennes*, p. 376.

a war, a country occupies territories against international laws. Thirty-four years later, this occupation continues despite the condemnations of the international community. The people living in these occupied territories see excessive obligations imposed on them, emergency laws and the denial of their right to self-determination. Destruction of houses, confiscation of land, imprisonment without trial, daily humiliation and, until recently, legalised torture under the name of "moderate physical pressure" are common practice. This population rebels and demands the creation of an independent state in the occupied territories as established by the United Nations. A cycle of violence and repression then begins, during which the invading power's forces regularly shoot and kill demonstrators and fatal attacks on the invading power's population. In any such situation, a humanist, and even more so a man of the left, would condemn the invading power. Imagine a country where the Prime Minister has been directly linked to the massacre of civilians, mainly women and children, in unarmed refugee camps. A country whose leader of the third political party in power treats members of one of the country's main national communities as "snakes", worse, "vipers", and proposes to annihilate these villains and thieves by shooting them with super-missiles. A country where armed extremists can organise pogroms against unarmed civilians with impunity. This would be an unacceptable situation. Yet that is the situation that is tolerated in the Middle East."

Pascal Boniface was shocked by the treatment meted out to those who dared to express criticism: "All those who oppose the policies of the Israeli government are suspected of not condemning the Holocaust or of being anti-Semitic… The intellectual terrorism that consists in accusing of anti-Semitism those who do not accept the policies of the governments of Israel (and not the State of Israel) may be effective in the short term, but catastrophic in the medium term… Fortunately,

Some intellectuals of Jewish origin such as Rony Brauman and Pierre Vidal Naquet have publicly disassociated themselves from the Israeli repression, avoiding the danger of lumping everyone together[338]."

Alain Menargues, the information director of *Radio-France International* (RFI, 400 journalists in Paris, 300 correspondents around the world), had also suffered the same kind of problems after the

---

[338] Pascal Boniface, *Est-il permis de critiquer Israël*, Robert Laffont, 2003, p. 233-238. Pascal Boniface was subsequently sidelined by the leadership of the Socialist Party.

publication of his book entitled *Sharon's Wall* in 2004. In it, he denounced the discriminations on which the Jewish state was founded and the construction of a security wall on the border with the Palestinian territories. After a vociferous press campaign, he was finally fired. After his forced departure from RFI, Alain Menargues did not seem convinced of his mistake, as the Jewish community monthly *L'Arche* reported in May 2005: "far from making honest amends for his anti-Semitic writings, he boasts about it, developing, moreover, a conspiracy theory, according to which his misfortunes come from the famous lobby whose name cannot be mentioned". That Ménargues had a truly unbelievable impudence! *L'Arche* continued: "We might have thought that such aberrations would have made the author a persona non grata for all citizens who identify with democracy and anti-racism. What was not our surprise when we discovered that his book, a collection of medieval anti-Jewish fantasies and texts copied from neo-Nazi and negationist authors, enjoys surprising publicity in the "Friends of the *Monde diplomatique*"". It was therefore "urgent to intervene with the board of *Monde diplomatique* to stop this scandal."

Alain Menargues' thesis was indeed untenable: for him, the "Sharon wall" was built not to protect Israelis from terrorism but to make a separation between the "pure" and the "impure": "This separation of the pure and the impure is an unequivocal commandment in Leviticus (the third book of the five books of the Torah)". Concerning the 613 commandments that govern the daily life of the Jews Menargues wrote: "These commandments are intended to make the "people of God a different people" from those around them: "You shall not do what is done in the land of Egypt, where you have dwelt, nor shall you do what is done in the land of Canaan, where I am taking you; you shall not follow their customs... For all these abominations are those which the men of those lands have committed, who dwelt there before you, and the land is defiled."(Leviticus 18, 3 and 27)" It is clear that Alain Menargues was displaying a delirious anti-Semitism, as the newspaper *L'Arche* saw it and asserted: "What you have just read is not an extract from Drumont's *Jewish France*, nor from Streicher's *Stürner*, but from the organ of the Friends of the *Monde diplomatique*. In this passage, the anti-Jewish hatred is based on total ignorance". *L'Arche* thus denounced in the strongest terms Mr Menargues' "anti-Semitic fantasies about "the pure and impure" in Judaism" and the myth of the "Jewish conspiracy" which he seemed to be feeding by speaking of "influential agents" who, he claimed, had organised a slanderous press campaign. "Perhaps Mr. Menargues would be so kind as to give his listeners the list of the negationist and neo-Nazi texts he used to write his book?"

Let Alain Menargues explain himself. In a long interview with Silvia Cattori on the website nord-palestine.org in November 2004, the former director of *Radio-France internationale expressed* his astonishment: "I've been in this profession for thirty years. None of my colleagues could have thought, before these attacks were unleashed against me, that one day I would be called a racist or an anti-Semite... I am very irritated to see how a fundamental freedom is disappearing in France... I cannot conceive that in my country there is an intellectual terrorism that gags people on pain of being destroyed". To the question: "Why don't more journalists tell it like it is?" Menargues replied: "Because some people have to make ends meet. There are many journalists who share the same opinion as me. But they are not free. Press chiefs are afraid of losing subscribers and advertising revenue."

His conclusion was as follows: "By accusing everyone, the word anti-Semite is trivialised. These excesses will eventually turn against the State of Israel and, unfortunately, against the Jewish citizens who accept all these abuses. In the wake of all that I suffered, I received thousands of emails of sympathy and also of exasperation. The intolerance of some runs the risk of stirring up the hatred of others". Menargues also mentioned the manipulations in the case of the self-stabbed rabbi and the burning of a synagogue: "If all journalists really did their job honestly, we could stop the torrent of lies poured out about everything concerning the Arab world". Like Pascal Boniface, he could have remembered his compatriots, but that would have been an "extreme right-wing" attitude.

The monthly community magazine *L'Arche* in May 2005 was alarmed by the reshaping of the political landscape. Indeed, Alain Menargues "had repeated his anti-Jewish ravings in several public interventions—starting with the extreme right-wing radio station *Radio Courtoisie*". This drift was therefore very worrying for the community, especially as "his "anti-Zionist" theses had been taken up in various extreme left-wing circles". Evidently, this convergence between the two extremes brought back bad memories for the Jewish community.

The dictatorship that has gradually imposed itself in France over the world of literature and French culture as a whole has greatly reduced freedom of expression. In November 2005, the French publisher of Israel Shamir's book *The Other Face of Israel was sentenced* to three months' imprisonment with probation and a fine of 10,000 euros. In addition, he had to pay 12,000 euros in damages and 1,500 euros in legal costs to the International League against Racism and Anti-Semitism (Licra). The publisher had 30 days to withdraw the book from sale, on pain of a fine of 100 euros for each copy remaining at the expiry of the deadline. The court had based its judgement on the fact that the book presented "the Jews" as the "dominators of the world", in the context of a "third world war" currently underway, according to the author. However, this was only one facet of the book, which focused extensively on the Palestinian question.

In 2003, Mr. Schoemann sent threatening letters with rifle bullets to about fifteen personalities known for their closeness to the Palestinian cause. "The next one won't come in the post," he wrote to each of the recipients. The 65-year-old claimed to have been deported at the age of two and, during the hearing, claimed that the civilian side was made up of "anti-Semites". In February 2007, Schoemann was sentenced on appeal to a fine of 500 euros for each of the complainants. "When you are Breton, Corsican or Muslim, you go to jail", denounced one of the lawyers, indignant at this lax verdict.

The pressure exerted against anyone who dared to criticise, and the resulting reprisals, were not a new phenomenon in France, and could even be exercised against the highest dignitaries of the state. The journalist François Brigneau, in the daily *National Hebdo* of 31 October 1996, recalled General de Gaulle's troubles after his words following the Six-Day War in 1967:

"General de Gaulle had a special friendship with the Hebrew state. His toast is often quoted: "Israel, our friend, our ally... "uttered in a vibrant voice." On 2 June 1967, however, de Gaulle decided on a total and immediate halt to arms shipments to the Middle East. On 5 June, the Israeli army attacked on all fronts. The Six Day War began with the crushing of the Egyptian air force on the runway: "Everywhere, the victorious soldiers of Peace (Shalom! Shalom!) occupied the Sinai Peninsula, the Golan and the West Bank. The embargo—which was not respected, and never would be—had not bothered them in the slightest. De Gaulle maintained it, however, condemning Israel and refusing to "take for granted the changes brought about on the ground by military action". On 27 November, during a press conference that remains famous today, de Gaulle dared to speak of a "warlike State of Israel determined to aggrandise itself" and of a "self-confident and domineering people". "Immediately, the shofars sounded from all sides, wrote François Brigneau. Chief Rabbi Kaplan accused General de Gaulle of "giving carte blanche to discrimination campaigns". Raymond Aron, who was considered a superior and moderate spirit, wrote: "General de Gaulle has voluntarily opened a new period in Jewish history, perhaps even in anti-Semitism". Six months later, in May 1968, a student riot, led by mostly Jewish ringleaders, organised by all the radio stations, turned into a revolt and shook De Gaulle's power. Eleven months later, the regime collapsed on the night of the lost referendum".

Indeed, the April 1969 referendum on regionalisation had led to the general's departure. In his book, François Brigneau presented testimonies taken from Samy Cohen's book *De Gaulle, the Gaullists and Israel* (Alain Moreau, 1974, p.209). "A book that is not hostile to the Zionists", Brigneau stressed. Six months after the referendum, François Mauriac had this to say: 'I saw, a few months before the referendum, how de Gaulle's policy towards Jerusalem drove some people crazy. And they were not individuals without means". In le *Libre Journal* de *Radio Courtoisie of* 19 December 2003, Brigneau recounted again: "Six months later, in the *Figaro littéraire*, François Mauriac revealed "what nobody dared to recall for fear of being accused of being an anti-Semite". One of the reasons for the victory of the "No" vote in the referendum was the General's policy towards Israel. I regret not having kept some letters from Jewish friends, fervent Gaullists, in which they suddenly became implacable opponents" (24 November 1969)".

Samy Cohen's book provided further testimonies, such as that of Leon Noel, ambassador, who denounced the "Israelis of France": "During the fateful referendum of April 1969, their opposition weighed so heavily that it is no exaggeration to say that they were largely responsible for the result". Edmont Michelet, former deportee, Minister of Justice and Minister of State confirmed this: "Those who decided the majority are the hundreds of thousands of Jews... They have in their hands a large part of the media."

Western policy towards Israel thus seemed to have been decided for a long time by influential Jews, both in the United States and in Europe. In the *Libre Journal* programme of 5 September 2006, François Brigneau presented the testimony of Forrestal, Roosevelt's last Secretary of the Navy and President Truman's Minister of Defence. On 29 November 1947, the United Nations voted to create a Jewish state. Regarding the partition of Palestine, Forrestal wrote in his *diary:* "26 July 1946: The Jews have unleashed a very vigorous propaganda to force the President [Truman]. On the date of 3 December 1947 he wrote: "It is altogether regrettable that the foreign policy of our country can be determined by the contribution of a group of private interests within the party." (p.225) François Brigneau continued: "A few weeks later, a press and radio campaign was launched against Forrestal, similar to those that once forced Ford to repentance and Lindbergh to ostracism. He was accused of unhealthy anti-communism and anti-Semitism. These are words that kill. A year later, President Truman accepted his resignation. On 23 May 1949, Forrestal threw himself from the 16th floor of the Bethesda Maritime Hospital in Maryland, where he was being cared for mental disorders. His diary was published in 1952.

Seventeen years before Edouard Drumond and his *Jewish France*, Roger Gougenot des Mousseaux had published a book on the same subject in 1869. Although he did not have the same style as his successor, some of his reflections are still strangely topical today. In *The Jews, Judaism and the Judaisation of Christian peoples*, he wrote in his introduction: "Singular audacity, indeed, the audacity of the Jew who,... raises his hand not only against the freedom of the press but against the very freedom of history, as soon as he feels the points that wound him". And further on:"... Who would not take him as an innocent victim? He complains, weeps, sighs, laments, mixes cries of pain with cries of fury; he fills, stuns the world with accusations... his pleas he redoubles with the insolence of his threats; he asks for help from his compatriots outside; he demands, invoking what he calls his rights, the intervention of foreign peoples... he treats these princes as if he were another power; he speaks to them in a tone of superiority, and whose obedience he doubts; he dares, in the face of liberal Europe, he dares to threaten them with his influence over the freedom of the press and the freedom of speech "[339]

## *Lies and slander*

The insults that "some" Jewish intellectuals hurl at those they do not like can be accompanied by lies and slander. Here is a text by the "philosopher" Bernard-Henri Levy, written point-blank between the two rounds of the 1995 municipal elections, to warn the voters of the town of Vitrolles against the candidate of the "extreme right". Bernard-Henri Levy republished *l'Appel de Vitrolles* in 2004, in his book entitled

---

[339] Roger Gougenot des Mousseaux, *The Jews, Judaism and the Judaisation of Christian peoples*. Pdf version. Translated into English by Professor Noemí Coronel and the invaluable collaboration of the Catholic Nationalism team. Argentina, 2013. p. XXXIII, XXXIV, and p. 470.

*Récidives*: "If Mr Megret were to win, we would see a proliferation of gangs and private militias. Rifles and sawn-off rifles would come out of the cellars? The young people of Vitrolles, most of them disgusted, would decide to go out and make a life for themselves and leave the town to those fools who decided to hand it over to these barbarians. Vitrolles would be a cursed city…". Bernard-Henri Levy described Mr Megret's programme as follows: "An ultraliberal programme. Which clearly means: a terrible programme for the weak; ruthless towards the marginalised; a programme in which only the strong are respected, and in which it is planned, as in all fascist programmes, to crush the humble, the crippled, the small. Mr Mégret does not care about the humble. Mr Mégret despises the marginalised… I know that there are men and women in Vitrolles who keep part of their hearts on the other side of the Mediterranean, in that Algeria where they grew up and which is covered in mourning day after day by the faceless terrorism of the Islamists. Well, I want them to know that Mr Mégret is one of those who approves of this terror? I want you to know that Mr Mégret's friends are accomplices of the murderers who are making Algeria a land of ruin and suffering. Mr Megret is the crime. Mr Megret is the war. Mr Megret is not the heir of those who made France, but of those who, over the centuries, have not ceased to unmake it… They are the enemies of France. And that is why we must, without ceasing, remind them of their unworthiness[340]." Evidently, none of this came about after the election of Bruno Megret to the mayoralty of that southern French commune. In any case, Bernard-Henri Levy was not afraid to make a fool of himself by republishing his article.

The "French" writer Albert Cohen also mentioned this tendency of "some" Jews to lie and slander in one of his novels entitled *Nut Eaters*. In it he describes the life of the Jews of Cephalonia, one of those Greek islands from which he himself hails. The novel is comic and burlesque, but underneath the broad strokes there are defining truths. *Nail-Eater* is a gruesome and colourful character: "Nail-Eater got out of bed fully clothed and proceeded to perform uncertain ablutions while blessing the Eternal,… he hastily mumbled his prayer, thanked God that He had made him man and not woman, (and) begged Him to transfer his sins to the heavenly account of his enemies… To his activities as a synagogal slaughterer of chickens, as a legal adviser, as a false witness of accidents, as a false creditor of bankrupt merchants and pisaouvas…

---

[340] Bernard-Henri Levy, *Récidives*, Grasset, 2004, p. 477, 478.

he added the lucrative profession of not slanderer of notables. His clientele of non-slanderers was not large but it was select[341]." In other words, he undertook, in exchange for hard cash, not to speak ill of important Jews and their families for some time.

We find the same pathological maledictiveness in Philip Roth's novel *Operation Shylock*, published in 1993: "Why is it that we Jews treat each other with so little regard? Why do we Jews, when we are among ourselves, lose the courtesy that is normal in all coexistence? Why do we have to magnify every offence, why must there be a fight every time there is a provocation?...? The lack of love of Jews for their Jewish comrades... the animosity, the ridicule, the pure and simple hatred of one Jew for another? Why is there so much division among Jews... Who has put it into the heads of Jews that one must always be talking, if not shouting or making jokes at someone's expense, or picking apart the faults of one's best friend over the telephone for a whole afternoon?[342]"

The great Russian writer Aleksandr Solzhenitsyn also mentioned this tendency, apparently widespread in the Jewish community. We saw, at the beginning of this book, how the Russian statesman Derjavine had studied the causes of the famine in Belarus in the early 19th century. Derjavine had concluded that the role of Jewish alcohol distillers and traders had had terrible consequences, which prompted him to order the closure of some distilleries, such as the one in the village of Liozno. After delivering his report to the Tsar in 1801, Derjavine was odiously slandered. A Jewish woman from Liozno had denounced him, accusing him of having raped her in a distillery, as a result of which she claimed to have given birth to a stillborn child. The senate ordered an investigation and Derjavine replied: "I was in that distillery barely a quarter of an hour; not only did I not beat up any Jewess, but with my own eyes, I did not see one. He strove to be received by the Emperor: "Let them lock me up in a fortress," he declared, before pleading with the Tsar. "How could you trust such a preposterous, such a far-fetched denunciation [343]?" The Jew who had written this slanderous

---

[341] Albert Cohen, *Comeclavos*, Anagrama, 1989, Barcelona, p. 38.

[342] Philip Roth, *Operación Shylock*, Debolsillo, Editorial Mondadori, 2005 Barcelona, p. 384, 385

[343] Alexandre Soljénitsyne, *Deux Siècles ensemble, Tome I*, Fayard, 2002, p. 62.

denunciation on behalf of the woman was finally sentenced to a year's imprisonment.

Less well known than Bernard-Henri Levy, the intellectual Albert Caraco explicitly expressed these unfortunate inclinations. The son of a Levantine financial intermediary, he was born in Constantinople in 1919 and spent his childhood in Berlin before fleeing to South America with his parents in the face of the Nazi threat. Returning to Europe after the destruction of Germany, he published some 20 books, including *Apology for Israel*, published in 1957, in which he abruptly declared, with respect for his fellow human beings: "Deceiving the spirits, slandering, lying, confident of their good faith... They have a white soul so that they can be darker and never die of their malice[344] " In *Eight Essays on Evil*, published in 1963, he wrote: "One can lie, provided one lies without stopping, always returning to the charge of those one slanders... The main thing is insistence... To strike ten times and even a hundred times, renewing the slander... Add to that an air of moderation so that the atrocities will be better accepted... The most tried and tested method is to pass off as madmen those who strive to understand[345]."

In the 4th century, Gregory of Nyssa was already attributing these defects to them: "Followers of the Devil, race of vipers, informers, slanderers, darkened brains, Pharisaic leaven, Sanhedrin of demons, execrable accursed ones, stoners, enemies of all that is beautiful[346]."

## *Repression against historians*

In 1990, in *Le Figaro* of 3 April, a former communist of Jewish origin, Annie Kriegel, denounced "an unbearable Jewish thought police". It is this police that, under the impetus of Rabbi Sirat[347], launched the idea of an anti-revisionist law that was finally voted in thanks to the former socialist Prime Minister of Jewish origin Laurent Fabius. Fabius rightly

---

[344] Albert Caraco, *Apologie d'Israël*, 1957, L'Age d'homme, 2004, p. 53.

[345] Albert Caraco, *Huits Essais sur le mal*, L'Age d'homme, 1963, p. 331, 332.

[346] François de Fontette, *Histoire de l'antisémitisme*, PUF, 1982, p. 29. Stoning was really in vogue at that time among the sons of Abraham.

[347] *L'Agence télégraphique juive* bulletin, 2 June 1986, p. 1.

\* See also http://www.ihr.org/jhr/v16/v16n2p-2_Faurisson.html.

claimed to be the sponsor of this parliamentary initiative. The media campaign organised around the desecration of the Jewish graves in the Carpentras cemetery had paralysed opposition to the final vote on the Sirat-Fabius-Gayssot law. This law significantly restricted freedom of expression in France, as it condemned any study or research into the official version of history established by the victors of the Second World War at Nuremberg in 1946.

In December 2005, in anticipation of a future international revisionist conference to be held in Iran, the famous Professor Faurisson reminded the public that the main revisionist historians were "either in prison, in exile or in a precarious situation" in such a way that they were forbidden to cross borders and transit through an international airport.

Historian Ernst Zündel, married to an American and living peacefully in the state of Tennessee, had been arrested in front of his home on 5 February 2003 and imprisoned on a false pretext. He was extradited to Canada where, for two years, he rotted in a high security prison in degrading conditions. He was finally handed over to Germany, where he was held in prison in Mannheim, awaiting trial for revisionism. In Canada, as in Germany, revisionists were denied the right to defend themselves and to question what was "public knowledge". Let us recall that Ernst Zündel had been the victim of a criminal arson attack in Toronto on 7 May 1995, which had destroyed his house. A few days later, he received a parcel bomb which the police had to defuse by exploding it[348].

Also in the USA, near Chicago, the German Germar Rudolf had been kidnapped, separated from his American wife and children, and handed over to Germany where he was imprisoned in Stuttgart. The Belgian revisionist Siegfried Verbeke had been arrested at Amsterdam airport in 2005 and handed over to Germany where he was held in Heidelberg prison. The famous British historian David Irving had been arrested while in transit through Austria and imprisoned in Vienna. These four people were facing prison sentences of several years "except perhaps David Irving, if, as his lawyer suggests, he recants, expresses his repentance and asks for the court's indulgence". Irving would indeed be

---

[348] For acts of violence committed in the USA, see Mark Weber, *The Zionist Terror Network, Background and Operation of the Jewish Defense League and other Criminal Zionist Group, A Special Report*, Institute for Historical Review, Revised and Updated Edition, 1993.

released in December 2006, a few days after the international revisionist conference in Tehran.

In September 2003, the Austrian revisionist Wolfgang Froehlich, a former far-right MP, was sentenced to one year's imprisonment and two years' probation after publishing a book denouncing the "lie" of the gas chambers. Other revisionists were in prison in Germany or Austria, Faurisson wrote, quoting lawyer Manfred Roeder. On 2 December 1999, Manfred Roeder was sentenced to two years in prison by a court in Grevesmuehlen for calling the Nazi genocide of the Jews an "imposture". In August 1995, German nationalist leader Bela Ewald Althans was sentenced to three and a half years in prison by a Berlin court after denying the Holocaust. On 15 December 1994, Althans had already been sentenced to 18 months in prison in Munich for denying on VHS videotape the death of millions of Jews by the Nazis. In November 1992, the chairman of the German nationalist NPD party, Guenther Anton Deckert, was sentenced to one year's probation in Mannhein for describing the figure of six million Jewish victims of Nazism as "cerebral ineptitude" and "absurdity". Fredrick Töben: an Australian citizen of German origin who was active as a revisionist in Australia and on the Internet. While passing through Germany to investigate on the spot the judicial repression of revisionism in that country, he was arrested and imprisoned. In Poland, the Czech Republic and other European countries, revisionists were also persecuted and sentenced. In Sweden, Ahmed Rami was also imprisoned.

Then there were the professional bans of all kinds in various countries, as well as the family dramas and suicides caused by repression. In Germany, in Munich, on 25 April 1995, the revisionist Reinhold Elstner had immolated himself to protest against the "Himalayas of lies" being poured out on his people. The German mainstream press ignored his heroic act and the German police had confiscated the bouquets of flowers laid at the site of the sacrifice and proceeded to arrest those who had expressed their sympathy.

In April 2000, the Swiss Gaston-Amaudruz, editor of a revisionist monthly, was sentenced to 12 years in prison by the Lausanne correctional court for having questioned the existence of the gas chambers and questioned the figure of six million Jews killed by the Nazis. In Switzerland, too, René-Louis Berclaz was imprisoned, while his compatriot, Professor Jurgen Graf, was sentenced in 1999 to a fine of 50,000 francs by the Paris correctional court for having sent a book entitled *L'Holocauste au scanner* (The *Holocaust under the scanner*) to French parliamentarians.

Another case worth remembering is that of Georges Theil, a former regional councillor of the National Front (FN), who was sentenced in January 2006 by the Lyon correctional court to six months' imprisonment and a fine of 10 000 euros for denying crimes against humanity, after having denounced in a television interview the "fantasy" of the gas chambers. He had already been sentenced in 2001 for similar acts to three months' probation and a fine of 50 000 francs by the Grenoble Court of Appeal. Jean Plantin, prosecuted in Lyon, and Vincent Reynouard in Limoges, had also received various convictions, including prison sentences. Robert Faurisson himself, convicted in 1981 and 1991, appeared before the Paris correctional court in July 2006 for having given a telephone interview on revisionist issues to the Iranian television station "Sahar". On 3 October 2006, he was sentenced to three months' probation and a fine of 7500 euros.

The siege seemed to be closing in. Bruno Gollnisch, the National Front's number two and an MEP, was also to appear before the Lyon court, having declared in October 2004: "There is no serious historian who fully subscribes to the conclusions of the Nuremberg trial. I believe that, with regard to the drama of the concentration camps, the discussion should be free. The existence of the gas chambers should be discussed by historians". This simple statement had provoked a reaction of general indignation in the press and was enough to bring him to justice. In January 2007, the Lyon correctional court sentenced Bruno Gollnisch to three months' probation and a fine of 5,000 euros for "denying the existence of a crime against humanity". He was also ordered to pay 55,000 euros in damages to the civil parties.

In the daily *Libération* of 28 December 2005, Jack Bensimon declared his satisfaction with the laws in force: "Today, thanks to this Gayssot law, it is no longer the Jews who must hide, but the anti-Semites, who must hide their anti-Semitism in their subconscious. As long as this remains the case, our country will be safe from the pogroms, the memory of which is still very much present in the collective Jewish, and even individual, subconscious."

Robert Faurisson recalled that, in France, Jewish armed groups roamed freely, attacking people with impunity and even within the walls of the Paris courthouse. From 1978 to 1993, he himself had suffered a dozen attacks that went unpunished. "If the Jews and the Zionists use physical violence and judicial repression in this way, it is because the revisionists have defeated them handily in the field of scientific and historical debate".

Jewish activists effectively acted with impunity. Through Betar\* and with the agreement of the Ministry of the Interior, the French Jewish minority had set up paramilitary formations, without any parallel in the rest of the French population or any foreign minority on French territory. Faurisson counted, from 19 June 1976 to 2 April 1991, some fifty cases of physical attacks committed by organised Jews. In the fifty cases identified, "the victims numbered in the hundreds. They included: deaths, serious injuries with coma, handicaps and serious after-effects, as well as acid attacks, acts of barbarism, eye gouging, severe beatings in the presence of police or security guards refusing to intervene, several hospitalisations and numerous ambushes". Most of these assaults were overlooked by the media or briefly reported. Some were condoned by Jewish publications or organisations, which, in general, after a few words of reprobation, implied that the victims deserved their fate and that, from now on, no leniency was to be expected if Jewish anger was provoked again. On the other hand, Faurisson stressed, "it is noteworthy how no Jew has ever been the victim of a single attack by an extreme right-wing or revisionist group[349]."

We know, on the other hand, that political assassination is a practice that is not repugnant to organised Jews, not to mention the attacks on Palestinians[350]. Hundreds of victims on the one hand, and on the other, victims whose total is zero. In the Jewish community press, calls for physical violence were commonplace. Jacques Kupfer, president of the Herout de France, warned of the Jewish response to the rise of French nationalism. In the *Tribune juive* of 25 May 1995, he wrote: 'I have never considered that anti-Semitism could be solved by declarations or philosophical discussions. But I do know how the problem of anti-Semites is solved: in a very physical way. Jewish youth must be prepared for it: no crying, no fear, no mourning".

---

[349] On the physical attacks committed against French patriots, see the book by Emmanuel Ratier, *Les Guerriers d'Israël: Enquête sur les milices sionistes* ("The Warriors of Israel: An investigation of Zionist militant groups," Facta, 37, rue d'Amsterdam, 75008 Paris, 1995).

\* Jewish self-defence militia.

[350] On political assassinations: Cf. *Les Espérances planétariennes*, p. 295-301. One can add the assassination in 1916 of Minister Stürgkh by Fréderic Adler, the son of Victor Adler, who led the Social Democratic movement in Germany. See also Nachman Ben-Yehuda, *Political Assassination by Jews, A Rhetorical Device for Justice*, New York, State University of New York Press, 1993.

The former socialist minister Bernard Kouchner (now a supporter of the liberal right) and his colleague Daniel Cohn-Bendit were equally combative, but they favoured the legal route: "Against the anti-Semitism that manifests itself in France, the culprits must first be prosecuted and condemned, as you rightly say. The problem will not be solved by force alone. Dani, we have our work cut out for us. Come on, this fight is necessary[351]."

Faced with the inexorable rise of anti-Semitism (since about 3000 years), the intellectual Michel Winock, professor of political science, presented the following analysis: "It is not the first time in France that an anti-Semitic crisis has manifested itself as a symptom of a democratic crisis. The last presidential election in 2002 was revealing. When the Republic falters, the Jews are the first to be affected. Today, the crisis is mainly due to the difficulties of integrating an immigrant or immigrant population, poorly educated, marginalised, too often discriminated against—a breeding ground for communitarian, anti-republican and anti-western propaganda. In this crisis… everyone at his or her own level has to get involved. A sense of openness, the ability to listen to others, continuous education, media responsibility, vigilance in the face of racism and anti-Semitism, and at the same time a firm commitment to secular values, the only ones that allow us to "*live together*" \*, beyond the differences that we must respect. It is an immense challenge: taking it up is the price of French pacification[352]." "Peace" is indeed at the heart of the Jewish conception of the world.

In the United States, the crackdown on anti-Semites was also intensifying. The *Rivarol* newspaper of 29 April 2005 reported the case of the American Matt Hale, 33, an Illinois law school graduate and president of the Church of the Creator, a nationalist movement that claimed to oppose "Zionist power" by systematically resorting to the courts as a means of struggle. Apparently, Matt Hale was becoming annoying. On 8 January 2003, Michaël Chertoff, the son of a rabbi and

---

[351] Daniel Cohn-Bendit, Bernard Kouchner, *Quand tu sera président*, Robert Laffont, 2004, p. 336.

[352] Michel Winock, *Eduard Drumond et Cie, antisémitisme et fascisme en France*, Seuil, Paris 1982, p. 385.

\*Living *together"*: *"Vivre ensemble"*: Politically correct euphemism in France, which serves as a media slogan for the population. Its definition would be: Ability and willingness of inhabitants, in an environment of social and cultural diversity, to share their living space in a harmonious way.

future justice minister of George Bush, ordered his arrest on the pretext that he had tried to organise the assassination of a judge. Under the new anti-terrorism legislation in force in the USA since the attacks of 11 September 2001 (the Patriot Act), he was held in solitary confinement for fifteen months and considered a terrorist like the Afghan and Iraqi Islamist prisoners held at Guantanamo Bay. In April 2004, he appeared in court dressed in the orange jumpsuit of the most dangerous criminals. The entire indictment was based on the testimony of a prosecution witness, Anthony Evola, who turned out to be an FBI agent undercover in Hale's entourage who ran his private security service, and who would testify to having been ordered by Hale to assassinate Judge Lefkow. Matthew Hale defended himself, denouncing "George Bush's police state" and the "Jewish-controlled media". He was sentenced on 6 April 2005 to forty years in prison.

"The Jews are always victims just long enough to become executioners", wrote Alphonse Toussenel in 1845, in the introduction to his book, *Les juifs rois de l'époque, histoire de la féodalité financière* (*The Jewish kings of the time, history of financial feudalism*). The ideal would be Lenin's Soviet law, which condemned anti-Semites to the death penalty. We could also take up the words written by Louis-Ferdinand Celine in his famous 1937 pamphlet, *Bagatelles pour un massacre*: "Every anti-Semite will have his head cut off". That would make it even easier.

## Cruelty

A "pacification" plan had already been established during the Second World War. "The Kaufmann Plan" went down in history to illustrate this desire to "pacify" individuals and nations. The text by Theodore N. Kaufmann, Roosevelt's advisor, was published in 1941 in the United States by Argyle Press under the title *"Germany must perish"*. The weekly *Rivarol* of 31 May 1996 published part of it:

"It now remains only to determine the best method, the most practical and expeditious way, by which the German nation is to be razed to the ground. And let it be understood, wholesale massacre and execution must be ruled out. Besides being impracticable, when applied to a population of some 70 million, such methods are inconsistent with the moral obligations and ethical practices of civilisation. There remains then but one way of ridding the world, for ever, of Germanism, and that is to stop the source from which these incontinent souls of war are born, by preventing the German people from reproducing forever in their kind. This modern method, known to science as eugenic sterilisation, is at once practical, humane and complete. Sterilisation has become a proverb of science, as the best method for the human race to get rid of what is bad for it: the degenerate, the insane, the hereditary criminal... When one realises that sanitary measures, such as vaccination and serum treatments, are considered to be of direct benefit to the community, certainly the sterilisation of the German people cannot be regarded as anything but a great measure, promoted by mankind, to immunise itself, for ever, against the virus of Germanism. The population of Germany, excluding conquered and annexed territories, is approximately 70 million, almost equally divided between males and females. To achieve the Germanic extinction project it would be necessary to sterilise some 48 million, a figure which excludes, because of the limited ability to procreate, males over sixty years of age and females over forty-five... Taking 20,000 surgeons, as an arbitrary figure, and on the assumption that each of them would get a minimum of twenty-five operations a day, it would not take more than a month, at most, to complete their sterilisation... Of course, after complete sterilisation, the birth rate in Germany will cease. With a normal death rate of 2 per cent per annum, German life would decrease by 1.5 million lives annually.

*Time Magazine* called these ideas "phenomenal"; the *Washington Post* spoke of a "provocative theory, interestingly presented", while the *New York Times* went so far as to headline: "A Plan for Lasting Peace for Civilised Nations". These ideas have undoubtedly helped influence American and British strategists in their massive bombing of German cities and civilian populations with gigantic quantities of incendiary bombs.

After Germany's defeat, many Jews, of course, left the way open for their revenge. After the fall of the Third Reich, more than five million German soldiers were imprisoned, crammed into barbed-wire fenced camps in the American and French occupation zones. The Canadian historian James Bacque published a very interesting book on this forgotten episode of history in 1989, *Other Losses*, in which he portrayed the appalling living conditions in these camps that resulted in the deaths of hundreds of thousands of prisoners: "The ground of the camps quickly became a filthy mire of faeces and urine, a veritable hotbed of epidemics. Poorly fed, without shelter, deprived of the most elementary sanitary facilities, the prisoners soon began to die of starvation and disease. From April 1945 to mid-1946, nearly one million people were annihilated, most of them in the American camps, the others in the French camps... For more than forty years, this tragic episode of the Second World War remained hidden in the Allied archives".

From 1947 to the early 1950s, James Bacque wrote that, "the Germans estimate that 1,700,000 soldiers, still alive at the end of hostilities, never returned home. All the Allied powers claim to know nothing of the whereabouts of these men. The United States, Britain and France accuse Russia of having committed atrocities in its internment camps[353]."

These figures do not include the countless casualties due to the evacuations of the 12 million Germans from the territories of East Prussia, Pomerania, Silesia and Sudetenland, now under Russian, Polish and Czech domination.

Let us recall the case of a certain Salomon Morel, commandant of the Swietochlowice-Zgoda labour camp from February to November 1945. At the age of 75, Salomon Morel had finally been charged in 1996 by the Polish justice system with "physical and psychological violence against German prisoners". His role in the crimes committed in the Swietochlowice camps had been clarified by the Institute of National Remembrance, an institution created in the 1990s in Poland after the fall of communism. This institution, chaired by a Polish Jew named Leon Kieres, was elected by the parliament and had set itself the goal of clarifying the dark pages of the Nazi and communist period.

The text initially published in Polish reported that poor living and hygienic conditions led to the dramatic spread of typhus, typhoid fever and dysentery[354]. Nothing had been done to prevent the spread of the epidemic, not even delousing the prisoners. Moreover, the prisoners lived in the terror instituted by the commandant: "On Easter Saturday 1945, the guards and Commandant Morel broke into the camp at night and beat the prisoners with whips, rifle butts and the legs of stools". On

---

[353] James Bacque, *Morts pour raisons diverses*, 1989, Éditions Sand, 1990 for l'Éd. Française, p. 16-18. (Read in Spanish *Crimen y Perdón*, by James Bacque, Editorial Machado, 2013, Madrid).

\* Theodore N. Kaufmann, *Germany Must Perish*, pdf version, Kamerad Publishing House, p. 41.

[354] The text translated from Polish into English was published in the newsletter No 55 (May 1997) of the Adelaide Institute (Australia). Jean Plantin's magazine *Tabou* gives a French version of the text in its issue No. 1, Éditions Akribeia, 2002.

that occasion, some thirty witnesses had suffered ill-treatment. Salomon Morel reportedly beat the Germans to death.

John Sack, an American Jew, wrote in his book *An Eye for an Eye*[355], that Polish Jews who had enlisted after the war in the Stalinist security services took revenge on any German who fell into their hands, but also on all opponents of Stalinism. Salomon Morel was one of them: "He would have shot them all. But the truncheon gave him greater emotional satisfaction. In Auschwitz, the SS were forbidden to beat Jews for their personal satisfaction, but Salomon Morel's guards feared no restraint of power. Sometimes, they distinguished "corporal punishment" from "general punishment", when they grabbed the German by the legs and arms and slammed his head against a wall as one does with a battering ram. They hunted the Germans by taking them to the kennels and beat them if they did not want to bark. They forced them to beat each other. They raped the women and trained the dogs to bite their genitals on command.

This was how, from February to October 1945, prisoners were treated in the camp run by Salomon Morel. Of the 6,000 prisoners, 1,800 had died due to mistreatment and a typhus epidemic. Pursued by Interpol for crimes against humanity, Salomon Morel had taken refuge in Israel in 1992, after having been a lifelong security services officer under the communist regime.

Little information is known about Jewish "avenger" groups after the war. Among the most famous was the Nakan group, whose name meant 'revenge' in Hebrew. The *Rivarol* newspaper of 12 April 1996 reported that an Israeli television programme called "An Eye for an Eye", broadcast on 25 February 1996, had hosted and interviewed Ava Kuvner, the former leader of one of these revenge groups. He recounted in detail and with some pride, the ambitious solution devised to liquidate six million Germans by poisoning the water of Munich, Nuremberg, Hamburg and other major German cities. This plan was reported to have been drawn up and warmly supported by Haïm Weizman, the future first president of the Hebrew state. It was Weizman who directed Kuvner to the competent chemists, confirmed Dan Setton in his 1995 book *Vengeance*. That project, perhaps too ambitious, failed despite many months of preparation. This is what Israel Shamir, an Israeli publicist and convert to Orthodox Christianity, says in his book *The Other Face*

---

[355] John Sack, *An Eye for an Eye*, Basic Books, 1993. www.johnsack.com

*of Israel*: 'Fortunately, the plot was uncovered and British officials arrested Kuvner in a European port. This story was published last year in Israel, in a biography of Kuvner written by Dina Porat, director of Tel-Aviv University's anti-Semitism research centre[356]." Shamir added that "Abba Kovner" had also tried to "poison the sources of the Rhine... You can read about it in his biography, without any hint of remorse or embarrassment, written by Israeli historian Anita Shapira[357]."

In the television programme, Kuvner boasted that he had succeeded in poisoning "thousands of SS" by introducing bread prepared with strychnine into the camps where they were imprisoned. Dan Setton put the number of German prisoners who had consumed poisoned bread at 15,000. The television programme was "strangely silent on the results of the operation". However, it was still surprising to hear criminals boasting about their actions under the pretext of "justice", regretting only that they had "not carried out their revenge". Haïm Weizman would give his name to the Weizman Institute, a counterpart of the French Pasteur Institute. No head of state visiting Israel is spared a reverent visit to this prestigious institute.

Israeli television had broadcast in 2000 another investigation into these Jewish 'avengers' operating in occupied Germany. Two elderly Israelis, Leipe Distel and Joseph Harmatz, members of the Nokim (Hebrew for *Avengers*), admitted to belonging to a death squad, directed from Tel Aviv, which aimed to poison thousands of German prisoners with arsenic in an American camp near Nuremberg. In 1946, after being hired to work in the camp bakery, they managed to soak 3,000 loaves of bread with arsenic. The records had preserved the medical reports of hundreds of prisoners with severe stomach ailments. The 74-year-old Joseph Harmatz had this to say on the subject: "We Jews have acted with morality on our side. The Jews have the right to take revenge on the Germans". Rafi Eitan, former director of Mossad operations, summed up the actions of the Nokim (there were probably hundreds of them) as follows: "They acted without regard and without further formality. They were content to execute all the Nazis they could find. For them, the acts were justified by the biblical rule: 'An eye for an eye, a tooth for a tooth'".

---

[356] *Haaretz*, 28 April 2001

[357] Israel Shamir, *L'autre visage d'Israël*, Éditions Al Qalam, 2004, p. 139, 333

Journalist Emmanuel Ratier reported in *Faits et Documents* that in April 2002, after years of delay, the German judicial authorities, in particular the Nuremberg prosecutor general, Klaus Hubmann, who had refused to bow to pressure, finally decided to open an unprecedented criminal investigation into the post-war Jewish death squads. It turned out that numerous members of the death squads had become Mossad agents and leaders. From Tel Aviv, Harmatz called the investigation "ridiculous": "These people are idiots, he said. I don't recognise Germany anyway. And I certainly have no intention of going there. The Israeli authorities will never allow them to come here to interrogate us. We've had enough of interrogations by Germans[358]."

After the war, the State of Israel wanted to put an end to these disorderly actions. A February 1985 issue of the *Crapouillot* reported that Colonel Schadmi, the head of the Haganah [359] in Europe, in charge of dismantling the existing networks, had to order the kidnapping of those "avengers" who refused to give up their activities and transfer them to Israel.

Elie Wiesel also mentioned some excesses committed by his fellow Jews in the German camps during the war: "How can one explain that the son of the great Polish Zionist leader Yitzhak Grinbaum, a kapo in Auschwitz, went to such lengths to torture, humiliate and beat his fellow Jews, especially if they were religious or Zionist? "These Jewish kapos who beat us up, why? To show the executioners that they can be just like them[360]?" We see here, after all, that Jews can be men like everyone else…

In his book on the Jews in Russia, the great Russian writer Aleksandr Solzhenitsyn also drew attention to the role of numerous Jews in the organs of Bolshevik repression: "They now had an almost unlimited power that they could never have imagined before. They did not know how to stop, to step aside, to find in themselves a restraint or the necessary lucidity." Solzhenitsyn quoted a Jewish historian, G. Landau, who wrote of the Bolshevik period, "We have been affected by something we did not expect to find in the Jews-cruelty, sadism and

---

[358] *Faits et documents,* 15 April 2002

[359] Haganah: the first paramilitary organisation fighting British troops for Israel's independence.

[360] Elie Wiesel, *Mémoires, Tome I*, Le Seuil, 1994, p. 111, 113.

violence that seemed alien to a people far removed from warlike life; those who yesterday did not know how to handle the rifle, were now among the murderers and executioners[361]."

These instincts were brought to the fore in other, older periods of history. In *The Other Face of Israel*, Israel Shamir recalled the 7th century conquest of Palestine by the Persians. In 614, Palestine was part of the Byzantine Empire, successor to the Roman Empire. The Jews of Palestine then allied themselves with their co-religionists in Babylonia to lend a hand to the Persians in their conquest of the Holy Land. 26,000 Jews participated in the offensive. After the Persian victory, the Jews perpetrated "a massive holocaust": "They set fire to the churches and monasteries, killing the monks and priests and burning the books". It was "the most horrible year in the history of Palestine until the 20th century," wrote Shamir, quoting Oxford University professor Henry Milman: "At last the long-awaited hour of triumph and revenge had come. The Jews did not miss their chance and washed the desecration of the holy city with the blood of the Christians". According to Shamir, they bought the Christians prisoners from the Persians, and murdered them in the Mamilla reservation. "In the city of Jerusalem alone, the Jews massacred between 60,000 and 90,000 Palestinian Christians... A few days later, having realised the magnitude of the massacre, the Persian soldiers prevented the Jews from continuing their abuses and outrages... The genocide of 614 after Jesus Christ was the most terrible, although it was not the only genocide perpetrated by the Jews during that chaotic era[362]."

Israel Shamir naturally mentioned other tragic episodes in Palestine, especially the massacre of the village of Deir Yassine, on the outskirts of Jerusalem: "During the night of 9 April 1948, the Jewish terrorist groups Etsel and Lethi attacked this peaceful village and massacred everyone, men, women and children". The leaders of these terrorist gangs, Menahem Begin and Itzhac Shamir, would later become Prime Ministers of Israel. Yet neither expressed any remorse, and even "Begin lived to the end of his life in a house with a panoramic view over Deir Yassine. For them there was no Nuremberg tribunal, no vengeance, no penance", but "a carpet of roses leading up to the Nobel Peace Prize".

---

[361] Alexandre Soljénitsyne, *Deux Siècles ensembles*, Fayard, 2003, p. 146.

[362] Israel Shamir, *L'autre visage d'Israël*, Éditions Al Qalam, 2004, p. 133-137.

When the massacre was unveiled, Ben Gourion, Prime Minister of Israel at the time, announced that "rampaging gangs of Arabs" had been the perpetrators. Three days later, the paramilitary groups were incorporated into the Israeli army being formed and a general amnesty absolved them of their crimes.

The same scheme, i.e. denial, followed by apologies and finally a gesture of clemency and promotions, was applied after the first atrocity committed by Prime Minister Sharon in 1953. That took place in the Palestinian village of Qibya, where Sharon's unit blew up houses with their inhabitants inside with dynamite, massacring some sixty people, men, women and children. When the affair was revealed, Prime Minister Ben Gourion began by accusing Arab gangs. This act, once again, did not ruin the career of Ariel Sharon, who would also become prime minister. Shamir cited a third example, that of the Kafr Kasem massacre, where Israeli troops had rounded up peasants to machine-gun them. "When it was impossible to deny the case and a communist deputy revealed the infamous details, the culprits were court-martialled and sentenced to long prison terms; they were released after a few months and the commander was appointed director of the "Israel Borrowing" bureau[363]."

An Agence France Presse report of 22 May 2006 noted that "most of the Israeli military and settlers involved in unlawful killings of Palestinians continued to enjoy impunity". In its annual report, Amnesty International reported on these human rights violations in Israel: "Investigations and prosecutions were rare. These, more often than not, did not result in convictions… In the exceptional cases where Israelis were found guilty of murder or violations of fundamental rights of Palestinians, the penalties incurred were light". The report also noted "recurrent" abuses perpetrated against Palestinians by Jewish settlers: "Israeli settlers have regularly attacked Palestinians and their property in the West Bank. They have destroyed crops, uprooted or burned olive trees, polluted water reservoirs and prevented farmers from cultivating their land in order to force them to leave". The report specified that, most of the time, the Israeli military and police did not intervene. "Instead, Israel used all means at its disposal—especially measures that violate international law such as assassinations and collective sanctions—against Palestinians responsible for attacks against Israelis or suspected of direct or indirect involvement in such attacks." Finally,

---

[363] Israel Shamir, *L'autre visage d'Israël*, Éditions Al Qalam, 2004, p. 143-146.

it mentioned that "allegations of torture of Palestinian prisoners were not the subject of serious investigations."

We see how the poisoning of water wells seems to be an old custom of these Jewish "avengers". It is also quite surprising to note how most Jewish historians tear their hair out over the terrible "accusations" of the Christians who, already in the Middle Ages, blamed the Jews for poisoning the water of the wells. But this is undoubtedly a legend, a myth propagated by anti-Semites to harm the Jewish people, always a victim, an eternal scapegoat.

Another accusation, equally absurd, was to claim that Jews practised ritual murder of Christian children (blood libels) in order to mix their blood with the unleavened bread eaten during the Jewish Passover (Pesach) feasts. These false, ignoble and horrible accusations were still numerous in the 19th century and even more recently. Such is the case of Tisza-Eszlar in Hungary, for example: in 1882, the synagogue of the town was destroyed after the disappearance of a fourteen-year-old girl. In June 1891, the body of a child was found in Xanten in Rhenish Prussia, the crime being attributed to the Jews' desire to collect blood. In 1899, a Jew named Hilsner was convicted of ritual murder in Bohemia. Naturally, these prejudices were persistent. The Beilis case, in 1911, was a high-profile one. Although the poor wretch was acquitted, the jury solemnly declared that ritual murders undoubtedly existed," wrote Leon Poliakov, "[364]".

Another high-profile case was in Damascus, a partly Christian city. In 1840, a Capuchin monk, Father Thomas, mysteriously disappeared. His body was found in March (after the feast of Purim) in the sewers of the Jewish quarter. The French consul, Ratti-Menton, blamed his disappearance on members of the Jewish community and supported legal action against prominent personalities accused of ritual murder. In Paris, Adolphe Thiers, who had just been appointed president of the Council by Louis-Philippe, expressed his solidarity with the French consul. But the financiers Fould and Rothschild intervened with all their might and promoted a press campaign against Thiers. The latter attacked them from the rostrum of the Chamber: "You claim in the name of the Jews and I claim in the name of France!" Again, historian Leon Poliakov gave us an idea of the power of the international Jewish

---

[364] Léon Poliakov, *Histoire des crises d'identités juives*, Austral 1994, p.210.

community at the time: "The Rothschilds finally won the cause, threatening to profit from the fall in rent. Thiers had to resign. The Jews then took up the struggle for the rehabilitation of the victims of the medieval slander and obtained it thanks to British intervention. But the warning had been given, and this affair marks the origin of Jewish defence organisations, starting with the Universal Israelite Alliance[365]."

This Israelite Alliance was created in 1860 by a Frenchman from the French Midi, "perfectly integrated": Adolphe Crémieux. In 1866, he had already rushed to Russia to defend the Jews: "In Saratov, a group of Jews was accused of ritual murder. Adolphe Crémieux went there and obtained their acquittal[366]". In 1870, he became the first Minister of Justice of the new French Republic, and, as we know, he immediately granted French nationality to his fellow Algerians, while the Prussian armies were still marching on the national territory.

If we go back in history, we find that there are dozens of blood libels all over Europe. In Spain, the famous case of the Santo Niño de La Guardia was the most emblematic. In Poland, in the 18th century, the Jewish community was in upheaval and was still torn by the conflict between the rabbis and the Sabbateans, the disciples of the "false messiah" Shabtai Tzvi and his successor, Jacob Frank. The Sabbateans, declared heretical by the rabbis, were severely persecuted[367], but countered by attacking the Talmud, "saying it was false and evil", reported David Bakan, adding: "They went so far as to accuse the Talmud of imposing the use of Christian blood, testifying and swearing that Jews perpetrated ritual crimes[368]." This is what Gershom Scholem, one of the greatest

---

[365] Léon Poliakov, *Los Samaritanos*, Anaya & Mario Muchnik, 1992, Madrid, p. 111. A book published on the subject in 2005, *La Sangre cristiana*, presented the confessions of a former repentant rabbi from Moldavia (*Refutación de la religion de los judíos*, 1803). He claimed that a few drops were enough. About the Damascus case, one can read that all the accused Jews confessed to the murder. Ten of them were condemned to death, and finally saved thanks to the intervention of Adolphe Crémieux, Moïse Montefiore and international financiers.

[366] Léon Poliakov, *Histoire des crises d'identités juives*, Austral 1994, p. 67.

[367] On the Sabbateans, cf. *Psychanalyse du Judaïsme*, H. Ryssen, Baskerville, p. 158-166.

[368] David Bakan, *Freud et la tradition mystique juive*, 1963, Payot, 2001, p. 132.

Jewish thinkers of the 20th century, also wrote: "During their public discussions with the Jewish rabbis in Lvov in 1759, the members of the sect did not shy away from resorting to the accusation of ritual crime, the most unbearable and painful accusation for Jewish sensibilities, even more so than those attacking their beliefs." But Scholem was quick to add that according to historian Meir Balaban, "the Sabbateans did so at the instigation of the Catholic clergy, who had an interest in possessing such a document for their own purposes[369]."

The last major case of ritual crime took place in 1946 in Kielce, Poland. A pogrom broke out following an accusation of ritual murder. In all, 42 Jews were executed by the mob, 5 by the police, and more than 70 were seriously injured. Kielce represented the most significant episode of anti-Semitism in Poland after the war: "Between November 1944 and October 1945 alone," wrote Gabriele Eschenazi, "some 350 Jews were murdered by the Poles. From liberation until the end of 1947, there were about 1500 victims." In Rzeszow in 1945, "news spread that a police patrol had found in a rabbi's house the tortured bodies of at least sixteen children. The Jewish community was forced to flee under police protection[370]."

In February 2007, another unpleasant case broke out in Italy and caused a major scandal. Professor Ariel Toaff had just published a 400-page book entitled *Pasque di sangue (Passover of Blood, the Jews of Europe and the Blood Libels)*. Professor Toaff, of Bar-Ilan University in Jerusalem, caused a media stir by acknowledging that ritual murders were practised by some Ashkenazi Jews in northern Italy.

The daily *Actualité juive* of 1 March 2007 summarised the affair: "*Pasque di sangue*, the book by historian Ariel Toaff, with a print run of only 1,000 copies, would perhaps have gone relatively unnoticed if another historian, Sergio Luzzato, also Jewish, had not written a glowing review of the book in the daily *Corriere della Sera*." The latter called the book "an unpublished and courageous intellectual act". He called the publication of the book "an unprecedented and courageous intellectual act." Ariel Toaff claimed that, during the Middle Ages, "between 1100 and 1500, some, perhaps several, crucifixions of Christian children had actually taken place" at the hands of "a minority

---

[369] Gershom Scholem, *Le Messianisme juif*, 1971, Calmann-Levy, 1974, p.144

[370] Gabriele Eschenazi, Gabriele Nissim, *Les Juifs et le communisme après la Shoah*, 1995, Éd. De Paris, 2000, p. 231-239.

of Ashkenazi fundamentalists." The newspaper gave further details: "pulverised, the blood was mixed with the unleavened bread and wine consumed on seder nights, (the Passover meal). One can easily imagine the shock wave produced by such statements. Ariel Toaff, a professor of medieval history, was none other than the son of the former Chief Rabbi of Rome, Elio Toaff, who was received by Pope John Paul II in the synagogue in Rome. The next day, all the Italian newspapers were talking about the book, whose thousand copies were sold out in a single day". Ariel Toaff then insisted, recalling in the daily La *Stampa* the persecutions of Jews during the Crusades: "From that trauma was born a passion for revenge which, in some cases, generated certain reactions such as the ritual murder of Christian children." The historian also mentioned "the trade in dried blood on both sides of the Alps, with vials stamped kosher by the rabbis." Immediately disavowed by transalpine historians, Ariel Toaff was disapproved of by his father, by the local Jewish community and "by the whole of Italian Judaism", as well as by the University of Bar-Ilan. After receiving various pressures, Toaff made some contradictory statements, and asked his publisher, El Molino, not to republish his work until he modified some chapters. The author also declared that the proceeds from the sale of the book would go to the Anti-Diffamation League, based in the United States, to express "his deepest regrets". Naturally, *Actualité juive* published another article by a Jewish historian who described the book as "hallucinatory".

In a book that we will examine in more detail later, Dr. Georges Valensin mentioned a certain inclination to cruelty in some of his fellow men. Referring to the retreat from Russia of Napoleon's Grande Armée, he gave the testimony of General Marbot, who wrote in his *Memoirs*: "Infamous Jews pounced on wounded or sick Frenchmen; they stripped them of their clothes and threw them naked out of the windows in a cold of minus 30 °C[371]". The testimony of Captain Coignet, who wrote in his famous *Cahiers,* is also well known about these events: "The Jews and the Russians slit the throats of a thousand Frenchmen; the streets of Vilna were covered with corpses. The Jews were the executioners of our

---

[371] Georges Valensin, *La Vie sexuelle juive*, Éditions philosophiques, 1981, p. 131.

Frenchmen. Fortunately, the Guard stopped them and the intrepid Marshal Ney restored order".

In 2002, Jacques Attali had, curiously, the exact opposite interpretation: "One hundred thousand Poles (among them Jews) die as heroes covering the retreat of the Grand Army[372]". Those who have read our previous books have noticed this propensity of many Jewish intellectuals to go against the truth when it bothers them, and to systematically accuse their victims of what they are probably guilty of. In 1869, Gougenot des Mousseaux noted this characteristic behaviour and detected in "the Jew", "his invincible boldness, his characteristic tenacity to deny all crimes, in the face of all evidence[373]".

Voltaire had also noticed a certain form of cruelty in the Jews. In the unredacted version of his *Philosophical Dictionary*, he wrote: "The seditious spirit of that people induced them to commit new excesses: their character was cruel in all ages, and their fate was always to be punished". He further noted that the Old Testament abounded with examples of massacres: "Almost all the songs… are full of imprecations against all the neighbouring peoples. It is only about killing, exterminating, disembowelling mothers and smashing children's brains against stones". (*Mélanges, Dieu et les hommes, ch.21*). Voltaire continued with his biting irony: "Jephthah immolates his daughter to his bloodthirsty god; Ehud murders his king in the name of the Lord; Yael nails the head of a general; Samson repeats the exploits of Hercules; the Jews want to practise pederasty with an angel and a Levite; a Levite tears his wife into twelve pieces; 400 000 soldiers are killed in a small territory; stories of 600 virgins and fables of cannibals; God takes revenge on the Canaanites by inflicting haemorrhoids on them; Samuel dismembers King Agag; Saul consults a pythoness; the fiddler David, at the head of his filibusters, plunders and slaughters without sparing the lives of nursing infants as the Jewish rite commands… It must be admitted that our brigands were less guilty in the eyes of men; but the

---

[372] Jacques Attali, *Los Judíos, el mundo y el dinero*, Fondo de cultura económica de Argentina, Buenos Aires, 2005, p.342.

[373] Roger Gougenot des Mousseaux, *The Jews, Judaism and the Judaisation of Christian peoples*. Pdf version. Translated into Spanish by Professor Noemí Coronel and the invaluable collaboration of the Catholic Nationalism team. Argentina, 2013, p. 244

ways of the god of the Jews are not ours" (*Voltaire, Examen important de milord Bolingbroke, ch.7 et 8*).

Voltaire went on and wrote: "There were, according to your Book of Numbers, sixteen thousand women for your soldiers, sixteen thousand women for your priests; and from the soldiers' share, thirty-two were taken for the Lord. What was done with them? What is the Lord's part in all your wars, but that of blood? (*Philosophical dictionary*, not expurgated).

In his *Testament of a Murdered Jewish Poet*, Elie Wiesel nevertheless tried to convince us that Jews were incapable of any act of barbarism. In it he recounts the adventures of his hero during the Spanish Civil War. He turned out to be "clumsy and unfit for combat". He would therefore be assigned to the service of "propaganda and culture". After describing the cruelties committed by both sides in the war, Wiesel insisted on exonerating the international volunteers: "The international volunteers, however, behaved honestly. Was it because there were many Jews in their ranks? For Jews seem incapable of committing certain ignominies, even when it comes to revenge. The Sterns, the Grosses, the Frenkels, the Steins-who came from scattered Jewish communities in Hungary, Romania and Poland-demonstrated magnanimity towards the vanquished," Elie Wiesel told us, finally concluding: "Their aversion to cruelty, they would never have attributed to their Jewish origins, but rather to their Marxist ideology[374]." Elie is an amazing guy.

## *The theology of revenge*

Revenge is not considered a noble sentiment in Christian civilisation. Israel Shamir claimed that it is not a noble sentiment in Muslim civilisation either: "In Christian and Muslim literatures, the idea of revenge rarely appears as the main theme of an important book. "Avenger' is a negative term in Christian culture and Muslim culture". Jewish culture, on the other hand, "is saturated with revenge, as it derives directly from the Old Testament. No wonder Israel has introduced revenge into its daily politics. Its attacks against the Palestinians are called *peulot tagmul*, acts of revenge". Shamir, who lived in Israel, had no difficulty in illustrating his words: "The invasion of Lebanon in 1982, with its 20 000 Lebanese and Palestinian, Christian

---

[374] Elie Wiesel, *Le Testament d'un poète juif assassiné*, 1980, Points Seuil, 1995, p. 209-211.

and Muslim, casualties, was an act of revenge for the attempted assassination of the Israeli ambassador in London. During the last Intifada, every Israeli terror action was labelled as 'punishment' or 'retaliation' by the Israelis and the US media[375]." Similarly, during the summer of 2006, the media portrayed the destruction of Lebanon under a deluge of fire as an act of retaliation in response to the kidnapping of two Israeli soldiers by Hezbollah.

Jean-Paul Sartre had already warned of the Jews' desire for revenge and as was well known to all: "During the [German] occupation, the democrats were deeply and sincerely opposed to anti-Semitic persecutions, but from time to time they sighed: 'The Jews will return from exile with such insolence and appetite for revenge that I fear a resurgence of anti-Semitism'[376]".

The essayist Viviane Forester, whom we have already mentioned in our previous books, also transcribed in some of her books the rages of some Jews. During the course of the Second World War, the national Jewish Resistance Committee in Poland sent a message to the whole world: "The blood of three million Jews cries out for revenge, and it will be avenged! Punishment will strike not only the Nazi cannibals, but also all those who did nothing to save a doomed people[377]."

Revenge also oozed from the book *Souvenirs* by the famous gangster Pierre Goldman, published in 1975. After taking part in the events of May 1968 in Paris, he spent some time in Venezuela before returning to France under a false identity. He went down the road of gangsterism and bloody armed robberies, although he admitted that these practices were far removed from his revolutionary ideal. He was arrested in April 1970 in possession of a false Venezuelan passport[378]. His father was a communist who had participated in the International Brigades: "He kills German [fascists]. With hatred, with joy, without hesitation. A carver and a sportsman, he fights and fights well. He deserved his French nationality and was never so Jewish as at that time… In communism, they dreamt of international brotherhood, an international and a

---

[375] Israel Shamir, *L'autre visage d'Israël*, Éditions Al Qalam, 2004, p. 245.

[376] Jean Paul Sartre, *Réflexions sur la question juive*, Gallimard, 1946, Folio, 1954, p. 68-69.

[377] Viviane Forrester, *Le Crime occidentale*, Fayard, 2004

[378] On Pierre Goldman: Cf *Psychanalyse du Judaïsme*, p. 134-136.

socialism where the Jewish people, their Jewish identity would not be abolished. No one was more Jewish than these new Hasmodeans, these new Maccabees, these sons of the people of the book who took up arms to write the sacred history of the Jewish rebellion".

Pierre Goldman's mother was a Jewish communist from Poland who would become a member of the French Communist Party: "In my cradle, there were leaflets and weapons hidden there," Golman wrote. In any case, he was frank about his identity affiliation: "To be French or not to be French was never a concern for me: for me, the question did not arise. I think I always knew that I was simply a Polish Jew, born in France... I was born an atheist and I was born a Jew[379] ", Goldman asserted.

He joined the Communist Youth Union in a spirit shaped by ideas of revenge: "I learned Marxism from Politzer (whom I knew to be a philosopher and a fighter, a thinker and one of the first communists to have taken up arms. I knew that this professor had been shot. I knew he was a Jew). I dreamt of the civil war, of the anti-fascist war, of a real return of time, of history... I was fed up, I was imbued, I was tormented by films and stories about that war, by images of the Holocaust".

The events in Algeria were the occasion to fuel his hatred: "I have a fierce, Jewish hatred for the pogromist policemen of the 1961 raids. I don't understand how the victims murdered in Charonne are not avenged". In Compiégne, he met the son of a former FTP: "Our plans: to steal weapons and kill some personalities known for their sympathies towards the OAS*. The Algerian war is over before we can act".

In Paris, he enrolled at the Sorbonne, but devoted most of his time to militant action: "I devote myself to mastering the subtleties of Marxist debate. I talk. But very quickly, I turn to organising the struggle against extreme right-wing groups (because hatred drives me to it)... This is what we will call the security service of the UEC (Communist Students' Union). We attacked those who were distributing fascist and monarchist leaflets[380]".

---

[379] Pierre Goldman, *Souvenirs obscurs d'un juif polonais né en France*, Points Seuil, 1975, p. 29-33.

\* Organisation of the Secret Army (OAS) (*Organisation de l'Armée Secrète*) was a French extreme right-wing terrorist organisation created in Madrid in 1961 after the attempted coup d'état against De Gaulle.

[380] Pierre Goldman, *Souvenirs obscurs d'un juif polonais né en France*, Points

Underlying his political combat were also certain criminal impulses. In Evreux, in the early 1960s, "he was associated with Jewish gangsters, pimps and a few biker gangsters". Goldman then enlisted on a Norwegian freighter and set sail for Mexico. Without proper papers, he was turned back at the border and ended up in an American prison: "In my cell, the man in charge was a Jew with a huge, ape-like body, though short and stocky, who took me in as a brotherly friend... This Jew, originally from Eastern Europe, like me, was in prison for armed robbery... He risked a sentence of twenty years, as he was a repeat offender, but he was indifferent to the imprisonment [381]." Pierre Goldman took very badly being confined with the whites; he would have preferred to be with the blacks. Indeed, his best friends in Paris were Guadeloupeans, and with them he would prepare his robberies a few years later. When he deserted France to avoid military service, he wandered between Prague, Berlin and Brussels, "in the bars frequented by the underworld and the West Indian lumpen".

In 1967, at the time of the Six Day War, he wrote, "I met two Jewish comrades, Marxist-Leninist and supposedly anti-Zionist, who hypocritically rejoiced at the might and warlike skill of Dayan's troops. I smiled to myself at this terrible and hidden complicity that we secretly shared as Jews. I thought of the holy ghetto fighters, of their absolute bravery. I thought of the Jews of the International Brigades, the Jews of the Manouchian-Boczov group, the Jews of the Red Orchestra and the Jews of the special services of the Stalinist Komintern... And I remembered my father's unabashed joy when he was vibrating at the triumph of the Jewish arms[382]."

The general atmosphere seemed propitious for big actions: "I decided to travel to Cuba as soon as possible. I had forged contacts with Guadeloupean comrades and, in the Parisian heat, we were preparing

---

Seuil, 1975, p. 39-43.

[381] Pierre Goldman, *Souvenirs obscurs d'un juif polonais né en France*, Points Seuil, 1975, p. 53.

[382] Pierre Goldman, *Souvenirs obscurs d'un* juif *polonais né en France*, Points Seuil, 1975, p. 62. We have already mentioned in this respect the cases of Herbert Marcuse, Marek Halter, Guy Konopnicki and Alexandre Adler in *Les Espérances planétariennes*, pp. 172, 173. Daniel Cohn-Bendit had this to say: "I remember I was passing an exam at the time. I went out every hour to listen to the news. I didn't say anything to anyone, but I was overwhelmed". (André Harris, Alain de Sédouy, *Juifs et Français*, Grasset, 1979, Poche, p.191).

violent insurrectionary fires and bloody liberation operations. He was, at the time, 24 years old, and was in contact with Guadeloupean and Congolese revolutionaries. "I stole a passport which I forged and waited... I thought, when I left France, that in Venezuela I would live experiences and great trials that would change me. Change or die, that was my obsession. To become what I never used to be. To tear myself away from this perpetual repetition in which I saw myself with disgust and revulsion. I also thought it was important that I should perish before the age of thirty and that I should die purified of the shameful dregs I was carrying[383]."

Living in hiding, he stayed away from the events of May '68 in Paris and left for Venezuela. There he spent some time with the guerrillas before returning to Paris: "I wanted to tear apart, to break the peaceful course of political relations in this country, to introduce violence into it, to provoke it. He was deeply fascinated by the idea of an armed struggle in France".

In 1969, he began his armed robberies with two West Indian accomplices, which ended with the murder of two pharmacists. One day he even confessed to the "hidden leaders of a large and proactive leftist organisation" (Maoist): "I experienced in crime, unique, pure moments of total, silent and mute fraternity, which had united me with unknown and armed blacks[384]."

The final judgement after his acquittal on appeal in 1976 caused great indignation. He was finally killed in 1979 by a mysterious "Honneur de la Police" group. A recent investigation into the "assassination of Pierre Goldman" claimed that this group was probably a front behind which the Spanish GAL (Grupo Antiterrorista de Liberación) was hiding. After his release, Goldman had been trafficking arms for ETA (Basque independence fighters) and drugs with Bauer (Mesrine's partner) between Spain and Sweden. Despite this chaotic CV, the Jewish community had managed to pass Goldman off as a martyr.

This is what Bernard-Henri Levy wrote in 1986: "Pierre Goldman was a Jew, one of our great Jewish writers, one who did much for the glory and exemplarity of our Judaism, and perhaps he died because he was

---

[383] Pierre Goldman, *Souvenirs obscurs d'un juif polonais né en France*, Points Seuil, 1975, p. 73.

[384] Pierre Goldman, *Souvenirs obscurs d'un juif polonais né en France*, Points Seuil, 1975, p. 80, 100.

too faithful to some of our texts and commandments, sometimes to the point of hallucination, even falling into the most extreme slips. In my opinion, he was, in his own way, a Righteous One whose loss mourns, our community[385]."

This proudly claimed Jewish solidarity was also detected by the Goyim, but at the time it was considered "anti-Semitic". In the newspaper *Je Suis Partout* of 17 February 1939, Robert Brasillach wrote, for example: "They willingly support each other, they refuse to stop being in solidarity with the scum of their people, and while a Frenchman disowns a Landru*, the finest and most intelligent Jew is always uncomfortable when something bad is said about Bela Kun in front of him", the famous Bolshevik leader who stood out in Hungary for his cruelty. It is true that Bernard-Henri Levy and Pierre Goldman come from a similar family background, for Levy wrote: "My father was a first-class anti-fascist, a volunteer at the age of 18 in Republican Spain, then in the French army to take part in the fight against the Nazis[386]."

Indeed, his vengeful spirit seemed to be directed much more against Europeans than against "capitalism" and liberal society, given the anti-racist relations and commitments of the gangster and the philosopher. But in the case of Pierre Goldman, it seems quite clear that his radical militancy reflected an identity crisis that often bordered, in Jews, on self-hatred and madness.

The founder of socialism in Germany, Ferdinand Lassalle, from an orthodox Jewish family, was himself tortured by his Jewish identity and the idea of revenge against the white man and European civilisation. This is what Leon Poliakov wrote about him: "As a teenager, he dreamed of the time of the Damascus scandal and of becoming the avenging messiah of the Jews[387]… He announced his hope of seeing the hour of vengeance come soon, and proclaimed his thirst for the blood of Christians." Lassalle changed his ambitions, however, and transcended his neurosis into communist messianism: "When his busy life made him the messiah of the German working class, his fury

---

[385] Bernard-Henri Levy, *Questions de principe*, deux, Grasset, 1986, Poche

* Landru, French serial killer of the early 20th century.

[386] Bernard-Henri Levy, *Récidives*, Grasset, 2004, p. 388.

[387] The Damascus case: in 1840, members of the city's Jewish community were accused of ritual crime.

seemed to be directed only against his brothers[388]." Indeed, like Marx, he began to vituperate against his fellows.

The idea of an avenging Messiah has recently been explored by Israeli academic Yacob Yuval of Hebraica University in his book *Two Nations in Your Midst*[389]. "Yuval cites numerous ancient Jewish texts to support his thesis," wrote Israel Shamir. "At the end of time (when the Messiah comes), God will destroy and exterminate all nations except the Israelites," according to Sefer Nitzahon Yashan, written by a 13th century German Jew." Shamir also cited for example Klonimus Ben Judah, who had a vision of the "hands of God filled with the corpses of goyim." One hundred years before the Crusades and the massacres perpetrated against the Jews, Rabbi Simon Ben Yitzhak was already imploring God to "wield the gladius and slit the goyim's throats[390]."

Rabbi Shmuel Boteach studied Jewish eschatology in an essay entitled *The Time of Hate*: "Judaism, he wrote, compels us to despise and fight the wicked at all costs… The only way to react to unrepentant evil is to wage all-out war on it until it is eradicated from the universe… For the sake of justice, the proper response to the evil one is to hate him with every fibre of our being and to wish him never to find rest, neither here, in this world, nor in the next[391]."

In his 1957 book, *Apology for Israel,* the thinker Albert Caraco expressed very explicitly in his aphorisms the great Talmudic thought: "I tell you, Romans: to be as cruel as our adversary, we have too much, too much to avenge" (p. 78). The honour of the Jews will be called vengeance and their redemption the sword, but a sword of justice" (p.176) "However much they curse us and however much they slit our throats, their children will be ours, on them we will take vengeance on the fathers" (p.247).

Caraco continued: "They pretend to resist the Jews, and well they do: they would give up for lack of resistance, for the hatred they feel for them gives them life and forces them to defend themselves, revived and diligent, prisoners of an insatiable fury, made into fire-breathers… They

---

[388] Léon Poliakov, *Histoire de l'antisémitisme, Tome II*, Point Seuil, 1981, p. 226.

[389] Two Nations in your womb, Tel Aviv, 2000, Alma/Am Oved.

[390] Israel Shamir, *L'autre visage d'Israël*, Éditions Al Qalam, 2004, p. 242, 243.

[391] Israel Shamir, *L'autre visage d'Israël*, Éditions Al Qalam, 2004, p. 270.

do not take revenge so badly on all those who offend them: they no longer treat them as men, but as objects, as mere accidents, denying them even the evidence, even burying them and defaming them dead or simply forgetting them forever, thus killing them a second time[392]."

## *The passion to destroy*

The novelist Romain Gary won the Goncourt Prize for the first time with his novel *The Roots of Heaven*, and a second time with *Life Ahead*. A Jew of Lithuanian origin, his real name was Roman Kacew. His father, Ariel-Leib Kacew, was a furrier in Wilna (Vilnius), Lithuania. He was thirteen when he left Warsaw to settle in Nice in the 1930s. He joined the Resistance in August 1940 and joined the Lorrraine Group of the Free French Air Force. In 1943, he wrote his first novel in English, encouraged by his roommate, Joseph Kessel, a volunteer fighter like himself. The book was immediately translated into French under the title *European Education*, an account of the Polish resistance, and his "overwhelming talent" was acclaimed by Raymond Aron, as transcribed in the review *Les Cahiers de L'Herne* devoted to the character (2005). Kessel, Aron, Gary: all in the same family. His early commitment to the Resistance would earn him a full and full-fledged diplomatic career. In the *Nouvel Observateur* of 26 February 2004, which devoted a few pages to him, we read: "He had to deal with more than one gerontoid of the old France who stared awkwardly at this meteco recycled into a diplomat". His first posting was to Sofia, Bulgaria.

Romain Gary was first and foremost a Jewish intellectual, to judge by his literary output. *Tulip*, his second novel, published in 1946, was dedicated to Leon Blum. According to *Les Cahiers de L'Herne*, Gary denounced "the atrocities of Nazism, nationalism, indifference, the rewriting of history, the role of the media, the teaching of hatred". The novelist expressed himself through his hero: Tulip "criticises the concept of the sovereign state, a loathsome sacred cow." (*Tulip*, p.53). In another of his novels, *L'Homme à la colombe (The Man with the Pigeon, 1958)*, the hero Johnny advocates a "world government" (p.44). In *The Roots of Heaven* (1956) and *The Star Eaters* (1966), he denounced the oppressive white man in the colonies[393]. Romain Gary

---

[392] Albert Caraco, *Apologie d'Israël*, 1957, L'Age d'homme, 2004, p. 150.

[393] Les Cahiers de l'Herne, Romain Gary, p. 143, 137

thus established himself as a true Jewish intellectual, manifesting the same obsessions as almost all of his peers, as we have shown in *Planetary Hopes (*2005) and *Psychoanalysis of Judaism (*2006).

In 1967, Gary joined the cabinet of General de Gaulle's Minister of Information. "A Gaullist, he nevertheless felt he was a man of the left. In 1968, he no longer identified with the majority in power, which is why he declared himself in favour of François Mitterrand in 1974. Moulded by cosmopolitanism, he took pleasure in turning the traditional values of European society on their head: "Resistance to social hierarchies and official culture… the change of values, the disregard of the noblest ideals, the constant permutation of high and low" formed the background to his works: "*Para Sganarelle* (essay, 1965) was, in this sense, a true manifesto, according to *Les Cahiers de L'Herne*… On its own, a book like *Lady L.* (novel, 1963) exemplified this carnivalesque turn, which placed a former prostitute at the pinnacle of the English aristocracy." (p.295). We recognise here perfectly the mark of the Jewish intellectual, obsessed with the subversion of traditional values. He was evidently an "Americanophile" and passionately "anti-racist". In the United States, he joined 23 anti-segregation movements and took the side of the Black Panthers.

This subversion of values was almost always observed, in one way or another, in Jewish intellectuals. Radical changes of situation are also often caricatured. In Steven Spielberg's film, *Twilight Zone: The Movie* (USA, 1983), for example, the racist Bill will find himself in the shoes of someone persecuted by racism. In the same style, Arthur Miller's novel *Focus*, published in 1945, cast an average American as a Jew, putting him through the daily anxieties of anti-Semitism[394]. Such role reversals were also staged in Joseph Losey's film *The Servant* (GB, 1963): a servant managed to dominate the aristocrat he worked for, who ended up falling into alcoholism.

In his *Apology for Israel*, published in 1957, Albert Caraco expressed this desire for the destruction of traditional society very well. His nineteen books were edited by Vladimir Dimitrijevic, a Serbian publisher. After the writer's suicide in 1971, Dimitrijevic published some of his posthumous works. In 1984, he declared: "His father and I were his only real readers… We are no longer used to hearing such a thunderous voice, such a beautiful and imperative language". In our

---

[394] Cf. *Psychanalyse du Judaïsme*, p. 223, 224.

opinion, and after having grappled with and exhaustively examined hundreds of books by Jewish intellectuals, we consider Caraco to have been the most arduous and fastidious reading of all. We have therefore endeavoured with this author, as with some others, by the way, to shape his thought by arranging his aphorisms in such a way as to make them easier to read.

Here then is the destiny of mankind, according to Albert Caraco: "Rome and Mecca are impure forever, pagan forever... The Church and Islam are bastards, and nothing will erase their bastardy as long as one member of the chosen race survives, carnally... God has only one home on earth: Jerusalem" (p.73, 244). "The Jews will bury Rome and Mecca and give their history a humiliating sense of the spirit that reigns in the pages of the Bible" (p.318). And he insisted: "We are at the time when Rome and Islam will come to an end, I do not give them a century of life." (p.246)

Caracus confirmed that the method of the Jews to achieve their goals was to uproot all traditional societies, to level all differences, all traditions in order to arrive at a world of "peace" in which only the people of Israel will subsist, which will have carefully preserved its memory: "The faith of the peoples, they will make it waver, without theirs varying, and when the world has neither faith nor laws, they will be among us to found one and enact others."(p.176). "He who will not want from us will not want from God. Our election never ceased, it is only through us that the Eternal God will test those who claim to serve Him". (p.322).

Islam evidently represented a rival of stature: "Where Islam prostrates itself, we pray standing; where Islam trembles, we are no longer afraid" (p.322). (p.322). As for the Catholic Church, from now on, its fate is already sealed: "The vengeance of Israel [will force] the Church to fear it, to arm itself, to fight at last to be guilty and to die an infidel... When the Jews overrun the Church, will the Church dare to pray for the Jews? Certainly not, but thus the Church will be doubly defeated." (p.186)

We also find in the thought of Albert Caraco, the "diabolical tendency" expressed by the Austrian writer Joseph Roth[395]: "The Church, wrote Caraco, wanted them to be the demons who serve it, but they are so with a view to bringing it down and gaining over the general ruin the virtues and power which are denied them" (p.165). (p.165). "He who does not

---

[395] On diabolical tendencies, cf. *Psychanalyse du Judaïsme*, p. 249-252.

close his ears to them is truly lost. In fact, they have no foundation except in ruin, they live on the death they sow… They are evil, and those who resist them are not good… The end of time has begun, the signs are already multiplying." (p.225)

Finally, Caracus evoked the typical images of the Jews to describe the messianic times, making them the spokesmen of wars and catastrophes: "Excess and chaos finish off what must die, the very rebirth requires violence, and the convulsions of the birth [of the Messiah] prelude his reign, war will force the century to change its shape" (p.226). (p.226). This is why "chaos is the sign of his reign" (p.172). (p.172). "What they cannot achieve, they reform; what they cannot reform, they destroy." (p.171).

Numerous Jewish intellectuals and filmmakers already showed their hatred of the Catholic Church in a more or less veiled way, through their literary or cinematic output. The American novelist Philip Roth, in *Portnoy's Evil*, did not hesitate to speak through his sickly character of "all the Catholic bullshit" and "those filthy Catholic schools". And further: "You can take it for granted, Alex: you will never in your life hear a *mishegoss*[396] as meaningless and as full of filth as the religion of the Christians[397]."

Albert Caraco incited the Jews to enter the Church in order to destroy it from within, although he did not insist too much on this point: "The Jews, he wrote, would be unwise to ruin the Church instead of dominating it… It is through Jesus that they will possess the universe and dominate it peacefully… They will remain Jews by becoming Christians, they will be free to choose the way instead of being under threat[398]."

These destructive inclinations were once again evident in the words of Elie Wiesel when he described the Germany of the Weimar Republic between the wars: "The defeated Germany gave the impression that

---

[396] Mishegoss: madness, foolishness

[397] Philip Roth, *El mal de Portnoy*, Seix Barral, Barcelona, 2007, on loan to Debolsillo, Mondadori, Barcelona, 2008 p. 95, 137, 38. (Sweetened translation by R. Buenaventura of "hideous Catholic bullshit", "fucking Catholic church" and "mixed-up crap and disgusting non sense as the Christian religion").

[398] Albert Caraco, *Apologie d'Israël*, 1957, L'Age d'homme, 2004, p. 126, 126, 148.

everything was permitted on its soil except taking itself seriously," wrote Wiesel. Idols were broken, statues were dismantled, religious habits were hung up, the sacred was mocked, and to make matters worse, laughter was sacralised for the sake of laughter[399]... The capital, in permanent effervescence, was reminiscent of the sinful cities of the Bible. The Talmudist in me blushed and looked away. Prostitution, pornography, depravation of the senses and the spirit, sexual perversion and so on; the city undressed, made itself up, humiliated itself without qualms, brandishing its degeneration as an ideology. Around the corner from *Chez Blum*, in a private club, men and women, or women with each other, danced naked. Elsewhere, people were taking drugs, whipping each other, crawling in the mud, transgressing all limits; it reminded me of the habits and customs of the Sabateans. Values were reversed, taboos were lifted, did people feel the storm approaching[400]?"

Two pages further on, Elie Wiesel wrote naively: "Berlin seemed dominated by Jews... Newspapers and publishing houses, theatres and banks, department stores and literary salons. The French anti-Semites who saw the Jew everywhere were right... at least in the German case. The sciences, medicine, the arts: the Jew was setting the tone, imposing it".

Even in antiquity, the Jews were the target of the same accusations. The Jewish historian Flavius Josephus collected the anti-Jewish writings of the time in his work *Against Apion*. Flavius Josephus quoted for example Lysimachus of Alexandria, a Greek scholar of the first century B.C.: "Moses... exhorted the Jews to be kind to no one, to follow the worst advice and to tear down all the shrines and altars of gods that they would find. The great historian of Judaism, Leon Poliakov, added in his *History of Anti-Semitism*: "Even in an author who speaks of the Jews and their institutions with much benevolence, Hecataeus of Abdera, we find this comment:" [Moses] instituted a way of life contrary to humanity and hospitality". Other Greek authors (Diodorus Siculus, Philostratus), as well as some Latin authors (Pompeius Trogo, Juvenal) take up the same accusations, which we see summarised in lapidary fashion in this famous passage from Tacitus: "The Jews... have among themselves a stubborn attachment, an active commiseration, which

---

[399] Elie Wiesel, *Le Testament d'un poète juif assasiné*, 1980, Points Seuil, 1995, p. 100.

[400] Elie Wiesel, *Le Testament d'un poète juif assasiné*, 1980, Points Seuil, 1995, p. 124.

contrasts with the implacable hatred they profess for the rest of mankind. They never eat or sleep with strangers. This race, although very given to depravity, abstains from any trade with foreign women… "And more laconically: "Everything that we worship, they hate; on the other hand, everything that is impure for us is permitted to them".

In the 4th century AD, Christian preachers launched violent diatribes against them. We have already seen what Gregory of Nyssa thought of them. John Chrysostom was of the same opinion: "Lupanar and theatre, the synagogue is also a den of thieves and a den of wild beasts[401]." But fifteen hundred years earlier, in ancient Egypt, the Jews already manifested the same regrettable inclinations. Elie Wiesel recalled how Joseph, sold by his Jewish brothers, had secured a position as a trusted advisor to Pharaoh: "At the height of his glory, Pharaoh gave him the nickname Tzofnat Paneach, the code-breaker[402]."

Jewish intellectuals often boast that they have endured through the centuries, while the Egyptian, Babylonian, Persian, Greek and Roman civilisations have long since disappeared. But they undoubtedly forget to tell us what part they played in the demise of these great civilisations.

This destructiveness manifests itself in our time on a daily basis, especially through television propaganda. For example, in 2006, a French television series, *Plus belle la vie (More beautiful life), gave* an idea of this relentless hatred. The newspaper *Présent* of 24 March 2006 presented a summary of the themes dealt with by this series, in which North Africans and blacks were naturally admired, "super nice", while the white, heterosexual male came off very badly. The series obviously exalted miscegenation: a mother of a family cheated on her husband with his boss, a black man, a good man in all respects. Another French woman, Juliet, fell in love with another black man. But he was an illegal immigrant. So she does everything she can to get him regularised. Finally, she found a solution, thanks to a homosexual policeman—a white man—who decided to steal a passport from his police station to give it to the illegal immigrant. The apology of miscegenation and homosexuality is indeed the trademark: it was the unmistakable Jewish

---

[401] Léon Poliakov, *Histoire de l'antisémitisme, Tome I*, Point Seuil, 1981, p. 19, 20, 33.

[402] Elie Wiesel, *Biblical Celebration. Retratos y leyendas del Antiguo Testamento*, Muchnik Editores, 1987, Barcelona, Spain.

stamp. The series also featured: a police officer having an affair with the son of a Marseille bar owner; two gay men fighting to adopt a child; a barmaid discovering she had North African origins; a depraved priest. White women encouraged to have abortions: a 15-year-old girl became pregnant. She would then ask her friend: "Should I keep it or snort it? Suck it up, big girl, especially if it's white": this is what the director and the scriptwriter were suggesting. White people are bastards, that's for sure. Wherever they go, they do evil. The opposite of the Jews, after all. In the series we could see them, for example, testing a new vaccine on poor black people in Africa. This unfortunate experience would decimate the population of the village. There was also that "extreme right-wing" militant who had been condemned for having run over a poor North African with his car, etc.... All these tasteless jokes were broadcast every evening at 8 p.m. on a public channel. We have Olivier Szulzynger to thank for these scripts.

The films and series that distil destructive messages are innumerable. We gave a non-exhaustive account of them in our two previous books. But we can cite here the American series *Cold Case*, which distilled an anti-Catholic message. One of the episodes told the story of a black girl who had been raped and murdered twenty years earlier. The culprit was finally arrested: it was a black priest. In another episode, the body of a child was found. The investigation established that he was an orphan and had been kidnapped by nuns. The nuns were, of course, very unpleasant and practised corporal punishment on the children. One of them bore a child, whom she gave to her former lover, to administer an electroshock treatment from which the child would never recover. A third chapter told the story of a child found dead. The investigation had led to three black men, but the main suspect had managed to escape. Twenty years later, the dossier was reopened and this time, the investigation would point to three characters, each more horrible than the last. First, a priest, obviously a paedophile, for it is well known that priests are all paedophiles, as the director makes very clear—although this is the classic Jewish inversion of the accusation, as we shall see later. The second suspect was the boy's own mother, a typical middle-class American unable to cope with her family responsibilities. Eventually, we discovered that the real culprit was a neighbourhood shopkeeper. It was he, the one who had made the despicable accusations against those black teenagers. This disgusting guy was an ignoble racist, who wanted the police to be more present in the neighbourhood, in order to drive up housing prices. These riff-raff will not back down from anything to make money!

A fourth chapter took place in the 1970s and featured a group of charming hippie revolutionaries. Their boss was a very cool, very nice black guy and his girl was a beautiful blonde. The latter was to be killed by a white bastard, who turned out to be an FBI informer.

In a fifth chapter, the hero's name was Ben: He was a handsome, seductive, seductive, disco king with whom all the girls were in love. Evidently, his success generated the hatred and envy of those little goyim wretches, for they are surely horrible anti-Semites. Ben was Jewish, and it was for this that he would be murdered. Fortunately, justice would be done. A very moving final scene showed the Jewish family in tears, once again victims of hatred. The producer of this series was none other than Jerry Bruckenheimer, a leading US director.

In 1925, in *The Surrealist Revolution*, the writer Louis Aragon had expressed this same destructive rage very explicitly, although it is also true that he was a fervent Stalinist: "We will ruin this civilisation that you love so much, he wrote... Western world, you are condemned to death. We are the defeatists of Europe: Look how this land is parched, ripe for all fires[403]."

Long before him, in the time of Napoleon III, Gougenot des Mousseaux quoted in his book a certain Ernest Desjardins, a university professor. He had surrendered to the evidence: "They introduce everywhere, by the very effect of their presence, the germs of destruction and dissolution, for their tendency is to rise wherever they are on the ruins of the others[404]."

## *Insolence*

Alexandre Minkowski was a rather famous doctor in France in the 1970s. A professor of neonatology, and a "non-conformist Jew", he had let off steam in a book entitled *The Barefoot Mandarin*, published in 1975. His parents "belonged to the Polish-Jewish intelligentsia". They had fled to Germany, where Jews were "in a privileged situation while

---

[403] Elisabeth Levy, *Les Maîtres censeurs*, Lattès, Poche, 2002, p. 238.

[404] Roger Gougenot des Mousseaux, *The Jews, Judaism and the Judaisation of Christian peoples*. Pdf version. Translated into Spanish by Professor Noemí Coronel and the invaluable collaboration of the Catholic Nationalism team. Argentina, 2013, p. 461

in France they were in the spotlight because of the Dreyfus affair (1894–1906)". Eventually, they settled in France.

Like most Jews, Alexandre Minkowski claimed to be a "perfectly integrated" Frenchman: he is a "Frenchman born in Paris and totally integrated". It was probably out of love for France that he joined the Resistance in 1940: "Contrary to my parents, who, as I said, considered it an honour to wear the yellow star... I found it annoying. Although he did not cite any armed action in which he had participated, his motivations seemed sincere. He did not understand why his colleagues at the hospital regarded him as an intruder: "I was just another Frenchman, surnamed Monkowski," he wrote. Evidently, he was outraged by the behaviour of those Frenchmen who refused to go and die again in the trenches for other people's interests. The fact was that very few of his friends were resisters: "My father had risked his life to come to France: "Hail France, Queen of Nations!" However, in Paris I discovered a village of bitter hens, the medical bourgeoisie at the head... Some brave voice made itself heard in an exceptional way in our faculty of cowards".

Resistance fighter Alexander Minkowski knew, however, his limits: "I always aspired to command, to be a boss. But strangely enough, not in the resistance". In 1944, once Germany's defeat was assured, he enlisted in the French army that was to invade the defeated country. The son of a bourgeois, a doctor and a hospital intern, he became a captain in a combat battalion: "In Alsace, I received a commendation that read: 'Good man-puller. He had half of his troops killed under his command"... The strongest thing is that he was so steeped in military values that my wife, after reading the text, had to make me understand the barbarity of this[405]."

The French bourgeoisie with whom he rubbed shoulders did not inspire him with confidence: "The xenophobia of the French bourgeoisie is legendary; it has resurfaced at the first signs of change under the German Occupation. It must be fought relentlessly. He also expressed his repugnance towards traditional France. His parents already had "some misgivings about the Catholic institution" which he "considers pernicious". There was still "a serious dispute with the Catholic Church". Speaking of a Catholic missionary priest in Indochina, he

---

[405] Alexandre Minkowski, *Le Mandarin aux pieds nus*, 1975, Points Seuil, 1977, p. 70-79.

brutally sentenced: "One can never be violent enough against those crusaders[406]."

In 1946, he moved to the United States to complete his medical training as a paediatrician. "I immediately felt at home," said this "totally integrated" Frenchman. He added: "Like my filmmaker friend Jean-Pierre Melville, I love the United States, physically and carnally[407]." We may note that on page 23 of his book, he further claimed to be a "citizen of the world". Although it was also true that he added that he was in favour of "a morality of ambiguity". And indeed, a few pages later he declared: "I am not a Zionist, I do not feel the need to settle in Israel. I am French.

In the United States, Alexander Minkowski was able to observe the behaviour of some of his peers at the top of the social scale: "As I earned very little money, I was hired as a domestic servant by a rich German Jew called Rothschild. The Rothschilds had a privileged position in Chicago, as they owned large clothing stores… He had a black chauffeur whom he beat with a fly swatter." Evidently, such derogatory behaviour may have encouraged anti-Semitism: "I found out later that the antagonism between Jews and blacks was almost definitive[408]."

In another book, entitled *The Impertinent*, the great bourgeois Alexander Minkowski told us how he was a fervent left-wing militant, and how he had committed himself to Pierre Mendes-France. Naturally, he praised the benefits of the multicultural society: "If we remember the cultural, artistic and commercial wealth of the Judeo-Arabic community of 14th century Spain (which the Catholic Monarchs put an end to, to the disgrace of their country and the civilised world), we can only hope for the return of that happy era. Perhaps this is an example for the salvation of Europe, and why not of the world? I propose to found with some volunteers a movement for a Judeo-Arab Europe[409]."

---

[406] Alexandre Minkowski, *Le Mandarin aux pieds nus*, 1975, Points Seuil, 1977, p. 24, 37, 43, 159.

[407] Alexandre Minkowski, *Le Mandarin aux pieds nus*, 1975, Points Seuil, 1977, p. 85, 90. Jen-Pierre Melville (Achod Malakian) is the director of *L'armée des ombres*, a film glorifying the "French" resistance.

[408] Alexandre Minkowski, *L'Impertinent*, Jean-Claude Lattès, 1984, p. 88.

[409] Alexandre Minkowski, *L'Impertinent*, Jean-Claude Lattès, 1984, 189

Surely this must be yet another "impertinence". Which makes us think that Minkowski would also deserve a few blows with a "fly swatter".

Sowing the seeds of discord and provoking "itches" seems to be the pastime of these "anti-conformist" spirits[410]". Daniel Cohn-Bendit, for example, represented in May '68 the insolent young rebel, hero of all French youth. Thirty years later, in November 1998, the editor of the weekly *L'Evénement du jeudi,* George-Marc Benamou, praised him on the front page in these terms: "Dany the ball-breaker". Dany, we were told, had "that provocative freshness" and managed to "drive the reactionary carcas out of their wits".

Alexander Minkowski had the same habit and proceeded in the same way: "Paradoxically, I would say that today it can be an advantage to be Jewish: as far as I am concerned, I can indulge with impunity in actions bordering on provocation... I have been publishing articles for several years against the excesses of the police and the judiciary, against the established order, against the medical bourgeoisie, against scandals. When Milliez does it—Milliez is a Catholic who comes from the Jesuits—he is publicly attacked, persecuted, etc. I am relatively protected insofar as our opponents are afraid of being seen as anti-Semites. Let's take advantage of it while we can, it may not last forever[411]!" In the latter Minkowski is probably right.

Roger Gougenot des Mousseaux had already noticed these characteristics of the Jewish spirit: "When the wind of time turns to unbelief, to persecution of the Church, like those of today, the Jew, forgetting the oppression under which he lived for so long and the generous hand extended to him by the Church, becomes arrogant, insolent, hateful; he fills the world with his complaints; he associates himself with any movement hostile to the Church and becomes by his revolutionary intolerance the most inconsequential of sectarians... it is bad when he is persecuted, arrogant and insolent; he hardly feels protected!"[412]

---

[410] Read *Psychanalyse du Judaïsme,* p. 69.

[411] Alexandre Minkowski, *Le Mandarin aux pieds nus,* 1975, Points Seuil, 1977, p. 44.

[412] Goschler, of Jewish origin, *Dict. encycl. allemand,* supra-page 453; 1861 in Roger Gougenot des Mousseaux, *The Jews, Judaism and the Judaisation of Christian peoples.* pdf version. Translated into English by Professor Noemí Coronel and the invaluable collaboration of the Catholic Nationalism team.

# THE JEWISH FANATICISM

Scorn and derision of traditional European society and contempt for the goy are frequently expressed by Jewish intellectuals. The famous American novelist Philip Roth wrote of the eating habits of non-Jews: "Let the *goyim* sink their teeth into every filthy creature that crawls and snarls on the face of the filthy earth, we will not so defile our humanity. Let *them* (if you know what I mean) gorge themselves on anything that moves, however odious and abject the animal, or grotesque, *shmutzig* (filthy) or stupid the creature in question may be. Let them eat eels and frogs and pigs and crabs and lobsters; let them eat vulture, let them eat monkey and skunk meat if they like—a diet of abominable creatures that perfectly suits a race so hopelessly vain and empty as to drink, divorce and fight with their fists. All these execrable-eating imbeciles know how to do is to bluster, insult, jeer and, sooner or later, to hit."

The Chinese deserved no more respect than the Europeans: "The only people in the world whom, it seems to me, we Jews are not afraid of are the Chinese. First, because in speaking English they make my father look like Lord Chesterfield himself next to them; second, because their heads are stuffed with fried rice; and, third, because to them we are not Jews, but *whites*—maybe *even* Anglo-Saxons. Go figure!... To them, we are a big-nosed WASP* variant[413] " It is clear that the Chinese fools will never understand the true nature of the Jews, their methods and their aims. But the American novelist found it hard to disguise his feelings: "The *Goyim* pretended to be something special, while we *were* really their moral superiors. And what made us superior was precisely the hatred and contempt they so lavishly showered on us![414]"

This mentality was confirmed by many other testimonies. The writer Israel Shamir is a former Jew who preferred to leave Judaism, contrary, according to him, to the morality of humanity. In *The Other Face of Israel*, he repeated this maxim pronounced by Rabbi Yaakov Perrin on 27 February 1994 and quoted by the *New York Times* on 28 February

---

Argentina, 2013, p. 317, 308

* WASP (White Anglo-Saxon Protestant), "White Anglo-Saxon Protestant", an American of Northern European descent who belongs to the Protestant church. WASPs are considered the ruling class in the United States.

[413] Philip Roth, *Lamento de Portnoy*, Alfaguara, Madrid 1977–1997, p. 78 and *El mal de Portnoy*, Seix Barral, Barcelona, 2007, on loan to Debolsillo, Mondadori, Barcelona, 2008, p. 87.

[414] Philip Roth, *Portnoy's Lament*, Alfaguara, Madrid 1977-1997, p. 54.

1994[415]: "The life of a hundred gentiles is not worth the toenail of one Jew".

Listen also to the response of the Chief Rabbi of the Lubavicth, when questioned about the possibility of extraterrestrial life: "It is possible that other life could exist, but these creatures would be of a lower level of intelligence than us, since they do not possess the Torah, the unique emanation of the wisdom of the Creator which was only revealed to the Jewish people[416]."

These words seem to reflect a widely shared mentality. For example, in *The Last Righteous*, the novelist André Schwarz-Bart told the story of poor Mordecai, who, attacked by Polish peasants, managed to defend himself—an incredible thing for a poor Jew—and defeat his assailants: "Mordecai, stunned and almost drunk with blood, suddenly discovered the Christian world of violence... That same night, on his way home, he knew that from now on, he would be able to outdo his fellow men, how derisory and insignificant, of a body closely linked to the earth, plants and trees, over all animals, harmless or dangerous—including those who bear the name of men[417]."

It is all these words that lead one to believe that the most insulting quotations from the Talmud, which one reads in the "anti-Semitic" books, are perhaps, after all, perfectly true: "Only the Jews are human, the other nations are the seed of cattle". The Talmud, as we know, is the reference book containing rabbinical interpretations, which must be placed above the Torah. As Bernard-Henri Levy put it, Jews must submit to "the commandment to love the Torah more than God, and to love the Talmud more than the Torah[418]."

Mockery and sarcasm are part of the dialectical arsenal of Judaism. Jewish intellectuals mock everything that is not Jewish, and have always ridiculed the traditions of the peoples among whom they live. A further example is Philip Roth, who mentioned in his book the work of the "most brilliant Irving Berlin", an American singer: "The two festivals on which the divinity of Christ is celebrated,... And what does

---

[415] Israel Shamir, *L'autre visage d'Israël*, Éditions Al Qalam, 2004, p. 380.

[416] *Actualité juive* of 4 September 1997, see *Faits et Documents*.

[417] André Schwarz-Bart, *El último justo*, Editorial Seix Barral, Barcelona, 1959, p. 41, 42.

[418] Bernard-Henri Levy, *Récidives*, Grasset, 2004, p.417

Irving Berlin do? He de-Christianises them both! He turns Easter into a fashion show and Christmas into a holiday in the snow. No blood and death of Christ: down with the crucifix and up with the woollen cap! The guy cheapens the Christian religion, but with all the gentleness in the world! So much gentleness, that the gentiles don't even know where the blow has hit them. They like it. Everybody likes it. Above all, the Jews[419]."

## The pacification of the world

The novelist and essayist Manes Sperber, who died in 1984, had broken with communist ideology in 1937, during the Moscow trials. He was an atheist Jew: "an atheist since he was thirteen". But he was nevertheless still imbued with a certain "love" for the Bible. In 1978, this Marxist expressed the same messianic hopes as religious Jews: "I used to believe with great optimism in a future that would reconcile all beings and all peoples, a future that would reunite all humanity; I still maintain this firm hope". Manes Sperber asserted that every Jew has a duty to work for the completion of Israel's project: "The coming of the Messiah depends on ourselves, on the work of all. No idea has ever dominated me so much, nor exerted so much influence on the path I have chosen: this world cannot remain as it is, it must become something totally different, and it will. This one demand and this one certainty have for as long as I can remember determined my existence as a Jew and a contemporary. Through his conversion to Marxism, he was merely prolonging Jewish eschatology in a secularised form: "When, later, I discovered Hegel and Marx, that great hope for a just world that will definitively overcome prehistory, I knew that I was following in the tradition of my messianic great-grandfather[420]."

Like many Jewish intellectuals, he recognised that he could not explain the destiny of the Jewish people in any other way than their divine election. For him, it was the only way to explain the very special destiny of the Jewish people: "I could never forget the threat that hung over the Jewish people as the chosen people; that is also why I could never rationally explain their unique destiny. Even today, more than ever, I

---

[419] Philip Roth, *Operación Shylock*, Debolsillo, Editorial Mondadori, 2005 Barcelona, p. 181. (*The guy cheapens the Christian religion: he turns it into shlokh, into shit. In the French translation by Gallimard, 1995.*)

[420] Manès Sperber, *Être Juif*, Éd.Odile Jacob, 1994, p. 34, 28, 32, 121

would be unable to say why we, precisely, have endured more than everything else, why we have survived so much". This fate according to him, "remains a historically and philosophically inextricable problem[421]."

The Jews do indeed seem capable of withstanding the onslaught of all their enemies: "The survivors of every catastrophe rediscovered their invincibility," wrote Sperber. Since antiquity, "we see how they never really considered themselves defeated, but on the contrary believed that they were destined for a later triumph that would be definitive. They claim an invincible God, their God, the only true God, who reigns over the universe[422]."

For them, the present is only a long corridor to a radiant future. Their whole existence seems to be dedicated to the advent of Israel's triumph and the eternal peace that will accompany it: "During the darkest time of their bimillennial exile, the Jews believed that the end times were approaching-they lived ahead of it," Sperber wrote. "The victors are not the nations that win the first battles, but those that emerge victorious from the last. Jewish eschatology promises that at the end of time an eternal peace will reign where all creatures will be reconciled[423]."

The messianic impulses of the Jews are sometimes expressed more brutally, as in the case of Albert Caraco. In his *Apology of Israel*, the most repeated terms under his pen are very explicit: "innocence", "vengeance", "glory", "insanity", "hope". Here are a few passages in which he expressed his thoughts.

Caraco stated his certainties in this way: "What are we? Whatever we want to be: slaves yesterday and pontiffs tomorrow". (p.82). "Watchers of the absolute, we are for you destiny and we will be your masters, your masters after God, your masters before God, we the slaves of the Face\*" (p.111). (p.111)

And, as we already know, for the people of Israel to achieve empire over the world, all nations must be destroyed: "Peace awaits us on the summits, in the royal solitude where we dwell with and before God,

---

[421] Manès Sperber, *Être Juif*, Éd.Odile Jacob, 1994, p. 17.

[422] Manès Sperber, *Être Juif*, Éd.Odile Jacob, 1994, p. 60, 133.

[423] Manès Sperber, *Être Juif*, Éd.Odile Jacob, 1994, p. 91.

\* Face, capitalised in the original text. Literally: the Face.

with the nations lying in the dust. Then we will intercede for them, we rightful pontiffs, born priestly race, servant of the Absolute". (p.81). "After twenty centuries during which their presence was silenced, the Jews have entered history, and that is why the times are drawing near," wrote Caracus (p.217). "Before three generations, there will be only one world, there will be no more borders and peace will reign". (p.259). "Without us, no light, through us, all light" (p.77).

The *pax Judaica* that is to be established in the world will be relentless. It is true that men have been unjust to the wretched Jewish people, so it is only natural that they should sate their lust for revenge: "They punished us, generous; they despised us, just; they will worship us, merciless". (p.77). Indeed, the Jewish people is "a people of leadership"(p.177). "Hungry for power and not for fame, this people despises forms and rages for the absolute, rages to convince the humble and seduce the rebellious, to reign over some and fulminate the others"(p.171). To go to righteousness by the ways of power, and to power by the ways of evil… by reason of the iniquity of men that made them hateful and miserable, such is the fate of the Jews, born for vengeance and born for salvation" (p.191). Let them have dominion, they will go to Grace and the Kingdom will be granted to them above the universe, so that all may rest in the shadow of Glory"(p.211). "Power is their flight and absolute dominion the only means of life left to them"(p.169). As always, it will be the common people who will rebel against this dictatorship, while the elites will betray: "The weak will throw up the Jews, so that the powerful will take them in, and the powerful who reject them will not be so for long. (p.132).

Thus, the Jewish people are a people at permanent war against the rest of humanity. "This people is under arms" (p.170). (p.170); it has been at war "for forty centuries". Clara Malraux, the wife of the writer André Malraux, a Jew originally from Berlin, also echoed this idea: "Defeat cannot be accepted with the memory of past victories and the hope of future victories. So it was for almost two millennia for the Jewish people[424]."

The strength of the Jews is to remain in the shadows and to act in secret: "They have the honour of reigning invisible". (p.158). "The shadow is their strength and equivocation their empire, absurdity their vengeance,

---

[424] Clara Malraux, *Rahel, ma grande sœur…*, Editions Ramsay, Paris, 1980, p. 54.

the world their hope, and when the world is Jewish, they will no longer walk alone, pitiful." (p.63). And Caraco went ahead, perhaps boldly, and warned: "Those who unravel their projects will no longer know how to realise them and will pass for madmen" (p.163). (p.163).

When the new masters will dominate the world, they will be able to reveal their true faces: "When they are equal to the evidence, they will lift their mask and truly no longer have to blush at themselves, nor the universe to have them as masters" (p.163). (p.163)

The mental universe of the Jews is totally permeated by these mad messianic hopes that feed their inordinate pride. The main work of the Jewish kabbalists, the Zohar, also contains passages that reflect very well the immense pride of the chosen people: "It is because God has affection for Israel and draws it to himself, that all the idolatrous nations hate Israel; for they are kept at a distance, while Israel is close to him[425]."

According to Stephen Sharot, this feeling of superiority was even more manifest in the Sephardic Jews, who claimed descent from the aristocracy of ancient Jerusalem and occupied the upper echelons of society in medieval Spain, whereas most Ashkenazi Jews were at that time small merchants and artisans in central Europe: "The feeling of superiority that animated the Sephardim came not only from their Jewishness and their Jewishness, as was the case with the Ashkenazim, but even more from their status and power within society[426]."

In his work *Sources*, the philosopher Vladimir Jankelevitch, explained bluntly that the Diaspora Jew was "twice as human as another man because of that power he has to be absent from himself and to be other than himself[427]."

Of course, Albert Caraco also expressed this extravagant pride: "Truly I tell you... it is God whom they strike through the Jews"(p.246). "It is God whom the Romans persecute through the Jews, God whom they hate and whom they wound"(p.84). "And truly I tell you: heaven has no more voice since this nation has kept its mouth shut"(p.188). "This people is the pivot of history"(p.234). In these conditions, "the choice

---

[425] Quoted by David Bakan, in *Freud et la tradition mystique juive*, 1963, Payot, 2001, p. 176.

[426] Shmuel Trigo, (under the direction of), *La société juive à travers l'histoire, tome I*, Fayard, 1992, p. 277.

[427] *Le Crappuillot*, February 1985

of the Jews is a self-evident fact… and whoever refuses to believe it will in the future have madness for a companion and darkness for an asylum… The world forged the masters, and when the trial is over, the glory will be better founded and the order more divine." (p.247)

In another work, *Races and Classes*, Albert Caraco wrote: "The Spirit of the world is gathered in his head, the world will have the choice between nothingness or the Jews" (p.374). (p.374). "Man needs God, but what is God, if He does not have the Jew for a priest" (p.375).

Finally, Caracus reiterated his faith in the divine election of the Jewish people and the need to destroy Christianity and Islam in order to achieve that world of "peace" described by the prophets: "The hour of the Jews begins: chosen or not, they are the point where the lever of subversion rests, before raising the world". (p.384). "That is properly the mission of the Jews". The lessons of the Jewish people "will hold for all peoples and for all centuries, it is now and before our eyes that the Election is confirmed[428]."

But the Messiah of the Jews has already appeared several times in history. Evidently, each time it turned out that this was a false messiah, that the times were not ripe, and that more patience was needed. The one who unleashed the most enthusiasm was undoubtedly Shabtai Tzvi, who lived in the Ottoman Empire in the 17th century and set all the Jewish communities of Europe abuzz[429]. In a novel entitled, *Satan in Goray*, Isaac Bashevis Singer, winner of the Nobel Prize for literature in 1978, described the debauchery of the Jewish people at that time. It was clear to all that the times had come, and that at last it was to be fulfilled that "the humblest and smallest of the nations of the earth was to overcome the other peoples and dominate them", Singer wrote: "The children of Israel were soon to be exalted above all other peoples[430]."

This is how the Jews then saw their imminent triumph: "The world was astonished. The people of Judea now enjoyed a high reputation. Princes and kings came to honour them and bowed down before them. Lands and heavens would rejoice on the day Sabbatai Zevi arrived in Istanbul.

---

[428] Albert Caraco, *Les Races et les classes*, L'Âge d'homme, 1967, p. 386.

[429] Cf. Hervé Ryssen, *Psychanalyse du Judaïsme*, Baskerville 2006, p. 158 et seq.

[430] Isaac Bashevis Singer, *Satan in Goray*, PDF, Digital publisher Epublibre, German25, 2017, p. 18, 26

Surely the Jews would celebrate the Feast of Weeks in the land of Israel. The Holy Temple would be restored, the tablets of the Law would return to the Holy Ark and a High Priest would enter the Holy of Holies. Sabbatai Zevi, the redeemer, would reign throughout the world... Every God-fearing man would have ten thousand heathen slaves to wash his feet and attend to him. Duchesses and princesses would be governesses and nursemaids to the Jewish children, as announced in the Book of Isaiah... The sick would be healed and the ugly would become beautiful people. All would eat on golden plates and drink nothing but wine. The daughters of Israel would bathe in streams of balsam and the fragrance of their bodies would flood the world. The sons of Israel would wear armour, with swords at their sides, bows and arrows at their shoulders, to harass the rest of Israel's enemies. The people of the nobility who were kind to the children of Israel would be spared, as well as their wives and offspring; all would become servants of the chosen ones[431].

The "English" writer Israel Zangwill summarised Shabtai Tzvi's adventure in his novel *The Ghetto Dreamers*, published in 1898. He described these mad messianic hopes in equivalent terms: "Fear no more, for you will exercise your empire not only over the nations, but also over the creatures that live at the bottom of the seas[432]."

Clearly, such speeches are likely to offend the susceptibility of the goyim, who are surely unwilling to accept the absolute domination of the chosen people. It is therefore necessary always to keep the background of these speeches secret when they are addressed to them, and to use ellipsis, emphasising rather the seductive concept of "universal peace".

Inspired by the mission of the Jewish people, the physicist Albert Einstein also worked to "pacify" us. In New York in 1931, he declared in an interview: "We should rewrite all school textbooks instead of perpetuating old grudges and prejudices. It may not be possible to eradicate all our warlike instincts in one generation. Perhaps not all of them should be done away with either, for men must still fight for something, but let it be worthwhile things from now on, and not fanciful

---

[431] Isaac Bashevis Singer, *Satan in Goray*, PDF Digital Editor German25, 2017, p. 75, 93

[432] Israel Zangwill, *Rêveurs de ghetto*, 1898, Éditions Complexe, 1994, p. 165.

geographical layouts, racial prejudices, or a greed that they dress up in the colours of patriotism[433]."

The rewriting of school textbooks was also one of the concerns of billionaire George Soros after the collapse of the Soviet empire: "We actively contribute to the training of teachers and the publication of new school textbooks to replace Marxist-Leninist works. We are printing millions of books every year in Russia[434]."

The sociologist Edgar Morin also sought to pacify us: "It is not enough to pacify states, we must pacify individuals, spirits and consciences. The problem of aggressiveness and racism lies first and foremost in the relationship between oneself and the other, and within oneself[435]." Edgar Morin's idea was that mass immigration and the apology of multicultural society were the best means to dissolve national identities, a precondition for the pacification of the world. From this perspective, it was essential to educate the European population, no doubt still too reticent about the great projects of Judaism. We see here how the word "shalom", meaning "peace", is at the heart of the Jewish worldview.

This is exactly what Elie Wiesel tried to make us understand in an article on Judaism, signed by him in the weekly *Le Point* of 21 July 2005 and dedicated to the great religions. He had entitled his article "The despised religion". Elie Wiesel was going to try to give us a better image of the Jewish people by responding to all these ignoble accusations: "We have never wished to conquer the world, as we have been accused of, he assures us… The Jewish people is not superior or inferior to the others… To be a Jew is to accept this past, sometimes full of threats, but also enlightened by the promise of the coming of the Messiah: History is heading somewhere to make itself better, to spread peace… Judaism is a religion that gives meaning to history: it has given the world messianism, the promise of a better future". He continued: "Judaism is fundamentally against fanaticism and extreme rigour. The beauty of the Talmud lies first in respect for the other. This may explain why there was no forced proselytising of Jews. A Christian does not need to convert to Judaism to deserve my respect. Same for Muslims, same for agnostics. I accept the other as he is.

---

[433] Cf. *Les Espérances planétariennes*, p. 121-126.

[434] George Soros, *Le Défi de l'argent*, Plon 1996, p. 115.

[435] Edgar Morin, *Un nouveau commencement*, Seuil, 1991, p. 39, 96.

In a magazine with a large circulation like *Le Point*, it is indeed important to present things in a more favourable light. The general public should know nothing of Israel's secrets. In fact, Jews have long been accustomed to concealing their true thoughts and twisting their words in order to avoid being subjected to terrible accusations. As when Shmuel Trigano, quoting the great Maimonides, wrote, for example: "The only difference between this world and the days of the Messiah is the subjection of Israel to the Nations[436]". His Jewish readers are not confused and instinctively understand the meaning of the formula.

## 2. Anti-Semitism

Even today, the mental universe of the Jews is still strongly marked by the persecutions that have marked their history and which seem to be an inevitability. The German novelist Joseph Roth wrote between the wars: "The flight from Egypt has lasted for millennia. One must always be prepared to leave in haste, with everything on one's person, bread and an onion in one pocket, phylacteries[437] in the other. Who knows whether one will not have to leave in an hour's time[438]?"

In *The Last Righteous*, André Schwarz-Bart chronicled Jewish suffering, from 12th century England to Nazi Germany, via the expulsions from France, Spain and the medieval pogroms in Poland and Russia. In 1917, the descendant of all these generations, Benjamin, is thinking of fleeing Poland, as his ancestor had fled Russia. He planned to flee to England, but hesitated: "An island, how to flee in case of extreme necessity? On the other hand, he was pleased with the word America", for it "reminded him of the biblical dance around the Golden Calf, to which his former chief carver of Zemiock compared the life of the American Jews... As

---

[436] Shmuel Trigo, (under the direction of), *La société juive à travers l'histoire*, tome I, Fayard, 1992, p. 263-266. Translated from English by Jean-Christophe Attias.

[437] Phylacteries or Tefillin in Hebrew: small leather wrappings containing strips of parchment with passages from the Bible, which Jews wear tied to their left arm and forehead during certain prayers.

[438] Joseph Roth, *Judíos errantes (Wandering Jews)*, Acantilado 164, Barcelona, 2008

for the word France, it had the disadvantage of being associated with the word Dreyfus, which Benjamin had heard pronounced a lot; it was said that the French had sent this Jew to the Devil's Island; the name alone gave one the shivers, so what was to be decided? Finally, after this discouraging tour of the world, Benjamin opted for the word: Germany[439]." And that is how he went to Berlin.

We see that the country in which a Jew chooses to live is the one that offers him the best opportunities and guarantees. He knows that he could be expelled at any moment, as has always been the case until now. Arthur Koestler informed us in one of his works of the agonising universe of the Jews and their tragic history, to legitimise their settlement in Palestine and the creation of the State of Israel: The history of the Jews "is a dreary tale that always begins with a honeymoon, only to end with a bloody divorce. At first, the Jews are flattered, granted charters, privileges and favours. They are welcomed as if they were alchemists, because they know the secret of turning the wheels of the economy". Koestler went on to give an insight into the reputation Jews had in the Middle Ages: "During the "dark centuries", the trade of Western Europe was largely in the hands of Jews, including also the slave trade, and the Carolingian cartularies use the words "Jew" and "merchant" as almost interchangeable terms[440]." Having reached the pinnacle of their power, the Jews are invariably expelled from the country they took over. "There is no example in history of a people who have been so persecuted on earth, who have survived their death as a nation, and who between the autos de fe and the gas chambers, have continued to toast "next year in Jerusalem" for such an astronomical interval of time and with the same unflagging faith in the supernatural[441]."

---

[439] André Schwarz-Bart, *El último justo*, Editorial Seix Barral, Barcelona, 1959.

[440] Encyclopedia Britannica, 1973, article "Jews", in Arthur Koestler, *La treizième Tribu*, Calmann-Levy, 1976, Poche, p. 198 (Translation from PDF Arthur Koestler, *Khazarian Jews, The Tribe number 13*, p. 185, on en.scribd.com)

[441] Arthur Koestler, in Victor Malka, *En Israël, Guide Bleu*, Hachette 1977, p. 13.

## *The scapegoat*

The main thesis promoted by Jewish intellectuals to explain anti-Semitism is that of the "scapegoat". The Jew will always and everywhere be the ideal culprit to be blamed when society is in crisis. Marxist historians have, of course, insisted on the economic aspect of the question. In *Anti-Semitic Hatred*, Serge Moati gave us, for example, the testimony of Simon Epstein, an economist who has been living in Israel since 1974: "Anti-Semitism always comes in waves. At the end of the last century, it was everywhere, and not only in France with the Dreyfus affair. At the beginning of the 20th century, it declined everywhere. It rises again in the 1930s and falls again after the Second World War. The cyclical nature of the phenomenon can therefore be linked to economic crises. The one at the end of the 19th century favoured the anti-Jewish crisis and the crash of 1929 contributed to the wave of the 1930s-40s".

A period of calm therefore seems inevitably to precede a phase of tensions: "The period of "calm" before the genocide bears many similarities to what we are currently experiencing[442]". These analyses that feed permanent anguish give legitimacy to calls for vigilance likely to unite the community.

Emil Weis, the animator of the Jewish film festival in Paris, defended a very caricatured Marxist analysis of anti-Semitism at the end of the 19th century: "This period corresponds to the advent of the industrial era and the decline of the great landowners. Hence the effort of the latter to mobilise and awaken the nationalist reflexes of public opinion in order to prevent the collapse of their own power. Unable to question or revise the archaic social structures, and clinging to their privileges, they placed responsibility for the crisis on scapegoats[443]."

But anti-Semitism is most of the time inexplicable, or rather: unexplained. At least under the pen of Jewish intellectuals. Here is another caricatured example taken from a book by Beatrice Phillippe entitled *The Jews in the Contemporary World*, which gave an idea of the anti-Semitism that plagued French Algeria after the Crémieux decree of 24 October 1870, which granted French nationality only to Algerian Jews: "France, true to its vocation, has "adopted 35 000 new

---

[442] Serge Moati, *La Haine antisémite*, Flammarion, 1991, p. 171, 172.

[443] CinémaAction, *Cinéma et judéité*, Annie Goldmann (dir.), Cerf. 1986, p. 44.

children"". However, that was only the beginning of the crisis: "The first outbreak of anti-Semitism broke out in 1882 in Algiers, then in 1883 in Oran and Sétif... The second outbreak would break out in the 1930s... Indeed, there were serious incidents in Oran in 1934, where 700 miserable Arabs set upon the Israeli population (23 dead, 38 wounded Jews and 3 dead and 35 wounded Muslims)[444]." Perhaps Béatrice Philippe could have added:"... just like that, just like that, without any reason". For she did not present any explanation for the angry attack by the Muslims of Algeria. She could have done less to explain that Adolphe Crémieux had also been the president of the Universal Israelite Alliance, and that, when he became Minister of Justice at the time of the proclamation of the Third Republic, he hastened to grant French nationality to his fellow citizens, at the risk of arousing the hatred of the Muslims towards France.

Serge Moati felt the same way. This is how he presented the anti-Semitism of Arab countries: "Most Arab countries, Israel's neighbours, often stir up anti-Semitic hatred under the pretext of anti-Zionism. For the past forty years, Jews, described as cowardly, hostile, deceitful, vengeful and hypocritical", have been the victims of numerous persecutions in these countries. On 1 June 1941, in Baghdad, a "spontaneous" pogrom left 600 dead, 240 wounded and 586 shops looted and 911 houses destroyed. Just a few months after the end of the Holocaust, in November 1945, the first riots and attacks on Jewish synagogues and shops broke out in Egypt, Syria and Libya. In December 1947, a second wave. Jews were massacred in Aleppo, Aden, Iraq, Persia and Pakistan. From 1945 to 1952, 150 000 Jews from Iraq fled clandestinely to Israel... In 1956, Jews were expelled from Egypt. In 1970, Jewish property was confiscated in Libya. In 1979, on the eve of the Islamic revolution, a thousand Jews were leaving Iran". He could also have added:"... just like that, without any reason". For indeed, he did not provide any explanation for these outbreaks of violence either. Although he noted that these anti-Semitic feelings remained, even after the Jews had left, he simply wrote: "The whole thing is surprising... Here, as in Poland, we are dealing with an 'anti-Semitism without Jews'. Arab anti-Semitism is more ideological and historical than social[445]." His explanation is, however, a little short.

---

[444] Béatrice Phillipe, *Les Juifs dans le monde contemporain*, MA éd., 1986, p. 18.

[445] Serge Moati, *La Haine antisémite*, Flammarion, 1991, p. 172, 174.

Anti-Semitism is a surprising thing. It is even a "great mystery", as Simon Epstein, quoted by Serge Moati, puts it: "Anti-Semitism is a great mystery. Instead of trying to explain it, why not observe it?" Indeed, this is the approach of almost all Jewish thinkers, who only show the manifestations of anti-Semitism without ever giving the causes of anti-Semitism. Therefore, anti-Semitism necessarily appears under their pen as something absurd.

In order to fill in the gaps in Beatrice Philippe's and Serge Moati's books on anti-Semitism in Arab countries, we could quote a single passage from Guy de Maupassant's travel novel, *Under the Sun*, published in 1887: "At Bu Saada, we see them squatting under filthy cubicles, bloated with fat, sordid and stalking the Arab like a spider stalks a fly. They call him, try to lend him a hundred quid and in return make him sign a paper. The man knows the danger, hesitates, resists. But the desire to drink, along with other desires, tempts him; a hundred pennies is so much pleasure for him! And finally he gives in, takes the silver coin and signs the greasy paper. At the end of three months he will owe ten francs, a hundred at the end of a year, two hundred at the end of three years. Then the Jew sells his land, if he has any, or else his camel, his horse, his donkey, in short, everything he owns. The chiefs, the *caids*, the agas or *Bach agas*, also fall into the clutches of these predators who are the plague, the bloody plague of our colony, the great obstacle to the civilisation and well-being of the Arab". This is probably a very fragmentary explanation, but it certainly allows us to launch the debate.

To try to understand the anti-Semitic reactions, we can refer to the luminous analysis of the great Primo Levi, who is well known to all schoolchildren in Western countries. In his famous book *Yes, This is a Man*, published in 1958, he recounted his experience in the concentration camps from which he miraculously escaped unharmed[446]. "Everyone now knows that *Yes, This is a Man* is a masterpiece of world literature and not only one of the most outstanding testimonies of the Holocaust". This is what Jean-Claude Zylberstein wants to tell us in a "note for this new edition".

In 1976, Primo Levi wrote an appendix to the school edition, "to answer questions put to him by high school students and adults alike. To the

---

[446] Professor Robert Faurisson, whose work has been translated and published all over the world, rightly pointed out that when miracles occur in a chain, they are no longer "miracles".

question: "How does one explain the fanatical hatred of the Nazis for the Jews?", he answered in eight pages, written in small type.

We will present here a summary, in the form of a friendly dialogue with the author:

"There is no doubt that this is originally a zoological fact: animals of the same species, but from different groups, show intolerance towards each other. This is also true of domestic animals: it is well known that if a hen from one henhouse is introduced into another, it is rejected for several days by pecks. The same is true of mice and bees and, in general, of all species of social animals. Now, man is certainly a social animal (as Aristotle had already stated): but woe betide us if all the zoological drives that survive in man were tolerated! This is precisely what human laws are there for: to limit animal impulses".

—This is all well said, Mr Levi, but how do you explain the Nazis' fanatical hatred of the Jews?

—Anti-Semitism is a typical phenomenon of intolerance. For intolerance to arise, there must be a perceptible difference between two groups in contact: this difference may be physical (blacks and whites, blondes and brunettes), but our complicated society has made us sensitive to more subtle differences such as language, or dialect, or even accent (our southerners know this well when they are forced to emigrate to the North); religion, with all its external manifestations and its profound influence on the way of living, the way of dressing or gesturing...

—This is all very interesting. But, if I may... how do you explain the fanatical hatred of the Nazis for the Jews?

—In antiquity], the Jews, a minority in all their affinities, were thus distinct, recognisable as distinct, and often proud (rightly or wrongly) of being distinct: all of which made them very vulnerable[447]. In fact, they were severely persecuted, in almost all countries and in almost all centuries... From the first centuries of Christianity, the Jews were accused of something much more serious: of being collectively and for eternity responsible for the crucifixion of Christ, of being, in short, the "deicidal people". This formulation, which appeared in the Easter liturgy in ancient times and which was only suppressed by the Second Vatican Council (1962–1965), is at the origin of several disastrous and

---

[447] I meant to say: "unpleasant".

constantly renewed popular beliefs: that the Jews poison wells and spread the plague; that they regularly desecrate the consecrated host; that at Easter they kidnap Christian children with whose blood they soak the unleavened bread. These beliefs have led to numerous bloody massacres and, among other things, to the expulsion of Jews first from France and England and then (1492–1498) from Spain and Portugal.

—And the fanatical hatred of the Nazis for the Jews, how do you explain it?

—Hitler's] fixed idea is that of a dominating Germany, not in the future but right now; not by a civilising mission but by arms. Everything that is not Germanic seems to him inferior, or worse: detestable, and the first enemies of Germany are the Jews, for many reasons that Hitler enunciated with dogmatic fervour: because they have "different blood"; because they are related to other Jews in England, in Russia, in America; because they are heirs of a culture in which reasoning and discussion precede obedience and in which it is forbidden to bow to idols, when he himself aspires to be worshipped as an idol...

—It is often said that Hitler also reproached the Jews for having too much power in Germany...

-... many German Jews have reached key positions in the economy, in finance, in the arts, in science, in literature: Hitler, a failed painter, a failed architect, turns his resentment and his frustrated envy on the Jews... [For him] the Jews are to blame for everything, for rapacious American capitalism and Soviet Bolshevism, for the defeat of 1918, for the inflation of 1923; liberalism, democracy, socialism and communism are satanic Jewish inventions that threaten the monolithic solidity of the Nazi state... Anti-Semitism... spread easily throughout Germany and much of Europe thanks to the effectiveness of the propaganda of the Fascists and the Nazis who needed a scapegoat on whom to unload all guilt and resentment; and that the phenomenon was brought to its paroxysm by Hitler, the maniacal dictator... It has been said that Hitler poured upon the Jews his hatred of the whole human race; that he recognised in the Jews some of his own faults, and that in hating the Jews he hated himself; that the violence of his aversion stemmed from the fear of having "Jewish blood in his veins"... Before Hitler came to power, German Jews were profoundly German, perfectly integrated into their country, and only Hitler and a few fanatics who followed him from the beginning considered them enemies.

—Numerous Jews have played a notable role in communism and the atrocities that were committed in its name, up to thirty million dead in the USSR, which is no mean feat. As many as thirty million died in the USSR, which is no small thing. Do you not think that the horrors of the Bolshevik revolution may have provoked a reaction in Germany, especially through Hitler's movement?

—Hitler's fixed idea that Judaism was confused with Bolshevism had no objective basis, especially in Germany, where it was well known that the overwhelming majority of Jews belonged to the bourgeoisie".[448]

The interlocutor, unconvinced, shakes his head slightly and asks.

—Tell me frankly, Mr Levi, do you really think these answers can convince our readers?

-... do not seem to me to be adequate explanations... The proposed hypotheses justify the facts only partially, they explain the quality, but not the quantity. I must admit that I prefer the humility with which some of the most serious historians (Bullock, Schramm, Bracher) confess that they do not understand the furious anti-Semitism of Hitler and, behind him, of Germany. Perhaps we cannot understand everything that happened, or should not understand, because to understand is almost to justify... in Nazi hatred there is no rationality: it is a hatred that is not in us, it is outside man, it is a poisonous fruit of the baneful trunk of fascism... We cannot understand it; but we can and must understand where it is born, and be on our guard[449].

—In the end, what you are proposing is not to ask questions about anti-Semitism, for fear that it might be understood, is that right?

—Exactly," replied Primo Levi with a big smile.

At last we were in agreement. At that moment, I stood up to give him a warm handshake.

—Mr Levi, thank you very much".

## The madness of men

---

[448] Primo Levi, *Si esto es un hombre*, Muchnik Editores, 2002, Barcelona, p. 116-119.

[449] Primo Levi, *Si esto es un hombre*, Muchnik Editores, 2002, Barcelona, p. 120.

In *The Testament of a Murdered Jewish Poet*, Elie Wiesel's hero recounted a terrible episode from his childhood in Russia at the turn of the century. One Christmas night, he and his family suffered unbridled hatred, and had to hide in a small room under the farmhouse: "To be a Jew in a Christian world is to know fear, and to become accustomed to it. Fear of heaven as well as fear of men. Fear of death and fear of life— fear of everything that breathes out there, of everything that is plotting on the other side. A dark threat hangs over us—over each of us... The enemy, the enemy. I was trying to imagine it. Egyptians in the time of the Pharaoh. Looters under Hamman. Crusaders under the shadow of icons, faces unhinged with hatred. The enemy does not change. Neither does the Jew".

The madness of men was to break out again: "I was to learn what men are capable of. Their madness was going to burst into our world: black and hateful madness, savage madness, thirsting for blood and murder. It approached slowly, stealthily, stealthily, like a herd of wild beasts surrounding a prey overcome by terror. Suddenly it breaks loose. A cry rises from the bowels, tearing through the silence and the darkness: Death to the Jews! Repeated by countless voices... Hearing them, enduring them and feeling them devastated my brain, my ears ached, my eyes and my whole body. I could not control my trembling; I crouched in my mother's bosom."

Meanwhile, on the outside, it was only massacres, rape and pillage, at least in Elie Wiesel's mind. "He felt towards the people of Krasnograd, therefore... towards the Russian people, therefore, towards the whole of Russia, a visceral, monstrous, merciless hatred[450]." Thus it was that his hero's family left Russia to settle in Romania.

Even during the war, when the Jews were so cruelly persecuted by the Germans, the Russian peasants did nothing to help them: "Why did the good people of Vitebsk allow these murderers to kill their Jewish neighbours? They could have protected them, taken them to safety. They did not. Forty years of communist education. I don't understand, I don't understand[451]." Stalin himself had gone "mad". Elie Wiesel

---

[450] Elie Wiesel, *Le Testament d'un poète juif assasiné*, 1980, Points Seuil, 1995, p. 39-43, 46.

[451] Elie Wiesel, *Le Testament d'un poète juif assasiné*, 1980, Points Seuil, 1995, p. 256.

realised this the day when, "in a burst of hatred, in a fit of insanity[452] ", Stalin began to attack Jewish intellectuals.

Wiesel confirmed this in his *Memoirs*: "Stalin is mad, his hatred has driven him mad. In Israel, where diplomatic relations with the USSR and its satellites no longer exist, the left is bewildered: it does not understand the ferocious and implacable anti-Semitism of Stalin and the Stalinians[453]."

The renowned sociologist Edgar Morin also believed that Stalinist anti-Semitism was the manifestation of madness. The Soviet system "went mad once between 1936 and 1937, when nothing seemed able to stop the mass arrests, until Stalin liquidated the two great successive enforcers, Yagoda and Yezhov; perhaps it would have gone mad a second time in 1953, had not Stalin's death stopped the delirium[454]."

In short, we must understand that communism went mad when it got rid of Jewish leaders who did not follow the party line, as in 1936–1937, or when it tried to exclude them from the administration in a more radical way. But in normal times, when the largely Jewish-led regime exterminated millions of peasants, of "bourgeoisie", as well as the Russian and Ukrainian nobility, it could be considered not so problematic.

In the daily *Le Figaro* of 9 July 1996, Henri Hajdenberg, president of the CRIF (Representative Council of Jewish Institutions in France) and vice-president of the European Jewish Congress, recalled another painful episode in Jewish history, in the Poland "liberated" by the Red Army: "From 3 May 1945, in Krakow, students broke the windows of Jewish houses and proclaimed anti-Semitic slogans. In August of the same year, in Krakow, accusations of ritual crimes reappeared. From 1945 to 1947, two thousand Jews were murdered in Poland. Half of the two hundred thousand who had returned from Russia were forced to go back into exile". In Kielce, on 4 July 1946, a pogrom broke out: "One wonders, Hajdenberg wrote, about the scandalous ease with which a population was prepared to murder Jews… It was not only a matter of

---

[452] Elie Wiesel, *Le Testament d'un poète juif assassiné*, 1980, Points Seuil, 1995, p. 14.

[453] Elie Wiesel, *Mémoires*, Tome I, Le Seuil, 1994, p.291

[454] Edgar Morin, *Un nouveau commencement*, Seuil, 1991, p. 38.

stealing their property, but, as the medical examinations showed, of smashing their faces.

Clearly, the Poles also went mad. And the Church, once again, was complicit in these atrocities committed for unknown reasons: "In a climate of civil war, with the installation of the communist regime and redoubled anti-Semitism, Cardinal Hlond, the Primate of Poland, thought only of denouncing the role of the Jewish communist leaders. The Vatican refused to condemn the pogrom. The emigration movement of the Jewish population accelerated brutally towards the displaced persons camps in West Germany, or towards Palestine".

The criminal madness of the anti-Semites was exposed by historian Norman Cohn, who explained modern anti-Semitism on the basis of the dissemination of the famous *Protocols of the Elders of Zion*. Norman Cohn showed how anti-Semitism "was revived and modernised in the 19th and 20th centuries by a few eccentric and reactionary Christians" before being revived "by racists, especially Hitler and his followers". *The Protocols of the Elders of Zion* "spread around the world and came to possess Hitler's mind and became the ideology of the most fanatical of his followers in Germany and other countries[455]". For Norman Cohn, of course, these were wild ideas, "fantasies so ridiculous", for "there is an underworld in which scoundrels and half-baked fanatics elaborate pathological fantasies in the guise of ideas, which they destine for the ignorant and the superstitious".[456]

The anti-Semitic delirium went so far as to accuse Jews of being the main protagonists of communism and liberalism. In his *Sociology of Anti-Semitism*, François "de Fontette" denounced this ineptitude: "Anti-Semites have often emphasised the close link, even collusion, which they claim occurred between the Jews and communism; so that the completely contradictory character of the accusations can be underlined once again, for while the Nazis had abundantly used this argument from 22 June 1941 onwards, they had not previously failed to denounce the pernicious influence of the Judeo-Masonic plutocracy in the Anglo-

---

[455] Norman Cohn, *The Myth of the World Jewish Conspiracy. The Protocols of the Elders of Zion*, Digital Editor pdf: Titivilius, 2016, p. 8

[456] Norman Cohn, *The Myth of the World Jewish Conspiracy. The Protocols of the Elders of Zion*, Digital Editor pdf: Titivilius, 2016, p. 8

Saxon countries, which for them was nothing more than the emanation of international capitalism and its ambition for world domination[457]."

The anti-Semites are sick, Eli Wiesel assured us through his poet, who did not believe the threat: "We spoke of the Nazis as an unpleasant but not very serious and not at all fatal disease. We said to ourselves: every society is full of scum, ours too; one day, they will be thrown into the dustbin of history. The threats, the ramblings, the obscene ravings of a Goebbels, a Goering or their ridiculous Führer did not even bother us. We thought: they bark and bark, but they'll get tired of it sooner or later[458]."

But as we all know, "anti-Semitic madness" was unleashed during the war. "Six million Jews were murdered in the death camps of a Europe gone mad," wrote Victor Malka. At the end of the conflict, there was nothing left for many Jews but the Zionist solution. The creation of the State of Israel and Jewish emigration seemed the only way out: "The survivors of the Nazi Holocaust, the last witnesses of Europe's criminal madness against the Jews, became the first[459]."

Anti-Semitism is a "strange phenomenon", wrote Shlomo Taub in *L'Impact* of 9 March 2007, a newspaper reporting on Israel and the Jewish world. Shlomo Taub was surprised by Nazi anti-Semitism, given that at the time the Jews were, according to him, perfectly integrated: "Towards the end of the 19th century, the Jews of Germany and Austria had for the first time in their history rejected the designation of a chosen people... They aspired to be like the Goyim, to be fully integrated into the society in which they lived and considered Germany as their home and refuge. At a time when the Jews had faithfully adopted the culture of the country, and when they felt more German than Jewish, anti-Semitic hatred reached its peak, with violent pogroms breaking out. This wave of barbarism occurred in the place and at the time when the Jews least claimed the idea of a chosen people". Jews were, as usual, accused of all evils because they were "an easy target for hatred and persecution" Finally, Shlomo Taub concluded, logically: anti-Semitism, "whose origins are so hard to understand" is a "strange phenomenon".

---

[457] François de Fontette, *Sociologie de l'antisémitisme*, PUF, 1984, p. 57.

[458] Elie Wiesel, *Le Testament d'un poète juif assasiné*, 1980, Points Seuil, 1995, p. 125.

[459] Victor Malka, *En Israel, Guide bleu*, Hachette 1977, p. 13, 27, 28

Manes Sperber analysed the question as follows: "Hatred of the Jews has always seemed to me to be an aggressive delirium of persecution... like a delirious fear of the other, an anguish which the hater tries to hide from himself. In his maniacal hostility, he persuades himself that he enjoys an insuperable superiority over those whom he hates and despises, but whom he fears because they are fiendishly malicious". And he added: "If this hatred sometimes constitutes for us the worst of dangers, it is nevertheless your disease. It is the evil that afflicts you. No doubt it has caused us untold suffering, but we continue to overcome it all the time". And in order to cure us, Manes Sperber advised us to thoroughly reform our society: "One can try to heal a total hatred when it is an individual phenomenon, with therapeutic education. To fight it as a social phenomenon, one must engage in combat against all religious, social and national impostures, which always arise in an age that hesitates to face its real problems[460]."

## *Innocence*

Innocence is a key term frequently found in the intellectual output of Judaism. Here, for example, is what Aharon Appefeld, an Israeli writer born in 1932 in Chernivtsi (Bukovina), who is considered by some to be "one of the greatest writers of our time", wrote. In his novel, *The Naked Inheritance*, published in 1994, he asked: "What is it in me, what makes me the enemy of mankind? Is it the way I am made, or my thinking?" Yet he acknowledged that he could not find an answer: "We always knew that our Jewishness was not a secret, that it was a catastrophe. There were times when, within our hearts, we cursed our fate, the fate of the persecuted innocent... whose only fault was the Jewish mystery within him[461]."

Albert Caraco also stressed the intrinsic innocence of the Jews. "The more innocent they are, the more unfortunate they are" he wrote in his *Apology for Israel*. "The Jews are innocent, hence their dullness; those who condemn them are cunning, cold monsters, worthy of the abysses of the seas[462]."

---

[460] Manès Sperber, *Être juif*, Éd. Odile Jacob, 1994, p. 24, 31, 149

[461] Aharon Appelfeld, *L'héritage nu*, 1994, éditions de L'Olivier, 2006, p. 34, 82

[462] Albert Caraco, *Apologie d'Israël*, 1957, L'Âge d'homme, 2004, p. 119, 227.

In a book entitled *On Anti-Semitism*, published in 2006, Stephane Zagdanski deliberately exaggerated: "According to the anti-Semite, it is very simple: the Jews are always and everywhere the cause of everything. They have martyred Christ, enslaved the Africans, invented capitalism, spread Bolshevism, falsified the disastrous figures of their own extermination, plundered the Palestinians. Now, as in the past, they own the money, the power and the media. According to the latest news, they are walling in an entire people[463] and gagging anyone who dares to question their demonic empire. In short, if they are universally hated, it is because they are unfailingly odious". And Zagdanski immediately added: "This self-justification of hatred is totally hallucinatory. It is precisely because they are not the cause of anything of which they are accused that Jews have been so hated in so many places throughout the ages[464]."

Let us now look at the situation in Hungary through the eyes of Gabriele Eschenazi. According to Eschenazi, the Jews are said to have shown great attachment to their country during the national liberation struggles of the Hungarian people: "Hungarian Jews participated massively in the failed revolution of 1848–1849, in which Hungary tried to free itself from Austrian rule". It is true that the Jews of the Austrian Empire at that time did not have the right of citizenship. In this case, their interests coincided momentarily with those of the Hungarians who wished to emancipate themselves from Austrian tutelage. This is what allowed the author to write that the Jews were "faithful patriots": "Such attachment to the Magyar nation cost them dearly. After the defeat, the Habsburg military government imposed a very high indemnity on the Jews, while restricting their economic and professional activities".

Finally, in 1867, the Austrians granted the Hungarians equal status. The Austrian Empire became two-headed, becoming the Austro-Hungarian Empire, with the Habsburgs as the reigning dynasty. It was also at this time that the right of citizenship was granted to the Jews: it seems that the Jews "considered themselves Hungarians of Mosaic faith", and declared themselves patriots: "In no other country in the East were so many Jews seen to renounce their surnames in order to adopt Hungarian surnames. The Weiss, Kohn, Löwy, Weinberger, Klein, Rosenfeld and Grünfeld became Vészi, Kardos, Kukacs, Biró, Kis, Radó and Erdélyi.

---

[463] An eight-metre high wall was built by Israel in 2004 to protect itself from incursions by Palestinian fighters.

[464] Stéphane Zagdanski, *De l'Antisémitisme*, Climats, 1995, 2006, p. 10.

They did not do it under duress, as happened in Poland, but because they wanted to be proud to be Magyars".

Thus, the Jews were able to evolve as they pleased in Hungarian society. One could say that their integration was a complete success, perhaps even a little too successful in the eyes of the Hungarians: "At the beginning of the 20th century, the city of Budapest represented a kind of New York for Hungarian Jews. It was called "Judapest". There was no modern profession in which Jews were not predominant. The figures from a study in the 1920s were significant. Despite making up 5.9% of the population, there were as many Jews engaged in commerce as there were Hungarians. They accounted for 59.9% of doctors, 50.6% of lawyers and 34.3% of musicians. In 1930, 61.7% of the commercial companies with more than 20 employees, as well as 47.4% of the largest industries, were owned by Jews. The Chorins, the Weiszes and the Goldbergers were the families that controlled the country's most important banking and industrial concerns".

They were indeed perfectly integrated, at least socially and financially. Unfortunately, "what seemed like an irresistible march towards successful integration was suddenly interrupted" by an event that traumatised Hungary. It was a new failure in the history of the Jewish people, definitely unfortunate. First there was the disastrous defeat of 1918 and the Treaty of Trianon which caused Hungary to lose 70% of its territory: "Moving from a multinational empire to a national state" deprived the Jews of their traditional function as agents of "Magyarisation" in the peripheral territories. Their patriotism was soon forgotten[465] ", as the Hungarians' desire to regain these territories led them to ally with Germany. As a result, "the trauma caused by the loss of the territories led to those who had hitherto been the most enthusiastic patriots of the empire being held responsible for the national defeat".

The author could have recounted the role of his fellow Jews in the 1919 episode of the Bolshevik Republic of Bela Kun, which bloodied the country for 133 days until it was overthrown by joint Romanian and French military action. He evidently kept a low profile about that

---

[465] Gabriele Eschenazi, Gabriele Nissim, *Les Juifs et le communisme...*, 1995, Éd. De Paris, 2000, p. 49-53.

adventure, although he acknowledged that, in that communist government, "Jews were in a large majority".[466]

This is how Jews—or "some Jews"—move from the role of bloodthirsty Bolshevik executioners to that of "scapegoat". In this way, the anti-Semitism of the Hungarians becomes incomprehensible. For example, a numerus clausus was instituted for university entrance: "It was a sign that their integration was no longer accepted, and that, after having been 'Hungarians of Mosaic faith', they were once again an ethnic minority[467]."

In April 1938, Hungary adopted the first anti-Jewish law in Eastern Europe, limiting the presence of Jews in all professional sectors to 20%. Two years later, the rate dropped to 6%, and with the vote on the third anti-Jewish law of 1941, Jews were forbidden to marry and have sexual relations with non-Jews. On 19 March 1944, the Germans, informed of Admiral Horthy's plans to switch sides and form an alliance with the Soviet Union, occupied the country. The Hungarians seemed to accommodate the situation: not only was there no resistance to the concentration of the Jews in the ghettos, but the Hungarian security services themselves assisted in their deportation. This shows how deeply Hungarians resented the Jews.

But Gabriele Eschenazi saw events in a different light. For him, the hostility of the Hungarians had no basis in fact. The Jews being innocent by nature, the Hungarians were therefore effectively guilty of having betrayed the Jews, who were more "patriotic" than the Hungarians. This is how he described the situation in 1945: "Most of the survivors found it difficult to feel Magyar after the betrayal of which they had been victims" (p.73); "the betrayal of the Hungarians seems incredible" (p.63); the country had abandoned its "most faithful patriots" (p.48).

The Red Army soldiers who entered Budapest victorious were naturally greeted as heroes by the Jews: "For the Jews, the arrival of the Soviet soldiers had meant their salvation, and the end of the terrible nightmare; they saw these soldiers marching through Budapest as heroes" (p.74). Jews then joined the new regime en masse. The author analysed the new communist dictatorship in Hungary as follows: "To rebuild the state

---

[466] On the Hungarian Revolution: *Les Espérances planétariennes*, p. 263, 274, 275

[467] Gabriele Eschenazi, Gabriele Nissim, *Les juifs et le communisme…*, 1995, Éd. De Paris, 2000, p. 54-56

apparatus, the communist party needed people who were competent and eager to build a new society, but who were not compromised by their past. The Jewish survivors of the Holocaust, who had been betrayed by the Hungarian right wing, fulfilled all the requirements. In this way, at the moment of greatest despair, unexpected prospects opened up for them". So, if we have understood correctly, in the "moment of greatest despair" the Jews establish a fierce dictatorship. But we must understand them: "It was the best way to finally integrate back into the country that had betrayed them" (p.81). (p.81). "With the disappearance of social classes, anti-Semitism would also disappear. We were at the dawn of a new world. The Jews wanted to forget their sufferings and the betrayal of their country." (p.83)

However, it is very important to point out that the communist leaders and executioners who took power were no longer Jews. Indeed, Eschenazi wrote: "The Party demanded, in exchange for the social contract it offered, that they completely repress their origins: they had to break with any form of Jewish identity, their religion, their old solidarities, their friends, the foreigner, and forget those who had left for Israel... That is why their involvement in the system was total... They compensated for the loss of their cultural identity. Their identification with the Party proved so powerful that their loyalty to the regime was often greater than that of other Hungarians... They made a career not because they were Jews, supported by a pro-Semitic communist party, as many Hungarians mistakenly thought, but because their persecuted past was considered a guarantee of loyalty by a regime that enjoyed no legitimacy in the country." Gabriele Eschenazi concluded, "This is how the myth of Jewish power began, slowly but surely, to insinuate itself into the new state[468]."

In short, if we understand correctly, the communist Jews, who had just installed a bloody dictatorship over the Hungarian people, were not really Jews at all. We must believe that the Hungarians were subject to "hallucinations", as Stephane Zagdanski would say. It is a reasoning analogous to that of today, which tells us that "the Jewish vote does not exist", "the Jewish lobby does not exist", "there is no Jewish community". We must retain from all this that when a novelist publishes a "great" book, he is a Jew; when a director releases a "moving" film, he is a Jew; when a violinist is "admirable", he is a Jew; but when a

---

[468] Gabriele Eschenazi, Gabriele Nissim, *Les juifs et le communisme...*, 1995, Éd. De Paris, 2000, p. 87, 88

torturer is guilty of unspeakable atrocities, he is just an ordinary man: probably a goy!

Jews are by nature innocent, and anti-Semitism stems from certain crude prejudices that must be constantly denounced. This is what Manes Sperber tried to explain to us: "The logic of hatred uses two methods: "totalitarisation" and "atomisation". The anti-Semite searches the daily news only for the names of Jewish swindlers. First he will say: 'all swindlers are Jews', and then he will totalise this generalisation by saying: 'all Jews are swindlers'. Finally he will atomise, stripping Jews of their quality as real people and reducing them only to the criminal acts of which they are accused[469]."

Totalitarianisation" is thus the procedure used by anti-Semites to unite Jews and Bolshevism in the same abomination. But in reality, we must understand that the Jews were the first victims of communism. This is what a certain Frederic Stroussi tried to explain to us in *Israel Magazine*, "the first French-language Israeli monthly", in April 2003: "While they were the first victims of Nazism, they were also among the first victims of Bolshevism. Only two years after the October revolution of 1917, the Jewish community suffered a veritable ethnic genocide. On 5 August 1919, a decree put an end to the autonomy of all Jewish organisations in the Soviet Union." Frederic Stroussi ended by explaining that the cheka had organised a "systematic repression of Zionist and Hebraist organisations: confiscated premises, suspension of publications and mass arrests."

Similarly, in Alain Brossat's book, we find the testimony of a communist militant who also relativised the overwhelming responsibility of Jewish doctrinaires, Jewish officials and torturers for the Soviet tragedy. Here is what one Chimen Abramsky declared: "During the first eleven years of the Soviet regime, [Jews] were treated if not as enemies, at least as second-class citizens, which is laughable considering the exceptionally high proportion of Jews in the Soviet state apparatus in the 1920s[470]." Here is another "paradox" raised by another Jewish intellectual.

Norman Cohn made the same analysis. While admitting that under the Soviet regime "it is true that Jews, in the sense of persons of Jewish origin, contributed a disproportionate share of the leadership (though

---

[469] Manès Sperber, *Être juif*, Éd. Odile Jacob, p. 145

[470] Alain Brossat, *Le Yiddishland révolutionnaire*, Balland, 1983, p. 18.

not of the total membership) of the two Marxist parties, the Bolsheviks and the Mensheviks", he then hastened to add, to reduce the scope of this truth, that "as for the Jews who were among the Bolshevik leaders, almost all of them were also shot in the 1930s [471]." Finally, the conclusion of his exposition was as follows: "Under the Soviet regime they [Jews] suffered even more than other Russians: in the 1920s more than a third of the Jewish population lacked civil rights, compared to 5 or 6 per cent of the non-Jewish population."

Gabriele Eschenazi wrote: "The myth of Judeo-communism is clearly an anti-Semitic ideological construct. Yes, there were indeed Stalinian Jews, but there were also Poles, Czechoslovaks and Hungarians… The refutation of the thesis of communism as a "Jewish power" presents no particular difficulty". We must therefore believe that the Jews "became the favourite scapegoat of the communist regimes[472]".

Historians such as Michael Checinski, quoted by Gabriele Eschenazi, did not hesitate to defend the thesis that Polish Jews were used "with total cynicism": "They were assigned the most thankless tasks so that popular resentment would be directed against them. Once the dirty work was done, these Jewish 'executioners' could be dismissed and condemned by the very regime that had used them" (p.227). (p.227). Again, we see how the suffering of the Jews must have been unbearable, and we must imagine their grief at the atrociously mutilated bodies of the Russian and Polish resistance fighters they had just tortured.

Arkadi Vaksberg also confirmed this, despite all the information he had provided: "The "excessive" share of Jews in the revolution, and the consequences that flowed from it, is an idea that owes much to the imaginary, to the myth[473]."

This selective amnesia is indispensable for the innocence of the Jewish people. Manes Sperber, who noted the same reflexes in the Jews of all ages after a period of persecution, wrote, not without a certain lucidity: "The people whose intelligence has been praised for millennia behaved

---

[471] Norman Cohn, *The Myth of the World Jewish Conspiracy. The Protocols of the Elders of Zion*, Digital Editor pdf: Titivilius, 2016, p. 80

[472] Gabriele Eschenazi, Gabriele Nissim, *Les juifs et le communisme…*, 1995, Éd. De Paris, 2000, p. 28, 35

[473] Arkadi Vaksberg, *Staline et les juifs*, Robert Laffont, 2003, p. 21.

as if they heard nothing, and quickly forgot what they could not have failed to hear". After each catastrophe, indeed, the survivors "rediscovered their invincibility. It was the invincibility of their faith.

Regarding the Second World War and the Holocaust, he wrote: "For the contemporaries of that cataclysm, there is no, there could be no comforting explanation, no consolation that would end the deep restlessness of the survivors... only a complacent and deficient memory would allow us to forget that the earth was crumbling beneath our feet[474]."

And here Sperber pointed out a key idea that allows us to better understand the very special mental universe of the Jews: "God was just, for he condemned his enemies to become murderers, and to them [the Jews] he granted the grace of being the victims, who in death would sanctify the Almighty. From John Chrysostom to the last pogromist mujik, the persecutors did not suspect the extent to which their momentary triumph reinforced the conviction of the persecuted that they were the chosen people[475]."

In short, the persecutions would simply be necessary to the Jewish people, not only because they confirm their divine election, but also because by turning the goyim into murderers, they allow the Jews to profit from the guilt of their enemies. There is undoubtedly something masochistic about these people. "My Master quoted the Talmud," wrote Elie Wiesel: "Better to be among the victims than among the murderers[476]"."

From this point onwards and taking this into account, the mechanism of accusatory projection allows the roles to be reversed and the adversary to be accused. Stalin thus becomes the ideal "scapegoat" who can be "accused of all evils". Stalin, the tyrant, the executioner, the dictator, the nationalist, is very useful in crystallising the horrors of the Soviet regime. Internationalist Jews have nothing to do with it, nor does communist ideology. Guy Konopnicki wrote: "On the contrary, it is the retreat of the revolution, the isolation of Soviet Russia and the nationalist awakening of Greater Russia decided by Stalin that founded that dreadful system which only a few mentally retarded people still call

---

[474] Manès Sperber, *Être juif*, Éd. Odile Jacob, 1994, p. 74.

[475] Manès Sperber, *Être juif*, Éd. Odile Jacob, 1994, p. 60.

[476] Elie Wiesel, *Mémoires, Tome I*, Le Seuil, 1994, p. 32.

the generous utopia of the last century... Nationalist ideology has bloodied that century through all sorts of great patriots such as Stalin in Russia, Pilsudski in Poland, Ceausescu in Romania and Khomeini in Iran. Not to mention the most nationalistic and therefore most murderous of all regimes, Nazism, with its return to Germanic cultural origins[477]." This is how a Jewish intellectual cleanses and purifies the Jewish people of their responsibility for the most terrifying and criminal regime in the entire history of mankind.

Removed from power in the USSR after Stalin's death, Jews around the world did not cease to cry out their grief all over the world afterwards. Elie Wiesél was also despairing at the brutal change of the Soviet regime in which many Jews had placed their hopes. He recounted the struggle of the Jews of the "free world" in the 1960s: "Tirelessly, they knock on the doors of senators, deputies, journalists and members of the clergy; they organise seminars, colloquiums and petitions: it is a matter of saving countless human lives by proclaiming their rights to dignity and hope. How many are there? Millions, it is said... What can we do for them? I mean: in addition to what we are already doing? I am about to advocate a stronger political fight, more vehement press campaigns, more committed speeches at the United Nations headquarters[478]."

Thus we see that the Jewish people can appear to be eternally innocent, and yet eternally persecuted. As André Darmon wrote at the end of his editorial in *Israel Magazine* in April 2003: "Killing a Jew or a child makes God weep, for this is the way to exterminate the bearers of universal ethics and innocence".

The slightest doubt, the slightest allusion to Israel's possible culpability, immediately provokes a wave of protests in all the media. We saw how Renaud Camus had paid dearly for it. Frederic Stroussi, in the same magazine, attacked Stephane Courtois, who had dared to write in the preface to his *Black Book of Communism*: "The death of a child of a Ukrainian kulak deliberately starved to death by the Stalinist regime is "worth" the same as the death of a Jewish child in the Warsaw ghetto". These simple words were enough to provoke the wrath of this Frederic Stroussi, who reacted in an exaggerated and totally disproportionate manner to these rather trivial and certainly justified words of the very

---

[477] Guy Konopnicki, *La Place de la nation*, Éd. Olivier Orban, 1983, p. 20, 21.

[478] Elie Wiesel, *Mémoires, Tome I*, Le Seuil, 1994, p. 485, 498.

thoughtful and moderate Stephane Courtois. He declared himself "stupefied" by such an affront. This speech, according to him, was nothing less than "abject" and represented an "obscene attack" on the Jewish people: "Why use the martyrdom of a Jewish child to insinuate, deceitfully and despicably, the idea that the Jews "overshadow" the other victims of totalitarianisms by monopolising all attention on them?"

In 1869, Gougenot des Mousseaux had noted this characteristic inclination: "With the utmost seriousness they demand special measures for their people. When we pull the ear of the Jewish child, *all the Jews of the world* shriek at this treatment, at this brutal attack. When one allows oneself the remark that the Jewish child may have deserved this, we are treated as reactionaries and obscurantists[479]."

In the following, we will discuss what can be called the "paradox of the Zohar": Anti-Semitism stems from the benefits that Jews bring to humanity. These benefits are so great that those who receive them are ashamed, and arouse in them hatred against their benefactors.

Elie Wiesel was indeed drawing on the "words of the Zohar", the Kabbalistic book, to present us with an interpretation of why there were outbreaks of anti-Semitism in ancient times: "Settled in Egypt, the sons of Jacob were at first prosperous, esteemed and happy. Then they began to envy them secretly. Then openly. But it was not dangerous. Then they began to fear them. To hate them. They thought they were too rich. They were too many, too annoying, too invasive. But it still wasn't dangerous. The time came when the Egyptians entered into a bloody war with their neighbours; and they were saved by the intervention of the children of Israel. Then, the danger that threatened the children of Israel became real. For that, the Egyptians could not forgive[480]."

Jacques Attali also expressed this curious paradox: "Christian anti-Judaism is consolidated, based on hatred of the one who brought the good word. Hatred of the one who rendered a service. This will be found

---

[479] Roger Gougenot des Mousseaux, *The Jews, Judaism and the Judaisation of Christian peoples.* Pdf version. Translated into Spanish by Professor Noemí Coronel and the invaluable collaboration of the Catholic Nationalism team. Argentina, 2013, p. 327

[480] Elie Wiesel, *Celebración Biblica, Retratos y leyendas del Antiguo Testamento*, Muchnik Editores, 1987, Barcelona,

much later in the relationship with money: hatred for the one who lends money to those who are not in favour of it.

others after having provided them with their God[481]."

Those who oppose the Jewish project can only be madmen who do not understand all the benefits that Jews bring to the rest of humanity. In his *Apology for Israel,* Albert Caraco wrote in turn: "We are punished because we were benefactors and because good disturbs order". (p.219) "They will never forgive the Jews for the favours they owe them, their vassalage devours them from within, their debt kills them and that is why we must be the stronger and save them from their own rage."

But sometimes, Jewish intellectuals hint that the innocence they boast of is perhaps less a virtue of the Jewish people than a subterfuge to dupe the goyim into achieving their ends. Albert Caraco, ever so explicit, stated it unequivocally: "Let them persevere in their innocence, and they will achieve with it what no people has ever dreamed of" (p.165). (p.165). "At the end of time, they will wear the robe of innocence and the royal mantle, those that power alone can whiten and that domination alone redeems" (p.175). "The Nothing or the Jews, that is the supreme choice[482]."

Stéphane Zagdanski already gave us a glimpse of the magic trick: Jews are "mystically indispensable to the world and therefore to its lie, holding it up as if they were an Atlas of joy and innocence, and for this very reason they are hated by the world and its lie[483]." In another passage of his book Zagdanski believed perhaps to be very fine when he wrote the following, "Anti-Semitic bad faith does not joke and does not tolerate for long to be mocked[484]."

Finally, we will leave the last word of this chapter to Manes Sperber, who in 1956 unburdened himself with an unusual sincerity: "The exile was only bearable to the extent that, for each punishment and wound, we found an interpretation that exculpated even God himself. To

---

[481] Jacques Attali, *Los Judíos, el mundo y el dinero,* Fondo de cultura económica de Argentina, Buenos Aires, 2005, p. 95.

[482] Albert Caraco, Apologie d'Israël, 1957, L'Âge d'homme, 2004, p. 25.

[483] Stéphane Zagdanski, *De l'Antisémitisme,* Climats, 1995, 2006, p. 334, 335.

[484] Stéphane Zagdanski, *De l'Antisémitisme,* Climats, 1995, 2006, p. 244. The sentence would be truer in the opposite sense.

achieve this reconciliation, all that was needed was an agile intelligence, a lively shrewdness and an art of interpretation[485]... "Finally, Manes Sperber accused anti-Semites of not understanding anything about Jews and Judaism: "All trampled minorities can be convinced that their enemies know practically nothing about them. This astounding ignorance which has always characterised anti-Semites is one of the strongest reasons for the contempt felt by Jews for their enemies[486]."

## *The accusatory inversion*

Like the Hungarians in the interwar period, the Poles had accused the Jews of having constituted a 'fifth column' of Soviet Bolshevism. This theory did not hold water, explained Gabriele Eschenazi: "This sui generis threat was not justified by any real facts... In reality, the Jews were the symbol of all the weaknesses and frustrations of the Polish nation... The Catholic myth of the Jewish 'demonic might' allowed the Poles, more than anything else, to justify their limits, their anxieties and their fears[487]."

The testimony of a certain Jerzy Szapiro, quoted by the author, provided a further element for understanding the phenomenon: "The Poles, said Szapiro, suffer from an inferiority complex; this is the reason why they blame others for their misfortunes. However, in their imagination, they feel superior; so they need, in order to justify their misfortunes, to find a scapegoat[488]."

We now know that the Poles are at least as deceitful as the Hungarians... Their perfidy is such that Polish historians went so far as to imagine the most absurd fables to discredit the wretched Jewish people. In 1940, for example, rumours circulated "that the Jews had not only welcomed the Soviet soldiers as liberators, but that a large number of them had joined

---

[485] Manès Sperber, *Être juif*, Éd. Odile Jacob, 1994, p. 103.

[486] Manès Sperber, *Être juif*, Éd. Odile Jacob, 1994, p. 147.

[487] Gabriele Eschenazi, Gabriele Nissim, *Les juifs et le communisme...*, 1995, Éd. De Paris, 2000, p. 166

[488] Gabriele Eschenazi, Gabriele Nissim, *Les juifs et le communisme...*, 1995, Éd. De Paris, 2000, p. 201

the new administration to replace the old Polish bureaucrats". That was the confirmation of the "Polish myth of the treachery of the Jews[489]".

Manifestly, Poles love to play the victim, Eschenazi explained: "The fact that the top of communist power was occupied by leaders of Jewish origin who came from the USSR with the Red Army during the "liberation" contributed to the paradoxical impression that in the end the Poles were the real "victims" of the Second World War, while the Jews were the "victors"… They came to believe in a totally surrealistic way that the Jews were the source of all Poland's ills: they were 'Judeo-communism'."

Because of their mistrustful, gauche minds, the Poles became confused and lumped everyone together: "In the collective imagination, leaders of Jewish origin occupied imminent positions within the communist system… Also, because Poles had a tendency to play the victim, they came to take out their frustrations on others. The Jew became the ideal scapegoat. Poland was oppressed: Whose fault was it? The Jews[490]."

The Poles are undoubtedly misguided, for the simple reason that the new Jewish leaders, as in Hungary, were in reality no longer Jews, but simply communists. It must be understood that "the "Jewish" Party leaders such as Jakun Berman, Hilary Minc or Roman Zambrowski… had broken with their Jewish origins and defined themselves solely as Communists and Poles". Just because Jews were "numerous at the head of the party" and "occupied the majority of posts in the central committee" did not mean that it was a Jewish dictatorship, for these Jews were, in reality, no longer Jews at all: "We are faced with a new paradox, wrote Eschenazi: by becoming Communists, the Jews ceased to be Jews for their own environment, but for the Poles, this conversion made them even more "Jews", even, Jews of the "worst kind[491]"." This is the real explanation. If the Poles had been less stupid, they would have understood.

---

[489] Gabriele Eschenazi, Gabriele Nissim, *Les juifs et le communisme…*, 1995, Éd. De Paris, 2000, p. 189, 192

[490] Gabriele Eschenazi, Gabriele Nissim, *Les juifs et le communisme…*, 1995, Éd. De Paris, 2000, p. 179, 180, 182

[491] Gabriele Eschenazi, Gabriele Nissim, *Les juifs et le communisme…*, 1995, Éd. De Paris, 2000, p. 183, 187

Gabriele Eschenazi quoted the testimony of a journalist named Wolicki, a member of the Party: "In the 1950s there were a large number of Jews in the political police. That is undeniable. In the 1960s, that was no longer the case. However, the myth was kept alive, even amplified. People believed that the police were full of Jews. I call this magical anti-Semitism. A pragmatic anti-Semitism says: "This man is a Jew, therefore he is a criminal". A magical anti-Semite says: 'This man is a criminal, therefore he is a Jew'" (p.224). Indeed, that is the problem: by hiding behind false identities, Jews have earned the natural suspicion of many.

Gabriele Eschenazi insisted on this point: 'The attitude of playing the victim is so deeply rooted in [Polish] society that it is difficult for any self-criticism to emerge. Failures and difficulties are still seen as the result of external factors (the enemy, a plot, the 'anti-Polish'). The Pole is "innocent" by definition. The 1968 exodus deprived society of its favourite scapegoat and from then on Poles began to be seen as pejoratively apoplectic towards other Poles. Any unsympathetic or unpleasant individual could be labelled a 'Jew'" (p.287). In reality, the author explained, "Poles unconsciously felt a deep remorse for all that had happened" during the war. "In order to escape the guilt that devoured them, they resorted to all sorts of justifications... "We could do nothing", "the Jews were with the Russians", etc."... In reality, although nobody wanted to admit it, the country carried an enormous burden on their conscience. (p.305). Here, from the pen of a Jewish intellectual, is an "accusatory projection".

The projection of guilt was also verified by the writer Manes Sperber, when he analysed the "myth" of greed, of which the Jews were always unjustly accused throughout history: "Possessing silver, gold and jewellery was the only—though not always effective—guarantee against expulsion and murder. The Jews thus bought the right to live, to settle in a place and temporary protection against the common people. The insatiable greed of those who had the power to sell them or deny them the right to exist condemned them to have to be tough to make a profit." Judaism "was threatened by enemies animated by a frenzied will to plunder and possess. These blackmailers found noble reasons to justify their attitude. Sometimes they wanted to avenge the crucifixion of Christ, sometimes to punish a desecration of hosts imagined for the occasion, or an invented ritual murder. It was the time of the lordly and clerical thieves[492]." Sperber insisted: "In their relations with the Jews, Christian princes behaved for more than a millennium singularly like the inhuman, gold-hungry being that the anti-Semitic caricature had made of the prototypical Jew[493]."

So that Manes Sperber could lament: "What have the enemies of the Jewish people not done—what means, what tricks, what poisons, what weapons have they used, what slanders have they spread? What laws have they enacted, what tortures have they invented[494]?"

But the Christian princes were not the only ones to blame: "More than half of the anti-Semitic pamphlets show that their authors are obsessed with money. And in almost all of them is manifested what the anti-Jewish polemicists call the Talmudic spirit, a term by which they designate the manner of treating a fact with contempt and of shamelessly twisting its real meaning." Shameless Manes!

The anti-Semite, as you will understand, hates in the Other "the defects which he would like to eliminate from himself. He forgives them and conceals them from himself more easily, imagining them grotesquely inordinate in the one he hates… The superiority of the Other in the areas in which he feels hopelessly inferior… Certainly, bad faith plays a role in this kind of argumentation, just as it does in the defamatory and slanderous rampage of totalitarian hatred. But it would be to ignore the meaning of this phenomenon if one did not take into account the paranoid logic that determines these procedures… It reverses the relationship of cause and effect, it breaks down the facts and patches them up arbitrarily, ignoring, denying or destroying evidence that opposes the preconceived interpretation" and "confers on the user an unalterable good conscience[495]".

The accusatory projection manifested itself again in Manes Sperber when it came to understanding the accusations of ritual murder: "The anti-Semite, more than any other, deserves the reproaches he makes against those he hates. What are we to think of the accusation of ritual murder, so often uttered against the followers of a religion which categorically forbids the consumption of any form of blood? According

---

[492] Manès Sperber, *Être juif*, Éd. Odile Jacob, 1994, p. 100.

[493] Manès Sperber, *Être juif*, Éd. Odile Jacob, 1994, p. 141.

[494] Manès Sperber, *Être juif*, Éd. Odile Jacob, 1994, p. 111.

[495] Manès Sperber, *Être juif*, Éd. Odile Jacob, 1994, p. 142-144.

to their dogma, Christians do drink the blood and eat the flesh of their Redeemer. Is there not a connection between this profoundly pagan rite and their absurd slander against us[496]?"

We see how the Jewish intellectual projects onto others everything he feels guilty about, including his own tendency to accusatory inversion. Alexis Rosenbaum is a professor of philosophy, and also a great Talmudist, as we can deduce from his way of analysing anti-Semitism in a book published in 2006 and originally entitled *Anti-Semitism*: "Is anti-Semitism the expression of a neurosis[497]?" he asked, before explaining: "The mechanism of projection is usually accompanied by an accusatory inversion. The mechanism of projection is usually accompanied by an accusatory reversal. The crimes one wanted to commit or was about to commit against Jews were attributed to them. We know, for example, that at the very time they were being persecuted in Nazi Germany, propaganda systematically attributed imaginary crimes to them: the Jew raped, mutilated, tortured, destroyed other religions, mistreated pure women, sought revenge for persecution, etc. From a psychoanalytical point of view, these events are symptomatic of a process of inversion between the victim and the executioner (or projective inversion). The latter persecutes the Jews because he imagines or convinces himself to be persecuted by them. This allows him to free himself from guilt while at the same time he blames the object of his hatred".

Alexis Rosenbaum went on to analyse Christian anti-Judaism through psychoanalysis: "In the imagination of the young Christian who identified with Christ as Son, the Jews could be perceived as a kind of fearsome ancestor still strangely present, that is to say as the transformed image of his own father. But according to Freudian psychoanalysis, the father is precisely the source of the Law, of the fundamental prohibitions to which the child must submit by limiting its craving for pleasure. The child's feelings are considered to be particularly ambivalent: because he confusingly perceives his mother as belonging to his father, his father is both an object of admiration and envy. This is why the Jews, the founders of monotheism and its laws, were susceptible to being the object of a deeply contradictory

---

[496] Manès Sperber, *Être juif*, Éd. Odile Jacob, 1994, p. 147.

[497] Alexis Rosenbaum, *L'Antisémitisme*, Bréal, 2006, p.63. Alexis Rosenbaum relied on the work of Otto Fenichel, *Elements of Psychoanalytic Theorie of Anti-semitism*, in E. Simmel, (dir), *Anti-Semitism. A social Desire*, IUP, 1946.

relationship, a kind of admiring hatred... The Jews were said to be the executioners of Christ, so that his blood was upon them. The child thus discovered in the holy story a surprising model of psychological solution to his conflicts: as a Christian, he could be exonerated from the death of Christ by shifting the burden of the crime onto the Jews... The Jewish people could be conceived as a means of alleviating any major guilt, as if they were a negative holy figure destined to pay eternally for the role they had supposedly played[498]."

"Anti-Semitism is characterised... by a strong tendency towards delusions, with personalities subject to obsessive and paranoid representations being fertile ground for it. In such cases, it is no longer a matter of ordinary xenophobia, but of a very particular fanaticism, which fabricates imaginary entities and favours desires for radical elimination. Let us remember that the multiplication of aberrant beliefs about Judaism has been prodigious throughout history. The passionate anti-Semite puts forward astonishingly wild and often ingenious theories, although he is never disturbed by the fact that none of the major accusations against the Jews has ever been proven. Obsessed either by the Semites or by the Zionists, it is almost impossible to reason with him[499]." Once again, it is enough to reverse the terms "Jews" and "anti-Semites" to realise Alexis Rosenbaum's problem.

Stephane Zagdanski also presented us with another good example of accusatory inversion. "The anti-Semitic logic is characterised by paranoid inversion, so that its most tenacious stereotypes are always stupid antitheses of what Jewish religion, culture and thought traditionally profess. And Zagdanski insisted on that point: "The privileged operation of anti-Semitism is paranoid inversion, and the preferred language of inversion is slander. This means that every anti-Semitic idea is the exact opposite of the truth... Every statement of anti-Semitism is an insult to common sense, every inflection of it an offence." The anti-Semite is "a great neurotic. He would do well to consult a psychoanalyst... He loses himself in obsessive calculations so as not to recognise his own delirium[500]."

---

[498] Alexis Rosenbaum, *L'Antisémitisme*, Bréal, 2006, p. 66-69.

[499] Alexis Rosenbaum, *L'Antisémitisme*, Bréal, 2006, p. 116.

[500] Stéphane Zagdanski, *De l'Antisémitisme*, Climats, 1995, 2006, p. 10, 157, 210, 224

The fact is that Zagdanski also protected himself in advance against any criticism: "This book is also a *schibboleth*\* for my own ears. Any criticism will sound like an alarm. As for praise, it will mostly be disguised insults. Whoever calls me paranoid will himself be strongly prone to delirium. Whoever reproaches me for mixing it all up will himself be tremendously confused. Whoever accuses me of not proving anything will be incapable of proving it. He who accuses me of this, is himself recusing himself". It is true that he had written at the beginning of his book: "I salute my fiery, my joyful, my voluble, my lively, my acrobatic, my highest thought. My blessed Jewish thought[501]."

We see, then, how the cosmopolitan intellectual projects onto others his own faults, all his faults, and thus his own tendency towards inversion.

Manes Sperber left us a wonderful and revealing picture of this Jewish inclination to see the world upside down: "When we were four years old—we were already learning to translate the Book—we spent our scarce free time practising two gymnastic exercises: standing on our heads and doing somersaults. All this to prepare us for the coming of the Messiah. When the great moment arrives, the earth will turn, then, of course, we will have to know how to stand on our heads for at least a quarter of an hour to get into the right posture. The dead, for their part, will roll underground to Jerusalem where they will rise again? The meaning of life, of suffering and of death, everything was determined by the End, the beginning of an eternal present[502]."

Our European forefathers had understood perfectly well that the profound nature of Judaism flowed from the precepts of the Talmud. King St. Louis, concerned about this, had ordered a trial of the Talmud. The trial was opened on 12 June 1240 at the Palais de Justice in Paris, under the presidency of Blanche de Castille. After much debate, it was decided to destroy the book. On 6 June 1242, twenty-four carts containing 1200 copies of the Talmud were burnt on the Place de Grève.

## Anti-Zionism as accusatory projection

---

\* Hebrew. A sort of password, like a password.

[501] Stéphane Zagdanski, *De l'Antisémitisme*, Climats, 1995, 2006, p. 338, 21

[502] Manès Sperber, *Être juif*, Éd. Odile Jacob, 1994, p. 118.

In the West, while no sensible politician or journalist would risk the slightest criticism of Jews, it is still tolerated, for the time being, to condemn Israeli policy. The Jews, however, prefer to do it themselves. In *Operation Shylock*, "a provocative book full of intelligence and humour", the famous American novelist Philip Roth realised how dangerous the state of Israel was for Jews all over the world: "The country that endangers the most Jewish lives today—the country called Israel—must be deactivated... The state which with its pervasive Jewish totalitarianism has become the main fear of the Jews of the world, replacing the gentiles; the state which today, with its lust for Jews, is, in so many terrible ways, deforming and disfiguring the Jews in a way that was once only available to our anti-Semitic enemies... What have they done? What are their merits? A bunch of rude people who go around in the street hustling and shoving you. I've lived in Chicago, in New York, in Boston. I've lived in Paris, I've lived in London, and nowhere have I seen such people walking the streets. What *arrogance*! What have you people here created that can compare with what you other Jews in the world have done? Absolutely nothing. Nothing but a state founded on force and the will to rule[503]."

Philip Roth was also indignant that the Israelis behaved in this way towards the Jews of the Diaspora: "But they don't reserve their arrogance for the Arab and his mentality, because they do the same with the *goyim*, the gentiles, and their mentality, or with you and your mentality. These provincial jerks look down on you! Can you imagine that?... They look down on all the 'neurotics' of the Diaspora. They look down their noses at all the "neurotics" in the Diaspora... And how superior they feel to the Jews who want nothing to do with weapons! Jews who grab Arab children and smash their knuckles with clubs? And how superior they feel to all of you who are incapable of such violence!... What *arrogance*, Philip, what *insufferable* arrogance! What you teach your children at school is to look down on the Jews of the Diaspora, to regard English-speaking Jews, and Spanish-speaking Jews, and Russian-speaking Jews, as a bunch of weirdos, worms, neurotics, panic-stricken prisoners... As if speaking Hebrew is the ultimate human achievement! I'm here, they think, and I speak Hebrew, this is my home and this is my language, and I don't have to go around asking myself over and over again: "I'm a Jew, but what is it to be a

---

[503] Philip Roth, *Operación Shylock*, Debolsillo, Editorial Mondadori, 2005 Barcelona, p. 91, 139-140

Jew? I don't have to be one of those terrified, alienated, self-hating neurotics who keep asking themselves questions? That's your great Jewish achievement: turning Jews into jailers and bomber pilots!... The Jews have a reputation for being intelligent, and they really are. As far as I know, the only place in the world where all Jews *are* idiots is Israel. I spit on them! *I spit* on them[504]!"

But "arrogance", "contempt" and the "will to dominate" are not only specific to Israeli Jews. The critique of domestic Zionism thus makes it possible to avoid talking about the influence of Diaspora Jews and projecting onto Israeli Jews the defects that anyone would attribute to Jews in general.

Philip Roth also accused his fellow Israelis: "We have wronged the Palestinians. We have displaced them and tortured them, we have killed them. The Jewish state, from the very moment of its creation, has dedicated itself to eliminating the historic Palestinian presence in historic Palestine, appropriating the land of an indigenous people. The Palestinians have been pushed aside, dispersed and conquered by the Jews[505]... I try to get it into their heads that there are Jews in the world who are nothing like the Jews here. But for them the Israeli Jew represents such a degree of evil, that they find it hard to believe me".

This transfer of blame is also evident when it comes to criticising the universal Jewish propensity for jeremiads. In this case, Philip Roth once again projected the faults of his fellow Jews in the Diaspora onto the state of Israel: "What justifies the fact that no opportunity to extend Israel's borders is missed? What justifies the bombing of the civilian population of Beirut? Auschwitz. What justifies crushing the bones of Palestinian children and blowing off the limbs of Arab mayors? Auschwitz. Dachau. Buchenvald. Belsen. Treblinka. Sobibor. Belsec... Power-mad Jews, that's what they are, that's all they are, and if they differ in any way from other power-mad Jews elsewhere on earth, it is in the mythology of victimisation they use to justify their addiction to power and their victimisation of us. The old American joke puts it exactly: "There is no business like *Shoah* business", instead of *"Show*

---

[504] Philip Roth, *Operación Shylock*, Debolsillo, Editorial Mondadori, 2005, Barcelona, p. 143-145.

[505] Philip Roth, *Operación Shylock*, Debolsillo, Editorial Mondadori, 2005 Barcelona, p. 404-405, 139

*business*", there is no business like Holocaust business, instead of *show business*".

Such statements, which the pro-Palestinian "anti-Zionists" rejoice in, are like trees that obscure the forest, relegating to the background the rise of the power of Jewish communities in the Western world, mainly through finance and the media system. It is the same projection syndrome that we discover in these words: "(...) the few Israelis who can still be trusted a little, because they still have self-respect and still know how to say something that is not pure propaganda". The trickery of these Israeli Jews, Roth wrote, serves "to reinforce the cornerstone of the Israelis' policy of arrogance, underpinning the ideology of the victim. They will not cease to paint themselves as victims or to identify with the past." Philip Roth once again railed against the "insufferable arrogance" of these Israelis, as if Diaspora Jews were free of these same defects, and finally warned the Jews of Israel "before the Zionists, in their irredeemable madness and vengefulness, end up involving the whole Jewish world in their brutality and bring upon it such a catastrophe that it will never recover[506]."

In short, the criticism of the State of Israel is very practical in order to make everyone forget that the heart of world Judaism is in New York, London and Paris, and not in Tel-Aviv. One might indeed wonder whether Israeli Jews are more cruel than the Bolshevik Jews were, and we would like to hear the same words and the same repentance for the atrocities inflicted on the Russian and Ukrainian people.

## *Lanterns and tall tales*

The persecutions of which Jewish communities claim to be victims are sometimes real, but sometimes also very dubious. Indeed, there are quite frequent cases of media hoaxes in this regard. A study published in the United States and translated into French in 2003 by the magazine *Tabou*[507] compiled several dozen allegedly anti-Semitic acts in the

---

[506] Philip Roth, *Operación Shylock*, Debolsillo, Editorial Mondadori, 2005 Barcelona, p. 152–157. In the French translation: "The tricks of these Israeli Jews serve to justify the power of the Jews, to justify the domination of the Jews by keeping alive for the next hundred millennia the image of the Jewish victim".

[507] Laird Wilcox, *Crying wolfes, hate crime hoaxes in America*, Editorial research service, Kansas, 1994, in *Tabou*, volume 4; Éditions Akribeia, 2003,

United States and abroad that were found to have been committed by Jews "with a disturbed mind". This study also compiled dozens of accusations of anti-Semitism against individuals who were sought to be discredited. The case was always highly publicised at first, and then carefully hushed up, once the superciliousness had been uncovered. Here are a few examples:

In August 1979, a Jewish dentist in New York State, Dr. Sheldon Jacobson, discovered a flaming swastika on the lawn of his home. A few days later, the police arrested the culprit: Douglas Kahn, a Jewish teenager angry that Jacobson's dog had done his business in his yard (*New York daily*, 29 August 1979).

In August 1983, a series of arson attacks terrorised the Jewish community in West Hartford, Connecticut. The fires affected two synagogues and the home of a local rabbi. All the media reacted at once to denounce anti-Semitism. Television broadcast images of an old woman in tears recalling the horrors of the Holocaust: "I never thought it would happen again", the frightened woman declared. The police put thirty-three inspectors on the case and the mayor offered a large reward. However, suspicion quickly focused on a 17-year-old Jewish student, one Barry Dov Schuss, who would eventually confess to the four arson attacks. Jack Schuss, the teenager's father, testified that Barry had some psychiatric problems and had already been treated. During his trial in January 1984, Schuss testified that he had "acted to keep alive an awareness of the danger of anti-Semitism". In his place any Goy would have been sentenced to fifteen years in prison, but Barry Dov Schuss only received a suspended sentence with five years probation. (*Chicago Tribune* of 1 September 1983, *Hartford Courant* of 15 and 17 December 1983 and 24 January 1984).

In March 1984, residents of Co-Op City, a housing complex in the Bronx, New York, found swastikas and anti-Semitic graffiti on 51 flat doors and walls. It was a "shock to the community". The incident was also highly publicised in the media, until two Jewish teenagers aged 14 and 15 were caught. Silence suddenly fell over this tedious case. (*Jewish Sentinel* of 31 March 1984)

On 24 November 1985, a release from the *Associated Press* in New York revealed that vandals had smashed the windows of eight Jewish-owned shops in Brooklyn. Horror! Journalists across the country

---

p. 64-120.

shouted their outrage, recalling the 1938 episode of Kristallnacht. Mayor Edward Koch offered a $10,000 reward to anyone who informed the police of the culprits' whereabouts. Calls for anti-fascist vigilance multiplied. On 9 December, the following could be read in the press: "A 38-year-old Jew with psychological disorders has been arrested..." (New York Daily News of 10 December). "(*New York Daily News* of 10 December 1985). It turned out that the accused, Gary Dworkin, was only railing against Israelis and Hasidic Jews.

In December 1985, the Milwaukee synagogue guard was sprayed with a caustic substance. The victim, Buzz Cody, a former Catholic convert to Judaism, stated that the men had dark skin and spoke with a Middle Eastern accent. Earlier in July, nine swastikas were painted on the community centre, as well as on Cody's flat, which was broken into and ransacked. Anti-Semitic graffiti and anonymous phone calls from a mysterious "Palestinian Defence League" made his life miserable. The investigation was soon completed, and in May 1986, Cody was indicted. He committed suicide within hours (*Milwaukee Journal* of 20 December 1985 and 17 May 1986).

On 15 July 1987, a Jewish woman from Rockville, Maryland was awakened in the middle of the night by a swastika burning in her yard. The culprit was a 19-year-old Jew, Gary Stein (*Washington jewish week* of 6 August 1987).

In January 1988, Laurie A. Recht, a 35-year-old legal secretary, allegedly received death threats because of her anti-racist activism. The media immediately turned her into a heroine, highlighting her courage and determination. In May, New Rochelle College presented her with an honorary doctor of letters degree in recognition of the adversity she had endured. In November, she claimed to have received further death threats: "The nigger lover, the Jewess. We have not forgotten you. With your corpse we will reveal our cause to the world. There is a bullet waiting for you. The FBI tapped her communications to apprehend the culprits and installed a camera outside her flat. In the end, it turned out that Laurie Recht had received no threat over the phone, and that instead the camera recorded her painting herself on the adjoining wall of her flat. In court, Laurie admitted the facts. She faced up to five years in prison and a fine of 250,000 dollars, but only received a suspended sentence with five years probation. (*New York Daily News*, 28 November 1988; *Agence télégraphique juive*, 1 December 1988).

*Newsweek* magazine of 8 May 1989 reported that a wealthy man, Morton Downey, had been assaulted by skinheads in the toilets of San

Francisco airport. They allegedly pinned him down in the bathroom to paint a swastika on his face and cut off a piece of his scalp before greeting him with a "Sieg heil". The airport inspectors found only minor cuts on his face, but not the events Downey told the press. Downey later admitted that the incident had been "a pre-planned publicity stunt".

On 25 March 1990, in Yorba Linda, California, hundreds of people discovered a leaflet allegedly distributed by the Methodist circle calling to "kill the Jews". A local newspaper reported: "One side depicts Jesus; it quotes a passage from the Gospel of Luke and this phrase: "Kill all Jews". The other side lists the reasons to distrust the Jews". Reverend Keneth Criswell, pastor of the local Unitarian Methodist Church immediately sent a letter to his community to assure them that the leaflets had been "falsely and fraudulently" attributed to the Methodist Church.

In late 1991, Nathan Kobrin, a Jew from Concord in California, claimed to be the victim of two arson attacks and pretended to have received anonymous letters and death threats over the phone. California newspapers applauded his courageous fight against anti-Semitism and he received numerous supporters. An investigator watching his home uncovered the hoax. On 31 January 1992, Nathan Kobrin, 36, confessed in Contra Santa Court that he was the perpetrator of the two fires and the false letters. He was charged with false testimony and sentenced to one year in prison (*Oakland Tribune* of 12 September 1991, *Northern Californian Jewish Bulletin* of 20 September 1991 and 17 July 1992).

In April 1993, a young Jewish couple, Jerome and Jamie Brown Roedel, reported the burglary of their home in Cooper City, Forida. The case was highly publicised because the walls had been covered with anti-Semitic graffiti. Again, there was great outrage and "shock within the community". Eight months of investigation were necessary to reach this conclusion: insurance fraud. Indeed, a few months earlier, Jamie Roedel had acquired valuable art objects. After organising the fake theft with several people, he claimed $47,000 from the insurance company. In the end, she pocketed $30,000, left her husband and started a new life with her lover. In December 1993, she was indicted for fraud (*Chicago Tribune* of 2 January 1994).

In 1994, openly racist and anti-Semitic leaflets were distributed in New York. The culprit was found to be a member of the national committee of the Anti Defamation League, the leading American "anti-racist" association (*New York Times*, 27 February 1994). After he was arrested, Donald Mintz explained that he had wanted to stir up a sympathy movement around his candidacy and raise funds. He lost the election after the scandal.

This study went up to 1994, so it was not possible to know about cases that occurred after that date. But everyone can get an idea of how frequent these dramas are in the United States and abroad. Let us remember this other case that broke out in 2004: swastikas had been painted on some twenty Jewish-owned shops in the New York boroughs of Brooklyn and Queens, as well as on some synagogues. The outrage was widespread. One rabbi offered a $5,000 bonus in exchange for any information. On 18 October 2004, the police finally arrested the culprit. It was Olga Abramovich, 49, who explained that she wanted to take revenge on her 78-year-old husband, Jack Greenberg, who had just divorced to marry a younger woman. The press and Jewish organisations then hushed up the whole story. Fortunately, the public quickly forgets what they see on television.

These "anti-Semitic" reports have been occurring for the same reasons for a long time. Let us listen to Arthur Miller, an American Jewish writer, famous above all as the husband of Marilyn Monroe, who was alarmed at the upsurge of anti-Semitism in the United States before the war. Synagogues and Jewish homes in Connecticut had been bombed. "The perpetrator was arrested a few weeks later. He was a young Jewish man of deranged mind[508]."

But more recently, in Israel, in May 1990, the desecration of two Jewish cemeteries had sent shockwaves around the world. More than two hundred and fifty Jewish graves had been discovered with inscriptions in Hebrew calling for the destruction of Judaism and the creation of a Palestinian state. "The Arabs will kill the Jews". Zevolon Hammer, Israel's minister of religious affairs, suggested that this episode could be linked to the desecration of graves in the Carpentras cemetery in France, which many had attributed to the extreme right. Two Jews, David Goldner, 41, and Gershon Tennenbaum, 32, were finally arrested in Haïfa. They explained their action by their desire to unite the Jewish people against the Arab states (*The Jewish Week* of 18 May 1990, *New York Times* of 17 May 1990). There were also many cases in Israel of fake attacks on Jewish settlers to provoke a reaction.

---

[508] Arthur Miller, *En el punto de mira*, Tusquets Editores, 1995, Barcelona, p. 12.

\* Bleu blanc rouge, from the French tricolour.

## THE JEWISH FANATICISM

In France, the news regularly presents the same super-tricks, creating "media bubbles". Here are a few examples:

In March 1990, Louisa Zemour, a militant of SOS-Racisme in Grenoble, was wounded by a "henchman of the National Front" who had disguised her face with a "blue-white-red*" scarf. (*Rivarol* of 15 June 1990).

In 1992, in the early hours of New Year's Eve, a Molotov cocktail set fire to the Villepinte synagogue in Seine-Saint-Denis. The attack was claimed by a mysterious group called "Pure France". It was a "shock within the community". On 10 January 1993, several ministers took part in the demonstration organised by the Chief Rabbi Joseph Sitruk to protest against this barbaric act. But in the end, it turned out that the author of the arson attack was a certain Michel Zoubiri, an Algerian Jew, who wanted to blame the attack on Patrick E, an amorous rival member of the National Front (*Rivarol* of 15 January 1993).

In January 2003, the stabbing of Rabbi Gabriel Fahri was highly publicised and politicised, before the case was finally buried: in fact, no attack had taken place. The medical expert's report mentioned "a doubtful wound", which had not resulted in any abdominal injury. Moreover, the 10-centimetre tearing of the clothing was "incompatible with the alleged assault". Due to the lack of witnesses, the whole case depended on the statements of the victim, who blamed a "man with a helmet", who allegedly shouted "Allah Akbar" with "a French accent". In reality, Rabbi Farhi had stabbed himself.

The arson attack on a Jewish social centre in Paris on 22 August 2004 was widely reported in the media. The culprits had left behind anti-Semitic graffiti, inverted swastikas and Islamist slogans with rude misspellings. The Mayor of Paris and the Prime Minister visited the scene of the fire to express their outrage. In the aftermath of the attack, the mayor allocated an additional 300,000 euros for the security of places frequented by the Jewish community in Paris. But the investigation eventually turned up a 52-year-old man, a member of the community, and a hard-working volunteer who enjoyed the meals served to the underprivileged. "Mentally fragile", he had not been able to bear the loss of the flat rented to him by the social centre.

Similarly, no French media reported the verdict of the 17th court of the Paris correctional court sentencing Alex Moïse to a fine of 750 euros. Moïse had reported anti-Semitic threats and insults received at his home, but the investigation had established that he had sent them himself. Alex Moïse, secretary general of the Zionist Federation of France (a full member of the CRIF) and former spokesman for Likoud France, was also one of the instigators of the bans on shows by the black comedian of Cameroonian origin Dieudonné M'Bala. In the 1990s, he had been the president of the coordination committee of the Sentier, the local Jewish self-defence militia.

Anti-Semitism is exaggerated in this way by the media system for three reasons. The first is that Jewish identity contains a part of anguish and paranoia that has been natural for three thousand years. The second is that it allows Jews all over the world to maintain and cultivate a fragile identity, always threatened to disappear by assimilation in the host country, and thus to reinforce the cohesion of the community. The third reason is that this incessant alarm allows many Jews to be encouraged to settle in Israel, whose demography is too small compared to that of the Arabs.

This is what Georges Friedmann confessed in 1965: "I have often observed how Ashkenazi Israelis, except for the *Kibbutzim*, and in general "the old ones", reacted positively to any news of manifestations of anti-Semitism in the world. They emphasised it and tended to exaggerate its importance[509]." Something similar was stated by a certain Jacques Kupfer, a Zionist leader, who looked favourably on anti-Semitism: "I wish there were more and more swastikas and bombs against synagogues, so that the Jews would finally get off their asses[510]."

More recently, Rabbi Melchior appealed from Israel to his fellow Jews in France, who he said were in an extremely dangerous situation, to move to Israel as soon as possible. On 8 January 2001, the Israeli Ministry of Integration awarded 9000 dollars to each Jew who made his or her *alyah*. The weekly *Le Point* of 27 April 2006 published an article on the subject after the publication of a book entitled *OPA on the Jews of France*. The book denounced the instrumentalisation of anti-Semitism for the benefit of the Zionist discourse and noted that indeed, the *aliyah* towards Israel was increasing: 3015 people in 2005. However, a quick calculation makes it possible to relativise the great fear of France's Jews, given that the "flight" represented only 0.3% of the Jewish population.

The second Palestinian Intifada in October 2000 had indeed provoked an outbreak of violence among young Muslim immigrants in the French

---

[509] Georges Friedman, *Fin du peuple juif?* Gallimard, 1965, p. 289.

[510] André Harris and Alain de Sédouy, *Juifs et Français*, Grasset, 1979, Poche, 1980, p. 328-344.

suburbs. From September 2000 to September 2001, the Representative Council of Jewish Institutions in France (CRIF) counted 350 anti-Semitic attacks. The Union of Jewish Students of France also recalled that 322 anti-Semitic acts had taken place in France between 1 January and 1 October 2004[511]. The Jewish community was shocked. Pierre Birenbaum noted that the situation was alarming: "The highest state authorities agree: anti-Semitism is spreading dangerously in contemporary French society". However, he himself acknowledged that the French government was firm on this point. In December 2001, during the annual dinner of the CRIF (Representative Council of Jewish Institutions in France), Lionel Jospin, then Prime Minister, said, in front of almost the entire government gathered there, that "just as we do not tolerate acts of racism, we do not tolerate acts of anti-Semitism[512]."

That the "almost full" government meets every year on the CRIF premises should reassure community leaders. But the concern and anguish remain.

It is striking to note that synagogues are the only "places of worship" in France, where they are enclosed behind barbed wire fences, metal barriers, glass and armoured doors. Any foreign observer, any "Candide" could legitimately say: "Well, here are people who don't seem to be appreciated". Perhaps they have something to reproach themselves for? Ernest Renan already wrote in 1873: "There may be a reason why this wretched people of Israel have spent their lives being massacred: when all other nations and all centuries have persecuted them, there must be some reason for it[513]."

---

[511] We don't know if they had counted the graffiti on school desks and letterboxes.

[512] Pierre Birenbaum, *Prier pour l'État, les Juifs, l'alliance royale et la démocratie*, Calmann-Levy, 2005, p. 137.

[513] François de Fontette, *Sociologie de l'antisémitisme*, PUF, 1984, p. 116. English Prime Minister Winston Churchill wrote in an article in 1937: "It may indeed be that they are unwittingly inviting persecution, that they are partly responsible for the hostility they suffer". The article, never published, was discovered in his archives by a Cambridge historian, according to Agence France Presse (March 2007).

# 3. Jewish identity

## *The hyper-patriots*

More often than not, Jewish intellectuals write that their fellow Jews are "perfectly integrated" in the country where they live. So well integrated that they would even be the quintessence of the nation and its best defenders.

At the end of the 19th century, Eastern European and Russian Jews wishing to emigrate were naturally attracted to France, the 'land of human rights'. Guy Konopnicki recounted the mood of those Jews who came to seek happiness in France: "When they bought their third-class ticket on the Shtetl-Strasbourg train, my ancestors were not only emigrating. They were looking for some of that flame that lit up all the Jewish villages in Poland and Russia at the time of the Dreyfus affair. A Jewish captain, a campaign of opinion to defend him, these things seemed like miracles, and no rabbinical magician was known who was able to get an innocent man out of Russian or Polish prisons".

Under these circumstances, these Jews became "hyper-patriots" in France: "For that reason, we became more French than the French," wrote Konopnicki. Our immigrant social environment nourished us with a dream France, as did the socialist professors[514]... Since then I have maintained a passion for the French Revolution". Konopnicki even drew a parallel between the 1789 Revolution and his own biblical references: "The founders of contemporary France were great cosmopolitans. That is why the scope of the French Revolution crosses time and space; today, there is no more important challenge than that proclaimed by it: the rights of man and of the citizen. The Revolution was not a purely French affair. It was universally proclaimed and rightly so: nothing like it had happened since the giving of the Law to the Hebrews on Mount Sinai... In executing Louis Capet, the conventions repeated the great gesture of Abraham... Robespierre wanted the Constitution to be a sacred act placed on the tabernacle, just like the Torah of the Hebrews[515] *". He might also have added that the countless

---

[514] Guy Konopnicki, *La Place de la nation*, Olivier Orban, 1983, p. 14.

* Assembly members of the National Convention of the First French Republic (1792–1795). It was the constituent assembly.

[515] Guy Konopnicki, *La Place de la nation*, Olivier Orban, 1983, p. 44-46.

massacres of the Revolution, especially against the Vandeans, repeated the relentless genocide committed by Joshua and the Hebrews in their conquest of the land of Canaan, so well described by the Torah.

In short, the French revolutionaries, under some unknown Masonic influence, had only taken up and secularised Hebraic eschatology. The novelist Pierre Paraf, co-founder of the LICA (League Against Anti-Semitism), dedicated a poem to this ideal: "To love all the oppressed/ To save the disinherited/ To raise on the highest peaks/ A temple to humanity/ Is the covenant of the alliance/ That the Eternal made with us/ Those virtues of your France/ Are the virtues of Israel[516]."

The essayist Pierre Pierre Birenbaum spoke of the immense happiness felt by the Jews when they settled in France at the end of the 19th century to enjoy the new "liberal regime": "The advent of the Third Republic was the golden age of the Jews, for they identified strongly with that liberal regime founded by Gambetta, and to which Adolf Crémieux and many other Jews had contributed so passionately... In many ways, that long period of happiness... justified as never before the famous metaphor 'happy as God in France', which was to spread like wildfire to the farthest reaches of Eastern Europe, thus bringing them the good news[517]."

The novelist Albert Cohen also expressed this immoderate and patriotic love of France. In his novel *Nut Eater,* he told the story of quirky Jews from Cephalonia and their mad pilgrimages. On the ship on which his hero and his friends were travelling to France at the end of the 19th century, an orchestra was playing the *Marseillaise*: "Neclavs Eater felt intensely French and a fervent enthusiast for Danton. He walked along the bridge giving military salutes to innumerable regiments of which he felt himself to be a tremendous generalissimo. Solomon would drink the winds to defend the fatherland! The Marseillaise was spreading ever more victorious wings, and Nail-Eater gravely assumed the functions of orchestra conductor.

---

*Conventionnaires: Assembly members of the National Convention of the First French Republic (1792–1795). It was the constituent assembly.

[516] Pierre Paraf, *Quand Israel aima*, 1929, Les Belles lettres, 2000, p. 45, 46.

[517] Pierre Birembaum, *Prier pour l'Etat, les Juifs, l'alliance royale et la démocratie*, Calmann-Levy, 2005, p. 89.

—If I were the leader of France," he declared with tears in his eyes, "I would have it played every hour in the streets to promote patriotism, and I would have the ringleaders shot,[518]!"

But Nail-Eater and his friends also loved England: "They did not forget that, following the pogrom of 1891, part of the British fleet stationed in Malta set sail at full steam for Cephalonia. And how quiet the Greek anti-Semites were when the tall, dear English riflemen landed, fair and stern! And this is true, and the Jews of the Ionian Islands will always remember the unselfish kindness shown to them by England."

Certainly, the English soldiers had shown great bravery on that occasion to save the poor Jews. Nail Eater was grateful to whom it was due: "On the walls of the kitchen of Nail Eater hung the portraits of the English royal family, of Sir Moses Montefiore, of Disraeli, and of a great number of Lords of the Admiralty[519]."

The Jews of France would naturally also be the most fervent patriots after Hitler's seizure of power in 1933. They would also be more warmongering than ever. This was what Jean-Pierre Bloch, former president of the League against anti-Semitism, declared. This great bourgeois was also a leader of the socialist party. "As a socialist, he was extremely patriotic. For example, I was one of the seven socialists who voted against the Munich Agreements. I believed that there was a 'party of betrayal'". All Jean-Pierre Bloch was indeed unanimous in inciting the French to declare war on the Germans. "I was immersed in hyper-patriotism[520] ", he said.

Manes Sperber, for his part, tore the French flag from our hands: "Faced with those Jews expelled from their homeland, those in France felt more French than the descendants of the Crusaders, and only Israelites out of philanthropic duty[521]." Unless it is the other way around.

---

[518] Albert Cohen, *Comeclavos*, Anagrama, 1989, Barcelona, p. 88, 89

[519] Albert Cohen, *Comeclavos*, Anagrama, 1989, Barcelona, p. 50. Moses Montefiore was an adviser and counsellor to Queen Victoria. He played an influential role in Europe, along with Adolphe Crémieux, the president of the Israelite Alliance.

[520] André Harris and Alain de Sédouy, *Juifs et Français*, Grasset, 1979, Poche, 1980, p. 63-65.

[521] Manès Sperber, *Être Juif*, Éd. Odile Jacob, 1994, p. 62.

At the beginning of the 20th century, the Austro-Hungarian Empire represented a stronghold in Europe for them. Indeed, the Jews had become the "kings of Vienna" and were at the forefront of banking, the press and the cultural world. Jewish artists, Jewish writers and Jewish musicians benefited from the ecstatic praise constantly heaped upon them by their journalist friends. There was a whole range of artists and writers in Vienna, each one more brilliant than the next. Michael Polack wrote in *Vienne 1900*: "There was Arthur Schnitzler, Hugo von Hofmannsthal, Leopold von Andrian, Richard Beer-Hofmann, Karl Kraus, Felix Salten and Theodor Herzl. Most of them came from the upper middle class, the gentry, even the aristocracy, and they shared certain values[522]."

In the Austrian capital one could come across the great Sigmund Freud, the writers Stefan Zweig and Arthur Schnitzler, the composers Gustav Mahler and Arnold Schönberg, and so on. They were all "perfectly integrated". So integrated that they were "more Austrian than Austrians themselves". The "queen of journalists", Françoise Giroud, naturally attracted by this Viennese society, took an interest in studying it: "Among the Emperor's subjects, the Jews of the Viennese bourgeoisie are perfectly integrated and the most faithful. It all began in 1867 with the incorporation into the constitution of freedom of religion and conscience, a sign of emancipation. Since then, the symbiosis has been going on, as in 15th century Spain. Since Jews had no chance of a career in the army or the civil service, they turned to the liberal professions and industry, and even had a strong presence in the financial aristocracy. Vienna's great liberal newspaper, the *Neue Freie Presse*, is owned by a Jewish family, the Benedikts. They are liberal and support the Emperor and the multinational state, because it is the guarantee of their security[523]."

This loyalty to the multinational empire was also mentioned by the philosopher Jacob-Leib Talmon: "The Jews were the only racial group in the Austro-Hungarian Empire that fully adhered to the Habsburgs' ideal of a multi-racial kingdom… They had every advantage in

---

[522] Michael Pollak, *Vienne 1900*, Folio Histoire, 1984, edition 1992, p. 14.

[523] Françoise Giroud, *Alma Mahler*, Robert Laffont, 1988, Presses Pocket 1989, p. 17.

remaining subjects of a multiracial and multinational Empire, which guaranteed the right of free speech to groups and entities of all kinds[524]."

In his biography of the writer Arthur Schnitzler, Jacques Le Rider corroborated these words: "The great majority of Viennese Jews had pinned their hopes on the metamorphosis of the monarchy into a democratic, pluralistic and multinational state… The Jewish subjects of the Habsburg monarchy have been particularly anxious to show their patriotism and loyalty to the emperor[525]."

Indeed, they are always very patriotic when they are at the helm. The famous writer Stefan Zweig wrote as follows: "Whoever wanted to do something new in Vienna could not do without the Jewish bourgeoisie; when once, during the anti-Semitic era, an attempt was made to found a so-called "national theatre", neither authors nor actors nor audience turned up; after a few months the "national theatre" failed miserably, and this example showed for the first time that nine-tenths of what the world celebrated as Viennese culture in the 19th century was a culture promoted, nurtured and even created by the Jewish community in Vienna[526]."

Françoise Giroud presented journalist Karl Kraus to us with admiration: he is an old, uncompromising social democratic polemicist, "who thrills audiences in his lectures by preaching purity and intransigence… Karl Krauss, set up as a judge, distributes anathemas, but those who loathe him and become enervated by his guilt cannot stop reading him: he is the king of Vienna[527]."

In her biography of Alma Mahler, Françoise Giroud had taken an interest in the wife of the composer Gustav Mahler, probably because she always surrounded herself with Jews. Her late husband, Franz Werfel, was a "genius" writer, as most Jews are. *The Forty Days of Musa Dagh* was "a beautifully inspired historical novel, Franz Werfel's first great success. An international success so resounding that the author's name would reach the ears of the Nobel Prize jury". Back in

---

[524] J.L.Talmon, *Destin d'Israël*, 1965, Calmann-Levy, 1967, p. 55.

[525] Jacques Le Rider, *Arthur Schnitzler*, Belin, 2003, p. 215.

[526] Stefan Zweig, *El mundo de ayer: memorias de un Europeo*, Acantilado, 44, Barcelona, p. 16.

[527] Françoise Giroud, *Alma Mahler*, Robert Laffont, 1988, Presses Pocket 1989, p. 64.

Vienna, "the Werfels inaugurate their twenty-eight-room house in Hohe Warte, which Alma has just bought. The crème de la crème of Vienna is present. Franz is now Austria's most famous author[528]."

Who was this Franz Werfel? "He is a typical Viennese, even if he was born in Prague, where his father owns a large glove factory". But Werfel was a convinced social democrat. "Sometimes he says: "How can I be happy while someone somewhere is suffering? He is a brilliant and inexhaustible talker… No one is more European and uniquely Viennese than he is". And it was this "typical Viennese", in November 1918, when Germany was defeated, who was haranguing the crowd in favour of the Bolshevik revolution: "Standing on the benches, he spent the day shouting to the rioters: "Raid the banks!", "Down with the capitalists[529]!"

The writer Arthur Schnitzler was indignant at the time against the mean-spirited recriminations of the anti-Semites. In June 1915, he declared bluntly: "They don't want to regard us as one of their own. They think I am not an Austrian like them… But I know very well that I am more in my country than these people. It is a well-known fact that the essence of Austria and Vienna is today felt and expressed more strongly by Jews than by anti-Semites".

Jacques Le Rider, in writing his biography of the writer, also failed to notice the paradox when, after stressing that Arthur Schnitzler was a "pure Viennese", he acknowledged a few pages later that his writings and plays were strongly anti-Austrian: "In January 1915, his play *The Call of Life (Der Ruf des Lebens)* was attacked as unpatriotic and anti-Austrian. The pillars of the Habsburg system, the Church, the army and the bureaucracy, did not seem worthy of consideration. Since *Lieutenant Gustel*, we know where we stand on the subject of "Schnitzler and the army". Clericalism and the Habsburg bureaucracy, fiercely depicted in *Professor Bernhardi*, had not risen in his esteem since the outbreak of the First World War[530]."

The "patriotism" of the Jewish intellectuals only really manifests itself when it is a matter of stirring up the people and the nation against

---

[528] Françoise Giroud, *Alma Mahler*, Robert Laffont, 1988, Presses Pocket, 1989, p. 168.

[529] Françoise Giroud, *Alma Mahler*, Robert Laffont, 1988, Presses Pocket, 1989, p. 150, 182, 157.

[530] Jacques Le Rider, *Arthur Schnitzler*, Belin, 2003, p. 222-225

another state, guilty of not giving the Jews the place they deserve. Their warmongering propaganda is then unbridled and unrestrained. In this case, the "patriotism" of the Austrian Jews was felt all the more strongly because their racial brethren in Russia were "persecuted", since they were not recognised as full Russians and had no possibility of dominating the country as they did in Austria. After the fall of the Tsarist regime in February 1917, the façade patriotic enthusiasm of German and Austrian Jews faded and naturally turned against their host country—an authoritarian empire and a Catholic monarchy—which offered fewer guarantees than the *Entente* countries and, with even more reason, than the new Bolshevik Russia. This was the famous "stab in the back".

Evidently, not all Viennese were gullible or had been fooled by the declarations of loyalty of those upstarts who had quickly taken the lead. There, as in France or elsewhere, anti-Semitism was widespread among the population. One of the leading Jewish writers of the time, the Englishman Israel Zangwill, painted an eloquent picture of the resentment of the Austrian population. In *Dreamers of the Ghetto* in 1998, he wrote bitterly: "Moses, Sinai, Palestine, Isaiah, Ezra, the Temple, the Christ, the Exile, the Ghettos, the martyrs, all this for the Austrian satirical press to make fun of nosy money changers and their opera glasses that need not hold[531]."

## *Dual ownership*

After several decades of 'perfectly successful' integration in republican France, some Jews were finally expressing their identity a little more openly. Thus Theo Klein, former president of the Representative Council of Jewish Institutions in France (CRIF), wrote in 2003: "I was born in France, I went to the municipal school, I express myself in French and participate spontaneously in French cultural life: I do my calculations in French, I dream in French, and just as I am naturally French, I am also Jewish", he wrote on page 94. This he wrote on page 94. But on page 99, Theo Klein revealed the following: "My attitude towards Israel has not changed: I am Israeli and I am happy to be Israeli. I participate from and for that history". He went on to explain: "A Jew is a man who has a common history with other Jews with whom,

---

[531] Israel Zangwill, *Rêveurs de ghetto, tome II*, 1898, Éd. Complexe, 2000, p. 293

despite their dispersion throughout the world, he maintains ties by virtue of that common history. Certainly, there are many ways of being a Jew. For me, it is a natural state that has never been questioned by anyone[532]."

In 2002, Elie Barnavi, Israel's then ambassador to France, wrote in his *Open Letter to the Jews of France* that the vast majority of French Jews "claim to have a strong attachment to the State of Israel". At the end of his book, on page 116, he encouraged the Jews of France to settle in Israel: "Come, join us, we need each other. Do not leave without hope of returning. We do not ask you to choose between one or the other identity, only to add ours to the one you already have, to which we understand that you are attached. By becoming Israeli, we are not asking you to stop being French[533]."

Similarly, Dominique Strauss-Kahn, a former minister and senior Socialist party official, declared on 13 May 2004 in France-Inter: "I believe that all Jews in the Diaspora and in France should help Israel, in fact, that is the main reason for Jews to have political responsibilities. Ultimately, through my functions and all the actions in my daily life I try to contribute my humble stone to the edification of Israel[534]."

In June 2006, Pierre Besnainou, president of the European Jewish Congress, clearly stated his position: "I have definitively settled the debate on dual loyalty: yes, I feel Franco-Israeli". He added: "European Jews today are fully credible and legitimate in their defence of Israel. We can afford to be the bridge between Israel and Europe… I consider that as a Jew we have a natural link with Israel… This dual membership puts us in the position of privileged interlocutors to foster dialogue… "But we know perfectly well what kind of "dialogue" M. Besnainou intended to engage in with the Palestinians and Iran. Pierre Besnainou continued: "It seems to me that it would be interesting and legitimate to grant Israeli nationality to Jews of the Diaspora who so wish, without them having to make their *alya*[535]. When we are in France, in Italy or elsewhere, we address the Jews saying: 'your' Prime Minister Ehoud Olmert, 'your' ambassador, 'your' president, why be uncomfortable

---

[532] Théo Klein, *Dieu n'était pas au rendez-vous*, Bayard, 2003, p. 101.

[533] Elie Barnavi, *Lettre ouverte aux juifs de France*, Stock, 2002, p. 116.

[534] Quoted in *Rivarol*, 27 October 2006.

[535] To make his *aliyah*: to settle in Israel.

with this issue? On the contrary, I think we should take it on board. If we are Israelis to others, why shouldn't the government recognise that affiliation for those Jews who want it? It is said that we are part of the same people, so why not make it official?"

This was already advocated by Guy Konopnicki in the 1980s: "Except in exceptional cases, within the framework of international agreements, it is not possible to have two nationalities. It is precisely in this respect that the generally accepted conception of national law is historically outdated: it no longer corresponds to the contemporary way of life[536]". As usual, we see how Jewish intellectuals only speak according to their own criteria and interests which they project on a universal plane.

But if we listen carefully to the historian Pierre Vidal-Naquet, dual allegiance could generate some kind of identity conflict, as he wrote in his *Memoirs*: "It is not by chance that in my scientific work the theme of splitting plays such an important role, for that is also how I live my Judaism[537]." The Chief Rabbi of France Joseph Sitruk expressed the same idea in the *Tribune juive* of October 2004: "I believe that all men are a little schizophrenic, especially the Jews".

In fact, it is precisely this ambivalence that is at the heart of the Jewish personality. Guy Sorman is originally from Poland: "I recuse myself as a Jewish intellectual. I don't feel that I belong to that category because Judaism is based on knowledge. I find it inappropriate to claim to be Jewish when knowledge is lost, as in my case… I only recognise myself as a French intellectual". But this is the concept of French identity according to Guy Sorman: "French, that is to say enriched in an extraordinary way by the crossbreeding that France has done and is doing… To be French is always to be multidimensional: one is at once Breton, Catholic and French, from the Cévennes, Protestant and French, or Polish, Jewish and French. No one is just French. If he only feels French, it is because he ignores his roots and his culture". His marriage to a "Norman and Angevin" Frenchwoman has not made him any less cosmopolitan. Once inside the square, he leaves the doors wide open to immigration: "Is it really so difficult to integrate a child from Sri Lanka or Algeria into the French nation through school? Of course the task is arduous, but no more so than making a Breton, an Auvergne or a Jew a

---

[536] Guy Konopnicki, *La Place de la nation*, Olivier Orban, 1983, p. 39.

[537] Pierre Vidal-Naquet, *Mémoires I, 1930-1955*. Seuil, p. 164

true Frenchman, as has been the case for several generations[538]." Guy Sorman is thus an "authentically French" intellectual, but one who thinks and reasons like an authentically Jewish intellectual, a tireless militant for the multicultural society.

In 1979, two journalists, André Harris and Alain de Sédouy, had conducted a series of interviews with various personalities in an attempt to understand the background to Jewish identity. Their book entitled *Jews and the French* revealed the paradoxes of Jewish discourse quite well.

The former chairman of Renault's board of directors, Pierre Dreyfus, was a Jew from Alsace, "the prototype of the integrated grand bourgeois". He declared, for example, on page 43: "I did not feel 99% French, but 100%". And on the following page he stated: "Although it is true that I did not receive any specifically Jewish education or culture, I always felt, throughout my life, in solidarity with the Jews, wherever they were unhappy". Mr. Dreyfus then went on to say that he was very concerned about the situation of Jews in Israel.

Jean-Pierre Bloch, whom we have already mentioned, was also "profoundly French", a "Frenchman like any other". He is an "integrated, honest Jew, with no possible contradictions". (pp. 63–65). On pages 71–72, he again declared his loyalty: "I protest against dual loyalty! I am a French citizen of Israelite confession... I feel deeply French. When I see patriotic sentiment being lost, I am outraged". But on the next page, he could not help himself and confessed: "Before, I used to say: 'I am a Frenchman of Jewish origin'". In reality, I have become a Jew again. I don't practise, but I go to synagogue on Yom Kippur".

Robert Munich is a general engineer in the air force. He is originally from Poland on his grandparents' side: "I feel more French than the French", he declared on page 75. And on page 250: "I am attached with every fibre of my body to Israel". He went on to explain why he continued to live in France: "I did not take this step because I believe that there is still a role to play for Jews in the Diaspora, especially in France... It is not easy to be a Jew. It's not the most comfortable way to

---

[538] Guy Sorman, *Le Bonheur français*, Fayard, 1995, p. 17-19. Daniel Cohn-Bendit declared: "What I like about France is its cosmopolitanism. The Blacks, the Arabs, the Jews. I love France, especially for that. (André Harris, Alain de Sédouy, *Juifs et Français*, Grasset, 1979, Poche, p. 188).

live. I am aware of that, but I accept it with pride". Finally he pointed out the main danger for the Jewish community: "If you want to live more comfortably, you can always escape, stop being Jewish: you change your surname, have an intermarriage and end up forgetting that you are Jewish." (page 252).

Annie Kriegel, an editorialist at *Le Figaro*, comes from a family of "very integrated French Jews", in her own words, and added with a certain sincerity that "paradoxically, however, I realise that although we were fully integrated, we only lived among ourselves... I can't remember, in my childhood, people coming to my house who were Christians. I had no problem with that. We didn't go to Christians' houses either[539]."

Henri Fiszbin is a former leader of the Paris federation of the communist party. On the state of Israel, he declared: "Although I feel very French, its inhabitants are my brothers". (page 226). Two pages later, he declared: "I feel deeply Jewish".

Emmanuel Rozencher is a physicist. The journalist asked him if of his two identities, the French one was the strongest within him. "No doubt about it. I am a republican in the style of the Third Republic: secular school, equality... "But then he confessed: "It bothers me to be so attached to Israel. But, even so, I detest the irrational... As long as I can stay in France, I will. I feel at home. But if the anti-Semitism were to become unbearable, we would go to America, not to Israel". (pages 257–260).

Journalist Ivan Levai has had a long media career. His parents had fled Budapest before the war. He was baptised at his mother's request and received no Jewish education. However, as a programme director at *Europe 1* radio, he had to deal with accusations during debates on the Israeli question: "At *Europe 1*, I had an incident one day. In 1968-69, I had invited two left-wing leaders, one from the Communist League and the other from another left-wing movement, *Long Live the Revolution*, and two others. Now, all four of them were Jewish. I didn't do it on purpose. That's just the way it was. Because one of the journalists of *Europe 1*—Fred Goldstein—who has since passed away and was a convinced Zionist, got very angry, creating a big incident because of that debate. He said to me: "I refuse to let four Jews come and fight in

---

[539] André Harris, A. de Sédouy, *Juifs et Français*, Grasset, 1979, Poche, p. 82-84.

front of a microphone...". "He even asked the rabbinate to put pressure on the management of the radio station to stop the programme. He was deeply shocked". Ivan Levai continued, "At the time, I was very angry with Fred Goldstein. I even remember saying to him: 'It is because of fanatics like you that anti-Semitism is reborn. Because I, here, am French! Being born a Jew is a mere curiosity, it's not on my identity card. It is you, Goldstein, who comes to remind me that I am a Jew, it is people like you who separate us from the others. I am perfectly integrated. Well today, even though I'm not an ultra-Zionist like him—in fact, he ended up moving to Israel—I wonder, when I read some of the emails I receive, if he wasn't right".

The journalist then asked him: "What are these emails like?" And Levai answered:"... You are not French, you have no right to defend this position... You give the floor to the anti-French... there are only Jews in the press... You shouldn't always invite people from the left to your programme... Give the floor to Mr. Le Pen... Obviously, Mr. Elleinstein whom you have invited is Jewish... And so are you", etc." All this did not prevent Ivan Levai from saying later on: "I feel French before I feel Jewish... Incredibly French, even. I like Israel, but not enough to go and live there[540]." After all these considerations, one can nevertheless think that Ivan Levai is above all Jewish, even, it must be said, "incredibly Jewish!".

Bernard-Henri Levy is also a very French intellectual who is well known outside our borders. This is what he explained to us after the publication of his book *La Ideologie française* in 1981, in which he dragged our greatest writers through the mud, accusing them of being impregnated with nauseating, more or less fascistic values. Levy defended himself beforehand against the accusations that ill-intentioned people might throw in his face: "It is in French and as a Frenchman, like any French philosopher, that I took the risk of carrying out this research on black France[541]."

Bernard-Henri Levy also wrote: "I am a Jew in France. I am a Jew and a Frenchman, a Jew who loves France". It was therefore clear, but the core of his identity remained monochromatic: "I am a Jew, I am a Jew with every fibre of my being. I am so with my lapses, I am so because

---

[540] André Harris, A. de Sédouy, *Juifs et Français*, Grasset, 1979, Poche, p. 268.

[541] Bernard-Henri Levy, *Questions de principe*, Grasset, 1986, p. 306; cf. *Les Espérances planetariennes*, p. 87 et seq.

of the dietary rules I have imposed on myself... I am so because of the way I write... I am a Jew by virtue of the invisible covenant that unites the Jews of the whole world... I am a Jew by virtue of my messianic patience[542]."

Elie Wiesel's "murdered Jewish poet", Paltiel Kossover, who was eventually arrested and executed along with other Jewish communist intellectuals in 1952, proclaimed the same thing. In his testament imagined by Elie Wiesel, Paltiel Kossover defended himself before the "citizen-magistrate" who was to condemn him: "I defend the Jewish cause, I defend it completely, totally; yes, I consider myself in solidarity with the Jews, wherever they are; yes, I am a Jewish nationalist in the historical, cultural and ethical sense; I am a Jew, above all, and I only regret not having affirmed it earlier and elsewhere[543]."

In the April 2003 issue of *Israel Magazine*, Dr. Itzhak Attia clarified it all: "Jewish solidarity is expressed as follows: '*Kol Israelarévim zé lazé*', each member of the people of Israel is the guarantor of another. This reality has numerous legal consequences and is above all the guarantee of our existence". Camille Marbo expressed the same in *Jewish Flames*, the "obligation of solidarity that Jews have towards one another[544]." This sense of belonging to the community was seen for example in the Austrian novelist Arthur Schnitzler, when he wrote in 1908 about the Vienna of Freud and Stefan Zweig: "I cannot deny that when a Jew behaves improperly or ridiculously in my presence, I feel so ashamed that I would like to disappear, to sink underground[545]."

"Each member of the brotherhood of Israel is responsible for all the others," wrote Israel Zangwill. This, by the way, did not prevent him at the end of his book from lamenting the condition of the Jews: "If a Christian does something wrong, the responsibility lies with the individual. If he is a Jew, it is to the nation. Why[546]?"

---

[542] Bernard-Henri Levy, *Récidives*, Grasset, 2004, p. 413–415.

[543] Elie Wiesel, *Le Testament d'un poète juif assassiné*, 1980, Point Seuil, 1995, p. 33.

[544] Camille Marbo, *Flammes juives*, 1936, Les Belles Lettres, 1999, p. 25, cf. *Psychanalyse du Judaïsme*, p. 86.

[545] Arthur Schnitzler, *Road to the Open Country*

[546] Israel Zangwill, *Rêveurs de ghetto*, 1898, Éd. Complexe, 1994, p. 17, 236

## THE JEWISH FANATICISM

Israel Zangwill (1864–1926) was born to parents who emigrated from Poland and Latvia to Whitechapel, a neighbourhood in London's East End where Jews from Russia and Central Europe crowded together. He was a prolific writer in the English language, known for his Jewish stories: *The Ghetto Children* (1892), *The King of Schnorrer* (1894), *Ghetto Tragedies* (1899), *Ghetto Comedies* (1907). We transcribe below a passage that demonstrates the strength of this sense of community. It is a dialogue between a father and his daughters who decide to tell him that one of them wants to marry a Christian.

"The father noticed that his daughters had a strange look on their faces:

—Do you have bad news? he exclaimed. Faces darkened, heads nodded.

—From Schnapsie? he shouted, startling himself.

—Sit down, sit down, he's not dead," said Lea contemptuously.

He sat down.

—What's going on? What's happening?

—He has made a commitment!

Those words in Lea's mouth sounded like a clarion call.

—Engaged! He gasped, imagining the worst.

—With a Christian! Daisy said brutally

He collapsed, pale and trembling. A tense silence fell over the room…

The daughters came to their senses and were now all talking at once…

-A horrible Christian freak…

It is a terrible disgrace for all of us[547]."

Let us recall the words of Golda Meir, Prime Minister of the State of Israel, which furthered this point: "Marrying a non-Jew is like joining the six million" exterminated Jews. In 1970, the Zionist Victor Tibika measured the degree of integration of Jews in the nations where he lived: "The Jew, except by conversion to another religion or the total abandonment of Judaism, is practically impossible to integrate[548]."

---

[547] Israel Zangwill, *Les Tragédies du Ghetto*, 1899, 1984, Éd.10/18, p. 98, 99

[548] Victor Tibika, *1967, Réveil et unité du peuple juif*, 1970, p. 34.

In *Tribe number 13*, published in 1976, Arthur Koestler gave some information about this religion and this "stubborn" people: "The Israelite religion, unlike Christianity, Islam and Buddhism, assumes membership of a historical nation, a chosen people. All Israelite festivals commemorate and celebrate events in national history: the departure from Egypt, the revolt of the Maccabees, the death of the oppressor Haman, the destruction of the Temple. The Old Testament is first and foremost a book of national history; although it gave the world monotheism, its creed is nevertheless tribal rather than universal. Every prayer, every rite, proclaims belonging to an ancient race, which automatically places the Jews outside the racial and historical past of the peoples among whom they live. The Israelite religion, as two thousand years of tragedies show, engenders their national and social segregation. It sets the Jew apart, invites him to be set apart. It automatically creates material and cultural ghettos[549]."

The novelist Isaac Bashevis Singer gave a very clear picture of this way of life in the ghettos. He described the life of these Jews in 17th century Poland. Christians were carefully kept away from the ghetto. "In the city itself there were very few Gentiles. These, on the Sabbath, did the necessary work forbidden to Jews. Among them were a bath attendant and a few others who lived in side streets, their houses surrounded by high palisades so that they would not flaunt their presence[550]."

## Duplicity

Jacques Lanzmann, a second-rate writer, demonstrated the duplicity so specific to Judaism. In his book *The Rat of America,* published in 1955, he told the story of a young Jew from Alsace who managed to slip through the Germans' netting during the Occupation. He was arrested one day by the militia and interned in Clermont-Ferrand: "In the afternoon, they came for me to take me to a German colonel.

—Fridman? Fridman? That's a Jewish surname... You're *Jewish*!

---

[549] Arthur Koestler, *La treizième Tribu*, C.Levy, 1976, Poche, 1978, p. 280-281. "All these Jewish practices are designed to separate us from the non-Jews; that is the fundamental idea". (Jean-Paul Elkann in André Harris, Alain de Sédouy, *Juifs et Français*, Grasset, 1979, Poche, p. 239).

[550] Isaac Bashevis Singer, *Satan in Goray*, PDF, Digital publisher Epublibre, German25, 2017, p. 23

—Colonel, I am not a *Jew*, I am an Alsatian.

I had repeated the lesson my father had taught me. I was Alsatian just as the Germans were Austrian at the end of the war.

—Colonel, I can give you proof of that.

I was terribly embarrassed and uncomfortable about having to pull out my glans in front of so many Germans. Not having been circumcised, I knew it was going to be convincing."

A few years later, in South America, the protagonist fell seriously ill. When a priest wanted to give him the last rites, he still found the strength to cry out: "I don't want to receive the last rites, I am not a Catholic, I am a Jew, a Jew... Leave me alone[551]!"

The novelist and businessman Paul-Loup Sulitzer left a similar testimony in his novel *Hannah*, in which he recounted the life of Helena Rubinstein, a Polish Jew who would go on to glory in the cosmetics industry. The beginning of the book recounted the abominable pogroms perpetrated in 1882 by the Cossacks against innocent Jews. This was Mendel Visoker. He was "the maddest of all the Jews in Poland... He is always on the road, seized by an imperious need to move": "Are you a Jew? —It depends on the day, Mendel replies in Russian. Not lately, no. I haven't been a Jew since recently, when I was asked to stop being one[552]." This reminds us of the words of the former health minister Bernard Kouchner, when he replied to his friend Cohn-Bendit: "I am a Jew when I want to be,[553] ", he said. In short, French by day and Jewish by night.

We have already seen in *Psychoanalysis of Judaism*, how Jews can, with an "astonishing plasticity", change their identity and put on surprising disguises: "Pure German, newly arrived Catholic Brazilian, old Indian Chief, moustachioed Cossack, Gangster turned Sister of Charity, Spanish or Dutch Catholic, Turkish Muslim Pacha, Polish aristocrat, Jacobin revolutionary, Buddhist monk or Chinese conspirator, the disguises of these Jews are always provisional and are no more than a mask which they will discard when the time comes."

---

[551] Jacques Lanzmann, *Le rat d'Amérique*, 1955, Pocket, 1977, p. 56, 142.

[552] Paul-Loup Sulitzer, *Hannah*, Stock, 1985, Poche, 1987, p. 58, 59, 42

[553] Daniel Cohn-Bendit, Bernard Kouchner, *Quand tu seras président*, Robert Laffont, 2004, p. 347.

Another example is Albert Cohen's novel *Nut Eater*. The protagonist Nut Eater is a forger who gives his children various names: "Such were the intimate of the three-year-old, whose official name was Lenin. The eldest, on the other hand, was called Mussolini. In this way, Slave Eater felt safe from any risk: in the event of social unrest, he would argue the appropriate name and, depending on the case, he would declare himself a convinced communist or a full-blown fascist[554]."

In *Dreamers of the Ghetto*, Israel Zangwill evoked the personality of Uriel da Costa (1585–1640), a tragic symbol of the Jewish condition. He came from a Portuguese Marrano family that had falsely converted to Catholicism and had gone into exile in Holland to return to the Jewish faith. Uriel da Costa then discovered that his new religion was very restrictive: "Astonishment gave way to dismay, dismay to indignation and horror when he realised in what a mess of rites he had entangled himself. He discovered that the Pentateuch itself, with its complex codex of six hundred and thirteen commandments, was only the cleared ground for a parasitic vegetation whose infinite ramifications reached into the innermost recesses of existence. How! Was it by this rabbinical fabrication that he had changed the majestic ceremonial of Catholicism?"

He criticised and refuted the authority of the rabbis: "None of their lessons refer to the immortality of the soul, their religion speaks only of the earth, it is very prosaic…". He had complained to Joseph that the rabbis cared little for immortality, but a more thorough search of the Pentateuch showed him that Moses himself had no regard for it either, and that he had never sought to bolster the morality of the moment with the terror of a posthumous tomorrow."

Finally, anathema was declared against him: "From that day on, no one, man, woman or child, dared to speak to him or walk beside him. Beggars refused his alms, hawkers spat in his path. His own mother and brother, now fully under the influence of their new Jewish environment, avoided being sullied by his presence and left him alone with his black servant in their house. Everyone avoided that great house as if it were marked by a cross pointing to the plague… He was considered dead and buried, forgotten… For years, he spoke to no one but his Moorish servant." In the end, he decided to make amends for his mistakes, recanting to the rabbis, "paying lip service to his ideals, laughing at them inside… In the peninsula he had disguised himself as a Christian;

---

[554] Albert Cohen, *Comeclavos*, Anagrama, 1989, Barcelona, p. 50.

he would also disguise himself as a Jew, a monkey among the ancient apes[555]."

This specifically Jewish duplicity was also observed in the 19th century "German" poet Heinrich Heine. While he ridiculed the patriotism of others and despite having converted to Christianity, Heine exalted the Jewish people. This made him say to Israel Zangwill: "I never returned to Judaism because I never left it. My baptism was just a dip. I signed H in all my books, never Heinrich, and I never stopped being "Harry" to my mother. Although the Jews hate me even more than the Christians, yet I have always supported my brothers[556]."

Joseph Goebbels, the Propaganda Minister of the Third Reich, was probably well aware of the nature of the Jews. When he was looking for a filmmaker to make a major film glorifying the National Socialist regime, he contacted Fritz Lang, who in 1926 had made *Metropolis*, the fabulous futuristic fresco that had fascinated the Fuhrer. To dissuade Goebbels from recruiting him as an official filmmaker, Fritz Lang claimed that his mother was Jewish, which was not true. Goebbels simply dismissed the objection by saying: "We decide what is Jewish.

Indeed, a Jew is recognised more by what he says, what he writes and what he does than by his name and surname, or his face. And since Jews are in the habit of hiding behind a mask, it is perfectly legitimate for the Goyim to define what is Jewish and what is not.

The thinker Albert Caraco expressed explicitly what seems to be deeply hidden within the Jewish spirit. His extremely heavy and twisted style is difficult to read. Nevertheless, we have been able to extract some eloquent passages from his aphorisms: "It behoves the Jews to lie, tirelessly, for if they did not lie, they would be dead... Lie, one day you will speak, the day when your choice will be the only one... Then you will lift the mask where the foreheads lie in the dust". (p.53,54). "Be guilty and liars, you will be invested with the kingdom and become Princes, you will be allowed to be here in this world the righteous that you are, masters in God's name of the whole universe." (p.54). They are "the people of the lie whose fable kills, they will lie to live... Without

---

[555] Israel Zangwill, *Rêveurs de ghetto*, 1898, Éd. Complexe, 1994, p. 102-115.

[556] Israel Zangwill, *Rêveurs de ghetto*, 1898, Éd. Complexe, 1994, p. 141. "Harry" instead of "Ari", lion in Hebrew.

their fable, the universe would be without hope, and before the Eternal, it justifies them." (p.65)

Caracus revealed one of the secrets of the Jews: "What saves them from death is to appear weak and guilty, as *long as they do not have the strength to overwhelm\**". And he insisted on this point: "Their strength is to appear weak"; "They never boast of their strength and always lament that they are weak, for it is by groaning that they will take the universe, which on the eve of triumph will still give them alms[557]."

Every Jew has therefore the imperative duty not to divulge the secrets of Israel: "He among the Jews who would lift the mask would cause unrest among the members of the sect" (p.52). (p.52). And then we can appreciate the literary style of Albert Caraco when he wrote: "We will gather you together, the time to annihilate you, and then we will remove the mask, the day when the children will tear down the grave of their fathers, in order to wound you in them. Forgive you? Good request! You will fight to the death and perish all the same if you do not fight the battle". (p.94) Finally, Caracus promised us great times of rejoicing and celebration when the Jews will have established their absolute domination: "Their innocence will do more harm than the ten plagues of Egypt, the fire of the heavens will be in their hands and the earth under their steps. Doubt not, the times are near, and near is the Salvation you fear more than death, nothingness and the devil[558]." Albert Caraco probably committed suicide too soon.

Such reckless revelations are evidently exceptional in Jewish literature. Following an old habit, other Jewish intellectuals have projected their own penchant for dissimulation onto others. The novelist Philip Roth wrote: 'Doctrinally speaking, dissimulation is part of Islamic culture; and the permission of dissimulation is widespread. Within this culture no one expects you to express yourself in terms that might do you harm, nor, of course, to be frank and sincere. You would be taken for a fool if you did. People say one thing, take one position in public, and then inside they are completely different, and in private they act very differently. They have an expression that applies to the case: "shifting sands", *ramál mutaharrika*... Dissimulation, two-facedness, secrecy...

---

[557] Albert Caraco, *Apologie d'Israël*, 1957, L'Age d'homme, 2004, p. 180, 186, 181.

\* *Tant qu'ils n'ont pas la force de raison garder*" in French in the original text.

[558] Albert Caraco, *Apologie d'Israël*, 1957, L'Âge d'homme, 2004, p. 100.

These are all things that… they hold in high regard. They are not of the opinion that people need to know what they really keep in their heads. In that they are very different from the Jews[559]… "Indeed, Jews are sincere, frank and honest. In fact, they have been known for that for centuries.

---

[559] Philip Roth, *Operación Shylock*, Debolsillo, Editorial Mondadori, 2005, Barcelona, p. 167.

# PART THREE

## PSYCHOPATHOLOGY OF JUDAISM

### Paradise Mombassa

In 22 November 2002, the *Paradise Mombasa* Hotel, an Israeli luxury hotel on the Kenyan coast, was attacked by a terrorist group affiliated with the Islamic group Al Qaeda. The resort had been built for the Israeli tourist market. The hotel reopened in 2005, but the new management is now trying to work with the European market in order to turn the page and erase the bad memories left by the Israeli clients on the local population. We have summarised here a translation of an article published in Hebrew on 14 October 2005 in the daily *Maariv*, the second largest newspaper[560] in Israel.

In the late 1990s, two Israelis, Yeuda Sulami and Itzik Mamman, came up with the idea of building a hotel on the Kenyan coast, facing the sea, and selling tour packages complete with flight, residence, activities and local adventures. The resort opened in 2001, was fully *kosher* and had its own synagogue. It was immediately very successful and soon 250 Israelis were landing each week at Mombassa airport. Business was booming for the owners, but the enthusiasm of the domestic staff quickly waned.

Especially the women in the entertainment team, who have a rather unpleasant memory of the holiday concept offered by *Mombassa Paradise*. Dorothy Maly, a dancer, recounted how once a week, on the day the clients arrived, five of them were taken to Mombassa airport: "We sang *Jambo, Jambo*! (Hello, Hello!) and *Evenu Shalom Aleichem*. The local Kenyans looked at us as if we had come out of the madhouse, but the Israelis were delighted. They loved the noise. When we got to the hotel, we started singing and shouting again. The manager ordered the girls not to leave the dance floor until the last of the guests left. If a

---

[560] www.makorrishon.co.il/nrg/online/1/ART/995/971.html

guest decided not to sleep, we had to stay with him until he went to bed. We had to make noise almost 24 hours a day. When we took a break, the manager would come and shout at us: "What's wrong with you, are you asleep? I'm going to deduct it from your salary, hurry up…"".

Rahima Raymond, a masseuse, said: "We were asked to stay with the guests until late at night. We had to go out with them, talk to them and entertain them. Sulami made it clear to us that we had to make the guests happy all the time. We used to dance with the men in the nightclubs so that they wouldn't be lonely. If we didn't do what they wanted, they would complain to the management: why don't the entertainment staff want to go out with us? We want to see the African night. They didn't care that we had families waiting in our homes. Of course they didn't pay us overtime. The next day, when they were still asleep in their rooms, we had to start the day again at eight in the morning. The motto 'the customer is always right' was literally applied".

One of the cooks, Josef Katan, also recalled: "They could take me out of the kitchen and tell me that now the guests wanted to have a good time and I had to go out with them. How could I bake biscuits and dance with them at the same time? The whole hotel was an entertainment team. The kitchen staff were part of the entertainment team, as were the reception staff, the gardeners and so on". He added: "There were, for example, religious Jews who could not sign the room service receipts from Friday to Saturday, the Sabbath day. We would write down their room numbers and wait until Sunday to bill them. After the Sabbath, some refused to pay. They would say: "You made it up, you forged my signature". In the end, the management always believed them and forced us to pay. I never believed that people could act like that".

Dorothy Maly further recounted that "to maintain "the true African spirit", the workers were forced to wear very light clothing. Unlike the other hotels, where the men served in uniform, the male staff were half-naked and barefoot. Women were asked to tie a small cloth around their chest and pubic area. Even when it was cool, we were not allowed to wear anything to cover ourselves. Sulami wanted us to look 'authentic'."

*Paradise Mombassa* is situated 8 kilometres from the main road. The dirt road leading to the hotel runs through a wild savannah, so the problem of transporting the hotel staff had to be solved. So transport was organised for the forty employees to the luxury resort in a transport truck for goods and animals. "It was a closed truck with no seats. People were packed so tightly that the back doors of the truck had to be left open. We felt like animals. Sometimes the truck almost ran out of oxygen, but we knew that if we complained we would have to stay in the hotel and not go home to be with our families. So we didn't say anything."

Even for meals, the employees had to make do as best they could. Saline Achling, a young waitress at the hotel, explained the manager's solution: "Sometimes Sulami was kind enough to let us eat the guests' leftovers. Our luck was that their eyes were bigger than their stomachs. They would go to the buffet and fill their plates to the top with salad and huge chunks of meat. They would touch the food and leave three quarters of it on the plates."

"*Akol kalul*', they said: 'all inclusive'. That was the philosophy of the resort. All hotel services were included in the holiday package marketed in Israel. The employees quickly understood what those words meant to Israelis. All day long, you could hear guests in the hotel shouting "*Akol kalul*"," said Saline Achling. There were those who grabbed my arm and shouted '*Akol kalul*' in my face. Even on the beach they were shouting "all inclusive, all inclusive" at people. I would ask them, "What is *Akol kalul*?" and they would reply, "All inclusive, even you", referring to me. I told them that I didn't belong to Sulami. The hotel belongs to him, but not me. And I thought to myself, "My God, will they behave the same way in their own countries?

Naturally, none of the guests forgot their right to a free massage once a day: "The first thing the men did when they arrived from the airport, even before taking their suitcases to their rooms, was to run to the massage room. They would walk into the hotel with their eyes open and ask with their suitcases on top of them, 'Where is the massage room? I took it upon myself to set up a schedule, as there was a competition among the men to be the first."

Dorothy Maly, the dancer, also worked in the massage room: "My job was to tell them, 'I'm Dorothy and I'm a masseuse at the hotel'. No sooner had I uttered this phrase than they started shouting "massage, massage!" Most of them could not speak English. They said "Ai Kam Nao" (I come now). A tourist from another country would have waited for two weeks, but in *Paradise*, they demanded this service immediately, sometimes even before breakfast. They would come and say, "I come for *akol kalul* massage. I want *harpaya*" (ejaculation). When I asked what "*harpaya*" meant, they replied, "not just *harpaya*, we want "all inclusive", "full sex", "full sexual intercourse". I told them that we were not in the habit of doing that, but then they answered: "Listen to me, women are also included! The director promised us in the Tel Aviv office that it was *akol kalul*. Sometimes, one of the managers would suggest that we give in to the whims of the clients".

Katherine Kaha, another masseuse, revealed her experience: "I would start giving the massage, and then the man would say, 'do it all over your body, you have to do it'. If I hadn't done what he wanted, he would have reported me to the management. I didn't like it, but I did it. In the end I got a dollar, sometimes two dollars. I felt terrible. I felt dirty."

An Israeli guest who used to visit the hotel from time to time gave the following testimony: "There were always problems with the massage. They took advantage of the massage to abuse the girls to the limit. It was pitiful. There were some groups that embarrassed me and I avoided being with them. They were so arrogant. They would come and feel like they owned everything, they thought they could do whatever they wanted or whatever came into their heads."

Rahima said: "One of the Israelis once said to me: 'You know I was with a little girl last night, she was only 13 years old. I slept with her, fucked her and gave her five dollars because she didn't even have money for clothes". I said, "She could be the age of your granddaughter. She didn't answer. "Here, in Africa, it is not customary after being with a girl to tell everyone. But the Israelis didn't hide anything and in the morning in the restaurant they told each other the details of the night: "Ah, I went with her, I fucked her all night long, over and over again, and I only paid one dollar"; "African women are very cheap and good"; "*Mechona tova, mechona tova*" (good machine, good machine). We understood perfectly what they were saying. When the first group of Israelis arrived, I thought the next group would probably be different. But no, it was exactly the same. Sometimes they would order food for the room, and when the girl came in, they would try to grab her and grope her. The waitresses were afraid and didn't want to go with the food to the rooms anymore. With me it was different, I made myself respected. Then they called me "big ass". For me that was better than being a sex slave.

Married men also took advantage of the girls in the hotel. I saw one of them say to his wife, "go to the dining room, I'll be over there", and disappear until the next day. We witnessed the wife shouting at her husband at breakfast. Once a man replied to his wife: "Women in Kenya are wonderful, they have such a little hole, so soft, and you have such a big, stupid hole!" "All this in the dining room, in public!" In cases like this, the rabbi would be called in to try to calm things down. There were times when the men would sit in the dining room while outside were donkeys from the hotel chasing each other for sex. When the male diners noticed this, they would stand up shouting and cheering the donkeys on: Good! Good! Forward, back! Come on, like this! "Once someone came to me and said in front of everybody: "I'm going to take my Viagra pills, and after that I'll have power, power to fuck. Power to fuck. What's your name by the way? "Rahima." OK, Rahima. I want to fuck you today! Another time, a client asked me: "Do you know a girl from the entertainment team called Charlie?" I went to the disco with her, I fucked her, but she was no good. I wanted to give her ten dollars, but I only gave her one dollar. I was screaming like crazy, when then little Charlie came in. He pointed at her and yelled, "There she is, that's her."

This prompted Karen Tiglo, a cleaning lady, to say: "We didn't know whether the Israeli guests were animals or people". Stela Matawa, a waitress, said: "Once a man came up to me and hit on me. Because I didn't agree, the next day in the dining room I heard him shouting to the others: 'That girl is no good, she's a shit, leave her alone, I invited her to the room and she was a nullity'".

Catherine Blunt had a traumatic experience with a 70-year-old Israeli guest who decided he was in love with her. "I didn't like him at all. We went to a disco together. I thought I was just accompanying him to relieve his boredom. On the way back, he and the taxi driver set me up. Instead of going back to the hotel, we arrived at a place where they rented rooms for one night. In the room he tried to force me to sleep with him, but I could not. When we got back to the hotel, he shouted at me that he never wanted to see me again, and that the next day he would report me to the manager because I had wasted his money. The manager suspended me for two weeks after the report[561]."

But the hotel management also went too far with the women. According to some of the female employees, Israeli managers not only failed to

---

[561] In October 2006, we learned that Israeli President Moshe Katzav was finally convicted of the rapes of his former secretary and a female employee. Married with five children, Moshe Katzav was also accused of sexual harassment of five other women, indecent acts, eavesdropping, obstruction of justice and prevarication. He claimed he was innocent and the victim of a "plot": "The press is conducting a witch-hunt against me and a public lynching," he told a military radio programme on 21 September 2006. "There is a plot that has been hatched against me for a long time by a gang of criminals," he denounced, but refused to make public the identity of the perpetrators of the plot.

condemn such behaviour, but some even participated in such abuse. "One of the hotel executives liked massages. He would say: 'Do it to me here and like this', just like with the clients. It had to be done... Another manager would take the women from the entertainment team to the room and say, 'I'm the manager, so no one will ask you where you're going'. I had to accept even though it was very bad. The next day, when I saw him in the hotel, he would walk past me without acknowledging me. After the entertainment team's show, a dancer would always disappear into one of the executives' rooms. At first, the girls thought it might have been a reprimand because the dance had been unsuccessful, but in the room they understood that the intentions were completely different."

Every week, on the day of the departure of the Israeli clients, when they were ready and boarding the bus to the airport, the bell would ring and the head of the entertainment team would become hysterical: "Get ready, the guests are leaving! He would order the women to gather at the exit gate and chase the bus of crying guests. They had to hit the bus with their eyes full of tears and shout: "Don't go, we love you, please come back, stay!" These manifestations of love were part of the all-inclusive tourist package and were supposed to leave the Israeli clients with unforgettable memories of their holiday.

Rahima recalled those scenes: "If you didn't cry you could lose your job. We were told to think of something really sad that had happened to us to really cry. But I didn't cry. Catherine Khaa confessed, "I didn't cry. How could I? I didn't like them. In fact, I hated them.

"It was a strange experience, says Saline Achling, the hotel's massage parlour manager, laughing and a little embarrassed. We were told to chase the bus, singing and crying to let the customers know that we loved them and wanted them to come back. I remember running after the bus like a madwoman, beating the bus with my fists and shouting at the customers: "Why are you leaving us, we miss you, we love you! The Israelis were watching us from the windows. Some were videotaping us.

## *Sex maniacs*

In 1981, Dr. Georges Valensin published an interesting study on *Jewish sexual life,* which gives a better understanding of the behaviour of these Israeli tourists, and of Jews in general. "Born into the important Jewish community of Algiers", Georges Valensin was a doctor of medicine at the university of Algiers. "He is generally regarded as one of the pioneers of modern sexuality studies and has published fifteen books on the subject." In the preamble to his work, the author explained that he "comes from old Spanish Sephardic families… through his father Levi Valensin and his mother Aboulker", adding further that "throughout my research I have tried to abstract from my origins and avoid any value judgements. Only the facts on the record count, even if some anti-Semites and prosemites use them to argue according to their wishes".

These were his explanations for the lack of composure and disinhibition of the Jews: "The young Jew, at the age of ten, was already made aware of the nature of sexual relations by reading the Talmud, which was very important to him if, as was often the case, his marriage was early. In that reading he would find very racy sexual stories; stories with many notes and passionate comments that helped him to talk freely about sexuality." Dr Valensin continued: "They willingly discuss their sexual problems with the rabbi, although the rabbi is asked not to be alone with a female counsellor or at least to be accompanied by his wife or a secretary. Many rabbis are trained as sex counsellors". Another sexologist, Kinsey, also explained how he had "been struck by the freedom of speech in sexual matters among young American Jews." Kinsey wrote: "Jews talk about sexual matters with much less reserve than other men, and that is probably why the legend has spread that they were very sexually active[562]."

But in reality, explained Dr. Valensin, "the abundance of detail provided in Kinsey's surveys has little to do with his actual activity[563]." Indeed, at the beginning of his book he presented the peculiarities of the conjugal life of Jews all over the world, especially the obligation of continence due to the "impure" state of women during their rules: "The observance of ritual purity has contributed much to the traditional continence of the Jews of old and some of today. In addition to the two weeks of abstinence from the day before the period until the ritual bath, there were further setbacks that could lengthen marital abstinence… The husband had to take his wife at her word; but she could take advantage of this and pretend that her period was imminent or that a red

---

[562] A.Kinsey, *Le Comportement sexuel de l'homme*, Éd. Du Pavois, Paris, 1950, p.617.

[563] Georges Valensin, *La Vie sexuelle juive*, Éditions philosophiques, 1981, p. 170.

spot had appeared suspiciously. Fickle menstruation could prevent the days of female purity from coinciding with the days of marital availability; but, above all, too close menstruation further reduced the possibility of relations: with a female cycle of three weeks, only six or seven days a month were free".

Dr. Valensin added: "Continence was also favoured by prudery... Maimonides praised Aristotle for teaching that sexual needs were shameful[564]. In the 15th century, Solomon Duran and other rabbis were proud that "the Jewish nation was the poorest of all in the number of fornicators[565]". Today, some of that Jewish continence still remains. According to Kinsey, the sexual activity of practising Jews is markedly lower than that of practising Catholics or Protestants[566]. A Talmudist rabbi wrote: "There is a member of man that is numb when he is hungry and insatiable when he is fed[567]". Practising Jews who are subjected to various sexual restrictions become accustomed to it and have less desire; their continence is easier".

Other factors specific to the Jewish condition contribute to this continence, explained Georges Valensin: "A woman often chosen among relatives is considered more like a sister or a mother, so that the chances of inspiring a husband are less than those of a foreigner, and being moreover that Jewish anguish does not predispose to great amorous emotions... The overly severe continence of many Jews of yesteryear and even today has resulted in early impotence. According to Stekel, a pioneer of Viennese sexology, impotence was at the beginning of the century a real social disease among Russian and Galician* Jews, all extreme practitioners: "I have often made this observation and it has been confirmed by several colleagues[568]". Reading several American Jewish novelists shows that they are more concerned than Aryan writers with problems of impotence; the interest they show in perverse or unbridled sexuality could be the result of the

---

[564] Maimonides, in *Encyclopedia Judaïca*, Jérusalem, 1971, volume VIII, p. 49.

[565] Rab. Borowitz, *Choosing a sex ethic*, New York, 1974, p. 96.

[566] A. Kinsey, *Le Comportement sexuel de l'homme*, Éd. Du Pavois, Paris, 1950, p. 595.

[567] M. Schvab, *Le Talmud de Jérusalem*, vol. I, p.42 of

* From Polish-Ukrainian Galicia

[568] Stekel, *L'Homme impuissant*, Gallimard, 1957, p. 246.

transference onto their heroes of their own desires which they are unable to satisfy". Dr. Valensin went on to explain: "Another factor in the impotence of Jews is the frequency of diabetes, which they suffer from, so that it has come to be called a Jewish disease. At the Israelite hospital on Long Island in New York, of the 359 Jews who came for consultations for sexual deficiencies, high sugar levels were found in a surprisingly high number of husbands[569]."

Finally, the chapter concluded: "We know that the volume of the penis increases with frequent sexual intercourse. L. Strominger was for forty years head of a urology department in Bucharest and noted that during the 1914–1918 war, examinations of many mobilised and civilian Jews had led him to the conclusion that their cocks were smaller than normal in volume; all these Romanian Jews practised a fervent Judaism[570]".

Let us recall here that the famous surgeon specialising in penis enlargement is the Jewish doctor Melvyn Rosenstein. The *Metroactive newspaper* of 8 February 1996 reported that he had been in trouble with the American courts. His licence had been revoked by the California Medical Board due to several lawsuits from his patients whose operations had gone wrong. With his 56 million dollars pocketed in two years, the famous "Dr Dick" had a good financial cushion for the rest of his life.

There is another interesting testimony that confirms the prevalence of sexual imbalance in the Jewish community. It is Xaviera Hollander's autobiographical book, *La Alegre Madam*, published in 1972, and whose original title is *The Happy Hooker*. It was a legendary *best-seller* of the 1970s, with 17 million copies sold worldwide. It is the story of the life of a 35-year-old woman who was for some time the manager of the most famous brothel in the United States. An only child, her mother was a beautiful "ash blonde of Germanic and French descent". Her father was a Dutch Jew, a doctor and owner of a large hospital in Indonesia before he lost everything with the arrival of the Japanese during the Second World War.

The family lived in Amsterdam. "In my house, sex was seen as something natural and beautiful, and I could often see my parents, semi

---

[569] S. Chumacher and C. Lloyd, Congrès international de sexologie, Paris, 1974.

[570] Georges Valensin, *La Vie sexuelle juive*, Éditions philosophiques, 1981, p. 31-33.

or fully naked, walking around the house". While still a teenager, the young girl was already very open sexually and used to seduce men: "My first attempt was with a brother of my mother's, my favourite uncle, who, as a child had adored me with a paternal love, but whose affection changed to a more carnal form, when I became a teenager." Another uncle's son, a young German who had come to visit his family and get to know Holland, was to be her "second family love affair".

Xaviera Hollander felt Jewish, probably in part because of the anti-Semitic repression suffered by her parents during the Japanese occupation of Indonesia. This is how she described one of her countless lovers. His name was Carl; he was an American who "did everything in his power to hide his Jewish background. He was even a member of the supposedly anti-Semitic New York Athletic Club, and once, when he took me to watch a high jump competition, he made me hide my Star of David". Hide it under your jumper," he murmured, "and they'll never know you're Jewish, because you don't look it. Other times, when we had guests over for lunch, he would make me hide one of the things I loved most, a beautiful copper menorah that my family had given me and which was the only thing I owned that had sentimental value to me, in this country[571]."

She later met Pearl Greenberg. It was she who persuaded her to use her insatiable sexual appetite and turn to prostitution. Xaviera proved her worth with "a fat, ugly Jewish man" and Pearl Greenberg was thrilled: "Pearl was so excited by the discovery that she spoke to everyone in Manhattan on the phone, announcing: 'I have this lovely Jewish girl* from Holland who loves sex and will do anything you want'. So this was the beginning of a pleasant if not very productive relationship with Pearl. She was what one knows as a *mensh* in Yiddish, kind-hearted, always in a good mood, spontaneous and tender[572]."

"I love to seduce boys who are seventeen or nineteen at the most. Most of the boys go to Puerto Rico with their fathers, so I had to approach them as if I were the maternal type, so as not to arouse suspicion… If I may be allowed not to be modest for a minute, I can say that I estimate

---

[571] Xaviera Hollander, *La Alegre Madame*, 1972, Editorial Grijalbo, México DF, p. 19, 22, 28, 58, 59

* *Yiddish medel* in the original version.

[572] Xaviera Hollander, *La Alegre Madame*, 1972, Editorial Grijalbo, Mexico DF, p. 68.

that twenty-five percent of the young Jews who were on holiday in Puerto Rico between February and April 1970 learned the art of love with me." After that holiday he decided to strike out on his own. "In the summer of 1970 I decided that I would not only be a Madame, but the best Madame in New York[573]."

From then on Xaviera Hollander started recruiting girls. The police, of course, kept after her, and she had to pay large sums in bail and increasingly heavy fines, in addition to lawyers' fees and bribes. Problems with clients also occurred: "A neighbour might report you for causing a disturbance; so might a rival Madame, in order to lessen competition; and sometimes it is a dissatisfied customer who, by way of revenge, calls the police. I think this is what happened the second time I was arrested. A lunatic named Nicky, whom I threw out of my house for being too much of a nuisance with the girls and bothering the other customers, went to the police station and filled out a complaint form.

—They have a house of prostitution there and they discriminate against Jewish people," he told them.

The truth is that I had removed him from my house because of his lunatic behaviour, but in no way because he was a lunatic Jew. But as a consequence the police got involved in the financial side of my business... and they told the judge that I was the most important Madame operating in New York City. It looked like things were going very badly at first, but my lawyer got the charge reduced to a misdemeanour, and when it was all over, I was able to get off with only a hundred-dollar fine. Plus, of course, a hefty legal fee[574]."

"Another pathetic case is that of German George, who needs to be cruelly degraded in order to get relief. He is a forty-five-year-old businessman, very rich... I met German George when he called at the house where I worked before I became Madame, requesting the services of a girl, who spoke fluent German, was reasonably strong and could torture a man. The Madame assured him that I was tailor-made for the act, and sent me to her flat in a luxurious high-rise on East Fiftieth Street. German George, after politely greeting me at the door, wanted to get

---

[573] Xaviera Hollander, *La Alegre Madame*, 1972, Editorial Grijalbo, Mexico DF, p. 124, 138

[574] Xaviera Hollander, *La Alegre Madame*, 1972, Editorial Grijalbo, Mexico DF, p. 107, 108

straight to the point, and the first thing he did, was to lead me to a locked wardrobe in the entrance hallway.

The man, pale and thin, peeped through the keyhole, and from the way he acted, I thought he kept the crown jewels in it. But when he opened the wardrobe door with a majestic gesture, I saw that it contained nothing except six or seven original S.S. mackintoshes…

The man asked me to undress, and he put one of the mackintoshes over my naked body and took out an imitation of the truncheon used by the S.S. "Don't forget to put on your belt" he reminded me as he put a swastika on my arm and handed me a toy gun. Don't forget to put on your belt" he reminded me as he put a swastika on my arm and handed me a toy gun. The scene continued as I left the room, while he lay on his bed naked with his head towards the closed door.

Outside the door I had to beat with my fists and shout in German: "It's the Gestapo! Open the door at once!"

But nobody answered. So she kicked open the door and stormed in, finding him lying there with his penis in his hand. Herr Cohen," she would order him in a threatening voice.

"No, no, I am Mr Smith," he said with a grimace, pretending to tremble.

"Don't lie to me, you're a Jew, Verdammte Jude, Schweinhund". Bam, bam, I punch him in the face.

Little German George shudders, gets an erection and is very excited. He starts badmouthing the "damned Jews" and how much he wants every last one of them to get what they deserve.

"Shut up, Jew!", I order him, and to make sure he obeys me, I sit on his face and force him to eat me. Then I get angry because he's not doing it right, and taking off my belt I pound him until he's about to climax, but at that moment he asks me to stop the action.

"Let's stop and start again," he says. So we repeat the scene again, and the third time, while I'm pounding him, Germán George ejaculates.

The poor man is happy and pleased to pay me, but these things make me sad, because I am Jewish too; and even though I was just a little baby during World War II, I hate to be confronted with situations like this.

Another depraved man, whose weakness comes from war, is a rabbi who can only do it with non-Jewish girls, even after they have painted his whole body with swastikas[575]."

## *Violations in psychiatry*

This predisposition towards sex must have been reflected in the large number of Jewish sexologists, and this "over-representation" was naturally also apparent in the professions of psychiatry and psychoanalysis. The following riddle is well known: "What is the difference between a small Jewish carver and a psychoanalyst? Answer: A generation". It is precisely these professions that are the ones that are regularly the subject of discussion in cases of rape of patients. The "Citizens' Commission for Human Rights" published a very strong report on the subject, entitled *Rape in psychiatry*[576]. A search on the internet allows one to determine that this "Commission" was a structure that depended on the famous Church of Scientology. Whatever one may think of this sect, the information gathered by this commission helps to understand why it is the target of attacks by the media mafia.

The actions taken by the US Medical Committee against 761 doctors for sexual assaults committed between 1981 and 1996 show a remarkable preponderance of the psychiatric and paedopsychiatric branch. Although they account for only 6% of physicians in the USA, they represent 28% of those convicted of sexual offences. Therefore, between 10 and 25% of mental health professionals are said to have sexually abused their patients. According to 1998 figures from the American Psychological Association, a hundred psychologists lose their licence to practise each year for "sexual misconduct". However, this disallowance to practice is often only temporary, and the American Psychological Association itself only expelled ten members, who can in any case continue to practice without a licence with their APA membership card. Psychiatrists, in fact, do not speak of rape, but of "sexual relations", and the board of the order regulating the profession treats the cases as simple "professional misconduct".

---

[575] Xaviera Hollander, *La Alegre Madame*, 1972, Editorial Grijalbo, Mexico DF, p. 196-197.

[576] http://h11.protectedsite.net/uploads/fr/FRE%20-%20rape.pdf

A British study showed that 25% of psychotherapists reported having had patients who had already had sexual relations with another therapist[577]. Dr. Roger Kahn's book gave higher figures for the United States: Although only 10% of psychiatrists admitted to having sexually abused their patients, 65% said that their new patients reported having been sexually abused by their former psychiatrist. Recall that "the profession is a largely Jewish monopoly", as Roger Kahn himself wrote[578]. The figures therefore show that a woman is "statistically more likely to be raped on a psychiatrist's couch than while *jogging* in New York's Central Park".

According to 1986 US research on psychiatrist-patient sex, 73% of psychiatrists who admitted to having sex with their patients claimed to have done so in the name of "love" or "pleasure"; 19% claimed it was to "increase the patient's self-esteem". Other excuses included "loss of control", impulsivity, "valuing the therapist" and "personal needs[579]". In short, psychiatrists liberate their patients by teaching them to overcome their sexual dysfunctions and reach orgasm. Some psychiatrists thus claim to decriminalise their crimes, but these acts "will never be truly therapeutic".

There is the example of Australian psychiatrist Paul Stenberg, who, according to an article in the *Courier Mail* in April 2002, said: The "therapy" he proposed to his patients consisted of taking them to a health spa weight training centre to have sex. He also suggested the use of heroin. In 2000, Stenberg voluntarily surrendered his licence, promising the medical council that he would never practise again. But only two years later, Stenberg was once again making headlines for further abuse of patients. "Anne" had asked for his help in trying to forget the years of sexual violence her father had inflicted on her and her sister. While her mother kept these horrors as a "family secret", Anne sought help in order to "master her memories". Paul Stenberg's therapeutic methods probably did nothing to appease her soul.

The justifications are always the same: "sex is a legitimate form of treatment". In 2001, Australian psychiatrist Clarence Alexander Gluskie, from Sydney, was struck off the medical register for having sex with a patient. He had, however, received the government's highest

---

[577] Doctor Bill médicare "for sex", *The Daily Telegraph-Mirror*, 8 July 1993

[578] Roger Kahn, *The Passionate People*, William Morris, Inc., 1968, p. 53.

[579] *American Journal of Psychiatry*, vol. 143, September 1986, p. 1128.

honour, the Order of Australia, in 1999. Gluskie had, as he put it, taken on the "role of father" during a woman's therapy sessions, encouraging her to regress to the state of childhood. In this way, the little girl she had become came to sit on his lap. According to him, children are often attracted to their parents. Gluskie claimed that "genital stimulation releases chemicals in the brain that promote bonding between children and adults".

APA psychiatrist Richard Simons offered an explanation for these outrages. According to him, "it is the patients who unconsciously provoke the therapists, either to abandon them or to mistreat them sadistically". These patients often suffer from "masochistic personality disorders".

Another example was this story from Missouri on 11 February 1998: psychiatrist William Cone was sentenced to 133 years in prison for sexually abusing several patients. Cone convinced them that they had to "revive their relationship with their parents", which required them to have sex with him. To convince them, he had prescribed them large quantities of psychotropic drugs, making them highly addicted. The prosecutor stated at his trial: "He is a predator. These people came to him for treatment and they were outraged. I have never seen a defendant cause so much pain and injury to so many people." One of his former patients testified, "I was incredibly attached to him. I was dependent on him. He told me, 'psychiatry works best when it is kept secret.' He forbade me to tell anyone about these sexual relationships and warned me that I couldn't trust anyone."

All the psychiatrists involved claimed that their patient consented. However, about 14% of patients abused by their therapist attempt suicide and 1% succeed. But the reality is that few patients dare to report it: only 1% of victims report the abuse they have suffered. Thousands of "psychiatric" patients have committed suicide and thousands more have been hospitalised as a result of the harm they have suffered. Thanks to the courage and determination of women who have come forward, some of these psychiatrist-violators have finally been brought to justice.

The jewwatch.com website has compiled a number of such cases in the US press. We see that abuse does not only affect the psychiatric professions. The *Arizona Republic* of 26 October 2001 reported that Dr. Brian Finkel, 51, owner of the Metro Phoenix clinic and an abortion specialist, had been jailed after complaints from some forty patients.

They accused him of having performed cunnilingus on them during consultations and even during abortions.

The *Detroit Now News* of 20 February 2002 reported that dentist Kenneth Friedman was accused by a dozen patients of having abused them in his office. The man pleaded guilty.

In France, the Tordjmann case is the most emblematic. A renowned sexologist, the highly publicised Gilbert Tordjmann was the founder and "pope" of sexology in France. The first complaint against him was made in 1999, but many more followed. Numerous patients complained of touching, masturbation, and "forced" caresses that went as far as penetration. Gilbert Tordjmann was charged in March 2002. In total, forty-four former patients claimed to have been abused by this "specialist". On 4 May 2005, *Le Figaro* reported that he had been sent to the Second Chamber. Naturally, Gilbert Tordjmann has always denied all these accusations: "A large part of the case has been dismissed", said one of his lawyers, who emphasised her client's profession as a gynaecologist to justify the intrusive "examinations". Thus, the sexologist would again ask for the case to be dismissed on the grounds that these gestures were indicated by medical practice[580].

The Hippocratic oath that all psychiatrists promise to respect prohibits sexual relations between doctors and patients, but one might think that for some 'therapists' this oath has little value. One might even think that some of them feel released from it when their patients are unaware of the sexual relationship.

This is how Californian psychiatrist James Harrington White proceeded. He drugged his patients before raping them and filming the scenes. He was sentenced to seven years in prison.

The famous doctor Jules Masserman, an eminent specialist, highly respected by his colleagues throughout the world and former honorary president of the world association of social psychiatry, had also caused a scandal in 1987 after being accused by several of his patients. Jules Masserman was in the habit of numbing his patients with amobarbital, a barbiturate capable of blocking memory. However, during one of his numerous sessions, Barbara Noel, one of the complainants, woke up to discover the horrible face of the guy gasping for breath on top of hers. "I've never felt such a sense of betrayal," Noel said. For years,

---

[580] Curiously, two years later, no information came out about this trial.

Masserman had drugged and raped her in her sleep. During the trial, he continued to claim that his accuser was "mentally ill" and a fabricator. Barbara Noel refused to give in and waged a seven-year legal battle, encouraging other women to testify publicly. The APA (American Psychiatric Association) eventually supported the Illinois Psychiatric Society's decision to withdraw Massermann's medical clearance, but that suspension was only effective for five years, and was not for rape but for drug use. The insurers had paid out more than $350,000 in compensation to his victims.

The *Associated Press* of 3 January 2002 reported another trial. That of Andrew Luster, 39, the grandson of cosmetics tycoon Max Factor, who had been arrested in 2000 on charges of raping two women after drugging them in a Santa Barbara bar and videotaping them. Police had found 17 videotapes of him having sex with apparently unconscious women in his home.

The case of Thierry Chichportich was also highly publicised. The "masseur to the stars", nicknamed the "man with the golden hands" by the world cinema elite. *Le Parisien* of 20 May 2006 reported that he was sentenced to 18 years in prison by the criminal court of Nice for the rape of 13 women. They had been lulled to sleep with tranquillisers administered without their consent. The first complaint was made after one of the victims woke up during the rape. The discovery by the police of the video recordings of his rapes and the drugs used led to his conviction.

Here is also what we can read in Dr. Valensin's book: "Jewish doctors, dentists and psychoanalysts have often been accused of abusing their patients. A century earlier, in Rouen, the dentist Levy had already been accused of rape under hypnosis of a young patient who had become pregnant; she turned out to be hysterical, and the rape dubious[581]. In January 1935, one could read in a Nazi medical journal: "Jewish doctors rape anaesthetised patients[582]...". On 14 August 1935, the *Volkisher Beobachter, a* Hitlerite newspaper, announced that the Hebrew doctor Ferdinand Goldstein from Constance had been sent to a concentration camp after having defiled a young German girl; hundreds of victims were attributed to him[583]."

---

[581] Brouardel, Annales d'hygiène et de médecine légale, t.I, 1879, p. 39.

[582] Deusch Volkgesundheit auss Blut und Boden, 1 January 1935

[583] Georges Valensin, *La Vie sexuelle juive*, Éditions philosophiques, 1981, p.

Xaviera Hollander's book also confirms this strong propensity: American Jews "are among my favourites, as well as my most assiduous clients. And although it is sad, I must also say that they are my most extravagant and depraved clients. Many of them seem to be going through psychoanalysis with problems that arose from having an overly domineering mother or a wife who is a Jewish-American princess trying to dominate them... Many of the Jewish doctors who come to my house are flamboyant, and usually wish they were slaves. However, I recently heard of a client who said to one of the girls: "Be absolutely still, don't say a word, act like you're dead". This is a necrophilia syndrome, which is the desire to copulate with a dead person[584]."

We find the same deviant behaviour in the films of some Jewish directors. Ingmar Bergman, a "Swedish" director, regularly shocked viewers. In *The Silence* (1963), a dialogue referred to copulation in a church. Swedish critics used the adjective "vomiting". After *Circus Night* and *Smiles of a Summer Night*, a journalist asked him: "Are you intentionally making pornography or do you just don't know how to do anything else?

Ingmar Bergman recounted in his memoirs that the discovery of a woman's corpse in a morgue when he was ten years old led him to associate nudity and eroticism with death for a long time. "That vision has inspired several Freudian scenes, notably in *The Hour of the Wolf*, when Ingrid Thulin lies naked on an autopsy table and wakes up when Max Von Sydow touches her, and in *The Silence* when the boy, watching his aunt dozing in her bed having rales, projects the image of her corpse. In *The Maiden's Spring*, the nudity of a young girl provokes the audience's discomfort, as she is a raped and murdered girl, and in *Cries and Whispers*, we are directly presented with the funeral washing of a dying woman[585]."

---

145.

[584] Xaviera Hollander, *La Alegre Madame*, 1972, Editorial Grijalbo, Mexico DF, p. 181-182.

[585] Jean Luc Doin, *Dictionnaire de la censure au cinéma*, PUF, 1998, p.55. Édouard Drumont noted in 1886: "Sarah Bernardt, with her macabre imagination, her white satin coffin in her room, is evidently a sick woman". (*La France juive*, tome I, p. 107)

This macabre inclination was also seen in the Mexican filmmaker and atheist Luis Buñuel. In *Un perro andaluz* (1928), a film made from dreams, and according to the automatic writing technique in vogue at the time of surrealism, a razor blade is seen cutting out a woman's eye and a girl plays with a severed hand. *The Golden Age* (1930) was a call to revolt against traditional society: a man and a woman tried to meet despite the successive obstacles put in their way by the police, nuns and representatives of the established order. In France, Prefect Chiappe banned the film for disturbing public order. In 1961, in *Viridiana*, Buñuel showed the "libidinous drive of an old man who, after making him drink a narcotic, abuses his young niece". The film was banned in Spain, Switzerland and Italy[586]. In *Belle de jour*, in 1966, based on the novel by the Jewish writer Joseph Kessel, one of the brothel customers was a necrophiliac and had a prostitute lie in a coffin.

Another report by the "Citizens Commission on Human Rights" provided further evidence of corruption in the psychiatric sector in the United States[587]. Insurance fraud would be very common. For example, a nursing home patient could be billed for mental therapy while in a coma, or daily "group therapy" sessions could be prescribed but were in fact music and tea talks. According to this report, 40% of psychiatrists in the US are prosecuted for professional misconduct during their careers.

This is how psychiatrist Robert Hadley Gross was sentenced to more than a year in prison in April 2004 for having billed his patients for procedures he had never performed, and for having accepted 860,000 dollars in commissions from hospitals to which he had transferred patients in the early 1990s. This scandal had set off a chain reaction in the country, and many private psychiatric hospitals had to pay millions in reimbursement, penalties and compensation.

Another New Jersey psychologist, Karl Lichtman, had defrauded 36 insurers of a total of USD 3.5 million for non-existent therapy sessions. In May 1996, he was ordered to repay USD 2.8 million to the private insurers and USD 200,000 to the administration.

---

[586] Jean Luc Doin, *Films à scandale*, Éditions du Chêne, 2001, p. 42.

[587] *Psychatrie, un secteur corrompu*:
http://h11.protectedsite.net/uploads/fr/FRE%20-%20fraud.pdf

Many unscrupulous psychiatrists have not hesitated to take advantage of the extensive medical coverage of mental disorders by insurers, which is mandatory under local and national legislation. Moreover, psychiatrists' associations exert strong pressure on children and adults to be examined during routine medical visits. Indeed, it should not be difficult to find something in every patient to prescribe, especially as the list of mental disorders has grown considerably longer. So nowadays, there is such a thing as "sleep terror disorder" or "nightmare disorder". The "Diagnostic and Statistical Manual of Mental Disorders" (DSM) identifies for children "difficulty in articulation", "disorder of written expression", "attention deficit disorder", "behavioural disorder", or "stuttering disorder", etc. The DSM used to classify 112 disorders, but in one of its latest updates it included 374 new ones. This new nomenclature is not anodyne, since it allows anyone to be hospitalised and makes money for insurers and the administration. The "bible of psychiatric billing" also makes it possible to absolve the guilty of their criminal acts by invoking insanity. So the thief will be able to claim before the judges that he is a "pathological thief", and the paedocriminal will say that he suffers from a "disorder of impulse and behaviour".

## *Paedocriminality*

A 2001 study in the United States revealed that one patient out of twenty sexually abused by a therapist was a minor. The average age was seven years for girls and twelve years for boys. The report entitled *Violations in psychiatry*[588] revealed for example the case of Donald Persson. This Utah psychologist was sentenced in 1993 to 10 years in prison for the rape of a 12-year-old girl. Psychiatrist Markham Berry pleaded guilty to the rape of six children. In 2000, Californian psychiatrist Burnell Gordon Forgey was sentenced to 15 years in prison for raping a teenage boy. In 1992, New York psychiatrist Alan Horowitz was sentenced to 20 years in prison for raping three boys aged 7 to 9 and a 14-year-old girl. Horowitz worked for a city organisation that helped children in poor neighbourhoods.

In recent years, the American website jewatch.com has collected numerous press articles implicating rabbis in this type of case. On 18 October 1996, the *Jewish Bulletin* of Northern California mentioned the case of Rabbi Robert Kirshner, a prominent figure in Californian

---

[588] http://h11.protectedsite.net/uploads/fr/FRE%20-%20rape.pdf

Judaism. He had been abruptly removed from his post in 1992 following accusations of sexual violence against eight women employees of the associations and the synagogue and two students at the Berkeley Theological Seminary.

The Los Angeles *Jewish Journal* also reported in its 15 December 2000 edition that one of California's most eminent liberal rabbis, Sheldon Zimmerman, had been suspended for "sexual indecency".

Rabbi Baruch Lanner of New Jersey was accused in March 2000 of having abused at least 20 girls during his career as an educator and leader of the Orthodox Union's National Conference. A 19-year-old girl accused him of abusing her almost every day in his office when she was 14 years old in 1995–1996. The rabbinical court tried its best to cover up the case, pressuring the parents not to report it to the courts, but the parents had finally stood by their allegations. (*Jewish Week*, 16 March 2000)

The *Jewish Journal of Greater Los Angeles* of 4 December 2001 reported that Rabbi Mordechai Yomtov, 36, a married father of four, had been arrested for sexual assaults on three children aged 8–10 in a primary school classroom.

We can also recall the case of that synagogue officiant, Jerrold Levy, accused of distributing paedocriminal pornography (*Sun-Sentinel*, 20 July 2001). Similarly, David Webber, 35, a former employee of the Calgary Jewish Community Council, was arrested on 22 February 1990. Numerous Polaroid photos of naked children between the ages of 10 and 14 were discovered in his flat. Before moving to Calgary, Webber had been the young director of the Beth Israel Synagogue in Edmonton, where he had already been accused of paedophilia.

*Newsday* of 20 February 2002 reported that Howard Nevison, 61, the "cantor" of the world's largest synagogue in Manhattan, had been arrested. The man was accused of having sexually assaulted his nephew between 1993 and 1997, when the nephew was between 3 and 7 years old. The boy did not want to testify against him, claiming that the cantor had a loud voice and terrifying eyes and had threatened to kill him if he spoke.

Another case, in 2002, 64-year-old Rabbi Richard Marcovitz, accused of sexual violence against two underage girls (*Channel Oklahoma*, 27 February 2002). Another rabbi, Juda Mintz, who lived in Georgia, faced between 27 and 33 months in prison for storing paedophile videos of children under the age of twelve on a dozen computers (*Newsday*, 26 February 2002).

The *New York Post* of 31 March 2002 reported the case of Sara Leven, who found her 17-year-old son Daniel hanged in her bathroom in 1993. The rabbi of the orthodox community, 57-year-old Ephraim B. Bryks of the Queens yeshiva in Montreal, despite being denounced by a family association, was never brought to justice.

In the *Jewish Bulletin of Northern California* of 21 February 1997 we read the following: Rabbi Sidney Goldenberg of Congregation B'Nai Israel was accused of sexually touching a 12-year-old girl. Several women in New York had contacted the district attorney in Santa Rosa, California, to say that they too had been victims of the rabbi as children. Charlotte Rolnick Schwab, a New York psychotherapist who published a book on the sexual criminality of some rabbis, claimed to have received hundreds of complaints from women across the country.

Rabbis and synagogue officiants are not the only ones incriminated. Israeli diplomats have also been in the news. Like this case reported in the *Jerusalem Post* of 6 July 2000: Brazilian police kept a close eye on the Israeli consulate in Rio de Janeiro, suspecting that the vice-consul, Aryeh Scher, was at the centre of a paedophile ring. The man managed to flee to Israel, but his accomplice George Schteinberg, a Hebrew teacher, was convicted of possession and dissemination of paedophile images via the internet. Reuters reported that police found hundreds of paedophile photos and videos in the home of George Schteinberg, a 40-year-old school teacher. Scher and Schteinberg also had intimate relations. The Israeli embassy and consulate declined to comment.

Tuvya Sa'ar, 65, director general of the Union of Israeli Journalists, was arrested for raping a 15-year-old girl in Tel Aviv. Sa'ar had years earlier been the director of Israel TV (*Haaretz*, 15 August 2001).

In January 2000, a teacher named Ze'ev Kopolevitch was accused of sexual violence by former students of a Jerusalem yeshiva, the Mercaz Harav yeshiva. The director of the institute, Avraham Shapira, was suspected of having covered up for the teacher (*Jerusalem Post*, 12 January 2000).

The head of the Jewish scout movement *Upper East Side's Boy Scout Troop 666*, Jerrold Schwartz, 42, was also charged with child molestation in Manhattan Supreme Court. The prosecutor presented five credible victims. "Ten minutes in the room with me; it's just punishment," said one of the 20-year-old victims during the trial. She was an alcoholic, addicted to cocaine and had nightmares ever since. The man attempted suicide several times by self-mutilation (*New York Post*, 19 December 2001).

We also know that film director Roman Polanski was forced to flee the United States in 1978 after he drugged and raped a 13-year-old girl. Today he is still wanted by the US justice system and faces up to 50 years in prison. That was the reason why he did not attend the 2003 Oscars gala where his film *The Pianist* was nominated. Woody Allen's paedophile tendencies are also well known, following Mia Farrow's statements in her memoirs (1997).

There are many more cases to report: Shlomo Nur, for example, was convicted of the 1998 rape of Linor Abergil, the Miss Universe when she had just received the crown in Italy (*Jerusalem Post*, 29 December 1999). He was sentenced in Tel-Aviv to 16 years in prison. Steven Gary Cohen was arrested in 2001 for having sex with a 14-year-old girl (*Westchester News*). Steven Berkoff, 64, convicted of rape (*Totally Jewish*, 16 August 2001).

Four years earlier, Samuel Cohen had raped for several months two girls, aged 7 and 8, who were the daughters of the babysitter who came to his home in Philadelphia. One of the girls had to be hospitalised after a particularly brutal rape (6 April 2000, philly.com).

The *Las Vegas Review-Journal* of 4 July 2000 reported that Russel D. Cohen, 41, pleaded guilty to raping children under the age of 14. His victims were young boys whom he paid to distribute leaflets. He was sentenced to 45 years in prison.

Recall also the case of 39-year-old Seth Bekenstein, accused in the press of being one of the leading distributors of paedophile videos in the US and the world (*San Ramon Valley*, 5 January 2002).

At the very edge of the law, a company called Webe Web in South Florida sold sex online with links to at least 14 pornographic sites. Webe Web, specialising in child erotica, was run by Marc Greenberg and Jeff Libman, both of whom photographed 12-year-old girls (NBC 6 and 8 November 2001).

News Making News reported on 29 March 2001 that David Asimov, the son of the famous science fiction writer Isaac Asimov, had just been sentenced to six months in prison for possession of child pornography, in Santa Rosa. He had previously been sentenced to five years in prison after pleading guilty, but was mysteriously released.

Another case appeared in the Israeli daily *Ha'aretz* on 4 November 2002: the Tel-Aviv magistrates rejected the request for the release of Ya'akov Ha'elyon, imprisoned for rape and sexual violence against a 14-year-old girl. Ya'akov Ha'elyon was the husband of Yael Ha'elyon, who was found dead at the foot of her building on a Tel-Aviv boulevard. Police concluded that she committed suicide by throwing herself from the eighth floor of her flat, probably after learning that her husband had been convicted.

This type of information hardly appears in the French and European press, or in very small print. For example, *Le Figaro* of 21 September 2006 reported discreetly in its international section: "In the United States: Howard Nevison, 65, the very popular rabbi of a synagogue in Manhattan, New York, has received a twelve-year suspended sentence for sexually touching a child. He was also banned from having any contact with children under the age of twelve". These cases do not make the front pages, nor do they make the news. The masters of the media prefer to project these accusations onto the priests of the Catholic Church, putting the spotlight on the Catholic Church when such cases occur.

In October 2005, the AFP (Agence France Presse) reported that a "renowned advertising executive" was on trial for the rape of his two granddaughters. The man, who was absent during the trial because he declared himself "ill", was sentenced on 7 November to three years in prison. The AFP did not disclose the name of the accused, which was extremely rare, but *Le Figaro* had broken the silence: it was Pierre de Blas, PDG (President and CEO) of several advertising groups and commentator on BFM, the economy radio station. *Faits-et-documents*, Emmanuel Ratier's valuable confidential letter, revealed that Count Pierre de Robinet de Plas was the son of a Vandea aristocrat, a pioneer of trade with the Communist bloc, and that he signed his novels with his mother's name, de Beer, thus vindicating his Jewishness, as he had already done in *Tribune juive*.

Emmanuel Ratier also revealed on 23 May 2007 that a rabbi had been arrested in southern India after an eleven-month manhunt. Rabbi Jay Horowitz, 60, was wanted by Interpol on a warrant issued by the New York police. The sexual predator had been sentenced to 15 years in prison in 1992 for the rapes of children and teenagers aged 10 to 17. Released in 2004, he was banned from leaving the country and would be extradited to the United States.

We know that the influence of Freud, the Freudo-Marxists of the Frankfurt school and psychoanalysis has been profoundly harmful in this area[589]. This is what the paediatrician Alexandre Minkowski commented in 1975, after having participated in a colloquium at Yale University: "In only fifteen years, under the influence of *permissiveness*, psychoanalysis and the liberation of complexes, sexual life is now very free, but also very precocious... We were told of high school classes where, out of twenty-five thirteen year old girls, only two were virgins and they were pointed at with the finger[590]!"

It is true that in the Jewish communities of old, marriage was always very early. In the novelist Isaac Bashevis Singer's *Satan in Goray*, Dr. Valensin wrote: "On the days between the holidays, marriage contracts were drawn up and good luck dishes were broken in every house where there was a girl over eight years old[591]." The novelist thus portrayed the customs of those 17th century Polish Jews who were convinced that Sabbatai Zevi was the long-awaited messiah: "Since the revelation of Sabbatai Zevi, the injunction against adultery was meaningless. It was rumoured that young men exchanged their wives... Levi was said to have forced Glucke, his brother Ozer's daughter, to lie with him and to have paid Ozer three Polish gold coins as a pledge that the sin would not be discovered. The young men studying in the house of instruction practised all kinds of depravity. They climbed on the women's rostrum in broad daylight, indulged in pederasty and performed acts of sodomy on goats[592]." Finally, the climax of the debauchery would reach the community: "From then on Goray indulged in all sorts of debauchery, becoming more corrupt every day... The practices of the faithful were truly an abomination... According to legend, they went into the castle's cellars and feasted on animals, tearing birds with their hands and devouring them. After the feast, fathers met their daughters, brothers

---

[589] Cf. our previous books: *Les Espérances planétariennes*, p. 69-81; *Psychanalyse du Judaïsme*, p. 351-366.

[590] Alexandre Minkowski, *Le Mandarin aux pieds nus*, Points Seuil, 1977, p. 96.

[591] Isaac Bashevis Singer, *Satan in Goray*, PDF, Digital publisher Epublibre, German25, 2017, p. 82

[592] Isaac Bashevis Singer, *Satan in Goray*, PDF, Digital publisher Epublibre, German25, 2017, p. 88

met their sisters, and sons met their mothers[593]." Incest is indeed a recurring theme that runs through Judaism in a hidden way.

## *Sexual ambiguity*

It is an undeniable fact that Judaism has a special link to homosexuality, if one looks for example at the film production of directors belonging to the community and the number of television programmes devoted to the subject. It is not only about perverting nations, as anti-Semites simplistically claim, but about the expression of the deep identity of Judaism, the main characteristic of which is ambiguity. Everything is ambiguous and doubtful in Judaism. Identity and cultural boundaries are blurred and shifting; and so is sexuality. We should not be surprised to see in cosmopolitan cinema an evident complacency with transgender characters and transvestites. The Freudian concept of "bisexuality", which proposes the idea that all men are a little bit female and all women are a little bit male, is actually a Jewish concept, enunciated by a Jew and applied primarily to the Jewish community, where hysterical ambiguity is widespread. This is simply because incest, which is the cause of that pathology, has been, and probably still is, widely practised within the Jewish community. This is what we have shown in our previous book, *Psychoanalysis of Judaism*.

Film production is particularly revealing of this typically hysterical ambiguity. *In and out* (USA, 1997) is a "hilarious" comedy: Professor Howard Brackett teaches literature at the university of a small town in Indiana, USA. He is loved by all his students and the local community, until one day his reputation is turned upside down when, during a TV show, a former student turned movie star publicly thanks his "gay" former professor. Obviously, the teacher is shocked by this statement. Parents, students and friends now look at him with suspicion. He therefore decides to quickly marry his girlfriend to nip the rumours in the bud. But this is without counting on that journalist who follows him everywhere with his camera, encouraging him to make his *"coming out"*. On the day of the wedding, in the middle of the ceremony at the altar, when he is about to say "yes" to his bride, he finally gives up and declares half-heartedly and resignedly: "I'm gay". The attendants are stunned and the bride suffers a nervous breakdown. The religious

---

[593] Isaac Bashevis Singer, *Satan in Goray*, PDF, Digital publisher Epublibre, German25, 2017, p. 105, 106

ceremony is interrupted (another Jewish obsession). The final scene is another great moment of cosmopolitan cinema: at the university, during the graduation ceremony, students and parents learn that the professor has been fired. Then they all stand up one by one to declare that they too are "gay"—everyone is gay! The film is by Frank Oz, a Jew.

*Drops of water on hot stones* (France, 1999) tells the story of Leopold, a fifty-year-old insurance broker who seduces Franz, a 19-year-old boy. It then features Anna, Franz's girlfriend, and Vera, Leopold's former lover, a transsexual for love. The film is by François Ozon (1999) and based on the play by Rainer-Werner Fassbinder. In *Eight Women* (2001), the "good Catholic" François Ozon shows adultery, homosexuality, incest, hypocrisy and social change. It is said to be a "great" film.

*First Summer* (*Presque rien*, France, 1999) is "a film about love that attempts to trivialise male homosexuality by showing very crude scenes", said Jean Tulard's *Guide des films*. The film is by director Sebastian Lifshitz. In the same vein, we can cite *Party boys* by Dirk Shafer (USA, 2002), *The man of his life* (*L'Homme de sa vie*, France 2006) by Zabou Breitman (France, 2006).

*Jessica's Temptation* (USA, 2001) is another example: Jessica Stein is a New York journalist who has it all. She is beautiful, sensitive and intelligent, but her bachelorhood weighs on her. After a series of awkward dates, Jessica notices an ad that piques her curiosity. Despite the fact that it appears in the "women looking for women" section, she decides to answer it. That's how she meets the attractive Helen Cooper in a bar. What if the man of her life turns out to be a woman? The film is by Charles Herman-Wurmfeld. Female homosexuality is also promoted in *All Daddies Don't Pee Standing Up*, a film by Dominique Baron (France, 1998): Simon is not a boy like the others. He has two mothers, Dan and Zoé, who conceived him by artificial insemination.

Let us also remember this 1998 film by director Jean-Jacques Zilbermann, which deals with homosexuality within the Jewish community: *L'Homme est une femme comme les autres (Man is a woman like any other woman)*. The title undoubtedly corresponds to a neurotic projection on the rest of the world, as homosexuality is probably much more prevalent than is believed among the Jewish people. The television presenter Stephane Bern surprisingly declared in *Libération* in May 2000 that "Jewish mothers made excellent homosexuals". The feminisation of Western societies and the rise of homosexuality are not fortuitous, but rather the consequences of a media power acquired by a large and influential group of Jewish intellectuals and journalists, who seek to fulfil their mission as "priestly people". It is therefore not only a conscious political action aimed at destroying the European world, based on a prophetic delirium typical of Judaism, but also the expression of a very characteristic neurosis.

In the film *A Madhouse* (*L'Auberge espagnole,* France, 2002), the director deliberately chose to have Cecile de France play the role of a lesbian with a well-furnished head and even intellectually superior to the rest. Yet another example is the Jewish director François Luciani's TV series *The Comrades (*2006), which tells the story of a group of friends after the "Liberation", all communists and affiliated to the Party. Everything was going well, until one day the Party leadership discovered the homosexuality of one of the "comrades". François Luciani aims to denounce the intolerance that exists within the Stalinist party under the orders of the USSR, which has become "reactionary" after the elimination of the "cosmopolitan" elements.

*American Beauty* (USA, 1999) is an entertaining film, but exceptional for its degree of perversion: In a perfect middle-class housing estate in an American city, a couple is in crisis. The wife is cheating on her husband with a real estate developer, while he is in love with a friend of his daughter, who is only fifteen years old. His daughter, who hates him, becomes infatuated with the new neighbour's son, a rather strange boy who spends his days filming everything with his camera. His father is an extreme right-wing military man who regularly beats him brutally. When he comes to suspect that his son has become the neighbour's dealer and lover, his blood starts to boil. His desperation will unveil… his latent homosexuality! Here again, homosexuality is presented benevolently with the brief appearance of a neighbourhood couple who seem to be the only really happy people in the neighbourhood. Apology for adultery, drugs, homosexuality, paedophile and incestuous ambiguity, denouncement of the "extreme right": we are confronted with a totally Jewish film. Sam Mendes was the director, and naturally, his film won five Oscars in Hollywood. "Ironic, provocative, uncomfortable" could be read everywhere.

*Far From Heaven* (USA, 2002) is also very characteristic of its genre: In a bourgeois housing estate in 1950s America, a woman discovers part of her husband's "dark past". One night, he calls home to tell her that he will be working late at his office. His wife then decides to surprise him by bringing him his dinner at work. Arriving on the fourteenth floor of the building emptied of its employees, she bursts into the office to discover her husband passionately kissing… another man! Fortunately, the beautiful American will find solace with her gardener: a big, burly black man who will take care of her. Homosexuality for the white man, and miscegenation for the white woman: what we see here is not so much the sexual ambiguity of Judaism as the Jew's characteristic hatred of the white race. Todd Haynes' film was naturally rewarded with four Oscar nominations: "a pure diamond", according to *Les Inrockuptibles* (Serge Kaganski); "moving, a masterpiece", for *Zurban* magazine.

In *My beautifull laundrette* (UK, 1990), director Stephen Frears expressed his hatred of the white race in this way: Omar, a young Pakistani, is commissioned by his uncle to revive a run-down laundrette in a London slum. Being very dynamic, he manages to renovate it and get the business up and running again. He hires an old friend, a poor English homosexual thug who becomes his lover. His gang of friends revolt against the fact that one of their own is working for the "Pakis". Evidently, they are very racist and very lazy. Fortunately, the Pakis are there to make the economy work and impregnate the English women, as can be seen in the film. Apology of miscegenation and homosexuality, denunciation of racism: the film received the Cesar for the best foreign film, despite being totally soporific.

If we go back in time, we find a "pearl" by Serge Gainsbourg: *Je t'aime moi non plus* (France, 1975), about "the sodomite love affairs of a flat-chested maid and a homosexual chauffeur". In the 1960s, Jewish directors were already trying to unload their obsessive tares and neuroses on the goy audience. In *The Slander* (USA, 1962), William Wyler shows two friends who run a high school for young girls and are accused of having sex. The rumour is amplified and the parents withdraw their daughters from the institute. "A daring subject for the time", wrote Jean Tulard in his *Guide to the Movies*. Wyler was effectively denouncing Puritanism and setting himself up as an apostle of the "liberation" of manners. In the same vein, *A Taste of Honey* (UK, 1961) tells the story of the relationship between two outcasts: a teenage girl pregnant from a one-night stand with a black man, and a homosexual. The director is Tony Richardson. In *Storm Over Washington* (USA, 1961), Otto Preminger also tried to raise awareness of homosexuality and dared to show gay bars. In the US president's entourage, an advisor who is threatened with revealing his homosexuality falls victim to intolerance and ends up committing suicide[594].

---

[594] Otto Preminger, after a long career, "did not publicly display his pro-Jewish and pro-Israeli commitment until the situation allowed it, i.e. from the 1960s

In a documentary film on the subject of a hundred years of homosexuality in Hollywood, *The Celluloid Closet* (1996), Rob Epstein and Jeffrey Friedman recalled the countless twists and turns directors took to circumvent the censorship of heterosexual puritanism[595].

Bisexuality, a concept that appeared with Freud and was popularised by other Jewish psychoanalysts, appears naturally in cosmopolitan cinema. In *Together alone* (USA, 1991) for example: "Bryan is blond, Brian is dark. They have just made love without a condom in the time of AIDS; can this mark of trust withstand the first lie? But Bryan is even more lonely when, before leaving, his partner announces that he is bisexual, married and a parent." The film is by P. J. Castellanta.

In *The Confusion of Genders (*France, 2000), director Ilan Duran Cohen tells the story of Alain, a forty-year-old lawyer, whose desires are confused. He oscillates between the security of stable relationships and the intoxicating desire of flirting. What should he do? Marry his love Laurence, a lawyer herself? Live with Christophe, a young man? Or indulge his fantasies about Marc, a prisoner he defends? Unless she gives in to the temptation of Babette, his girlfriend.

Although psychoanalysis is widely discredited in most parts of the world, its latest adherents in France still have a foothold in the media system. The 2006 Interralié prize was awarded to Michel Schneider's book on Marilyn Monroe, *Marilyn, last sessions*, a work very revealing of the underlying tendency of Jews to project their own neurosis onto the "universal". *Le Nouvel Observateur* of 14 September 2006 published a summary of the book: "Has she committed suicide? Likely, has she been murdered? Not out of the question. Marilyn's psychiatrist, Ralph Greenson, "whose real name was Romeo Greeschpoon, the most famous psychiatrist in the world," as Philippe Sollers wrote, was the only man who could help the film star. Greenson "identifies his patient's unhealthy fear of homosexuality, perhaps unaware of his frigidity, and gives himself totally to a very profitable rescue attempt. Schneider sharply points out that instead of taking Marilyn down the traditional

---

onwards (*Exodus*, 1960). Jerry Lewis acted in the same way with *The Nutty Professor* in 1963" (Jean-Luc Doin, *Dictionnaire de la censure au cinéma*, Presse Universitaire de France, 1998, p.83). Fourteen years after *Exodus*, Preminger returned with *Rosebud* and took the side of the Palestine Liberation Army.

[595] Jean-Luc Doin, *Dictionnaire de la censure au cinéma*, PUF, 1998.

father-life-love-desire path, he plunges her into her mother-homosexuality-excrement-death anguish."

Let us also look at the obsession with transvestites and transsexuals in the films of cosmopolitan directors. For example, in *Torch Song Trilogy* (USA, 1989), Harvey Fierstein, the film's screenwriter, also played the main character: a homosexual who sings in a transvestite club. A travésti artist, openly gay and Jewish, Arnold lives intensely, between his flirtation with Ed who left him for a woman, his love affair with young Alan, his engagement to David, his adopted son, and his stormy relations with his Jewish mother.

Tootsie is a film by Sidney Pollack (USA, 1983): Dorsey is a demanding but unemployed actor. In order to get a part, he disguises himself as a woman and becomes Tootsie. His disguise will get him a role in a TV series and a lot of fans. But he soon finds himself in a dilemma: how to tell his colleague, who has made him her confidant, that he is in fact a transvestite and that he is in love with her?

*All about my mother* (Spain, 1999) is a film by Pedro Almodóvar: Manuela, a nurse, lives alone with her 17-year-old son Esteban. Esteban is tragically killed by a car. Manuela (Cecilia Roth) then travels to Barcelona in search of her son's father. Her search leads her to meet Agrado, a transsexual, Huma, a theatre actress, and Rosa, a young woman who works for a Catholic charity. She is impregnated by Lola, Estaban's father, who turns out to be a transvestite, and in the process transmits AIDS to him. Almodóvar also gloats by showing us a very multiracial Spain, which is also very symptomatic. The film, produced by Michel Ruben, was presented on DVD in France by Claude Berri (Langman). Almodóvar was naturally rewarded at the 1999 Cannes Film Festival with the prize for the best mise-en-scène. "I dedicate this award to Spanish democracy. I have known religious fundamentalism, police brutality and hatred of what is different," he explained on the podium. In *Tacones lejanos* (1991), Almodóvar already showed a scene of rape by a transvestite. Perhaps it is in that film that a character is seen ejaculating on a crucifix.

*Chouchou* (2003) is a film by Merzak Allouache, a "French" director born in Algeria: Chouchou is a young Maghrebi who disembarks clandestinely in Paris to join his nephew. He finds a job as a handyman in the office of a psychoanalyst, in addition to receiving her clients. In the meantime, her nephew has become "Vanessa", a romantic singer in a cabaret, and Chouchou decides to cross-dress in her spare time. The film came out of the imagination of its screenwriter, Gad Elmaleh, who is also the main character in the film. In *Mrs. Doubtfire, Daddy for Life* (USA, 1993), Chris Columbus tells the story of a divorced couple. The husband, who wants to see his children again, disguises himself as a nanny and is hired by his ex-wife. The screenplay is by Randi Mayem Singer.

Transsexuality is the main theme of *Thelma*, a film by Pierre-Alain Meier (France, 2002): Vincent is a disillusioned taxi driver from Lausanne. One night, in the forest, he meets the beautiful Thelma in the middle of a dispute with a man. She gets into his taxi and offers him, in exchange for money, to help her take revenge on a former lover. Vincent does not know that Thelma was formerly a man called Louis. *My Life in Pink*, by Alain Berliner (France, 1997), is the evocation of difference through the story of Ludovic, a boy persuaded to be a girl.

As early as 1959, in *Some Like It Hot* (USA), the talented Billy Wilder told a story of transvestites in a hilarious comedy: Two unemployed jazz musicians, unwittingly involved in a gangster's score, transform themselves into musicians in order to escape. They travel to Florida with a female orchestra, and fall in love with a charming creature (Marilyn), who wants to marry a millionaire.

Obviously, not all films about homosexuality, transvestites and transsexuals are directed by Jews. *Tenue de soirée (*France, 1986), for example, was directed by Bertrand Blier. He is not Jewish, but perhaps he was under the influence of his wife (Anouk Grinberg). *The Adventures of Priscilla, Queen of the Desert* (Australia, 1994) tells the story of three Sydney cabaret "madwomen", two transvestites and a "trans", who decide to tour the centre of the country in an old bus they christen Priscilla. Naturally, Stephan Elliott's film won the Audience Award at Cannes in 1994. Jim Sharman, the director of the legendary film *The Rocky Horror Picture Show* (USA, 1975), a dreck that makes no sense other than to cast a transsexual as the main character, is not Jewish either. But the three producers Michael White, John Goldstone and Lou Adler certainly are. Certainly, there is a kind of symbiosis, a convergence of interests between these two lobbies predominant in all media systems of Western democracies.

It is also worth noting, as an anecdote, that the Eurovision Song Contest was won in 1998 by a pioneering Israeli singer, called "Llady Dana international". This girl, formerly called Yaron Cohen, was a transsexual. One can also mention Steven Cohen, a South African artist, "white, Jewish, homosexual and transvestite" whose contemporary dance performances revolve around the concept of transvestism.

The sexologist Elisabeth Badinter, wife of the former socialist minister of justice and very rich heiress of the Publicis group, reflected Jewish neurosis very well when she said that the sex of an individual was more the product of his or her upbringing than a natural attribute. All the hysterical ambiguity consubstantial to Judaism thus appeared when she wrote in 1986 in her book entitled *One is the Other*: "It is not because of some innate force that the baby will know that he is a boy and that he will be male. The parents teach him that, and they could very well teach him otherwise. From the moment they know they have a boy, they start a process that, depending on what they consider to be masculinity, will encourage certain behaviours and avoid others. Choice of name, style of clothing, manner of carrying the child, type of play, etc., constitute the major part of the child's training for the development of his or her gender identity". Elisabeth Badinter continued, "In the case of a transsexual child, mother and child remain attached to each other: the mother lives with the child in such a close symbiosis that she treats him as if he were a part of her body and he feels as such. Mothers of transsexuals have in common the fact that they feel totally attached to the child, who lives in permanent bodily contact with her. The child has access to her nakedness and intimacy. He sleeps in her bed as if there is no boundary between their bodies. This contact satisfies a need of the mother from which she derives great pleasure and which is never satiated[596]".

Naturally, Elisabeth Badinter omitted to inform us that, like Freud, she drew her knowledge from the study of Judaism and the behaviour of the Jewish mother, who probably imagines herself to have given birth to the long-awaited Messiah.

Dr. Georges Valensin pointed out that the transsexual phenomenon had been inaugurated by an influential Jewish sexologist in inter-war Germany, Magnus Hirschfeld: "He conducted some 10 000 interviews of homosexuals in Germany, more valuable than Kinsey's. In the 1920s, he founded the Berlin Institute of Sexology, where the first surgical sex transformations and homosexual information meetings were held. In the 1920s, he founded the Berlin Institute of Sexology, where the first surgical sex transformations and homosexual information meetings took place. Hirshfeld was to create a school; he was surrounded by a

---

[596] Elisabeth Badinter, *L'un est l'autre*, Éd. Odile Jacob, 1986, p. 292, 293

team of co-religionists. He started the rehabilitation of homosexuals and was the first to use the term "third sex" to designate them[597]." His institute was closed down as soon as Hitler came to power and his works were used for the famous book burnings.

It is not surprising to see how the pornographic industry is largely dominated by Jewish producers. It is common knowledge that the Jewish community has exercised a near monopoly over this industry since its inception. Georges Valensin provided interesting historical data in this regard: "In Sweden, Ingmar Bergman, a follower of introversion and obsessed with sexuality, is an Israeli". Indeed, *The Silence* (Sweden, 1963) had been censored for showing a masturbation scene. He added: "German cinema before the Nazis had enjoyed a surprising boom thanks to the Jews. Sternberg directed *The Blue Angel*, whose eroticism was shattering. Fritz Lang was the author of *M, the Vampire of Düsseldorf*: the story of a sexual criminal and paedophile played by his co-religionist Peter Lorre who brought an innate Jewish anxiety to the screen… Pornographic cinema also had its Israelis in France. Bernard Nathan, with his *Sister Vaseline*, inaugurated this type of cinema for the general public; today, its most prominent representative is Joseph Benazeraff, producer of forty pornographic films in fifteen years[598]." Dr. Valensin continued and did not hesitate to quote other authors: "Already in the middle of the last century, a German writer claimed that, in Hamburg, "the most obscene engravings and books were sold by the Jews"; as peddlers, it was easy for them to propose them between two romantic almanacs or even between pious images[599]." We also know that, in 1886, Edouard Drumont again levelled the same accusation in *La France Judaise*. Georges Valensin even quoted anti-Semitic authors and publications: "In 1934, the Cardinal Primate of Poland, asked to protest against Hitler's racial persecutions, replied that he would only intervene when the Jews stopped propagating communism and pornographic images. In Berlin, in 1921, the journalist Hugo Bettauer edited a weekly specialising in

---

[597] Georges Valensin, *La Vie sexuelle juive*, Éditions philosophiques, 1981, p. 170.

[598] Georges Valensin, *La Vie sexuelle juive*, Éditions philosophiques, 1981, p. 164.

[599] J. Gross, Hoffinger, *Le sort des femmes*, Leipzig, 1857

libertine stories; a nationalist student killed him because he saw him as a Jew corrupting the youth[600]."

In the 1930s, the more conscientious goyim were already concerned about the extraordinary aggressiveness of Jewish cinema. In the United States, *the Legion of Decency demanded* the establishment of a veritable "code of decency" to monitor the content of recorded fiction and to verify that "American values" were respected. Part of the Catholic hierarchy was involved in this campaign. In 1933, the Archbishop of Cincinnati (Ohio), Monsignor John McNicholas, declared: "I join with all those who protest against these images which represent a grave threat to family life, to the nation and to religion". In the spring of 1934, the Cardinal of Philadelphia, Monsignor Denis Dougherty, called on all Catholics in the United States to boycott Hollywood productions "dominated by Jewish businessmen" and some 11 million of the faithful responded to his call[601]. The results of the boycott were not long in coming: theatres emptied and movie profits plummeted. President William Hays' Hays Code, which dictated strict rules of decency, was enforced in 1934. Productions were to be subject to censorship by the Production Code Commission, chaired by Joseph Breen, a Catholic who exercised some power over Hollywood's moral and political standards for twenty years and whose policy was continued by McCarthy's in the 1950s.

Fifty years later, almost all the levees have collapsed under the combined pressure of cosmopolitan high finance and the libertarian movements, whose activists think they are "revolutionaries", but in reality do nothing more than parrot the cosmopolitan slogans of their leaders and doctrinaires. In 2005, the Catholic reaction to the wave of television and film filth was expressed by William Donohue, president of the League of American Catholics. When Mel Gibson's film *The Passion of the Christ*, so criticised by the official media, was released, he did not hesitate to declare in front of the television cameras: "Hollywood is controlled by secular Jews who hate Christianity. It's no secret and I'm not afraid to say it. That's why they hate this film,

---

[600] H. Andics, *Histoire de l'antisémitisme*, Éd. Albin Michel, 1967, p. 213. in Georges Valensin, *La vie sexuelle juive*, p. 168.

[601] See Thomas Dougherty, *Pré-code Hollywood: Sex, Immorality and Insurrection in American Cinema*, New York, Columbia University Press, 2000. And also: *Courrier international*, 3 février 2000.

because it talks about Jesus Christ". He added: "I love family, while Hollywood loves anal sex[602]."

This has been going on since ancient times, if some historical testimonies are anything to go by. In 15th century Spain, for example, the Franciscan Alonso de Espina published in 1487 his *Fortalitium fidei contra Judeos in* which he mentioned this particularity along with the other complaints against the Jews: "Spirit of treason, ritual crimes, poisoning doctors, destruction of Christians with the outrageous practice of usury, false Jews and sodomites, etc.". The *Book of Alboraique*, published in 1488 by an anonymous author "resumed over a dozen pages the popular accusations directed this time at both new-Christians and Jews: deceitful, vain, cowardly, blasphemers, sacrilegious and sodomites."

Again, in 1623, Vicente Acosta, a Portuguese Jewish convert, published a 428-page book against his former fellow Jews. His work was immediately translated into Spanish under the title *Discurso contra los Judios*. The Jews were described as "greedy, rebellious, and liars by nature... It would be impossible to enumerate all their vices: envy, pride, their noble pretensions, their ostentatious luxury, which they display daily in Portugal and even more so in Madrid, as well as their insolence and their *"outrages"*. Sodomy (to which he devotes a separate chapter) stems from their natural lasciviousness and the idleness in which they indulge... In fact, the Jews of North Africa regularly sodomise their wives and children[603]!" Daniel Tollet, who published the book in which we collect these testimonies, pretended not to take these grotesque accusations seriously. But we have seen, in *Psychoanalysis of Judaism*, that these practices were indeed encouraged by the Talmud. It is said that Jewishness is transmitted by the mother, but sometimes one has the impression that it is rather transmitted by the c.... Finally, you have understood.

We can quote again in this chapter the testimony of "Madame" Xaviera Hollander, in an episode of her troubled life. This time we see her on holiday at her stepsister's house in South Africa: "One day, while I was resting by the pool, and thinking that I would go mad if I did not satisfy

---

[602] *Faits-et-Documents* du 15 janvier 2005

[603] Daniel Tollet, *Les Textes judéophobes et judéophiles dans l'Europe chrétienne à l'époque moderne*, Presses universitaires de France, 2000, p. 30, 34, 39.

my sexual appetites, I noticed that the big German shepherd was lying next to me, and very nervous. This dog had confused me quite a bit the first five days after my arrival at the house, following me around and sniffing my legs. Apparently his sniffing turned him on sexually, and I had reached a point where I couldn't be too choosy, so I decided that—grotesque, or not—my first South African lover would be him... I began to rub his penis, which came out of his skin, red and glistening, and the sight of which really thrilled me[604]... "We will not go any further into this interesting experience, but the reader should know that the caresses were enough to appease Xaviera's excitement.

The dubious customs of the Jews had already provoked the sarcasm of Voltaire, who wrote in the "Jews" section of his *Philosophical Dictionary*: "Jewish law forbids women to mate with horses and asses, so that to impose this prohibition it was necessary that Jewish women should have been engaged in such affairs... Men are forbidden to offer sperm to Moloch, and lest they should think that this is a metaphor, the law repeats that it refers to the semen of the male. The Jews claim it is not true, but in that case "Tell me sirs, why are you the only people on earth whose law has imposed such a prohibition? Would a lawgiver have dared to enact this strange law if the crime were not common[605]?"

The *New York Times Magazine* of 25 March 2001 wrote an article about a certain Tobias Schneebaum, who also wanted to "cross all borders", and give himself up to new "liberating experiences", far from the rigid norms of this Christian society. In 1973, this homosexual had made his first trip to the jungle of New Guinea. There he would spend several years in the company of his new friends from the Arakmbut tribe. He wanted, as the newspaper reports, "to escape the oppression of Western civilisation and to transgress one of the last taboos: cannibalism". This is an extreme example of what Jewish neurosis can generate.

## *Feminism*

Elisabeth Badinter is one of the great figures of feminism in France. In *One is the Other*, published in 1986, she noted with satisfaction the

---

[604] Xaviera Hollander, *La Alegre Madame*, 1972, Editorial Grijalbo, Mexico DF, p. 37, 38

[605] Voltaire, *Dictionnaire philosophique*, Librodot PDF, p. 613 and in French at voltaire-integral.com/19/juifs.htm (unredacted version)

disappearance of the patriarchal family model on which Christian civilisation was founded: "Paternal and marital power is in the process of disappearing. The ideological, social and political power of man is seriously eroded... In most Western democracies, the patriarchal system has received the coup de grâce during the last two decades... The 20th century has marked the end of manly values in the West".

And of course, there will be nothing to regret: "They were archaic manly values," wrote Badinter, equating "manliness" with the warrior values of the West and especially with the Second World War: "manliness has shown its most odious face, that is to say its most murderous face[606]."

The feminist movements in vogue in Western countries in the late 1960s must be seen in the context of decolonisation and the liberation of third world peoples. Feminists said that they were "exploited just as the colonised of old were exploited by the white man". In the minds of these feminists, most of them women of the Hebrew people, the white man was indeed the personification of evil. "In the US, they compared his condition to that of the black community. There, under the leadership of Betty Friedan or in France... militant feminists listed the exploitations of which they were victims: sexual, domestic, economic, social and political." In a footnote, Badinter noted that Betty Friedan had founded the first major feminist movement in the United States: NOW (National Organisation of Women). In France, Anne Tristan

---

[606] Elisabeth Badinter, *L'un est l'autre*, Éd. Odile Jacob, 1986, p. 214–217. Elisabeth Badinter, like William Reich (cf. *Planetary Hopes*, p. 73, 74) noted that Soviet policy in this area, so "advanced" at the beginning, had later favoured the traditional family: "Although the young Soviet Union had passed laws to liberate women and to withdraw from men all prerogatives over their family members, the experiment failed. Russian society experienced a sexual counter-revolution that made it increasingly resemble those of other European countries. Under Stalin, the traditional family was defended with the same zeal as in Nazi Germany. All of Lenin's liberating laws were abandoned in favour of repressive provisions." Elisabeth Badinter wrote in a footnote: "From 1932, at the Kiev congress, abortion was denigrated. There was talk of preserving the race. In 1944, abortion was abolished... In 1936, a new divorce law made it punishable by fines, and in 1944 an even harsher law was passed. Illegitimacy was again criminalised and stigmatised on mother and children. The father was no longer responsible. The laws of 1936 and 1946 gave advantages to mothers of six children, etc." (p. 213, 214).

created in May '68 "Feminine-Masculine-Future[607]." In the 1970s, the press would begin to talk about the Women's Liberation Movement, which at first was no more than a nebula of small, ephemeral formations.

From the 1970s onwards, feminists praised solitude. "Inspired by Virginia Woolf, they demanded the right to have "a room for themselves", even "a bed for themselves", or a place to live free... At that time, many feminists decided to live on their own... In the "Common Agenda for Women", Gisele Halimi suggested in 1978 that the suppression of the patriarchal family perhaps necessitated the suppression of cohabitation of the couple for a generation". Some, like Jerry Rubin, a former American anti-establishment ringleader, went so far as to advocate renouncing love in order to, "love myself enough and not need anyone else to make me happy." These continuous press campaigns, repeated throughout the media system, have evidently had consequences: "The number of one-person households has increased dramatically in the last thirty years[608]."

These Jewish activists played a leading role in the passage of laws legalising abortion. In the United States, "the pioneer of Birth Control" was Margaret Sanger. Her law was passed in 1973. In West Germany it was passed in 1974 and in France in 1975 under the impetus of Simone Veil. "Female contraception dealt a mortal blow to the patriarchal family by leaving the domain of procreation to the other party... The balance of power has been completely reversed to the detriment of the father, who is thus deprived of an essential power". On the other hand, if the wife's fidelity escaped the husband's vigilance, men had less to fear from bastards. This revolution, together with the loss of traditional sexual role references due to women's willingness to share economic power with men, weakened the patriarchal system. Elisabeth Badinter welcomed the explosion of the traditional family: "Until a few decades ago, marriage was synonymous with security, respectability and fertility. Nowadays, it has lost these three essential characteristics... The considerable loss of influence of religion has allowed the development of two new customs that were unknown in earlier times: divorce and common-law unions[609]." Let us recall here that the precursor of the

---

[607] Elisabeth Badinter, *L'un est l'autre*, Éd. Odile Jacob, 1986, p. 217, 218. The real name of Anne Tristan, a hysterical anti-fascist militant, is Anne Zelansky.

[608] Elisabeth Badinter, *L'un est l'autre*, Éd. Odile Jacob, 1986, p. 319-321, 333

[609] Elisabeth Badinter, *L'un est l'autre*, Éd. Odile Jacob, 1986, p. 230, 231. On

divorce law in France in 1882 was another Israelite named Alfred Naquet.

The consequences of this cultural revolution on the European birth rate were not long in coming, especially with the drop in births brought about by the invention of the abortion pill RU 486. This abortion pill, designed and produced by Professor Etienne Beaulieu, made billions for the Roussel-Uclaf monopoly and its "brilliant" inventor. A coincidence: Professor Beaulieu was also an Israelite: "Born in Strasbourg on 12 December 1926, he was the son of Leonce Arrodi Blum, born in Alsace, and his wife Therese Lion, born in Caen. Leonce Blum was the son of Rabbi Felix Blum. After the Popular Front, the Blum surname was difficult to bear, so the Blums requested a change of surname, which was granted by decree in 1947. From then on, they took the surname Beaulieu[610]."

Dr. Georges Valensin reported on these abortion practices, noting this testimony from the inter-war period: "Israeli doctors were accused of immorality because they easily lent themselves to limiting births. According to the *Libre Parole* of 1 December 1935, the ablation of ovaries to sterilise their clients was commonplace[611]."

After Sigmund Freud, the Freudo-Marxists of the Frankfurt School and the battalions of feminists also sought to trivialise homosexuality by defending the idea of the bisexual nature of all human beings. This is what Elisabeth Badinter wrote in a chapter entitled "the advent of the androgynous": "In reality, we are all androgynous since humans are bisexual, in various aspects and to varying degrees. Masculine and feminine intersect in each of us". Traditional education, which has hitherto had the function of producing "men" and "women", must now, according to her, make room for new norms: "It was up to education to repress ambiguities and to teach to reject the other part of oneself. A "virile" man, a "feminine" woman… The imposed norm was contrast and opposition". There is however "a whole range of possible intermediates between the two ideal types. In reality, the training more or less achieves its aim, and the adult always retains within him an indestructible part of the Other. The model of resemblance is conducive

---

divorce law: see *Planetary Hopes*, p. 79.

[610] Henry Coston, *Les Financiers qui ménent le monde*, 1989 Edition, p. 520.

[611] Georges Valensin, *La Vie sexuelle juive*, Éditions philosophiques, 1981, p. 145.

to the integration of our androgynous nature". And he added: "It is now widely accepted that the personal fulfilment of the individual passes through the recognition of his or her bisexuality[612]." Evidently, the impersonal form "it is widely accepted" referred mainly to the world of Jewish intellectuals who analyse their own personal cases.

Therefore, differences between men and women should not exist, or as little as possible. "Now that social references are fading away, that the plasticity of sexual roles is imposed, and that women can choose not to be mothers, the specific differences between the One and the Other are becoming increasingly difficult to perceive... Apart from the irreducible chromosomal difference, we are reduced to distinctions of more and less. Certainly there are more male hormones in the One and female hormones in the Other, but both sexes produce male and female hormones. Males have greater muscular strength and more aggressiveness than females, but these differences vary greatly between individuals". There are therefore in reality "several intermediate types between the types defined as female and male," wrote Badinter who cited in support of his thesis Professor Etienne Beaulieu, who also argued that there was "a great initial similarity and a certain plasticity in the differentiation of the two sexes," and "that there are no impassable boundaries between the masculine and the feminine[613]."

Another leading sociologist, James Levine, "who studies new fatherhood in the United States" supported these views and noted "the gradual blurring of the line between motherhood and fatherhood" pointing out that, in divorce cases, "the percentage of fathers gaining custody of their children has been rising steadily over the past decade". Feminists have put an end to the "sexual division of labour".

Elisabeth Badinter further quoted sociologist Edgar Morin, who considered "the feminisation of men and the virilisation of women" as "progress on the road to humanisation". And he added in *The Lost Paradigm* (p.87): "There is no doubt, in our opinion, that man humanises himself by developing his genetic and cultural femininity[614]."

"The ideal is to give birth to a unisexual human being," continued Elisabeth Badinter. "By finally becoming aware of physical and psychic

---

[612] Elisabeth Badinter, *L'un est l'autre*, Éd. Odile Jacob, 1986, p. 269.

[613] Elisabeth Badinter, *L'un est l'autre*, Éd. Odile Jacob, 1986, p. 249.

[614] Elisabeth Badinter, *L'un est l'autre*, Éd. Odile Jacob, 1986, p. 257, 288.

bisexuality, which has long been denied, we can reduce the otherness of the two sexes to a minimum. For the moment, the only difference that remains, like an intangible rock, is the fact that it is the women who bear the children of the men and not the other way round... By distancing themselves from motherhood, women implicitly take a step towards their partners". But this last difference is going to disappear, and soon, perhaps, men "will be able to bear a child without a mother, much as certain women bear children without a father." Elisabeth Badinter put "the possibility of the pregnant man" on the table: delusion? Science fiction? "Maybe not. The two main people responsible for the first French test-tube baby have already cast doubt on its impossibility." In April 1985, answering a question in a women's magazine, "Is the pregnant man really feasible?", Professor René Frydman had replied, "Two years ago, I would not have believed it. But now, frankly, I don't know any more." A few months later, in another magazine, Frydman was "clearly more affirmative": "Technically, it is possible... the myth of male pregnancy may one day become reality." (*Actuel*, February 1986)

That would put an end to sex differences and therefore also to "discriminations". "Bisexual humanity brings the sexes as close together as possible. In this way, it allows the expression of all personal differences. It is no longer divided into two heterogeneous groups, but consists of a multiplicity of individualities that are both similar and distinguishable through infinite nuances[615]."

We recognise here the egalitarian fanaticism of Judaism: always the same obsession with levelling out the differences between human beings. Feminists claim that there are no differences between the sexes, as in the old days, Marxists promised that social classes would be abolished, and just as today, democrats predict a world without borders that will reunite and encompass mixed humanity. The aim is always to dissolve identities, be they sexual, social, or national, and then to coagulate the atomised particles in order to unify the world and bring about the advent of an ultimate "peace", which will be the peace of Israel, the *pax Judaica*: dissolve and coagulate.

One of the great Jewish thinkers of the 20th century, Martin Buber, an early Austrian atheist and Zionist, expressed this permanent tension of Judaism towards unity very well: "It is this tension of the Jew towards

---

[615] Elisabeth Badinter, *L'un est l'autre*, Éd. Odile Jacob, 1986, p. 244, 303.

unity that makes Judaism a phenomenon of humanity, and the Jewish question a human question... The aspiration for unity is everywhere. Towards unity within the individual. Towards unity among the divided members of the people and among the nations. Towards the unity of man and all living things, towards the unity of God and the world... It is this tension towards unity that is at the origin of the creativity of the Jew. In his effort to access unity from the division of the self, he conceived the idea of the One God. From the effort to bring unity out of the division of the community, he conceived the idea of universal justice. From the effort towards unity out of the division of all that lives, he conceived the idea of universal love. From the effort towards unity out of the division of the world, he conceived the messianic ideal, which, in a later epoch, again with the participation of the Jews,... he called socialism[616]."

But this "tension towards unity" of which Martin Buber spoke translates above all into a destructiveness towards the rest of humanity, it being undeniable that the "creativity of the Jew" acts as a powerful solvent of the traditions of the peoples in the midst of which it has installed itself. Some might see in this definition of Judaism a certain "tension" towards totalitarianism. Others might even see in it the mark of the devil: "*Solve et coagula*" is the motto tattooed on Satan's arm: "*Solve et coagula*".

Elisabeth Badinter admitted that the ideal unisexual society she wanted to drag us into was an innovation in human history. The "new reflection on the sexes is made all the more difficult and risky by the fact that it has no pre-existing model on which to base itself[617]." To put it bluntly, these militant Israelites don't quite know where they are taking us. But the important thing, clearly, is to oppose the natural state of affairs: "The control of nature is receding and, with it, the difference between the sexes... Equality is in the process of being realised; it generates the similarity that puts an end to war... The 20th century has inaugurated in our part of the world something resembling a new era," wrote Badinter, dismissing the objections: Moralists "will see in this change, so contrary to the natural order, nothing but a manifestation of decadence analogous to so many others that history has known[618]."

---

[616] Martin Buber, *Judaïsme*, Édition Verdier, 1982, p. 34-37

[617] Elisabeth Badinter, *L'un est l'autre*, Éd. Odile Jacob, 1986, p. 249.

[618] Elisabeth Badinter, *L'un est l'autre*, Éd. Odile Jacob, 1986, p. 245, 250.

\* An uninterrupted flow without punctuation or typographical differentiation

These statements could be compared to those of the novelist Albert Cohen, in a passage from *Beautiful of the Lord*. At the end of the book, Cohen imitated James Joyce's stream-of-consciousness\*, pouring over several pages a revealing messianic-mundane verbiage: "Israel is the people of unnature bearing a mad hope that the natural abhors the noblest portions of humanity are of Jewish soul and stand firm on their rock which is the Bible oh my Jews to whom I silently speak know your people venerate them for having willed schism and separation for having waged the struggle against nature and its laws[619]."

"The fact that more and more of our bisexual nature is being brought out into the open ends up disorienting us," acknowledged Elisabeth Badinter. "The new model that is being constructed before our eyes is distressing. Actors in a revolution that has only just begun to take shape, we have lost our old references without being sure of the new ones... We have been taken by surprise by this formidable change of civilisation that we have brought about... We want to break with the old civilisation, but at the same time we fear the new[620]."

And we must recognise that, so far, this civilisational revolution has not been conducive to the fulfilment of Western men: "The years that have just passed seem to indicate that only a minority of men react positively to the new model. As a general rule—in this first stage of an evolution that has just begun—they express in various ways that they do not want to be the twins of women... Not feeling sufficiently anchored in their own sexual identity, men fear that the performance of traditionally feminine tasks will awaken homosexual drives in them[621]." Elisabeth Badinter relied here on another sexologist: According to R. Stoller, masculinity is indeed not present at birth: "As the feeling of being male is less anchored in men, homosexuality is felt as a mortal threat to their identity."

In the face of this "deadly threat", Western men are hardly reacting: "It may be surprising how silent men have been since the beginning of this

---

in which the character's thoughts and impressions emerge (from Molly Blum's famous soliloquy in Joyce's *Ulysses*).

[619] Albert Cohen, *Bella del Señor*, Editorial Anagrama, Barcelona, 1992, p. 562, 563.

[620] Elisabeth Badinter, *L'un est l'autre*, Éd. Odile Jacob, 1986, p. 249, 247

[621] Elisabeth Badinter, *L'un est l'autre*, Éd. Odile Jacob, 1986, p. 280, 282.

extraordinary mutation that started twenty years ago. No books, no films, no deep reflections on their new condition. They remain mute, as if tetanised by an evolution they have no control over... There is no collective male awareness of the new relations between the sexes. They deny it, put up with it or return in silence. The silence of half of humanity is never a good omen". Their response "will surely depend on how they will solve their identity problems. Will they be able to cohabit better with their inner femininity or, on the contrary, will they be more anxious about their self-confidence and their virility[622]?" Elisabeth Badinter concluded her book with this sentence, "The end of man? No, a new man." This itself was already the ambition of the Bolsheviks.

On the back cover of Badinter's book, Rachel Assouline of the magazine *L'Événement du jeudi* reviewed the book: "The most ingrained preconceptions about relations between men and women are blown out of the water. If the talent of an essayist is measured in terms of the intellectual itch and exhilaration she provokes, then Elisabeth Badinter is particularly good". Once again we note the typical inclination of Jewish intellectuals to provoke "itching[623] ", their morbid need to provoke the goyim. They are the ones who are then surprised to be "persecuted". As Vincent Acosta wrote in 1623, in his *Discourse against the Jews*: "They are greedy, malicious, envious, murderous, perfidious, hated by God and man, inventors of all sorts of evils, rebellious, without faith, without love, without truth... mortal enemies of mankind[624]."

## Incest

The question of incest is an important theme in the literary and cinematic output of Judaism. In *Psychoanalysis of Judaism,* we saw how the Torah offers numerous examples of incestuous relationships. Of course, incest is strictly forbidden in Judaism, as stipulated in the Torah (Leviticus, 18), and in the Babylonian Talmud (Yebamot, 2a). This is what Gérard Haddad tried to explain in his book *The Talmudic*

---

[622] Elisabeth Badinter, *L'un est l'autre*, Éd. Odile Jacob, 1986, p. 341.

[623] On "itching": read *Psychanalyse du Judaïsme*, p. 69.

[624] Daniel Tollet, *Les Textes judéophobes et judéophiles dans l'Europe chrétienne à l'époque moderne*, Presses universitaires de France, 2000, p. 45.

*Sources of Psychoanalysis*[625], with a certain ambiguity, by the way. For everything is ambiguous in Judaism, and it is undeniable that Jews know how to deal with biblical texts. In his book on *Jewish Messianism*, Gershom Scholem, one of the greatest specialists on Kabbalah, explained that the Hasidic Jews also knew how to interpret the law in their own way, and recalled that the Jews belonging to the heretical sect of the Sabbateans had adopted a rule of conduct that allowed them to systematically violate all the prohibitions of the Torah, especially that of incest, which they had declared abrogated[626]. What gives rise to an equivocal interpretation in the Talmudic Jews is interpreted more clearly by the Hasidic Jews, and in a perfectly explicit manner by the Sabbatean Jews. On this subject we refer to our previous book, *Psychoanalysis of Judaism*.

The Jewish American researcher David Bakan went on to provide confirmation that such practices were common in Jewish communities. In his book, *Freud and the Jewish Mystical Tradition*, he questioned "the role of incest in Jewish history" in an attempt to understand Freud's "repeated references to it". "Because of their endogamy, the problem of incest was a characteristic feature of Jewish communities, so that the role of Jewish mysticism (i.e. Hasidism) was partly to provide the means to deal with the intense feelings of guilt arising from incestuous desires." Jews, indeed, especially in Eastern Europe, usually lived in small communities, "so that the choice of a partner was extremely limited", and it was naturally forbidden to marry a goy. The traditional arrangement of marriages by the elders of the Jewish community was partly due to "the fact that the elders knew the essential information about degrees of kinship."

We know, moreover, that Sephardic and Ashkenazi Jews married their children very young, at the age of 12 or 13[627]. "The custom of early marriages was perhaps justified, not only by the realism generally applied to the sexual impulses that existed in Jews, but also by the need to alleviate incestuous tendencies". David Bakan concluded: "Incestuous temptations are perhaps, as Freud indicates, universally

---

[625] Gérard Haddad, *Les Sources talmudiques de la psychanalyse*, Desclée de Brouwer, 1981, Poche, 1996.

[626] Gershom Scholem, *Le Messianisme juif*, 1971, Éd. Calmann-Levy, 1974, p. 135–137.

[627] Cf. *Psychanalyse du Judaïsme*, p. 350.

widespread, but they were especially marked in Jews, which prompted the elaboration of intense countermeasures and, consequently, an excessive feeling of guilt[628]."

The customs of the Jews are undoubtedly quite different from European customs. We saw, in *Psychoanalysis of Judaism*, that the Talmud was quite explicit on the subject. The reading of these texts is tiresome, so we will simply mention two exemplary and astonishing passages from tractate Sanhedrin 55a-55b (Babylonian Talmud): "In all crimes of incest [committed by the child], the passive adult incurs no guilt unless the other party is at least nine years and one day old. Hence the Baraitha supports Rab's assertion that nine years and one day is the minimum age of the passive partner for the adult to be liable." (Sanhedrin, 55a, note 1). "A girl of three years and one day of age, whose father arranged her [marriage] engagement, is committed to intercourse, since the legal status of intercourse with her is that of full intercourse. In the event that the childless husband of a girl three years and a day old dies, if her brother has sexual intercourse with her, then he acquires her as his wife." (Sanhedrin, 55b).

The question of incest is, however, rather seldom alluded to in the literary output of Judaism. We know that the Jewish people love to keep mystery and secrecy alive, and incest is precisely one of the secrets, if not "THE" secret of Judaism. However, it appears here and there, anecdotally, in the pen of a few novelists. In the study on Romain Gary that we have already seen, the *Cahiers de l'Herne* informed us that his work reflected in many ways the neurosis of Judaism: "Incestuous fantasies are displayed in all their ambivalence. With the young women he meets, Momo [the hero of one of his novels], hesitates between a love affair and a maternal quest. Under the pretext of universal love, Jean sleeps with a woman who could very well be his mother". Sexual ambiguity is naturally present: "The difference between the sexes becomes uncertain: Lola, born a man, has chosen a feminine identity and it is no longer clear whether Rosa, aged, is still a woman[629]." (*Life Ahead*).

See now what Elie Wiesel wrote, in *Talmudic Celebration*, when he took a random example to explain the Talmud: "Sometimes the Talmudic sentence drags with it ten others, sometimes a few lines are

---

[628] David Bakan, *Freud et la tradition mystique juive*, 1963, Payot, 2001.

[629] *Emil Ajar, Romain Gary*, Les Cahiers de l'Herne, 2005

enough to tell a story. An example? A woman wanted to consult Rabbi Eliezer about a serious problem, but he refused to help her. She then turned to Rabbi Yeoshua, who was more benevolent. What was the problem? *B'ni hakatan mibni hagadol*, my younger son has my older son for his father. About this incestuous woman afflicted with remorse and the desire to confess, would Dostoyevsky not have been able to write six hundred pages[630]?"

Elie Wiesel cited in his book the case of Rabbi Elisha, who lived in the second century, at the time of Hadrian and the war in Judea. Wiesel told us that he was the "symbol of abjuration and betrayal... He had pockets full of anti-Jewish pamphlets... Worse still: he began to campaign for forced assimilation... He sympathised with the occupier, became a collaborator and finally an accomplice of the Roman army." That Rabbi Elisha "was Akher-he represented the dark forces of the Jews, the forces of man's Evil... He was called first Rabbi Elisha, then Elish ben Abouya, then ben Abouya, and finally Akher." What could be the origin of this unacceptable dissent? "The first hypothesis points to the guilt—of course—of? his mother. Jewish mothers are always to blame for what happens to their beloved children." And Wiesel elliptically added: "Like a good Jew, he loved his mother—a little too much[631]."

We know that Jacques Attali also evoked the question surreptitiously in 1994, in a passage of his novel entitled Il *viendra* (*The Coming*). In his first novel, in 1989, he had also alluded to it. *Eternal Life* is a more or less incomprehensible novel, and in any case terribly boring, which did not prevent the author from winning the Grand Prix *du Roman de la Société des gens de Lettres* (*Grand Prix du Roman de la Société des gens de Lettres*). It is a book for the initiated. The author expressed himself in ellipsis so that only Jews could understand what the story was all about. This is what you can read on the title page: "Over there, on a desert island—or up there, on some distant star—a people cut off from everything by some great catastrophe repeats the history of mankind from its origins, including the persecution, exile and massacre of a minority that stands out for its traditions, its magical powers and the eternal life it is supposed to have... Memory and prophecy become confused, and this "testimony from beyond the grave" begins to resemble and mingle with the oldest stories humanity has ever lived

---

[630] Elie Wiesel, *Célébration talmudique*, Éd. Seuil, 1991, p. 12

[631] Elie Wiesel, *Célébration talmudique*, Éd. Seuil, 1991, p. 182-191.

through, recalling the barbaric excess of the worst genocides and the wildest hopes of the makers of eternity." And "humanity" in question, you have understood it clearly, looks strangely like a small, well-known village.

The book began well enough, promising some pearls such as this for the researcher: "In that little canton of the Universe there survived in penitence seventeen million men and women imprisoned by their enigmas, ashamed of their triumphs, grieved by their forgetfulness, terrified by their hopes, drunk with their loneliness". (p. 15). The whole hysteria of Judaism can hardly be summed up in fewer words.

Unfortunately, the rest of the book is a gibberish with no head or tail, in which Jacques Attali tried to make his fellow human beings understand that he was really referring to them, only to them and to no one else but them. For example, he explained that "the "Siv" have become renowned professors, prudent bankers, efficient and recognised high-ranking civil servants" (p. 63). (p. 63). Attali ended by declaring at the end of his book that the Jews were definitely the only "humanity" worth its salt: "Now it's up to you, it's up to you. I am relying on you. I beg you, protect yourselves: you are the last flame of Humanity[632]."

But in this absurd story, it was also a question of a "Great Book of the Secret", of a "Great Speaker". The heroine's name was Golischa: "Of her father I knew nothing: neither his name, nor his face, nor his history. She had heard from some of the officers of the Guard that he had been an adventurer, killed before his birth in an ambush... One day, he even heard one of his servants claim in restricted circles that his grandfather was also his father, which explained the mother's prostration and the daughter's seclusion[633]." In short, her grandfather had slept with his own daughter.

Let us complete this chapter on incest with an analysis of film production, even if it is most likely incomplete. Indeed, to do so, we would have to watch all the films of the Jewish directors again, but this time with the sharper vision provided by this new knowledge of the particular mental universe of the Jewish intellectuals.

---

[632] Jacques Attali, *La Vie éternelle*, Éd. Fayard, 1989, p. 241

[633] Jacques Attali, *La Vie éternelle*, Éd. Fayard, 1989, p. 16

## THE JEWISH FANATICISM

Years ago, when we saw Roman Polanski's film *Chinatown* (1974) for the first time, we did not detect anything specifically Jewish, for the simple reason that we did not pay attention to it. Let us briefly recall the story: In Los Angeles in the 1930s, drought forces small farmers to sell their land. The land is bought up at a bargain price by large landowners with the complicity of the municipality, which drains the valuable water at night. Jack Nicholson, a private detective, investigates this case, which is not to everyone's liking. He receives a strong warning and a good cut on the nose. With the bandage on, he is asked: "Does it hurt?" Only when I breathe! At the end of the film, the beautiful Faye Dunaway, slapped in the face by Nicholson, finally reveals who this young girl is that she is hiding in plain sight: she is both his daughter and his sister. She had a daughter with her monster of a father, the big landowner. In this film, Roman Polansky has typically projected onto the Goyim a problem that torments the Jewish community. It is public knowledge that Polansky is still wanted by the US justice system in connection with a paedophilia case.

Let's look at the film by the famous director Joseph Mankiewicz, *Suddenly, Last Summer* (1960): A wealthy American (Katherine Hepburn), traumatised by the death of her son, enlists the services of a famous doctor to perform a lobotomy on her niece (Elizabeth Taylor), who is in a psychiatric hospital and whom she reproaches for having separated her from her "beloved son". The incestuous relationship—here, between mother and son—is strongly suggested. Here, too, the director has projected his obsessions onto a Christian family in a typical way. It should be noted that the only sane character in the story is the "great surgeon named Cukrowicz", but Joseph Mankiewicz cast him as a handsome Aryan (Montgomery Clift) to mislead the viewer.

Louis Malle's film *The Breath at the Heart* (1971) also dealt with incest. This leads us to believe that Louis Malle, in the light of the rest of his production, which is at least "compromised", is of Jewish origin. The story is that of a bourgeois family in Dijon in 1954, which marks the end of the Indochina war. The father is a busy gynaecologist; Clara, the mother, looks after her son Laurent, the youngest, who is suffering from a heart condition. She accompanies him on a cure, and their complicity leads to an incestuous relationship. Louis Malle "criticises a straitjacketed society", applauds criticism... This is what the leftist Jean-Luc Doin said about Louis Malle in his book *Films de scandale*: "He irritates the biemensens by depicting a mother-son incest against a jazz background in *The Heartbeat* (1971) and the fiery love affair between a British MP and his son's girlfriend in *Wounded* (*Fatale*, 1992)[634]."

In 1997, the cosmopolitan director Milos Forman presented *Larry Flint*, a film about the scandalous life of the pornographic press magnate who became the US standard-bearer against the moral order. Its recent re-release has allowed us to see that the question of incest is also present. We see this pornography "pope"—portrayed with the features of a goy—brought to justice by the representative of the "moral order" for having caricatured him in a newspaper having sex with his own mother in the bathroom. Once again, the accusatory projection is verified. In France, Catholic associations had succeeded in having the film's poster, depicting a crucified man on a woman's crotch, withdrawn.

In *Coming out of the Closet* (France, 2001), Francis Veber told the story of a drab accountant with no personality who was about to be fired. Following the advice of his neighbour, an old homosexual, he decides to pass himself off as a homosexual to try to keep his job. All around him, the looks of others change and everything works out well for him. It seems that director Francis Veber "denounces the reign of political correctness". The film trivialised homosexuality and presented people who were still a little reticent as intolerant and brutal jerks, probably hiding a "repressed homosexuality". In the 47th minute of the film, a dialogue between two employees addressed the subject of incest, about a film that had been shown on television the day before: the story of a girl in love with a man who finally discovered that he was her father. Jewish filmmakers often introduce such winks of the eye into their films that only the initiated notice.

Serge Gainsbourg's *Charlotte for Ever* (1986) told of the troubled relations between a drunken father, Stan, and his fifteen-year-old daughter. This attraction to young people was also seen, for example, in Stanley Kubrick's 1962 film *Lolita*, based on Vladimir Nabokov's novel: Humbert, a divorced and attractive literature professor, rents a room in the house of Charlotte, a cultured widow. She tries to seduce him, but he is attracted to her teenage daughter Lolita. He ends up marrying her mother so that he can stay close to her daughter. When

---

[634] Jean-Luc Doin, *Films à scandale*, Éditions du Chêne, 2001, p. 38. In a book of dialogues with Louis Malle, published in 1993, we learn that the director is originally from northern France. His father was the director of a sugar factory belonging to the Beghin family. Françoise, his mother, was a Miss Beghin (Philip French, *Conversation avec Louis Malle*, Denoël, 1993, p. 207).

Charlotte dies, Humbert takes Lolita back to the United States on a regrettable journey that raises suspicions all around him.

The theme was also addressed in Elia Kazan's *Baby Doll* (1957): In a backwater in America, Archie, a guy who's been a bit lost since his company went bankrupt, is married to a sexy girl who has decided to wait her twenties to consummate the marriage. However, he can't stop a rival from seducing his pretty, immature wife.

Of course, not all filmmakers who have dealt with incest are Jewish, although one may doubt their origins, as Jewishness is often lived in secret. In *La Luna* (1979), the left-wing filmmaker Bernardo Bertolucci told the story of Caterina. This famous opera singer leaves the United States for good after the death of her husband. She settles in Italy with her son Joe. When she discovers to her horror that Joe is taking drugs, she realises that she has been too negligent and decides to take care of him.

The very provocative and anticlerical Mexican (ex-Spanish) filmmaker Luis Buñuel directed the 1961 film *Viridiana*: the ending of the film suggested an incest scene between a young woman and her cousin. But censorship forced the filmmaker to beat around the bush. This is what Jean-Luc Doin wrote in his *Dictionary of censorship in cinema*: "In a first version, Buñuel showed the heroine knocking at her cousin's door. The door opened, she entered, and the door closed. As the censors rejected this incest-like epilogue, Buñuel showed Viridiana joining her cousin and lover in a game of cards. The cousin said in conclusion: "I knew you would end up playing with us". An insidious ending as it suggests a *ménage à trois*.[635]"

The film *Festen* was directed by Danish director Thomas Vintergerg (1998): In a very respectable family, everyone is invited to celebrate the sixtieth birthday of the head of the family. But terrible secrets are soon revealed: the father sexually abused his daughter and son for years.

Incest was evoked in *Sitcom*, a film by François Ozon that shows a very peaceful French family until the day when the father has the strange idea of buying a rat and offering it to his children. From that moment on, everything goes wrong: the son discovers that he is homosexual and starts having sex with the maid's husband, a black man; the daughter becomes sadistic and tries to commit suicide; the mother has incestuous

---

[635] Jean-Luc Doin, *Dictionnaire de la censure au cinéma*, Presse Universitaire de France, 1998, p. 307.

desires with her son, while the husband remains impassive, as if gone and absent. In a rather symptomatic scene, the man turns into a giant rat and assaults his wife in the bedroom. Finally, he is stabbed to death by his daughter. The last scene of the film is the following: the mother, son and daughter meditate on his grave. Reflected in a mirror, the upside-down, satanic crucifix appears on the tombstone. And once again we see the convergences between militant homosexuality and the obsessions of Judaism. The film is "biting, hilarious and totally iconoclastic" according to *Le Parisien* (15 July 2006). It is true that when it comes to sullying family values, dragging Catholicism through the mud and spitting on the values of European civilisation, a cosmopolitan journalist always comes out to call it "genius", "disturbing", "irritating", until the "biemenspensants" try to shake off these odious parasites.

We should also mention in this chapter Jonathan Litell, winner of the Goncourt Prize in 2006 for his novel *The Benevolent Ones*. The author described the suffering of the Jews during the Second World War through a rather special character: a homosexual, paedophile SS officer who allegedly had sexual relations with his twin sister. As we see, again, homosexuality and incest are very present in Judaism. But here, as elsewhere, Jewish intellectuals project their neurosis onto others, onto "all humanity". It seems quite clear to us that, by incarnating himself in the character of an SS officer, this Jonathan Littell has merely projected his identity disorder and his unconscious hatred of his own people onto the Nazis. On the other hand, the *Benevolent Ones* are mythological creatures out of hell "who rage against Orestes after he kills his mother". We have already seen what Xaviera Hollander wrote: American Jews"… are my most extravagant and depraved clients. Many of them seem to be going through psychoanalysis with problems arising from having an overly dominant mother or a wife who is a Jewish-American princess trying to dominate them… Many of the Jewish doctors who come to my house are flamboyant, and usually wish they were slaves." (*The Merry Madame,* p. 181). This is why Jonathan Litell, who unconsciously wishes to kill his mother and the entire Jewish people, has incarnated himself as a sadistic SS and chosen *The Benevolent Ones* as the title of his novel. All this nonsense and misrepresentation will not prevent him from becoming a "prince of literature". It is said that more than 200,000 Jews have already bought his book…

In the same vein, we could also look at Woody Allen's film, *Disassembled Harry* (USA, 1997). The director plays the role of an anguished Jewish writer who feels bad about himself. He asks a prostitute to tie him to a bed, to hurt him by whipping him, before finishing with a fellatio: another "benevolent!"

Elisabeth Badinter left a rather explicit passage on the subject of incest when she analysed the evolution of our European societies subjected to the delusions of cultural Judaism. She confusedly tried to justify incest, pretending to see it as a natural evolution of society, and finally presented its practice as a liberation: "We perceive less and less the extensive system of social exchange which gave its positive character to the law of exogamy, i.e. to the prohibition of incest. Since women no longer have any exchange value or peace value, the necessary incest prohibition loses one of its most important justifications. After the biological explanations for the incest ban—we now know that endogamous unions are no more harmful than other unions—the social advantage of necessary unions now also declines. But humanity has not run out of arguments to avoid what it abhors: the maintenance of the taboo is justified in another way. The discourse is no longer that of biology or anthropology, but that of psychoanalysis. Madness is today the last barrier against incest. Sexual relations between brothers and sisters, and especially between parents and children, are declared pathological and the cause of unhappiness. But for the first time, some people are daring to claim the right to incest out in the open, while others are trying to play it down. This is how Wardell Pomeroy... calmly states that "the time has come to recognise that incest is not necessarily a perversion or a form of mental illness, and that it can even sometimes be beneficial". Elisabeth Badinter added: "The prohibitions weigh less and less, and, as the temptations to defy them grow greater and greater, these will perhaps make the universal incest taboo fall into disuse[636]."

In his book on anti-Semitism, we had Stéphane Zagdanski warning us to "decipher" his words and restore the meaning of his sentences. On the subject of "anti-Semites", he wrote: "To decipher: they selfishly indulge in the dark pleasures of incest to which we have been denied access. It must be understood that the anti-Semite is very concerned about incest, which is logical, since he suffers from a deficiency of his limits[637]."

---

[636] Elisabeth Badinter, *L'un est l'autre*, Éd. Odile Jacob, 1986, p. 239.

[637] Stéphane Zagdanski, *De l'Antisémitisme*, Climats, 1995, 2006, p. 206. Cf:

Dr Georges Valensin recalled that psychoanalysis, which brings everything into the realm of sexuality, came from the brain of a Jew, that of Sigmund Freud: "Gifted with a Talmudic spirit, with his need to delve and discuss, he discovered sex everywhere. Psychoanalysis was a Jewish affair[638]." Indeed, Freud, who was steeped in Judaism, had grown up in a believing family in Moravia. "He had probably read the Zohar, according to which "the whole core, the whole sap and strength of life comes from the genital organs"."

In Vienna, where he lived, Jews "were extremely numerous, especially in the middle and intellectual classes", where he recruited his clientele. George Valensin wrote: "His own Jewish origin must have kept away a good part of the Christian patients, less neurotic than the perpetually restless sons of Israel... Many circumcised clients could account for the exorbitant importance given to the castration complex by the father of psychoanalysis: penis envy, another Freudian discovery, could be explained by the extreme predilection for boys in Jewish families; girls must have deeply regretted not being a boy".

Regarding incest, Dr. Valensin said with a gentle euphemism: "The Oedipus complex, the love for the parent of the opposite sex, occurred more intensely in the Jewish family, because the latter lived more closed in on itself". That is indeed the case: "closed in on itself". We can therefore conclude with Georges Valensin: "Freud has generalised the inhibitions, probably much more frequent in Jews restrained by their morals... Through psychoanalysis, Christianity was to become even more impregnated with Judaism[639]."

---

*Psychanalyse du Judaïsme*, p. 357.

[638] Dr. Valensin mentioned what we had analysed in *Psychoanalysis of Judaism* about the Jewish origins of Sigmund Freud's inspiration: "He gave a new impulse to the study of dreams; there were already 24 professional dream interpreters in Jerusalem according to the Talmud, which is full of dream stories with a divinatory meaning". (Encyclopedia Judaïca, vol. XIII, art. *Les rêves*). "In Marrakech, a traveller was surprised to observe that in the Jewish quarter dreams were a constant topic of conversation". (J. Benech, *Essai d'explication d'un mellah*, Marrakesh, 1936, p. 114). The interpretation of dreams was a common practice in Babylonia and Sumer.

[639] Georges Valensin, *La Vie sexuelle juive*, Éditions philosophiques, 1981, p. 171, 172.

It is true that the psychoanalyst had replaced the priest in caring for souls, but with the difference that one did it for free while the other demanded to be paid. It is amusing to note how these "sick people[640]" constitute the majority of the battalions of those who claim to cure humanity. But this is only one of the many "paradoxes" of Judaism. The truth is that all those Jewish psychoanalysts do not practice their profession so much to cure their patients as to try to cure themselves through them. It is not by chance that Freud built his career on the analysis of hysterical pathology, since, on the one hand, he himself was directly affected, and, on the other hand, he could see that the malady was widespread in the Jewish community, for the simple reason that incest, which is the cause of it, seems to be much more common in the Jewish community than in the rest of society. With his theory of the Oedipus complex, Freud had only projected a Jewish specificity onto the whole of humanity, for in reality, the famous "Oedipus complex" is above all the "Israel complex", that of a mother sleeping with her own child. When he claimed that neuroses had their origin in the repression of sexual impulses by Christian morality, he was in fact projecting his own neurosis and the neurosis of Judaism onto a civilisation that he consciously hated. Indeed, he himself had warned us on landing in America: "You do not know that we bring you the plague!"

## *Jewish anguish*

Jewish neurosis is translated, on the religious level, by a megalomaniacal project with universal pretensions. The aim is to work for the unification of the earth, the disappearance of races, religions and nations, in a great planetary intermingling, leading to a world of "Peace", the prelude to the coming of the Messiah. On the individual level, this neurosis sometimes presents a face that can inspire compassion when expressed with sincerity. The famous American novelist Philp Roth left a testimony in this regard, in *Portnoy's Evil*, a novel published in 1967. In that book, which sold five million copies

---

[640] Jacques Attali mentioned the expulsion of the Jews from Egypt in these terms: "According to tradition, this departure took place in -1212. Egyptian texts of the time also mention the expulsion of a sick people, or of a people with a leper king, and an uprising of foreign slaves". (*Los Judios, el mundo y el dinero*, Fondo de cultura económica de Argentina, Buenos Aires, 2005, p. 29).

worldwide[641], the author truly comes across as a sex maniac. The first pages explain to the reader the nature of "Portnoy's disease": "A disorder in which altruistic and moral impulses are experienced with great intensity, but are perpetually at war with the most extreme and sometimes perverse sexual desire. Spielvogel says of this: "Exhibitionism, voyeurism, fetishism and autoeroticism abound, as does oral intercourse... Spielvogel considers that these symptoms can be traced back to the bonds that have prevailed in the mother-child relationship". In this case, you have naturally guessed it, it is a Jewish mother.

Philip Roth was obviously deeply affected by this: "Doctor Spielvogel, this is my life; and it happens to be all in a Jewish joke. I am the son of a Jewish joke, but not a joke at all! Please, who made us so crippled? Who made us so morbid and so hysterical and so weak?... Doctor, what name would you give to this illness I'm suffering from? Is it the Jewish suffering I've heard so much about? Doctor, I can't bear it any longer, I can't bear to live so terrified for nothing. Grant me the blessing of manhood! Make me brave! Make me strong! Make me whole! I'm sick and tired of being a nice Jewish boy, of pleasing my parents in public, while in private I fuck the *putz\**. *That's* enough[642]!"

The Roth family learned one day that a fifteen-year-old boy named Ronald Nimkin, a neighbourhood kid, had hanged himself in the bathroom. In the building, the women commented on the fact: "You couldn't find a boy more in love with his mother than Ronald! And Philip Roth indignantly exclaimed: "I swear, I'm not making it up, it's not a manipulated memory, it's exactly the words those women use... My own mother... greets me with the following telephone greeting: "Well, how is my love?" Her love calls me with her husband listening... And it never crosses her mind that, if I am her love, who is he, the *schmegeggy\** with whom she lives?" Jewish mothers, "in love" with their children, probably imagine they have given birth to the long-awaited Messiah of Israel. Philip Roth added: "What was wrong with these Jewish parents, what were they capable of making us young Jews believe, on the one hand, that we were princes, unique in the world, like

---

[641] We must understand that it was a great success within the Jewish community.

\* Penis

[642] Philip Roth, *El mal de Portnoy*, Seix Barral, Barcelona, 2007, Debolsillo, Mondadori, 2008, p. 35.

unicorns, geniuses, more brilliant than anyone else ever was and more beautiful than any other children in history? Redeemers, pure perfection[643]... "

This could partly explain why so many journalists have the habit of praising their fellow writers in the most indecent manner, describing their works as "genius", "incomparable", "splendid", and so on. The novelist gave vent to his resentment against his parents: "Because I've had it up to here with all this talk of 'goyische patatín' and 'goyische patatán'. If he is bad, he is a Goyim, if he is good, he is a Jew. Don't you realise, my dear parents,... that such a way of thinking is a bit barbaric, that in reality all you are doing is revealing your fear? The first difference I learned from you, I am sure, was not between night and day, nor between cold and heat, but between the Goyische and the Jewish... you narrow-minded *schmuck*\*\*—what hatred I have for your narrow-minded Jewish mentality[644]!"

Philip Roth's novel is naturally overloaded with pornographic scenes. At the end of the book, his hero travels to Israel, hoping that his obsessive neurosis will finally subside. On a beach in Tel-Aviv, he shares with us his amazement: "I leave the room and go to splash in the sea with the happy Jews. I'm swimming in the area where the crowds are most crowded. I'm frolicking in a sea full of Jews! Frolicking Jews, who are jumping around! Their Jewish limbs are bobbing in the water, no less Jewish! The Jewish children are laughing as if they were the masters of the place!... The fact is, yes, this place belongs to them! And the lifeguard, another Jew! Beach up, beach down, as far as the eye can see. All Jews, and more pouring out as if from a cornucopia in the beautiful morning. I lie down on the beach, I close my eyes. From above I hear an engine noise: nothing to fear, it's a Jewish plane. Below me, the sand is warm, and it's Jewish. I buy a Jewish ice cream from an ice-

---

[643] Philip Roth, *El mal de Portnoy*, Seix Barral, Barcelona, 2007, Debolsillo, Mondadori, 2008, p. 94, 116

\* Cuckold

[644] Philip Roth, *El mal de Portnoy*, Seix Barral, Barcelona, 2007, Debolsillo, Mondadori, 2008, p. 72, 73

\*\* Stupid

cream man who is no less Jewish". What a thing", I say to myself: "a Jewish country!"... Alex in Wonderland[645]."

Everything is going well, but unfortunately his Jewish neurosis seems to haunt him to the end. While he is with a young Israeli army lieutenant in his hotel room, he discovers that he is impotent: impotent in Israel[646]! Finally, all these misfortunes lead him to consider his wretched condition as a Jew: "We, the fallen psychoneurotic Jews... "

In *The Modern World and the Jewish Question*, published in 2006, the planetary sociologist Edgar Morin also projects his faults onto others, after having experienced some unpleasantness with his own community over his statements on Israeli policy. He pretends to discover that "Jewish psychopathology" is a recent phenomenon: "After the anti-Semitic psychopathology obsessed with the omnipresent and threatening Jew, there has appeared an obsessive Jewish psychopathology that detects the omnipresent and threatening anti-Semitism[647]."

But we know perfectly well that this Jewish anguish, which often has the appearance of pure paranoia, has been deeply rooted in the Jewish soul since ancient times; and anti-Semitism, which the Jews are happy to exaggerate out of all proportion, has little to do with it. Let us listen to the writer Georges Perec: "Being Jewish is not linked to a belief, a religion, a practice, a culture, a folklore, a history, a destiny, a language. It is rather an absence, a question, a hesitation, a restlessness: an unsettling certainty behind which looms another certainty, abstract, heavy, unbearable: that of having been designated as a Jew, and therefore a victim[648]."

Three years ago, before the publication of the first volume of this study of Judaism, we had dismissed this testimony as yet another manifestation of the "perfidy" of the Jews, always ready to make jeremiads to deceive the goyim. We now think that it is impossible to understand the Jewish soul without taking into account this existential anguish that undermines most Jews, at least the intellectuals. Let us also

---

[645] Philip Roth, *El mal de Portnoy*, Seix Barral, Barcelona, 2007, Debolsillo, Mondadori, 2008, p. 253, 254

[646] "I couldn't keep an erection in the Promised Land!"

[647] Edgar Morin, *Le Monde moderne et la question juive*, Éd. Seuil, 2006, p.152

[648] Georges Perec, *Je suis né*, Éd. Seuil, 1990, p. 99

listen to Georges Friedmann, who wrote in 1965: "Jewish restlessness is a psychological, ethical, social fact… The range extends from weak, intermittent manifestations to the typical forms of anxiety, anguish and neurosis[649]."

In 2002, a certain Joseph Bialot published a book of memories. On that occasion, the newspaper *Le Monde* generously devoted an entire page to it. The author, born in 1923 in Warsaw, had settled in Paris with his family in the working-class district of Belleville. Naturally, he too had experienced the death camps. "The Jews of Western Europe, perfectly integrated, were totally unprepared for the horror". Like hundreds of thousands of others, he was able to return alive to tell the tale. But Joseph Bialot put it frankly: his trauma was not so much due to the concentration camp experience as to the upbringing he had received: "Above all, I had to cure myself of a family neurosis due to 'overprotection'". Indeed, this communist party member had been seeing a psychoanalyst for nine years.

"There are perhaps two ways of dealing with Jewish neurosis, psychoanalysis and Zionism." This was what Michael Bar-Zvi, the author of a *Philosophy of the Jewish Nation*, declared on *Radio J* in 2006.

Jacques Kupfer, who was a Betar leader in France in the 1980s, provided a corroborating testimony. In 1979, this Jew of Russian-Polish origin was thirty years old and was determined to convince, through conferences and meetings, French Jews to settle in Israel, to make their "*alyah*" as they say. He defined himself as a Jew, exclusively Jewish: "I am only Jewish, not French at all… I don't give a damn about France… If it wasn't for my father, I would have been in Israel a long time ago… It's not of my own free will that I'm staying in France: I don't want to leave my parents, who are too old to rebuild their lives". For him, Jews all over the world are destined to live in Israel. And to the journalist's question: "How do you explain that very few French Jews go to Israel?", he replied: "Because they are sick! I say this without malice, because I too have traces of this disease. Two thousand years in the ghetto, I repeat: it is a disease that makes it very difficult to transplant oneself". And he insisted on that point: "The Jewish people are sick from two thousand years of *gola*[650]."

---

[649] Georges Friedmann, *Fin du peuple juif?* Éd. Gallimard, 1965, p. 341.

[650] André Harris and Alain de Sédouy, *Juifs et Français*, Grasset, 1979, Poche,

The historian Henri Minczeles, who was studying the development of Zionist ideas in Russian communities in the early 20th century, also raised the question. At that time, Leo Pinsker had published a book entitled *Self-Emancipation,* which presented "an attempt to solve the Jewish problem through territorialism". The book was the prelude to the formation of the group Am Olam (The Eternal People), which influenced the Zionist movement in its early days: "A forerunner of Zionism, Pinsker characterised the Jewish people as a community of sick people. To remedy this anomalous, almost desperate situation, it was necessary to seek out virgin spaces of inhabitants, wherever[651]."

The writer Romain Gary also highlighted in one of his novels this neurosis so specific to Judaism: "Incarnated by a character admitted to a psychiatric clinic due to "genuine personality disorders", *Pseudo* explores in a privileged way the fluctuating borders separating reason and madness... Momo himself experiences occasional crises of violence that overwhelm him: "It's as if I had an inhabitant inside me[652]."

The dossier of the *Nouvel Observateur* of 26 February 2004, devoted to the publication of a biography by Myriam Anissimov entitled *Romain Gary, the cameleon,* revealed another facet of the character: "Gary has often lied without blushing, elevating dissimulation to the rank of the rights of man". He told, for example, that he was the "son of Ivan Mosjoukine, a dignified and beautiful actor famous in 1930s Russia." The journalist replied: "Myriam Anissimov is categorical: impossible. Mina Kacew, Romain's mother, never set foot in the theatre where the writer claims they loved each other". Later, in *The Promise of Dawn,* Gary would make Mina a renowned Paris designer. "Her mother was actually a humble milliner who toiled in the grimy suburbs of Wilno, Poland. The biographers' work is ruthless," added the journalist, who also wrote: "Lying was for him a courtesy, a calling card." Nor were the deeds of arms of this "hero of Free France" mentioned...

Like Romain Gary, Elie Wiesél also had an "inhabitant" inside him—a "*dibbouk*"—as he confessed in his last novel *A Mad Desire to Dance,*

---

1980, p. 328-344. "*Gola*: Exile.

[651] Henri Minczeles, *Histoire générale du Bund*, 1995, Denoël, 1999, p. 26.

[652] *La Vie devant soi*, p. 56 *in Emil Ajar, Romain Gary*, Les Cahiers de l'Herne, 2005

published in 2006: his hero, who "suffers from a madness due to an excess of memory" confessed to a psychoanalyst: "Like the dibbouk, I take refuge in my madness like in a warm bed on a winter's night. Yes, that's right. It is a dibbouk that haunts me, that lives inside me. He who takes my place. He who usurps my identity and imposes his destiny on me... Where does my great uneasiness come from, these changes, these sudden metamorphoses, without explanations or rites of passage, this being in the doldrums close to stultification, this vacillation of being that characterises my malaise?" Wiesel asked himself with anguish, through his character: "Am I paranoid, schizophrenic, hysterical, neurotic[653]?"

And like Romain Gary, Elie Wiesel was also prone to fabulation. We are familiar with the regrettable tendency of many Jewish intellectuals to distort reality and talk nonsense. In *Psychoanalysis of Judaism*, we dwelled at length on the testimonies of Elie Wiesel, Samuel Pisar and Marek Halter. Let us quote here the historian Pierre Vidal-Naquet, who declared one day about Elie Wiesel: "Rabbi Kahane, that Jewish extremist... is less dangerous than a man like Elie Wiesel, who speaks nothing but nonsense... You only have to read *The Night* to realise that some of his descriptions are not accurate and that he ends up becoming a holocaust peddler... For he is also lacking in truth, an immense lack of historical truth[654]."

But other, more sensible Jewish writers, too, let themselves be fooled by the imagination of these fabulists. Thus, in the preface to a book on the drama of the Second World War, Arthur Koestler naively repeated some humbug that no one today believes: "Hundreds of books were devoted to the preservation and cleansing of the master race, while at the same time melting and transforming corpses into soap[655]." Even in April 2003, we could read Frederic Stroussi writing earnestly in *Israël Magazine*: "SS Letton Cukurs had the hobby of throwing Jewish babies in the air and shooting them in the head, as with saucer shooting." Readers of *Psychoanalysis of Judaism* will know that fabulation is one of the symptoms of hysterical pathology. But it is true that, on these subjects, authors often have the unfortunate habit of copying each other.

---

[653] Elie Wiesel, *Un Désir fou de danser*, Éd. Seuil, 2006, p. 29, 13

[654] Pierre Vidal-Naquet in *Zéro*, April 1987, p. 57.

[655] Fred Uhlman, *L'ami retrouvé*, 1971, Éd. Gallimard, 1978, Folio, 1983, p. 11.

Romain Gary was also a "great depressive", according to the *Nouvel Observateur* of 26 February 2004, in which we read: "Tormented, hiding his great kindness behind coarse manners and a fanciful irony, emotional to the point of lying prostrate for hours without saying a word, unhealthily disordered", he was obviously suicidal. In his letters to René Agid in 1955, he wrote: "A missing button, a very small shoe, a lost key, and I see the irremediable peace of suicide as the only solution". The idea of suicide was indeed recurrent in his books. At the end of one of his novels, his hero named Tulipe committed suicide "in utmost protest" against "the little village next door, where the peasants were happy despite living next to a concentration camp[656]." Typically, the Jewish intellectual tries to blame the goyim by holding them responsible for all their ills. The whole world is guilty of complacency with the Nazis. The image is present in many Jewish intellectuals. See again Elie Wiesel: "What can we say about the death of a million Jewish children in an indifferent and complacent world[657]?"

It should be remembered that the actress Jean Seberg, the beautiful little *Herald Tribune* salesgirl in Jean-Luc Godard's *The Edge of Escape* (1960), Romain Gary's partner, had followed the writer in his political delirium and financed the Black Panther Party activists. He would end up sinking into madness and committing suicide in 1979. The hysterical pathology that characterises Judaism so well is indeed extremely contagious. Gary committed suicide on 2 December 1980. "It is undeniable that, through my mother, I have a Jewish sensibility. It comes through in my books and when I reread them, I feel it myself[658]." That is what we thought.

Although there are no statistics on the subject, we can safely say that suicides are very common in Judaism. The famous writer Stefan Zweig, one of the few Jewish writers with a talent for writing, had fled Austria in the 1930s and committed suicide in Brazil in 1942, devastated by the victories of his people's enemies in Europe. But if we look more closely, we realise that his suicidal instincts were already deeply buried in him from the beginning. Like the other Jews, this "citizen of the world" felt

---

[656] *Emil Ajar, Romain Gary*, Cahiers de l'Herne, 2005, p. 78-80

[657] Elie Wiesel, *Célébration talmudique*, Éd. Seuil, 1991, p. 210. See the chapters on 'guilt' in our previous books.

[658] *Emil Ajar, Romain Gary*, Les Cahiers de l'Herne, 2005. Interview published in the Jewish monthly *L'Arche*, 26 April 1970, p. 40–45.

a strong sense of identity rupture. Although Zweig made no secret of his Jewishness, he also claimed, like his fellow Jews, to be an "integrated" Jew. Identity obsession, a constituent element of Jewish neurosis, appeared, for example, in *The Dangerous Pity, a* novel in which a respectable Hungarian Castilian turned out to be a Jew who went to great lengths to conceal his past. This story, wrote Jacques Le Rider in the June 1995 literary review *Europe*, "is a moving testimony to a profound inner crisis and also a symptom of an almost pathological regression" (p. 42). (p. 42).

In his unfinished novel *Clarissa,* Stefan Zweig portrayed a Jewish neurologist named Silberstein who resembled the author in every respect. Silberstein went so far as to confess: "Actually, I am nervousness made man. I owe it to my Jewish ancestry. From my childhood, it grew into morbidity" (p. 49). (p. 49). In a youthful story from 1901 entitled *In the Snow,* Stefan Zweig already gave a glimpse of an almost morbid tendency and suicidal resignation: In this story, a Jewish community in a German village near the Polish border was fleeing before the arrival of a band of scourgers hostile to Jews. The fleeing caravan of Jews was caught in a snowstorm at night. Suddenly, they all succumbed to the temptation to take refuge in a collective death, leaving themselves freezing to death.

The June 1995 issue of *Europe* magazine, devoted to Stefan Zweig, featured an article by Monique Bacelli who made the same analysis of Stefan Zweig's last novel written in 1940, entitled *Chess Novel*: Zweig, the journalist wrote, "is shipwrecked in a neurotic splitting". In fact, the author wrote in the novel:"… I had nothing at my disposal but that senseless game against myself, my anger, my desire for revenge, fanatically pounced on it. Something inside me cried out for justice, and inside me I had no one to fight me but my other self". The theme of revenge is a recurring one in Judaism, but here we will note above all that Stefan Zweig's suicidal tendencies were not only dependent on the political events of his time, but were also constitutive of his personality.

Like all other Jewish intellectuals, Zweig was tormented by the universalism of Judaism. He opposed the Zionists' project to return to Israel and wrote: "There have always been two parties within the Jewish community, the one that believes that salvation is in the temple, and the one that believes that when the temple was destroyed during the siege of Jerusalem, the whole world would become the temple. I believe that "Jew" and "human" must remain identical, and I regard as a great moral danger any arrogance tending to isolate the Jewish community". This idea that assimilates "Jew" and "humanity" corresponds perfectly to the words of Elie Wiesel and the other Jewish intellectuals.

A great admirer of Freud, Zweig systematically sent his books to the master of psychoanalysis. In 1926, he presented Freud with several short novels that would later be published, and Freud showed great interest in commenting on them: *"Twenty-four Hours in the Life of a Woman*, whose heroine gives herself to a young baron in an attempt to save him from his suicidal passion for gambling, transposes, according to him, the problems of a mother who introduces her son to sexual relations in order to save him from the dangers of onanism: play would be no more than a substitute for masturbation and the "feminine impulses" described would be characteristic of the "libidinous fixation" of all mothers on their children. As for *The Destruction of a Heart*, it would revolve around the jealousy of a father who discovers his teenage daughter's sexuality, while she was originally his property" (p. 33). Interestingly, wrote Lionel Richard (*Europe*), Zweig had no reservations about these interpretations of Freud through the prism of sexuality alone… In his letter of thanks to Freud on 8 September 1926, he merely expressed his admiration once again.

Once again, we see how Jewish intellectuals are obsessed by incestuous drives. It is a fact that the suicide rate of psychiatrists and other psychologists is the highest of all professions in the medical sector. It was certainly not Nazism that killed Stefan Zweig, but rather Judaism that drove him to suicide.

A contemporary and compatriot of Stefan Zweig, the novelist Arthur Schnitzler had also suffered the suicide of his daughter. "Schnitzler was a pessimist, a sceptic, a tormented man who suffered censorship, anti-Semitism, and life-shattering dramas. His daughter Lili committed suicide in Venice in 1928. She was nineteen years old. In her novel *Der Weg ins Freie*, the main character Georg von Wergenthin is a divided aristocrat, a "dandy completely broken inside, a symbol of chaos and the end of a society." Regine Robin further wrote: "Fantasies of fragmentation also in Kafka whose hybrids and doubles are the emblematic figures. Everywhere an untraceable identity, uncomfortable comings and goings, nostalgic points of fixation, conversions and reconversions, points of anchorage in an often phantasmagorical Jewishness. Eternal oscillation between universalist socialist messianism and nationalist Jewish messianism of the Diaspora or Zionism". Here again is Jiri Langer from Prague, Kafka's friend, "in revolt against the nothingness of the Judaism (*Nichts von Judentum*) of his assimilated bourgeois family[659]."

We have already seen in our previous books how frequent suicides were around the person of Elie Wiesel, recounted in the two volumes of his biography. In his *Testament of a Murdered Jewish Poet*, he evoked the suicide of a certain Bernard Hauptmannn after the Nazi election victory in 1932. Again, one might think that anguish at the extent of resistance to Judaism drove this communist leader to suicide. But finally Elie Wiesel had to admit it: "Traub claimed that Bernard had been attracted by the idea of suicide for some time". The whole egocentrism of Judaism is verified in the following sentence: "Inge, on the contrary, maintained that Hauptmann's gesture was directed at humanity and not at himself. He had killed himself because, according to him, we had just witnessed the decadence, the death of the human species[660]."

The decline of Judaism is the death of the human species. Manes Sperber put it very well: "The genocide perpetrated against the Jews was a crime against the human species[661]." One can see here, once again, how Jews only reason according to their own standards and identity, and how they seem closed in, isolated, incapable of understanding that one can see the world other than through Judaism. Moreover, they always feel the need to project onto a universal plane a problem that concerns them in particular. Thus, when in 2003 it seemed that Iraq and Saddam Hussein were threatening Israel, Elie Wiesel leapt into the limelight to declare that the whole of humanity was under threat. The same speeches resonate today as Jewish communities around the world prepare, through the Western media, for war against Iran. In *Biblical Celebration*, Wiesel wrote: "Working for his people, the Jew helps humanity[662]."

Jewish neurosis can be translated in cinema by a compensatory creation. The persecuted little Jew, the intelligent but unfortunate *"schlémiel"*, who is beaten up after school, has imagined characters capable of

---

[659] CinémAction, *Cinéma et judéité*, Annie Goldmann (dir.), Cerf, 1986, p. 10.

[660] Elie Wiesel, *Le Testament d'un poète juif assassiné*, 1980, Points Seuil, 1995, p. 135.

[661] Manès Sperber, *Être Juif*, Éd. Odile Jacob, 1994, p. 81.

[662] Elie Wiesel, *Célébration biblique*, Éditions du Seuil, 1975, p. 142.

transforming themselves into beings endowed with extraordinary powers. This is how superheroes were born. Robert L. Liebmam wrote: "The idea that Jewishness is an utterly disadvantageous condition, and one from which it is natural to want to flee, is at the heart of the invention of Superman. Superman is the brainchild, in the early 1930s, of two young Cleveland Jews, [Jerome Siegel and Joseph Shuster], who did not consciously see their Jewishness as playing a role in the creative process; the stories in the "Superman" cycle contain no explicit reference to Jewishness, but the schlémiel-Superman theme is tied to Jewish religious and cultural traditions. The Clark Kent-Superman dualism that is at the centre of the fantastic story... corresponds to a typically Jewish imaginary; that the Man of Steel was imagined by two Jews is not the result of chance or coincidence." Compared to Kafka, who transformed a young man into an insect, Superman is incontestably a step forward.

The famous legend of the Golem fits into the same mental universe of Judaism. In Péretz's version, which has been reprinted many times, the Jews of Prague in the 16th century were threatened with certain and imminent destruction. Their rabbi then moulded a clay figure which he brought to life by blowing into its nostrils and whispering "The Name" in its ear. It was transformed into an invulnerable and invincible Avenger who slaughtered the "goyim" and stopped the pogroms, thus saving the surviving Jews.

In Charlie Chaplin's *The Dictator*, "the Jew takes over by transforming himself into his non-Jewish enemy, taking his place...; also in Superman, the little man empowers himself by shedding his Jewishness and adopting non-Jewish characteristics." And Robert Liebman added: "I am convinced that the dreams of non-Jews must be very different from those of Jews."

Analysis of Jerry Lewis's film *The Nutty Professor* (1963) reveals the same projective process. It is the story of an insignificant little man who discovers the formula for a magic potion to transform himself into a superman and seduce the woman he is in love with. "Julius Kelp is the quintessential *schlémiel*," wrote Liebman. He is short-sighted, humble and clumsy. Buddy Love, on the other hand, is not only handsome, efficient and self-assured, he is also extraordinarily talented and athletic; in short, he has superhuman characteristics. "Neither the character's ethnicity nor religion is mentioned, but it seems clear that Jerry Lewis (born Joseph Levitch) is inspired by Jewish stereotypes. His name and profession make it clear that Julius Kelp has been the typical good Jewish student of novels and films; Buddy Love, more sensual than cerebral, hard-drinking, womanising and brawling, is the mythical image of the introverted young Jewish 'goy': a hot-blooded brute whose life is a non-stop sensual party. The preoccupations and fantasies Lewis gives his character are the same ones that Philip Roth, in *Portnoy's Evil*, would say years later are typically Jewish. His Portnoy… is an inveterate ladies' man who in his youth thought himself disadvantaged with women because of his Jewishness[663]."

Naturally, in this competition between the shy and the "gallant", the young woman will prefer the *schlémiel*, the shy little Jew. In *Dreams of a Seducer* (1972), Woody Allen taught Jews that they should be themselves. In *Annie Hall* (1977), being Jewish was even a sexual advantage.

The study of the cultural production of Judaism also shows that Jews seem to suffer deeply from the lack of love from the rest of humanity, which does not seem to understand the mission of the "chosen people". Jewish directors thus compensate for this suffering by imagining the Jew finally recognised for what he is: a being of genius, definitely genius, who deserves to be acclaimed and roundly applauded.

This image was seen at the end of the film *The Last Underground* (1980) by François "Trufffaut" (Levy): Lucas Steiner, a theatre director who was forced to hide in a cellar throughout the war, finally reveals himself to his audience at the moment of the "Liberation". After a performance, he takes the stage with the actors and is frantically applauded by the fervent Goyim who recognise his genius. We find this image at the end of Woody Allen's film, *Disassembling Harry* (USA, 1997): the hero of the film, a novelist, is applauded at length by all his characters. The little Jew is greeted in the midst of his characters with a *standing ovation*. In Norman Jewison's *Rollerball* (USA, 1975), the action takes place in 2018; at that date, nations have been abolished, and politicians have been replaced by technocrats. A civilisation of leisure has developed, with a game that grips the planet. Jonathan (James Caan) is the most popular of all these new heroes. The crowd chants his name endlessly. Let's look at the film *Barton Fink* by the Coen brothers (USA, 1991): At the beginning of the film, the young playwright is frantically applauded by the audience: it is the beginning of a great career in Hollywood. This image is also seen in a curious way in a short novel by

---

[663] CinémAction, *Cinéma et judéité*, Annie Goldmann (ed.), Cerf, 1986, p. 115-121. In Jerry Lewis' other films, the characters multiply their identities (*The Family jewels*, 1965; *Three on a Couch*, 1966; *The Big Mouth*, 1967).

Jacques Lanzmann, entitled *The Seventh Heaven*: A certain Moses has the nerve to christen his thoroughbred horse "Long live the Jews" so that the crowd cheers him with fervour[664]. This need to be loved and recognised is evoked in Woody Allen's film *Zelig* (1983): "One of Woody Allen's last films," wrote Dominique Cohen, "tells the story of Zelig, a chameleon of a man who always wants to look like the Other in order to be loved. He goes so far as to enlist in the SS when Nazism gains the support of the majority[665].".

Jews, as we see, need a lot of love. The novelist Philip Roth imagined in *Operation Shylock* that the Jews would one day leave Israel and be welcomed back into the Central European countries where they once lived. This passage from his book is symptomatic of the tortures of the Jewish soul, thirsting to be loved and recognised at last: "Do you know what will happen at the Warsaw railway station when the first trainload of Jews arrives? A crowd will come to meet them. There will be jubilation. There will be tears. They will shout: "Our Jews are coming home! Our Jews are coming home!". The spectacle will be televised live to the whole world. And what an historic day for Europe, for Judaism, for the whole of humanity… A historic day for human memory, for human justice and also for atonement. The conscience of Europe will only begin to regain its whiteness in those railway stations, when there the crowds weep and sing and express their jubilation, when there the Christians fall on their knees in prayer at the feet of their Jewish brethren[666]… "

Looking at the good, there is in them above all the need to blame the Goyim in order to bring them to their knees, to the feet of the Jews. The famous Yiddish writer Sholem-Aleichem has bequeathed to us his hopes for Israel. Born in Russia in 1859, he was the master of Yiddish literature, a language hitherto disdained by scholars. In *The Adventures of Menahem-Mendl*, published in 1913, he wrote: "The war that will break out—I am speaking of the Great War—will take place neither on the seas nor on land but in the air… Its great advantage is that it will not last. When the first fissure appears, a sign of weakening, a shriek will be raised that will shake the whole world—and at that moment, there

---

[664] Jacques Lanzmann, *Le Septième Ciel*, J. C: Lattès, Poche, p. 17

[665] CinémAction, *Cinéma et judéité*, Annie Goldmann (dir.), Cerf, 1986, p. 51.

[666] Philip Roth, *Operación Shylock*, Debolsillo, Editorial Mondadori, 2005 Barcelona, p. 49.

will have to be peace, concord, universal happiness—and then, our time will also come, brothers, children of Israel. It will be the others who will take our side. Enemies will become good friends. We will no longer be insulted. The Poles will go unnoticed with their boycott. They will be ashamed to confess that they boycotted us in the past. And countless will be those who will be ashamed and regret that they made our blood flow. But all that will come in their day, one day[667]… "

Jews often find it hard to understand why humanity rejects them, which hurts them all the more when they are intimately convinced that they are the representatives of the Good on earth, of the Good, the Beautiful and universal morality. René Neher, a former resistance fighter, expressed "this desire to ensure that morality is respected in the world. It remains our raison d'être… Anti-Semitism, which arose for essentially religious reasons, will eventually disappear. One day, people will recognise that we do not wish evil on anyone[668]."

The famous "Nazi hunter" Simon Wiesenthal, who died in Vienna in 2006 at the age of 96, had also contributed to the enforcement of morality in the world. His tireless search after the Second World War led to the arrest of some 1100 "criminals", some of them nonagenarians, who were all brought to justice and convicted. His greatest achievement was to have brought to justice Adolf Eichmann, the mastermind behind the "Final Solution". Simon Wiesenthal began this long hunt "as soon as he left the Mauthausen extermination camp". But it should be remembered that he had been in five other death camps, from which he had miraculously emerged alive, as had hundreds of thousands of other survivors. His thirst for revenge motivated him to the end of his days, but he always denied the rumours about the "Wiesenthal commandos" who had discovered and liquidated hidden Nazis. This great man naturally received countless awards for his actions. Moshe Katzav, the Israeli president, declared on the occasion of his death: "He represented the morals of humanity, he represented the free and democratic world".

The moral demands of the Jews are such that humanity is not always able to understand the lessons of the Jewish people. Sometimes, in order to make themselves better understood, they use other arguments in which we feel a certain threat: "You will love the Jews, wrote Albert

---

[667] Cholem-Aleikhem, *La Peste soit de l'Amérique*, 1913, Liana Levi, 1992, p. 195.

[668] Serge Moati, *La Haine antisémite*, Flammarion, 1991, p. 165.

Caraco, not when you have to put up with them, but fear them" (p. 177). (p. 177). "Hated while they are despised, they will be loved when they are formidable, for so they must become to free the people from hatred" (p. 180). (p. 180). "They will be forgiven when they are triumphant, for so they will become the saints they were. Without the power, they will not have the Grace[669]."

## Dementia

Jewish neurosis can also manifest itself in an even more ecstatic form. Especially in the Hasidic stream, where this neurosis is externalised without complex during religious ceremonies. Created in the 18th century by Baal Shem Tov ("Besht"), this stream later had a great influence on Ashkenazi Judaism. The English writer Israel Zangwill informed us, in *The Ghetto Dreamers*, that Besht's grandfather was a Shabb—a Sabbatean—a heretical Jewish adherent of the famous sect of Shabtai Tzvi.

The Besht was born in 1700 (5459) in Ukop, in Bukovina, in the north of present-day Romania. At the age of 42 he began touring Podolia and Wallachia preaching his teachings. The Kabbalists interpret his date of birth as follows: "The properties of numbers are marvellous, inasmuch as five, which is the symbol of the pentagon, is the key to everything. It follows then that we find five by subtracting the first two from the last two, and while the first multiplied by the third equals the square of five, likewise, the second multiplied by the fourth gives the square of six, and likewise, the first added to the third equals ten which is the number of the commandments, and the second added to the fourth equals thirteen which is the number of the principles of faith. Even Christians, who call that year 1700, indicate that it marks the beginning of a new era[670]."

Soon the followers of the Besht were the talk of the region. Israel Zangwill described them as follows: "They were regarded as a bunch of debauched, fanatical dancers. To tell the truth, a ceremony in the city I managed to attend dampened my hopes considerably. The worshippers were shouting, beating their breasts, pulling their curls, jumping up and

---

[669] Albert Caraco, *Apologie d'Israël*, 1957, L'Âge d'homme, 2004, p. 187.

[670] Israel Zangwill, *Rêveurs du ghetto*, tome II, 1898, Éd. Complexe, 2000, p. 21

down like savages, even foaming at the mouth. I could not see what sublime idea was hidden behind all this madness[671]."

After the Besht's death in 1760, his disciples continued to preach his teachings and succeeded in bringing together most of the Jews of Central Europe. In *Chassidic Celebrations*, Elie Wiesel paid tribute to the great Tzaddikim[672] of the Chassidic movement, such as the great Maggid of Mezeritch, who died in 1772: 'Like all Chassidic teachers, he lived his whole life waiting for the coming of the Messiah'. And Rabbi Levi-Yitzhk of Berditchev, who died in 1809: "He prayed with such self-abandonment that the faithful, frightened, instinctively turned away. He gesticulated, howled, danced, jumped up and down, pushing and knocking everyone down. Nobody existed for him... More than anything else in the world, he believed in the coming of the Messiah. When they were drawing up the wedding contract for his son, the scribe noted that the wedding was to take place on that date in Berditchev. Levi-Yitzhak angrily tore it up: "Berditchev? why Berditchev? write! The wedding will take place on this date in Jerusalem, unless the Messiah has not yet arrived; in that case, the ceremony will take place in Berditchev[673]"."

Rabbi Nahman of Bratzlav, who died in 1810, was another "phenomenon". Like most Jews, he had been married very young, at the age of thirteen: "He is never himself, but he is always himself; it seems like a splitting of the self: the saint sometimes behaves like a comedian". A bit like Elie Wiesel, in short. "As a teenager, he discovered his body and had to fight his desires... "For me, a man or a woman is the same thing. I react the same to both." Rabbi Nahman led an "intense life, with "dizzying falls and ascents", accompanied by fasting and insomnia. He suffered in silence—"he would grit his teeth so hard he could grind a piece of wood", sometimes "shrieking and howling in a half-voice". He had an unbalanced life, punctuated with

---

[671] Israel Zangwill, *Rêveurs du ghetto*, tome II, 1898, Éd. Complexe, 2000, p. 39

[672] The Tzaddik is the Righteous in Hebrew. He is the opposite of Rasha, which means wicked: "He who abandons the community is a Rasha" (Elie Wiesel, Célébration biblique, Éditions duuil, 1975). (Elie Wiesel, *Célébration biblique*, Éditions du Seuil, 1975). The head of a Hasidic community is also called "Tzadik", or rebbe.

[673] Elie Wiesel, *Célébration hassidique*, Éd. Seuil, 1972, op. cit., p. 94, 112, 113.

flashes and painful and exalting visions… Unstable temperament, hypersensitive, lively and precocious intelligence, he felt and received life as a wound".

Elie Wiesel then introduced us to Rabbi Menahem-Mendl of Kotzk, who died in 1859: "In Kotzk, you don't talk; you shout or shut up. They spend their time fighting desire, trying to thwart it; they do the opposite of what they feel like doing. They eat when they are not hungry, they deprive themselves of water when they are thirsty. They pray later, or earlier than usual: The Rabbi says: "When you feel like shouting and you don't shout, that's when you really shout[674]"."

One passage in the book enlightened us about the countless contradictions and paradoxes we encounter in the course of reading almost all Jewish authors: "Hasidism is not afraid of contradictions: life is full of them, only death annuls them… ambiguities, confusion of places and dates, paradoxes and controversies abound in the legend of Baal-Shem". Regarding the fabulation so prevalent in Jewish authors, Elie Wiesel wrote: "The real and the imaginary, both the one and the other are part of the story: one is the bark, the other the sap[675]."

In the *Testament of a Murdered Jewish Poet*, Wiesel had his hero, Paltiel Kossover, say: "Ever since I was a child, I was as attracted to the madmen as they were to me. Maimonides is right: a world without madmen would not exist[676]." Indeed, in another of his books, *A Mad Desire to Dance*, Wiesel repeated what Maimonides had sentenced in his time: "The world will be saved by madmen[677]." Recall that Moses ben Maimon, Maimonides, author of two seminal books in the 12th century, the *Guide for the Perplexed* and the *Mishneh Torah*, is the most influential personality in all of post-Talmudic Judaism.

Alexandre Minkowski had left a corroborating testimony to these inclinations in his book, *The Barefoot Mandarin*. His parents practised psychiatry. His father, the son of a Warsaw banker whose ancestors were rabbis, had "made a notable name for himself in French

---

[674] Elie Wiesel, *Célébration hassidique*, Éd. Seuil, 1972, op. cit., p. 182-184, 250.

[675] Elie Wiesel, *Célébration hassidique*, Éd. Seuil, 1972, op. cit., p. 22, 23.

[676] Elie Wiesel, *Le Testament d'un poète juif assasiné*, 1980, Points Seuil, 1995, p. 148.

[677] Elie Wiesel, *Un Désir fou de danser*, Éd. Seuil, 2006, p. 14

psychiatry... Bergson was his teacher and a thoughtful friend." His mother was an assistant in a psychiatric hospital in the canton of Zurich. Alexandre Minkowski explained: "My father received mentally disturbed patients in an adjoining room". His mother, a little worried, "said, however: "We love the mentally ill[678]."

All this may explain why a filmmaker like Milos Forman, in *Someone Flew Over the Cuckoo's Nest* (1975), tried to make us believe that the alienated were not really as crazy as they seemed, and that they were mostly victims of an oppressive society. That was the aim of the anti-psychiatry school, which had its glory hours in the 1970s with David Cooper, Aaron Esterson and Ronald D. Laing: there are no mentally ill people; it is society that generates them. Again this inability to get out of oneself and the same need to project a very particular problem onto a universal plane. But perhaps one day Israel's perseverance will succeed, and as Israel Zangwill predicted: "There will come a day when God will straighten out the twisted[679]."

"Twisted" is undoubtedly the most appropriate epithet to describe certain artistic production. One only has to look at the paintings in art galleries, or the sculptures in the squares and roundabouts of our cities, to realise the neurotic disorder. But it is true that "beauty—physical, external, material beauty—is not highly prized in Talmudic circles", as Elie Wiesel admitted. The praise of physical ugliness was seen, for example, in this Rabbi Yeoshoua: "He did not have a graceful physique. The texts remarked on this trait by illustrating it with an anecdote. Seeing him one day, a Roman princess was impressed by his lack of grace and asked him the following question: 'How can so much wisdom find its place in such an ugly body? He replied: "Where does your father keep his best wine, in golden jars or clay amphorae? Wine spoils in gold or silver, but its taste will be better preserved in a simple pitcher, even if it is ugly". A logical answer, but the princess insisted:" I know many people who possess wisdom and beauty at the same time." Rabbi Yeosshoua remained calm: "True. But they would probably be wiser if they were less beautiful."[680]."

---

[678] Alexandre Minkowski, *Le Mandarin aux pieds nus*, 1975, Points Seuil, 1977, p. 19, 20, 13.

[679] Israel Zangwill, *Rêveurs du ghetto*, tome II, 1898, Éd. Complexe, 2000, p. 255

[680] Elie Wiesel, *Célébration talmudique*, Éd. Seuil, 1991, p. 274, 95.

Sigmund Freud, who came from a family of Hasidic Jews, had no choice but to acknowledge: "The harmony between the culture of spiritual and physical activities, as achieved by the Greek people, was denied to the Jews[681]."

This neurosis, which is expressed in literature and film through sexual depravity, can also manifest itself through the most bloodthirsty and crazed forms of violence, as in gore films. The film *Hostel* (USA, 2005), to take just one example, tells the story of two American students on holiday in Europe. With a young Icelandic man they meet in Amsterdam, they decide to travel to Slovakia, a country full of beautiful, promiscuous girls who have been described to them as a paradise of debauchery. They arrive by train at the station of a small Slovakian town, promising, so they are told, and are immediately seduced by young beauties. But in reality they have just walked into a trap, and soon they are in for a real nightmare. One by one, they will be kidnapped by a group of sadistic men and suffer the worst tortures. In the middle of the countryside, a disused and abandoned factory has been transformed into a huge slaughterhouse for human flesh. Torture takes place on every floor and in every form: with scissors, with pincers, with chainsaws. Western mental maniacs pay fortunes to indulge in this pleasure, and these horrible Slovaks give them what they want. Fortunately, the last American student manages to escape, albeit with a few fingers amputated. His torturer has slipped in a pool of blood and the chainsaw has fallen on him just as he was about to rip our hero to shreds. He manages to escape from the factory of death in the company of a young Japanese girl disfigured with a welding machine and holding one eye in her hands. The car chase through the small narrow streets of the city ends badly for the Slovakian pursuers: stuck in a dead end, they are attacked and stoned to death by brave gypsy children. Obviously, director Eli Roth doesn't like the Slovaks very much; perhaps a bad memory? When the film was released, they made it clear to him that it was reciprocal. Note that the film was produced by one of his friends: Quentin Tarentino. The final scene concludes with the murder in a German station of one of the executioners, whose throat is slit by our hero over a toilet bowl. Toilet bowls often appear in this type of film...

---

[681] Sigmund Freud, *L'Homme Moïse et la religion monothéiste*, 1939, Gallimard, 1986, p. 215.

Recall that the inventor of gore cinema was one Herschell Gordon Lewis, who made his name by revolutionising the horror genre with *Blood Feast*, released in 1963. The man was later arrested for swindling in a shady deal with a car rental agency. His conviction ended his career in "vomit cinema".

Through film and literature, Jewish neurosis is able to express itself more and more freely. Indeed, it is clear that Jews feel a morbid need to communicate their malaise to the rest of humanity. In *The Great Fear of the Biemensants*, published in 1931, Georges Bernanos, who denounced Jewish fanaticism during the Dreyfus affair, had already perceived this constant and tiresome agitation: "It is clear that, in the long run, the frenzied and convulsive agitation of the Jewish world would eventually bring a people already infected by this oriental neurosis to the verge of a nervous breakdown". And Bernanos added, perhaps without realising the accuracy of the diagnosis: "This is how a hysterical woman triumphs over the best man[682]."

In his insufferable *Apology for Israel*, Albert Caraco confirmed that some Jews were aware of this continuous and permanent agitation: "Bloody, victim or dominator, executioner, never at peace with this world" (p.137), "They have come to make the world change and their people live in trembling, far from rest where the Eternal One does not want to remain, and their excesses no one on earth represses... Rest flees from them when they reach it. As soon as the walls do not contain them, does not the universe seem to gurgle" (p. 65). Caracus could have said: "that the universe runneth", as the novelist Albert Cohen wrote to describe the Jews of the Ionian islands: "All the Jews, velvety or ragged, runnelling and gesticulating, were throwing themselves to the four corners of the earth... And the whole island was a buzzing... a great runrhoning hall. They prayed to God, they begged Him to have the goodness to help their dear little village[683]."

The young Austrian writer Otto Weininger also made a similar comparison: "The symbol of Jewishness is the fly: there are many analogies: the sugar, the ubiquity, the buzzing, the invasion and the false pretence of fidelity in the eyes[684]".

---

[682] Georges Bernanos, *La grande peur des bien-pensants, Edouard Drumont*, 1931, Grasset, Poche, 1969, p. 323.

[683] Albert Cohen, *Comeclavos*, Anagrama, 1989, Barcelona, p. 15, 36

[684] Otto Weininger, *Sexe et caractère*, L'Age d'homme, 1975, p. 140. As a

This buzzing, accompanied by the itching already mentioned above, reminds us of the words of Daniel Cohn-Bendit, Georges Steiner and Emmanuel Lévinas when they genuinely acknowledged that Jews were there to annoy others, to prevent them from living peacefully[685]. It is the same incessant buzz and bustle around planet earth of a certain ruling class, such as Hannah, the heroine of a novel by Paul-Loup Sulitzer who is none other than Helena Rubinstein. At the end of the book, Hannah managed to found her empire in the cosmetics industry: "I have to be in New York by 15 February. But before that, I'll go back to Rome and Milan, which are opening, then I'll go to Madrid and Lisbon for the same reason. And then Berlin, Paris and London. America immediately after that[686]."

The highly influential Jacques Attali also has something to say about this. Let us recall that this grey eminence of President François Mitterrand, and later ones as well, theorised the political project of Judaism, but secularised it so that the general public could more easily adhere to it. In all his books, Attali delectably describes the "nomadic world" that he and his ilk are preparing for us, and in which the "hypernomads" will, he believes, form the new ruling class of the planet. His latest book, published in 2006 and very significantly entitled *A Brief History of the Future*—in the great tradition of Jewish prophetism—contains a passage that presents these "hypernomads" in more detail: "Hypochondriacs, paranoids and megalomaniacs, narcissists and egocentrics, all at once, the hypernomads... will thus invent the best and the worst of a volatile, carefree, selfish and precarious planetary society. Arbiters of elegance and masters of wealth and the media, they will profess no allegiance, neither national, nor political, nor cultural[687]."

The "mission" of the Jewish people seems to have its conclusion in that finally unified world, in which the Jews will be recognised by all as the ruling class. Albert Caraco strongly expressed his faith in the mission of the Jewish people and in the final victory: "They march more furiously from century to century, more threatened and triumphant

---

curiosity, the fly symbolises Beelzebub, "the lord of the flies". In David Cronenberg's film *The Fly* (1986), Jeff Goldblum fuses with a fly.

[685] A kind of lame fly syndrome. Cf. *Psychanalyse du Judaïsme*, p. 69.

[686] Paul-Loup Sulitzer, *Hannah*, Stock, 1985, Poche, 1987, p. 617.

[687] Jacques Attali, *Breve historia del futuro*, Ediciones Paidós Ibérica, 2007, Barcelona, p. 176, 177.

among the bonfires and the graves, with a hundred peoples on their arms and victory for asylum". And Caraco continued, always in his inimitable style: "Who would forgive you, O Jew, to be right against the whole world? Before you the best are sometimes criminals. You falsify all measures and the universe groans under the weight of your debt. The madmen who despise you are the same who raffle the shreds of your legend[688]."

The madmen, evidently, are all men who do not understand the greatness of the mission of the Jews: "A billion humans cannot bear to be wrong before a handful of Hebrews". (p. 271). "The Temple will be raised again," Caracus assured, and those who do not want the Jews will be "driven into the abysses", then "the wound will be closed." (p. 254). And "when the Temple will be raised, it will be immolated again." (p. 231).

Such certainties do not come without a certain dose of madness, as Albert Caraco himself acknowledged: "They communicate to the species a voracious insanity... They sow division, fanaticism springs up in their footsteps... Confusion lifts them up and order brings them down... No certainty calms them and no temper appeases them... Their rage serves the designs of the Eternal, and their madness pleases God... They close the ways of the future and their insanity watches over the world". And finally, "Let them not cease in their madness and exhaust it all to the end[689]."

Their faith in the final victory is clearly unshakeable, and all the penalties that could be inflicted on them would only serve to reinforce their convictions. Let us recall again what Manes Sperber wrote: "God was just, for He condemned His enemies to become murderers, and to them [the Jews] He granted the grace of being the victims, who in death would sanctify the Almighty. From John Chrysostom to the last pogromist mujik, the persecutors did not suspect the extent to which their momentary triumph reinforced the conviction of the persecuted that they were the chosen people[690]."

---

[688] Albert Caraco, *Apologie d'Israël*, 1957, L'Âge d'homme, 2004, p. 256.

[689] Albert Caraco, *Apologie d'Israël*, 1957, L'Âge d'homme, 2004, p. 143, 144, 153, 226, 26, 145.

[690] Manès Sperber, *Être Juif,* Éd. Odile Jacob, 1994, p. 60.

As Rabbi Akiba, who lived at the time of Emperor Hadrian, said: "all Jews are princes", therefore it is right that the world belongs to them. This is also what Rabbi Shimon bar Yohai, to whom the Zohar, the book of Kabbalah, is sometimes attributed, and who lived during the reign of Marcus Aurelius, said. In *Talmudic Celebration*, Elie Wiesel referred to these words: 'What he says about the pagans—or the Gentiles?—sounds unpleasant today. "Only the Jews are human. Worse still: "The best of the heathen, you have to crush his head like a snake". As for the Jews, he goes on and on extolling their merits. "God offered them three gifts: the Torah, the country of Israel and the world to come; and all three can only be acquired through suffering", and as we know, the suffering of the Jews is extremely painful. About Rabbi Hillel and Rabbi Shammai, the first two teachers of the Talmud who lived at the time of the Roman conquest, Elie Wiesel wrote: "I love their extreme passion for truth, I love their truth even in violence. Fanatics? Yes, they are. But, although everything in me is opposed to fanaticism, I don't entirely dislike theirs[691]."

Two thousand years later, the philosopher Bernard-Henri Levy expressed his fascination with the perseverance and obstinacy of Judaism through the centuries in his 1979 book *The Testament of God*. Let's listen to him waxing ecstatic about the mystery of the destiny of the Jewish people: "An ageless insubordination, literally immemorial, which for two thousand years has constantly asserted the longest, most stubborn and tenacious denial that human chronicles have recorded to this day. An absolutely unique case of rebellion against any logic, oblivion or genocide, of stubbornness in saying no, in denying the verdict of the facts, in defying the machine of the centuries in its procession of reprimands and murderous fatalities".

But this stubbornness of the Jewish people is above all like the fly that keeps banging against the glass when the window is open. This "singular, incredible experience" exalted Bernard-Henri Levy: "I am talking about the Jewish people, of course. Of that indomitable people whose perseverance to be remains one of the most profound enigmas for contemporary consciousness... I affirm now, without ambiguity, that I identify with this community. I choose to wear and defend its colours with ardour and pride[692]."

---

[691] Elie Wiesel, *Célébration talmudique*, Seuil, 1991, p. 154, 237, 37.

[692] Bernard-Henri Levy, *Le Testament de Dieu*, Grasset, 1979, p. 8, 9.

The influential press director Jean Daniel said nothing else: "The Jewish mystery is a moving phenomenon that can raise mystical questions and lead some people to believe in the election of a people[693]." One hears here the echo of the philosopher André Glucksmann:"... Two millennia of being a living question for its environment. Two millennia of innocence, having nothing to do with anything[694]." We will transcribe here the medical diagnosis we set out in *Psychoanalysis of Judaism*: "Whatever the place and the time, the symptoms always translate the hysteric's permanent desire to constitute an enigma for scientific logic and to offer his body to the scrutinising and knowing gaze of the doctor".

It is truly exceptional to read, from the pen of a Jewish intellectual, a somewhat rational analysis. The one we were able to discover in the April 2003 issue of *Israël Magazine* is too rare not to be mentioned. Dr. Itzhak Attia, "director of French-speaking seminars at the International School for the Study of the Holocaust at the Yad Vashem Institute", demonstrated in his analysis of the anti-Semitic phenomenon an exceptional acuity. While most Jewish thinkers analyse anti-Semitism as a "disease", typically projecting their own faults onto their enemies, Itzhak Attia seemed, on the contrary, to identify the specificity of the Jewish people: "What is it in me that provokes so much fear and hatred in non-Jews?"he asked himself, before going on to write: "The anti-Semitism that has followed in our footsteps since the beginning of our existence... is neither a disease awaiting a possible cure, nor a scourge that we have to endure irremediably, but the distorting mirror of our identity, the specific identity of the people of Israel". Good riddance!

However, Itzhak Attia seemed to be frightened by his own audacity and immediately resumed the messianic discourse of Judaism which states with certainty that the Messiah will soon come, that the Jews will be delivered from all their tribulations, and that "universal peace will reign over the post-modern global village where all humanity lives".

Judaism is an eternal flight forward. Itzhak Attia expressed it in very explicit words, with a clarity unusual for Jewish intellectuals, probably because he was doing so in a magazine reserved for the Jewish community: "Despite the fact that reason cries out to us with all its might the absurdity of this confrontation, between a small insignificant

---

[693] Jean Daniel, *La Blessure*, Grasset, 1992, p. 259.

[694] André Glucksmann, *Le Discours de la haine*, Plon, 2004, p. 73, 86, 88

people like Israel and the rest of humanity... however absurd, incoherent and monstrous it may seem, we are indeed engaged in an intimate combat between Israel and the Nations, which can only be genocidal and total, for our respective identities depend on it". You read that right: between the Jewish people and the rest of humanity, the combat can only be "genocidal and total". And indeed, this is what we had already understood. Judaism is a war machine against the rest of humanity. Jews inevitably arouse hatred that turns out to be as old as Judaism itself.

However, in their folly, it does occasionally happen that some Jews become aware that the children of Israel may have made some mistakes. Thus, Theo Klein, former president of the Crif, publicly acknowledged: "The Jews have made a considerable contribution to the development of the world; they have probably also contributed to some mistakes[695]... "The man did not say much more, but he was surely thinking of the atrocities committed by his fellow Jews in Bolshevik Russia, which represents the greatest massacre in the history of mankind after the Maoist tragedy. I could also have mentioned the overwhelming responsibility of Jewish traders in the European and black slave trade, or the role of eminent Jews in triggering the Second World War. But as Albert Caraco rightly said in his indispensable *Apology for Israel*: "The world, sooner reduced to ashes than the Jews rejected" (p. 77). (p. 77).

But there is at least one day of wisdom in Judaism: Yom Kippur. In *A Stroller in New York*, published in 1951, Alfred Kazin, a well-known literary critic in the United States, gave some information on the rites of this secrecy-loving people. On the day of Kippur, a day of fasting and prayer, the Jews go to the synagogue: "I had wrapped my arm in the black straps of the phylactery; I tied it on my forehead". At the moment when the faithful bow their heads, each man "beats his breast as a sign of bitterness and repentance for every sin committed during the year". It is at that moment that the Jews begin in chorus a "long litany": "Truly, we confess, we have sinned. We have broken the law. We have acted treacherously. We have stolen. We have slandered. We have committed injustice. And we have acted cruelly. We have been presumptuous. We have been violent. We have said what was false. We have counselled evil. We have spoken lies. We have scorned. We have

---

[695] Théo Klein, *Dieu n'était pas au rendez-vous*, Bayard, 2003, p. 102.

rebelled. We have blasphemed. We have acted wickedly. We have transgressed the law[696]."

But Judaism is not just a religion, for, as we know, many Jews are atheists or agnostics, and do not consider themselves any less Jewish for that. In fact, neither is it a race, although an expert eye can recognise the "Jewish type", i.e. a characteristic physiognomy resulting from centuries of inbreeding. The Jews, indeed, avoided for centuries relations with the non-Jewish world, and it was unthinkable to marry outside the community: God's "chosen people" had to preserve their blood from any impurity from outside.

Today, however, intermarriage exists, contributing to the renewal of the blood of Israel. What is important in these mixed marriages is that the mother is Jewish, since the orthodox rabbis recognise as Jewish a person born of a Jewish mother. But sometimes a Jewish father or even a Jewish grandfather is enough to identify fully with Judaism. Jewishness is therefore a feeling of belonging to a people, a common memory to which one is connected. It is also the adherence to a political project based on the messianic hope of a tribal religion, whose aim is to establish on earth a perpetual "peace" on the ruins of peoples and nations.

At this point, however, the emergence of psychoanalysis is still not fully understood. A second-rate writer, Michel Herszlikowicz, is, as far as we know, one of the few Jewish intellectuals to have dared to approach the precipice. In his *Philosophy of Anti-Semitism*, he wrote furtively, as if frightened by his own audacity: "Psychoanalysis leaves anti-Semitism behind when it investigates the non-Jewish origin of the Jewish people[697]."

Stephane Zagdanski also expressed this idea, but reversed the formula: "In this book I provide an interpretation of the why of age-old anti-Semitism. I trace the genealogy of this hatred incubated for centuries in

---

[696] Alfred Kazin, *Retour à Brooklyn*, Éditions Seghers, 1965, p. 135.

[697] Michel Herszlikowicz, *Philosophie de l'antisémitisme*, Presse Universitaire de France, 1985, p. 154.

the form of a deep religious neurosis, gangrenous with violently symptomatic eruptions[698]."

Indeed, Judaism is essentially a neurosis, a sickness of the spirit; a perfectly identified sickness that has its origin in incest. This pathology, which was at the heart of Sigmund Freud's work, corresponded exactly to what the father of psychoanalysis could observe and observe around him, in his own community. In fact, it is Judaism as a whole, the Jewish "mission" with universal pretensions in its various political, intellectual and artistic expressions, that seems to be a manifestation of hysteria. Egocentrism, paranoia, anguish, introspection, manipulation, identity plasticity, "mission", selective amnesia or fabulation: everything in Judaism corresponds point for point with the symptoms of hysteria. This is what we demonstrated in our previous book.

At the beginning of the 20th century, the famous Viennese Jewish journalist Karl Kraus had also approached the abyss. The man had a low opinion of Freud: "Psychoanalysis is that mental illness of which it claims to be the cure[699]." The truth is that Judaism is that mental illness which psychoanalysis claimed to be able to cure. And the feverish expectation of the messiah is just another symptom: it corresponds to the typical imaginary pregnancy of the hysterical woman. For for the Jews themselves, the Jewish community is a woman, the bride of God, who must "beget" and give birth to a Messiah. This is what Manes Sperber wrote about the *Song of Songs*: "We read this text as a fragment of the love story between God and the Jewish people. The woman was the people, who had committed a sin against God by not opening the door in time. Now God had gone away, had temporarily denied the woman his grace. And the people look for God again among the strangers in the night[700]."

The question now is whether the aggressiveness of Judaism can be neutralised, in order to rid humanity of evils that could prove worse than Marxism, psychoanalysis and globalist ideology put together. It is first necessary to recognise that, after centuries of mutual misunderstanding, Christian, Muslim and Hitlerite anti-Semitism have failed to resolve the "Jewish question". The fact is that Jews feed on the hatred they arouse

---

[698] Stéphane Zagdanski, *De l'Antisémitisme*, Climats, 1995, 2006, p. 20, 11

[699] Françoise Giroud, *Alma Mahler*, Robert Laffont, 1988, P. Pocket 1989, p. 65.

[700] Manès Sperber, *Être Juif*, Odile Jacob, 1994, p. 37.

everywhere and among all the peoples of the world. This hatred, we must understand, is indispensable to their genetic and spiritual survival, for it enables the community to close ranks and to cross the centuries, when other civilisations have disappeared for good.

For their part, the rabbis do all they can to reassure Jews that their Jewishness is inscribed in their genes, that even a renegade Jew is still a Jew, and that it is therefore perfectly futile to try to break out of the communal prison. To claim that a Jew can only remain a Jew is to work to consolidate the walls of that prison. On the contrary, everything possible must be done to welcome the sick among us. We must love the Jews, and love them sincerely in order to free them from the prison in which they are imprisoned. Only in this way can we free ourselves from their control and at the same time free them from the evil that dwells in them and threatens all humanity.


This evidence can be illustrated by the startling image of a trial of a serial killer in the United States that had been broadcast live on television. The man, who had murdered some thirty young women, appeared in court, dressed in the orange uniform of dangerous prisoners. The courtroom was packed, with all the parents of the victims who had come to testify. We then saw a young Asian man, mad with rage, trying to get close to the monster, uttering terrible threats, his face unhinged with hatred. We can imagine his sister or his wife being killed, and his reaction was certainly legitimate. But however strong his hatred, his violent outbursts did not seem to impress the psychopath who remained perfectly impassive. Not a shudder, not a single emotion appeared on his face. In the midst of the shouting, a woman managed to make herself heard; a woman whose daughter had surely suffered the worst atrocities. Her words held the attention of the whole room, and there was silence: of course not, she did not hate the man; on the contrary. One had to try to understand the suffering that had led him to commit all those crimes. There is something good in every man, even if he is a murderer, she said with conviction... This elderly lady expressed herself with such dignity and faith that the prisoner burst into tears. The camera then zoomed in on her face, and her eyes were bathed in tears.

Paris, June 2007.

## Other titles

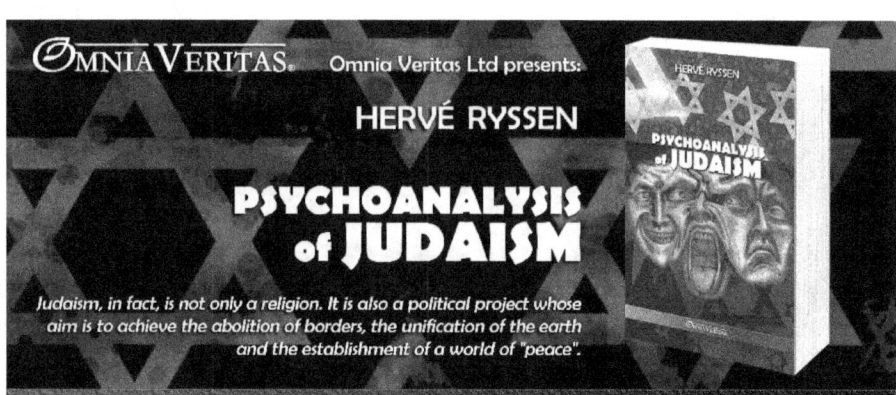

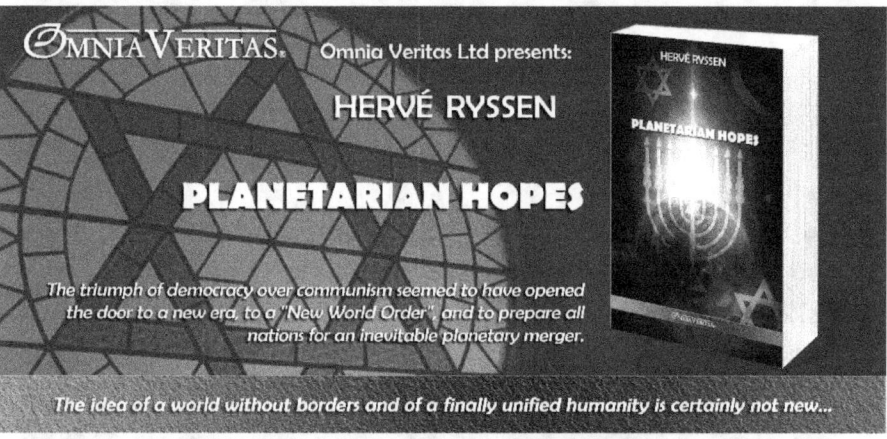

# THE JEWISH FANATICISM

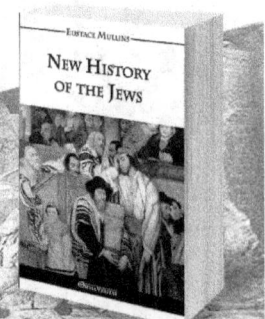

www.ingramcontent.com/pod-product-compliance
Lightning Source LLC
Chambersburg PA
CBHW071949220426
43662CB00009B/1064